THE GOOD NEWS OF JESUS CHRIST IN THE GOSPELS

THE GOOD NEWS OF JESUS CHRIST IN THE GOSPELS

George Mlakuzhyil S.J.

2021

The Good News of Jesus Christ in the Gospels – Published by the Indian Society for Promoting Christian Knowledge (ISPCK), Post Box 1585, 1654 Madarsa Road, Kashmere Gate, Delhi-110006.

Imprimi Potest: Rev. Fr. Sebastian Jeerakassery S.J., Delhi Jesuit Provincial (July 16, 2020).

Online order: http://ispck.org.in/book.php

Also available on amazon.com

Cover Design: Mr. Bejoy P. Mukkathu

RAINBOW is the symbol of "THE GOOD NEWS OF JESUS CHRIST." Sunlight, when refracted, is seen as a *multi-coloured rainbow* in the sky. Similarly, "Jesus Christ's Good News" is reflected upon in the light of faith and interpreted contextually "in the Gospels."

The *revelation* (represented by the rays of light) of JESUS CHRIST enlightens the four *Evangelists*, symbolized by the winged Man (*Matthew*), Lion (*Mark*), Ox (*Luke*) and Eagle (*John*).

The *painting of Jesus Christ* and the *symbols* of the *Evangelists* are from *Internet sources*.

ISBN: 978-81-949231-6-9

Laser typeset by

ISPCK, Post Box 1585, 1654, Madarsa Road, Kashmere Gate, Delhi-110006 • *Tel:* 23866323

e-mail: ashish@ispck.org.in • ella@ispck.org.in
website: www.ispck.org.in

Dedicated to

JESUS CHRIST

Who called me to be His Companion
and to announce the Good News to all
specially to the poor and the marginalized

A.M.D.G.

CONTENTS

Preface

Already as a student of theology in Vidyajyoti, Delhi, I was fascinated by *Jesus Christ* and *his diverse portraits* in the four Gospels. Therefore, during my Biblical studies in Rome, I paid special attention to the *various faith interpretations of Jesus Christ's person, message and mission* by the four Evangelists. Gradually I realized that, in spite of the remarkable differences in the portrayals of *Jesus Christ in the Gospels*, he is "*the good news*" in all of them.

Jesus Christ not only *proclaimed the good news* of the *reign of God* but also *manifested* its *presence in and through his actions and attitudes* towards all. Because he was a *divinehuman* person, he was both very human and divine in his relationships with all men, women and children. All who met him experienced the *loving presence of God* in him. *Jesus Christ in the Gospels* is *a loving and compassionate Saviour* to the poor, the hungry, the sick, the suffering, the dying, the despised, the marginalized, the exploited, the sinners, etc. He is a *living liberator* and a *loving life-giver* in the Gospels of Matthew, Mark, Luke and John.

Based on my personal experiences of various people during the past three decades of teaching the Gospel of John and Christology in Vidyajyoti College of Theology in Delhi and Regional Theology Centres (RTCs) and giving seminars, workshops and Retreats in Navjivan Renewal Centre (NRC) in NCR and elsewhere in India, I have realized that "*the good news of Jesus Christ in the Gospels*" is very appealing to all and especially to the Seminarians, Priests, Pastors, Religious, Christian faithful and people of all faiths. May this book help them and others to meet the *living and loving Jesus Christ* and to enter into an intimate relationship with him, which will spiritually nourish their lives and energize their mission in our motherland.

Gratitude is the attitude of an appreciative heart. I feel grateful to many persons who have helped me in various ways in writing and publishing this book. First of all, my heart-felt thanks to *Jesus Christ* who has accompanied me during the past sixty years as a Jesuit and particularly during the time of composition of this "Gospel Christology."

I am indebted to Fr. Soosai Mani S.J. (Provincial), Fr. Varkey Perekkatt S.J. and Fr. Sebastian Jeerakassery S.J. (former Provincials) for encouraging me to write this volume and to my Jesuit companions for their brotherly support. I am grateful to the Vidyajyoti librarian (Fr. K. T. Chandy S.J.) and library staff for their timely help and to Fr. K. T. Thomas S.J. (St. Xavier's, Delhi) for correcting the first draft of this book. I thank most sincerely Mr. Bejoy P. Mukkathu for preparing the attractive Cover Design. Finally, I am obliged to Rev. Dr. Ashish Amos of ISPCK, Delhi, for publishing this volume (despite the difficulties due to Corona virus pandemic).

1 July 2020
(60 years a Jesuit)

George Mlakuzhyil S.J.
Jesuit Residence,
St. Xavier's, 4 Raj Niwas Marg,
Delhi 110054.
Email: georgemlakuzhy@gmail.com

INTRODUCTION

The New Testament has *four Gospels* which deal with *Jesus Christ.* But it must be noted at the outset that the Gospels are *not* plain *reports* about *Jesus of history* but *post-resurrectional faith interpretations of Jesus Christ.* They are the *most reliable presentations of Jesus Christ* adapted to the various readers/audiences and Christian communities by the four Evangelists.[1]

Mark starts his Gospel as "*the good news* of *Jesus Christ, Son of God*" (Mk 1,1). The word "Gospel" (*euangelion*) means "good news" (glad tidings). The entire Gospel is intended to be "*good news*" for the readers. In Mark's rendition, "*Jesus Christ, Son of God*" is truly "*the good news*" (Mk1,1; cf. also 8,35; 10,29).

Even though all the *four Gospels* deal with *the same Jesus Christ*, there is an impressive *diversity in their presentations* of his person and mission. There are many differences not only in the content but also in the interpretations of his significance. This is because the Gospels are *not biographies of Jesus* (in the modern sense of the word) but *post-Easter contextual faith-interpretations of Jesus Christ* adapted to the concrete situations of the intended readers of each Gospel. Therefore, they do not contradict one another but *complement* each other. For example, even the same Christological "*title*" (e.g., "*Christ/Messiah*") applied to Jesus in the four Gospels highlights *different but complementary* dimensions. Jesus is a *mysterious* Messiah in Mk, a *Davidic* Messiah in Mt, a *prophetic* Messiah in Lk and a *universal* Messiah in Jn (as we shall see below). This '*unity in diversity*' (complementary diversity) in the Evangelists' interpretation of the person and mission of Jesus Christ is an incentive to develop *diverse contextual Christologies* for various groups in India.[2]

The *purpose* of *this book* ("THE GOOD NEWS OF JESUS CHRIST IN THE GOSPELS") is *not* to give an elaborate exegetical explanation of the entire text of the four Gospels (that's for commentaries to do) but *to highlight the presentation of Jesus Christ as "the Good News" in each of the Gospels* from a narrative and theological/faith perspective.[3]

All the four Gospels deal with "*Jesus Christ*", that is, not only the "Jesus of history" (historical Jesus) but also the "Christ of faith" (the risen Lord in whom the Christians believe). Both Matthew and Mark begin their Gospels by introducing "*Jesus Christ*" (Mt 1,1; Mk 1,1) and John mentions "Jesus Christ" already in the Prologue (Jn 1,17). By the time the Gospels were written (65-100 CE), the early Church had combined "Christ" with the *personal name* "*Jesus*" to form his *full name* "*Jesus Christ*" (Mt 1,1.18; Mk 1,1; Jn 1,17; 17,3), which meant that the Christian communities believed Jesus to be the Christ. In fact, "Jesus Christ" in the Gospels means more than "Jesus, the Christ" (that "Jesus" is "the Christ"), for it is linked to his being "the Son of God" (Mk 1,1; cf. also Mt 1,18; Jn 1,17-18; 17,1-3). In short, "*Jesus Christ*" stands for "*Jesus, the Christ, the Son of God*". All the four Gospels reflect the *disciples'/Christians' post-*

resurrection faith in *Jesus* as *the Christ* and as the divine *Son of God* (e.g., Jn 20,31).

> All the canonical Gospels (written between 65 and 100) present Jesus as a man who was *Messiah, Son of Man, and Son of God* (and sometimes specifically *Lord*) during his public *ministry*. The Gospel reader is made a party to a revelation connected to the baptism of Jesus by John the Baptist where God identifies Jesus as his Son (Mark 1,11; Matt 3,17; Luke 3,22; cf. John 1,33-34).[4]

Although all the four Gospels acknowledge *Jesus Christ* as *the Messiah and the Son of God* during his *public ministry*, only Luke has a *boyhood Christology*: As a *boy* of 12 years, Jesus was aware of God being his Father (2,49). But both Matthew (1,20-25) and Luke (1,34-35) have also a *conception Christology* since they "associate Jesus' Christological identity as *Emmanuel* ["God with us"], the Holy One, and the Son of God with the moment of *conception* through the Spirit without a human father."[5] Only John has a clear *pre-creation Christology*: "In the beginning was the Word and Word was with God and the Word was God. He was in the beginning with God" (Jn 1,1-2), that is, "the Word of God" *existed even before the creation* of the cosmos. This *eternal divine Word* that 'assumed' human nature is *Jesus Christ* (Jn 1,14.17).

The *four Evangelists* narrate and interpret the story of *Jesus Christ* in their own *unique* ways. As creative *artists* in their own right, they paint *four distinctive portraits* of Jesus.[6]

> *Each* of the four Gospels — *Matthew, Mark, Luke, and John* — paints *a unique portrait of Jesus Christ*. Each provides *special insight* into who he is and what he accomplished. The Gospels exhibit both *unity* and *diversity*, bearing witness to the *same Jesus* (unity) but viewing him from *unique perspectives* (diversity).... These are not contradictory portraits but *complementary*

> ones. Having four Gospels gives us a deeper, more profound understanding of *Christology* — the nature of *Jesus' person and work.*[7]

We pay careful attention to each of the Gospels' narratives in order to understand the *unique insights* into and *different dimensions* of the *person and mission of Jesus Christ* highlighted by each Evangelist. To do this, we examine not only the *statements* by Jesus or others *about his identity* but also observe closely his *actions* (miracles, etc.) and *attitudes* towards God and others.

> The gospels invite readers to enter their world, to listen to Jesus' words, to watch his great deeds, to appreciate their understanding of him, and to ask ourselves the same questions as the people in the text: 'who is this man?' (Mk 4,41), or 'what shall I do with Jesus?' (Mt 27,22).[8]

The *Gospels* are *faith interpretations* of the words and deeds, the mission and person of Jesus Christ primarily *to deepen/strengthen* the Christians' *faith* in him and secondarily to attract others *to believe* in "*the Saviour of the world*" (Jn 4,42), who is "*the Christ, the Son of God*" and *the Giver of (eternal) life* (Jn 20,31).

The *four Gospel portraits of Jesus Christ* stimulate and invite us to enter into *contemplation* and *reflection* on his captivating *person*, his challenging *message* and his life-giving *mission,* and prepare us to *reinterpret* them *in the Indian context.*[9]

In this book "**THE GOOD NEWS OF JESUS CHRIST IN THE GOSPELS**" we deal successively with "**Mark's, Matthew's, Luke's and John's Good News of Jesus Christ**" **(Chapters 1-4)**.[10]

Chapter 1

MARK'S GOOD NEWS OF JESUS CHRIST

The first words of Mark's Gospel are: "The beginning of *the good news* of *Jesus Christ, Son of God*" (Mk 1,1). The term "*Gospel*" (*euangelion*) means "*good news*." The whole "Gospel" of Mark is meant to be "the good news" of "Jesus Christ, Son of God." Who is "Jesus Christ"? What does Mark mean by describing him as "Son of God"? What is the "the good news"? To find satisfactory answers to such deep questions, we have to examine the entire Gospel of Mark.

Mark's Gospel has a **theological-geographical plan**, which consists of **three major Parts**, preceded by an **Introduction** and followed by an **Appendix:**

- **1.0. Introduction: Jesus Christ, Son of God (1,1-13)**
- **1.1. Jesus, the Mysterious Messiah (in Galilee and Beyond) (1,14-8,30)**[11]
- **1.2. Jesus' Passion Predictions of the Son of Man (on the Way to Jerusalem) (8,31-10,52)**[12]

1.3. Jesus, the Son of God's Passion (in Jerusalem) (11,1-16,8)[13]

1.x. Appendix: Later Additions (16,9-20).

1.0. Introduction: Jesus Christ, Son of God (Mk 1,1-13)

1.0.1. "The beginning of the Gospel of Jesus Christ, Son of God" (Mk 1,1)

Here the "gospel" (*euangelion*) refers to the "good news" (glad tidings) of "Jesus Christ," where "Christ" (*Christos*, "anointed one") is not used as a title (cf. 8,29; 12,35; 14,61; 15,32) but as a part of Jesus' name. "Jesus Christ" is further identified as "*Son of God*" (*hyios theou*) (1,1; cf. also 15,39),[14] which denotes his *divinity* and *filial relationship with God*. Thus the very first verse in Mark's Gospel announces the Messianic and divine identity of Jesus to the readers, even though the human characters in the Gospel will take a long time before they come to know who Jesus is/was (cf. 8,29; 15,39).

1.0.2. John the Baptist's Preaching of Jesus, the Mighty Lord (Mk 1,2-8)

John the Baptist is the messenger of God to "prepare the way of the Lord" (Mk 1,2-3), as foretold by the prophets (cf. Mal 3,1 and Is 40,3). Even though "*the Lord*" in the citation in Mk 1,3 originally referred to God, here it is applied to Jesus, the Son of God (1,1), who shares in the *divine Lordship*. Therefore, John the Baptist proclaims him as "*mightier* than I the thong of whose sandals I am not worthy to stoop down and untie" (Mk 1,7). John tells the people: "I have baptized you *with water* (*hydati*), but he will baptize [immerse] you *in the Holy Spirit*" (*en pneumati hagiô*) (1,8). Hence Jesus, *the Lord*, is far *greater* than John the Baptist.

1.0.3. Revelation of Jesus as God's Beloved Son at His Baptism (Mk 1,9-11)

Jesus came from Nazareth to be baptized in the Jordan by John (1,9). Immediately after Jesus' baptism "he saw the heavens opened and the Spirit descending *into him* (*katabainon eis auton*) like a dove" (*hôs peristeran* 1,10), indicating that he was inwardly animated/anointed by the heavenly Spirit of God, and he heard the heavenly voice, "You are *my Son*, *the beloved* (*sy ei ho hyios mou ho agapêtos*), *with you I am well-pleased* (*en soi eudokêsa*)" (1,11). Even though it was a personal revelation made by God to his beloved Son, the affirmation of the latter's *divine filial identity* and of his being *the beloved* of God are revealed by Mark to his readers (1,1.11).

1.0.4. Jesus' Testing by Satan in the Wilderness (Mk 1,12-13)

The indwelling Holy Spirit drives Jesus out into the desert (1,12) "and he was in the wilderness for forty days, *being tempted/tested (peirazomenos)* by Satan" (1,13). It gives us an indication about Jesus' future battle against Satan [his adversary] in establishing the kingdom of God (cf. 1,15.23-24). The *paradox* of Jesus' being *tested/tempted* points to his being *human*, even though he was declared by God (the Father) as his *beloved Son*. The fact that "the angels ministered to him" (1,13) implies that he was *victorious* over Satan.

1.1. Jesus, the Mysterious Messiah (in Galilee and Beyond) (Mk 1,14-8,30)

1.1.1. Jesus' Proclamation of the "Good News" of "God's Reign" (Mk 1,14-15)

After John the Baptist's arrest, Jesus (the Spirit-anointed Messiah and the beloved Son of God) comes to Galilee "proclaiming *the good news of God*" (*kêryssôn to euangelion tou theou:* 1,14):

> "The *time is fulfilled*
> and the *reign of God is at hand* (1,15a).[15]
> *Repent* and *believe* in *the good news*" (1,15b).

"*The good news of God*" that Jesus announced to the people of Galilee is that the time of waiting is over and the divinely appointed "*time* (*ho kairos*)" (God's opportune moment) is here because "the reign of God" *is at hand* (1,15).

> The decisive manifestation of the saving God about which the prophets spoke is now taking place… Mark wants to indicate that with Jesus' arrival, the time of waiting has come to an end and the Kingdom of God has broken into history.[16]

The proper response expected of the people to this profound event was to reorient their lives through "repentance" (change of mind and conversion of heart) and "faith in the good news" (1,15).

> The initial proclamation of the kingdom establishes the dominant theme of the narrative so that everything Jesus does (preach, teach, heal, and expel demons) is in the service of the kingdom of God. Accordingly, the narrator portrays *Jesus* as *the Messiah, the Son of God and the herald of God's kingdom.* Jesus is God's eschatological agent who announces that *God is bringing his rule* over creation and history under his ministry.[17]

1.1.2. The Call of Jesus' First Disciples (Mk 1,16-20)

Passing by the Sea of Galilee, Jesus finds four fishermen at their place of work (Simon and Andrew casting a net in the sea and James and John mending the nets with their father). He calls them to "follow" him and "immediately" (i.e., without any hesitation) they leave their nets and father and follow Jesus

(1,16-20). It shows that they are fascinated by the person of Jesus who has taken the initiative to invite them to become his disciples. "The story emphasizes the gravity of discipleship with its severe demands of leaving behind family and financial security."[18]

1.1.3. Jesus' Compassionate Healings and Authoritative Exorcisms (Mk 1,21-45)

In Mk Jesus begins his ministry in Galilee, immediately after the call of the first disciples (1,16-20), with many *healings* and *exorcisms* that demonstrate his *compassion* and *divine authority* through which he inaugurates *God's reign* among the sick and the possessed (1,21-45).

> In 1,21-45, Jesus performs several healings and exorcisms that effectuate the presence of God's kingdom for the sick and the demon-possessed of Galilee. In rapid succession, he expels an unclean spirit from a man in the synagogue of Capernaum (1,21-28), heals Simon's mother-in-law (1,29-31), cures the sick and the demon-possessed of Capernaum (1,32-34), inaugurates a preaching tour of Galilee during which he expels demons (1,32-39), and cleanses a leper (1,40-45). Through Jesus' mighty deeds, the kingdom of God makes an impressive entry into Galilee and sounds the death knell of Satan's rule.[19]

Jesus *teaches with authority* (1,21-22.27) and *casts out demons and cures the sick* to manifest that *the reign of God* is being established in and through him. Jesus heals Simon's mother-in-law (suffering from fever) by taking her by the hand and raising her up from the sickbed (1,30-31). He cures all kinds of physically and mentally sick persons brought to him by the people (1,32-34). He commands the demons ("unclean spirits") to come out of the possessed persons and they obey him instantly (1,23-27.32-34). Also, he silences them when they announce his identity as "the Holy One of God" (1,24.34). This reveals Jesus' *divine authority* to cure the sick and cast out the demons.

It is *Jesus' intimacy with God* in and through *prayer* that enables him to *discern the Father's will* about his preaching and healing ministry and to *share* in the *divine authority and power* to accomplish the *liberative* mission among the marginalized (1,35-39).

Lepers were the most marginalized in Jewish society since they were regarded as unclean and untouchable. They were excluded from the social and religious life of the community. So when a leper comes up to Jesus and falling on his knees, beseeches him: "If you will, you can cleanse me" (1,40), Jesus, moved to compassion, stretches out his hand and touches him, saying: "I will; be cleansed" (1,41). By *touching the untouchable*, Jesus cleanses the 'unclean' leper and restores not only his physical health but also his social life (1,42-44). The holistic *healing touch of Jesus* transforms the outcast leper into an enthusiastic proclaimer of the good news to all in the town (1,45).

1.1.4. Jesus' Controversial Deeds and Words (Mk 2,1-3,6)

The healings and exorcisms in Mk 1,21-45 are followed by a series of *controversial deeds and discussions* with the Jewish religious leaders (2,1-3,6).

a) Jesus' Healing a Helpless Paralytic and Forgiving His Sins (Mk 2,1-12)

When Jesus sees a helpless paralytic lying on a pallet (carried by four men, being lowered through the roof of the house where he was preaching in Capernaum) (2,2-4), he tells the paralytic: "My son, your sins are forgiven" (2,5). When the scribes blame

Jesus of committing blasphemy (2,6), he shows them that "the Son of Man has *authority* on earth *to forgive sins*" (2,10) by *curing the paralytic* through the power of his word: "I say to you, rise, take up your pallet and go home" (2,11). The immediate healing of the paralytic reveals Jesus' *divine power* to *cure the sick* and his *authority* to forgive sinners, at which the people are amazed and they glorify God (2,12).

b) The Call of Levi and Jesus' Eating with Tax Collectors and Sinners (Mk 2,13-17)

Just as Jesus calls four fishermen to become his disciples (1,16-20), he tells a *tax collector Levi* sitting at the tax office: "Follow me" (2,14), which he promptly does.

Jesus' *table-fellowship with sinners and tax collectors* in Levi's house (2,15-16) scandalizes the scribes and the Pharisees since the latter would not sit at table with the former (the socially marginalized, labelled as 'sinners' and despised by the Jewish leaders). He answers them that, just as the physician is for the sick (not for the healthy), *his mission* is "to call sinners" (not the righteous) to repentance and communion in the Kingdom of God (2,17; cf. 1,15). This *kingdom-communion* is symbolized by *Jesus' dining* with the "tax-collectors and sinners," thus integrating them into *Jesus' community* of disciples.[20]

c) Question about Not Fasting by the Disciples (Mk 2,18-22)

When Jesus is questioned why his disciples do *not fast* (whereas those of John the Baptist and the Pharisees do) (2,18), his answer is because the *bridegroom* is in their midst (2,19). *Jesus' ministry* is like a *bridegroom's wedding feast* during which the guests are not expected to fast. But "when the bridegroom is taken away from them," which is an allusion to Jesus' death, "then they will fast" (2,20). The *newness in Jesus* is like *new wine* in fresh wineskins (2,22); it must not be poured into old wineskins (irrelevant rituals and outdated practices). With the coming of Jesus, a *new era of God's reign* has begun.

d) Jesus' Defence of the Disciples' Plucking Grain on the Sabbath (Mk 2,23-28)

When the Pharisees find fault with the hungry disciples' plucking grain on the Sabbath as a forbidden work (2,23-24), Jesus defends them as not violating the Sabbath by citing the example of the hungry David and his companions who ate the bread of the Presence in the Temple (2,25-26; cf. 1 Sam 21,1-7). Jesus affirms that the original purpose of the Sabbath was the *wellbeing of humans* ("The Sabbath was made for man, not man for the Sabbath" 2,27). He also claims: "the Son of Man is Lord even of the Sabbath" (Mk 2,28), indicating humans' authority to interpret the true meaning of Sabbath laws and other laws in favour of human welfare.

e) Jesus' Healing of a Man with a Withered Hand on the Sabbath (Mk 3,1-6)

Jesus *cures a man with a paralysed hand* on the Sabbath because it is lawful to do good and save life on the Sabbath, even though it would displease the legalistic and hard-hearted Pharisees (3,1-5). Jesus' restorative and liberative action on the Sabbath provokes the hypocritical Pharisees to link up with the power-greedy Herodians and plot with them how to destroy him (3,6). He is ready to courageously face conflicts arising out of his determination to do life-promoting actions in favour of the underprivileged (like the physically challenged persons).

1.1.4.© These episodes [in Mk 2,1-3,6] represent a conflict that runs through the narrative. Who speaks and acts with God's authority? Jesus or the religious leaders? Does Jesus have *God-given authority* to forgive sins, to associate with sinners, to dispense his disciples from fasting, and to act with supreme freedom on the Sabbath? Or is he blaspheming and violating God's commandments? The readers of Mark's Gospel, of course, know the answers to these questions, but not the characters in the narrative. The beginning of Jesus' ministry, then, develops its Christological portrait in several ways. *Jesus, the Son of God,* is *the powerful herald of the kingdom* whose word is effective in deeds. Endowed with a teaching authority superior to that of the scribes, he forgives sins, associates with sinners, and acts as one who is lord of the Sabbath. Despite this portrait, the characters in the story are *ignorant of Jesus' identity*, even though demons continuously cry out that he is the Son of God (3,11).[21]

1.1.5. *Mystery of God's Kingdom and Jesus' Authority (Mk 3,13-5,43)*

a) Jesus' Choosing of the Twelve (Mk 3,13-19)

Going up the mountain, Jesus "called to himself those whom he desired and appointed Twelve to be with him and to be sent out to preach and to have authority to cast out demons" 3,13-14). It is Jesus who *chooses the Twelve* for a *twofold purpose*: "*to be with him* and *to be sent out*" on his *mission* of *preaching* and *driving out demons*. Just as Jesus was proclaiming the good news of the reign of God (cf. 1,14-15) and authoritatively exorcising those possessed by the unclean spirits (cf. 1,21-28), the Twelve will be authorized and empowered to do the same (cf. 6,7-13). Jesus' authority is shared with the Twelve apostles for the service of the people and not for domination.

b) Jesus' Power and Beelzebul (Mk 3,20-27)

Jesus is misunderstood both by his family and by the scribes from Jerusalem. His family members believe people's rumours that he is out of his mind and so they come to seize him (3,21). The scribes accuse Jesus of being "possessed by Beelzebul" and of casting out demons by the power of "the prince of demons" (3,22). As a wise teacher, Jesus asks them: "How can Satan cast out Satan?" (3,23). He shows the contradiction in the scribes' false allegation of having recourse to Satanic power to drive out demons (3,24-26). Jesus has the stronger divine power (of the Holy Spirit) to bind the strong Satan and throw him out (as is manifested in his exorcisms) (3,27). He declares the stubborn scribes to be guilty of the unpardonable sin of blasphemy against the Holy Spirit (3,28-30).

c) Jesus' Mother and Brothers (Mk 3,28-34)

When the crowd informs Jesus that his mother and brothers (cousins) are waiting outside to meet him (3,31-34), he tells the people: "Who are my mother and my brothers? ... Whoever does the will of God is my brother, sister and mother" (3,33.35). Here Jesus does not deny or reject his family relationships but insists that the right criterion to belong to God's family is to accomplish His will (which Jesus does throughout his life: cf. Mk 14,36; cf. also Mt 6,9-10: "Our Father... your will be done"). Those who *do the Father's will become children of God* and thus enter into *a new brotherly/sisterly/motherly relationship with Jesus* (3,34-35).

d) Jesus' Parables of the Kingdom of God (Mk 4,1-34)

Jesus teaches the people about the *kingdom of God* through *parables* (4,1-2). The *sower* sows some *seeds* but only those seeds that fall on *good ground* yield *much fruit* (4,8.14.20). Like the *growing seed*, the kingdom of God will grow gradually and mysteriously under the hidden action of God until the eschatological harvest (4,26-29). Or like the smallest *mustard seed* which becomes a great shrub with many branches that provide shelter to the birds of the air (4,30-32), God's kingdom will slowly but surely grow.

> For those who believe in his proclamation of the in-breaking rule of God, Jesus is the one who discloses the mystery of the kingdom (4,11). In a series of *parables* that the crowd cannot understand, he reveals, to those [disciples] who are the nucleus of his new family, that the hidden kingdom will be revealed in power (4,1-34). Thus the narrator presents *Jesus* as one who *knows the mystery of God's rule.* Furthermore, his parables are allegories that provide important Christological information since they disclose that the *sower* is *Jesus*, and the *seed* is the *proclamation of the kingdom*. Thus the parables teach that despite the insignificant beginnings of his ministry, the seed that Jesus sows will *bear fruit* when the kingdom of God appears in power.[22]

e) Jesus' Power to Perform Miracles (Mk 4,35-5,43)

(i) Calming of the storm (Mk 4,35-41)

It is surprising that, despite the great storm in the Sea of Galilee and the high waves beating into the boat, Jesus was asleep in the stern, as if unconcerned about his disciples' safety! When they wake him up, he *calms the raging storm* with a word/command ("Peace! Be still!") and he asks the disciples: "Why are you afraid? Have you no faith?" (4,35-40). Their lack of faith is the reason for their fear. Awe-stricken, they say to one another, "*Who then is this*, that even *the wind and the sea obey him?*" (4,41). They wonder about *Jesus' identity* because of *his power and authority* over the chaotic forces of nature!

(ii) Exorcism of the Gerasene demoniac (Mk 5,1-20)

Jesus' casting out the legion of demons from the uncontrollably violent man, living alone among the tombs in the Gentile country of the Gerasenes, manifests *Jesus' divine power over the evil spirits* which destroy the humanity of a man and segregate him from his community (5,1-9). The possessed man had become the mouthpiece of the demon who cried out: "What have you to do with me, *Jesus, Son of God, the Most High?* I adjure you by God, do not torment me" (5,7). It is noteworthy that, when Jesus tells the *cured demoniac* to go home and tell his friends "how much *the Lord* [God] has done for you" (5,19), the healed man goes and proclaims to the people of Decapolis "how much *Jesus* had done for him" (5,20). It means that "*Jesus*" is *his "Lord"* who has *freed* him from the destructive powers of the demonic forces.

(iii) Healing of the woman with a flow of blood (Mk 5,24-43)

On the way to Jairus' house, a woman suffering from a haemorrhage for twelve long years comes behind Jesus in the crowd and touches his garment with great faith in her heart ("If I touch even his garments, I shall be made well"), and she is immediately healed of her illness (5,25-33). Jesus addresses her endearingly, praises her faith, wishes her peace and assures her of lasting wellness: "Daughter, your faith has made you well; go in peace and be healed of your disease" (5,34). This episode reveals not only *her unfailing faith* but also *Jesus' divine healing power and his touching humaneness.*

(iv) Raising of Jairus' daughter (Mk 5,21-24.35-43)

Jairus, a ruler of the synagogue, entreats Jesus to come and save his dying daughter (5,22-23). When he gets the shocking news of his daughter's death, Jesus reassures him: "Do not fear, only believe" (5,35-36) and Jesus goes with him to his house. After putting all the mourners out, Jesus *raises the dead daughter to life* by taking her by the hand and telling her: "Little girl, I say to you, arise" (5,41). Through his *human touch and divine word*, Jesus restores life to the twelve-year-old girl. When she gets up and walks, Jesus asks her parents to *give her* something *to eat* (5,42-43), which manifests his *human concern* for her.

It is to be noted that all the *four miracles* narrated above (4,35-5,43) manifest *Jesus' mysterious power* over *storm, Satan, sickness* and *death.* They reveal Jesus not only as *powerful in word and deed* but also as *compassionate* to those *struggling* and *suffering* in various ways.

1.1.6. Jesus, the Shepherd-Messiah (Mk 6,1-8,30)

a) Rejection of Jesus at Nazareth (Mk 6,1-6)

Many in the Synagogue at Nazareth are *astonished* at *Jesus' teaching* with *wisdom* and doing *miracles* ("mighty works") (6,1-2). But others are *scandalized* because he is a village *carpenter*, the son of Mary and brother of James, Joses, Judas and Simon, which shows that familiarity breeds prejudice and leads to contempt (6,3). However, Jesus is aware that *rejection* by his own people is the fate of every *prophet* (6,4). Because they refused *to believe*, Jesus "could do no mighty work there" (6,5). "And he marvelled because of their *unbelief*" (6,6). In short, *the* disbelieving *people* in his native village *reject Jesus* as '*teacher* and *prophet*'!

b) The Mission of the Twelve (Mk 6,7-13)

Jesus *sends out the Twelve* two by two *with his authority* over unclean spirits but *with no material provisions* (like bread or bag or money) for their ministry, except a staff and a pair of sandals for their journey (6,7-10). They are also told that they may, like Jesus, experience *rejection* by some people (6,11).

Mark tells us that the Twelve went out and *preached repentance* (change of mind and heart), *cast out* many demons and *cured* several sick persons (6,12-13). From this, it is clear that *the mission of the Twelve* was an *extension of Jesus' ministry* of *preaching and healing the* (physically and mentally) *sick* in Galilee (cf. 1,14-15.21-39; etc.). Ostensibly, their mission was successful and they did not experience rejection by the people (cf. 6,30).

c) Beheading of John the Baptist (Mk 6,14-29)

There is a *division of opinion* among the people about *Jesus' identity* whether he is *Elijah* or a *prophet* or *John the Baptist* who was beheaded by Herod Antipas but raised from the dead by God (6,14-16).

The Markan purpose of *sandwiching* the narrative of the *murder of John the Baptist* (6,17-29) between the *sending* of the Twelve (6,7-13) and their *return* (6,30) seems to point to the *parallel* between the recent fate of the Baptist and the future fate of Jesus and the Twelve.[23]

The gory story of the *beheading of the Baptist* (6,21-28) who dared to question king Herod's immoral and adulterous union with his brother's wife Herodias (6,18) shows how (Herodias') hatred (6,19-25) and (Herod's) false sense of honour led to the brutal butchery of justice (6,26-28). Readers start getting a *premonition* that something similar might be in store for Jesus!

d) *Messianic Miracles, Misunderstandings and Controversies (Mk 6,30-8,26)*

(i) Feeding of the five thousand (Mk 6,30-42)

When Jesus saw a great crowd, "he had *compassion* on them because they were like *sheep without a shepherd*; and he began to teach them many things" (6,34). Seeing the leaderless multitude in front of him, Jesus felt compassion for them deep within ("he was moved in his inward parts" [*esplagchnisthê*, *splagchna*, bowels, womb]." It is his human compassion that moves him to teach the hapless crowd.

In the evening the disciples request Jesus to send the hungry people away so that they may go and buy some food from the surrounding villages (6,35-36). He tells them: "*You* give them something to eat"[24] but they plead helplessness to "buy two hundred denarii worth of bread" (6,37)! On being asked how many loaves they have, they reply: "Five, and two fish" (6,38). Taking their five loaves and two fish, Jesus blesses them, breaks them and gives them to the disciples to distribute them to the crowd and all of them eat till they are fully satisfied, and at the end of the meal twelve baskets of residual pieces are collected (6,39-42). Jesus' miraculous feeding of the five thousand fulfils God's promise to the people of Israel: "I will set up over them one shepherd, my servant David, and he shall feed them: he shall feed them and be their shepherd" (Ezek 34,23). "In this initial feeding scene, then, the Markan narrator presents *Jesus* as *the Shepherd-Messiah* who feeds Israel by *teaching* as well as by *multiplying the loaves*."[25] Thus Jesus' teaching the crowd and feeding them with his disciples' food are valuable *lessons* that they must be *ready to share* their food and knowledge with the hungry and the illiterate, without excluding anybody among the poor.[26]

(ii) Walking on the stormy sea (Mk 6,45-52)

After sending the crowd away and despatching the disciples by boat to Bethsaida, Jesus goes up to the mountain to pray alone till evening (6,45-47). Realizing that the disciples in the boat are struggling against strong headwinds, he comes to them walking on the stormy sea, but they are terrified, thinking him to be a ghost (6,48-50). He reassures them saying, "Take heart, it is I (*egô eimi*, "I am"); have no fear" (6,50). When he gets into their boat, the strong wind ceases, and they are "utterly astounded" (6,51)! The disciples are stupefied at the sudden stopping of the storm as soon as Jesus enters their boat but they fail to understand its deeper significance, namely, with the *presence of Jesus*, the *divine "I am"* (*egô eimi*) with them, they need not be afraid of any destructive force around them (cf. 6,50-52).

(iii) Healing of the sick in Gennesaret (Mk 6,53-56)

Crowds carried seriously sick persons on pallets and brought them to Jesus wherever he went (village, city, countryside or market-place) in Gennesaret. *Touching* even the fringe of his garment was enough for the sick to be made well (6,54-56). Here *Jesus* is presented as a *powerful and universal healer.*

(iv) Controversies with the Pharisees and scribes (Mk 7,1-23)

When the Pharisees and the scribes criticize Jesus' disciples for eating without washing the hands, he condemns their hypocrisy of holding on to the traditions of the elders while neglecting God's commandments (e.g., to honour the parents and help them in their needs) (7,1-13). Jesus tells the people and his disciples that it is not what goes into the stomach that defiles anybody, but what comes out of the heart. Food that is ingested just passes through the digestive system, but the produce of the heart, viz. evil thoughts, sinful words and immoral deeds – these are the real spoilers (7,14-23). Here Jesus gives *priority* to the *purity of the heart* (inner) over ritual purity of the hands (external).

(v) Exorcism of the Syrophoenician woman's daughter (Mk 7,24-30)

When Jesus is in a Gentile house in the region of Tyre and Sidon, a Greek woman (of Syrophoenician origin) comes and falls at his feet and pleads with him to cast a demon out of her daughter at home (7,24-26). Jesus tells her: "Let the children be fed first, for it is not good/right (*kalos*) to take the children's bread and throw it to the puppies" (*kynaria* 7,27). But she replies to him: "Lord, even the puppies under the table eat the crumbs from the children's bread" (7,28). Her smart and remarkable response challenges Jesus to *broaden his mission* beyond the Jews ("children") to *include the Gentiles* ("puppies")! Touched by the *Gentile woman's faith* in his universal healing power, he gives her what she wants – the complete cure of her daughter without even moving an inch from his place. (7,29-30). Thus, Jesus extends his *healing mission to the Gentiles.*

(vi) Healing of a deaf and dumb man (Mk 7,31-37)

In the region of the Decapolis, a *deaf and dumb man* is brought to Jesus "to lay his hand upon him" (7,31-32), that is, to heal him by touching and blessing him. So Jesus puts his fingers into the deaf man's ears and applies his spittle upon the dumb man's tongue so that he can feel Jesus' healing actions (7,33). Looking up to heaven in prayer, Jesus tells the deaf and dumb man: "Be opened" (*ephphatha* 7,34) and thus his *hearing and speaking faculties* are *restored* to the great astonishment of all (7,35-37).

(vii) Feeding of the four thousand (Mk 8,1-10)

Just as Jesus fed the five thousand because of his compassion for them (6,34), now he is concerned about the large crowd because they have been with him for three days and they have nothing to eat and if they are sent away on an empty stomach they will faint on the way (8,1-3). Even though the disciples feel helpless to feed such a big crowd in the desert (8,4), Jesus takes the disciples' seven loaves and a few fish and, after giving thanks to God and breaking them, he gives them to the disciples to feed the four thousand miraculously (8,5-9). The lesson Jesus teaches his disciples is: "Share what you have with the starving and trust that the Lord will do the rest."

> Between the feeding of the five thousand [6,30-42] and the feeding of the four thousand [8,1-10], Jesus heals great crowds of people at Gennesaret (6,53-56), criticizes the Pharisees and scribes for placing the traditions of the elders above the commandments of God (7,1-23), travels into gentile territory and exorcises a demon from the daughter of a Greek woman (7,24-30) and heals a deaf [and dumb] man in the district of Decapolis (7,31-37). *Markan Christology* unfolds in several ways in this section. First, Mark notes that at Gennesaret great numbers of people were *healed by simply touching* the tassel of Jesus' cloak (6,56). Second, the *power of Jesus* is *so great* that he *can exorcise a demon even from a distance*. Third, Jesus shows himself to be the *authentic interpreter of God's will*, who obeys God's commandments. Finally, having declared that *food does not defile a person*, Jesus *extends his ministry to Gentiles* in the land of Tyre, Sidon, and the Decapolis. With an allusion to the messianic text of Isa. 35,5-6, people declare, "He has *done*

everything well; he *even makes the deaf to hear and the mute to speak*" (7,37).[27]

(viii) The Pharisees' demand for a sign (Mk 8,11-13) and the disciples' lack of understanding (Mk 8,14-21)

Even though Jesus has performed many miracles of feeding, healing and exorcism (cf. 6,30-8,10), the *Pharisees demand a spectacular sign* (wonder) from heaven, which reveals *their closed minds*, because of which he refuses to perform any sensational sign for them and decides to depart from them and to go away to another place (8,11-13).

Similarly, despite the *disciples* having witnessed Jesus' feeding thousands with barely a few loaves of bread and gathered "many baskets full of broken pieces," yet they *do not understand who Jesus is*, because their "hearts are hardened" (8,14-21)! They *fail to recognize* that *Jesus* is *the caring Shepherd-Messiah.*

(ix) Healing of a blind man at Bethsaida (Mk 8,22-26)

As in the case of the healing of the deaf and dumb man (cf. 7,31-37), a *blind man* is brought by people to Jesus so that he may *touch* him and heal him; Jesus takes him by the hand and leads him out of the village and *applies his saliva on his eyes* and *his vision is restored slowly* (8,22-25).

The *healing* of the *blind man* in *two stages* seems to symbolize the gradual growth in the *disciples' faith in Jesus.* In the *first stage,* the blind man sees but not clearly, for he has only a *blurred vision*, seeing vaguely *men like walking trees* (8,22-24), but in the *second stage*, he *sees everything clearly* (8,25). Similarly, the disciples *begin to recognize Jesus as the Messiah* (cf. 8,27-30) but *fail to understand* what kind of a Messiah he is, namely, that he is *the suffering Son of Man* (cf. 8,31-33). Only after his passion-death-resurrection will the disciples perceive the *true nature* of his Messiahship, namely, as *the suffering Messiah.*

(x) Peter's confession of Jesus as the Messiah (Mk 8,27-30)
On the way to Caesarea Philippi, Jesus asks the disciples: "Who do people say that I am?" (8,27) and they report that he is John the Baptist or Elijah or one of the prophets (8,28). Now he asks his disciples a direct question: "But who do *you* say that I am?" As the leader of the group, Peter confesses their faith in him by declaring: "*You are the Christ*" (8,29). His declaration of Jesus as the expected (royal) *Messiah* ("the anointed one") is partially correct but *inadequate* because he is also *the suffering Messiah* (cf. Jesus' passion-predictions at 8,31; 9,31; 10,32-34).

> Jesus is the Shepherd-Messiah who heals, feeds, and teaches his people, the one who brings Jew and Gentile together. But he is also the Messiah who must suffer, die, and rise from the dead before he returns as God's glorious eschatological agent. To speak of Jesus apart from his destiny as the Son of Man, therefore, is inadequate.[28]

1.2. Jesus' Passion Predictions of the Son of Man (on the Way to Jerusalem) (Mk 8,31-10,52)

Jesus' *three passion predictions* and *three miracles* narrated in 8,31-10,52 are not understood by his disciples and therefore he *instructs* them on *discipleship* and its *demands*, especially on the *necessity and meaning* of *suffering* so that they would gradually become *Christ-like.*

1.2.1. First Passion Prediction and Demands of Discipleship (Mk 8,31-9,29)

a) Jesus, a Suffering Messiah/Son of Man (Mk 8,31-33)
When Peter confessed the disciples' faith in Jesus as "the Messiah"

(8,29), Jesus charged them not to tell this to anyone (8,30) lest he should be misunderstood as a royal Davidic Messiah. "And he began to teach them that the Son of man must (*dei*) suffer many things, and be rejected by the elders and the chief priests and the scribes, and be killed, and after three days rise again" (8,31). This is the first time that Jesus tells the disciples plainly that he has to suffer, die and be raised from the dead, which indicates that he is *the suffering Messiah/Son of Man.*

> In effect, the Gospel of Mark redefines Messiahship in terms of suffering, death, and resurrection. It replaces the royal Davidic Messiah who defeats Israel's enemies in this age with a Messiah who must fulfill his destiny as the Son of Man. Only after he has passed through suffering and death will the Messiah return in power with God's holy angels at the end of the ages (8,38). Prior to Jesus' death and resurrection, however, his disciples are unable to comprehend this mystery of the Son of Man.[29]

Peter's "rebuke" of Jesus (8,32) and Jesus' "rebuke" (reprimand) of Peter (8,33: "Get behind me, *Satan*![30] For you are not on the side of God, but of men") show that Peter is far from understanding the suffering dimension of the Messiah in the salvific plan of God.

b) Suffering, an Indispensable Part of Discipleship (Mk 8,34-38)

Jesus teaches the disciples and the people on the *necessity of suffering* (8,34: "If any man would come after me, let him deny himself and take up his *cross* and *follow* me"). A *true follower/ disciple* must be ready and willing to "*lose his life*" for the sake of Jesus and the Gospel. Only then will he "*save his life*" (8,35). Hence *suffering (cross)* is an *indispensable demand of discipleship and* an *integral part of God's plan of salvation.*

c) Jesus' Transfiguration (Mk 9,2-13)

When Jesus was *transfigured* (his appearance changed and even his clothes shone white, accompanied by Elijah and Moses in conversation) on a high mountain before Peter, James and John (9,2-4), a heavenly voice from the cloud declared to them the *true identity of Jesus* and demanded that they should listen to him: "This is *my Son, the beloved; listen to him*" (9,7). The disciples must *listen* to what Jesus, *God's beloved Son*, has already revealed to them and will reveal regarding the *suffering destiny* of *the Son of Man* and that of *his true disciples* (cf. 8,31-38; cf. also 9,12.30-32; 10,32-34).[31]

d) Jesus' Exorcism of a Possessed Dumb Boy (Mk 9,14-29)

The *disciples fail* to exorcise the demon from the dumb boy (9,17-18) because of their *lack of faith* (9,19: "unbelieving"; 9,23: "All things are possible to him who believes"). Now the father of the boy cries out in supplication: "I believe; help my unbelief!" (9,24). Jesus rebukes the unclean spirit and commands it to come out of the boy and, after crying out and convulsing him, it comes out of him, leaving him seemingly dead (9,25-27). "But Jesus took him by the hand and lifted him up, and he arose" (9,28). This reveals not only *Jesus' divine power over the demon* but also *his human compassion* for the suffering boy and his hapless father (cf. 9,20-24).

When the disciples ask Jesus why they could not cast out the demon, he tells them about the absolute necessity of *prayer*: "This kind cannot be driven out by anything but prayer" (9,28-29). It is the divine power, experienced through prayerful communion with God, that can drive out the demonic power that enslaves persons. No disciple/Christian can be an agent of lasting societal transformation unless s/he is a *prayerful person* attuned to the heart of Jesus/God and continually drawing the divine energy for the difficult mission of liberation.

1.2.2. Second Passion Prediction and Demands of Discipleship (Mk 9,30-10,31)

a) Second Passion Prediction (Mk 9,30-32)

Even though Jesus had told the disciples about the necessity of his suffering, death and resurrection (cf. 8,31-33) and even though during his transfiguration the Father had asked them to "listen" to his beloved Son's teaching about his impending passion (cf. 9,7), the *disciples failed to understand Jesus' second prediction* of his betrayal, death and resurrection after three days, and they were even *afraid to ask* him for an explanation (9,31-32). A *suffering Messiah* was simply beyond their comprehension at that time!

b) Servant-Leadership (Mk 9,33-37)

On the way to Capernaum, the disciples discuss with one another who is the *greatest* among them (9,33-34), indicating their ambition to be the *first*. Jesus instructs the Twelve, "if anyone would be *first*, he must be *last* of all and *servant* of all" (9,35). Here "servant of all" stresses the "*servant-leadership*."[32] *Service* is the *ideal of Christian leadership*.

Children had the lowest status in society; they were considered as the "last of all". Jesus had a special love for them. He tells the disciples: "Whoever receives *one of such children* in my name receives me; and whoever receives me, receives not me but him who sent me" (9,37). Jesus identifies himself with the "last of all" (9,35.37). Whoever welcomes Jesus (present in the "last of all" in society) welcomes God who sent him (9,37).

c) *Inclusiveness and Tolerance (Mk 9,38-41)*

When John (one of the Twelve) forbids an anonymous man (not belonging to the group of disciples) casting out demons in the name of Jesus (9,38), he tells his disciples to be *broad-minded* in their attitude to the so-called "*outsiders*" (9,39), "for he that is not against us is for us" (9,40). He asks the disciples to be *inclusive and tolerant*, not exclusive and inimical, in their relationship with others (irrespective of their caste, creed or cult) who work for the liberation of the suppressed sections of society from the enslaving evil forces and powers (the demons of today).

d) *Temptations to Sin (Mk 9,42-50)*

Jesus warns the disciples against "*scandalizing*" (causing to stumble/sin) the "little ones" who believe in him (9,42). It is better to drown oneself in the sea than to cause others to sin (9,42)! Jesus also instructs the disciples to *avoid temptations* to personal sin. His statements about maiming one's body (cf. 9,43-48) are to be understood metaphorically and not literally.

e) *Divorce, a Violation of God's Will (Mk 10,1-12)*

Questioned about the legality of *divorce*, Jesus tells the Pharisees that arbitrary and discriminative divorce of wife manifests the husband's hardness of heart (10,1-5). Since God created human beings "male and female" and intended husband and wife to "become one flesh" (10,6-8; cf. Gen 2,24) through marriage, divorce is *against the original will of God*: "What therefore God has joined together, let not man put asunder" (10,9). Here *Jesus* presents himself as the *authentic interpreter of God's will.*

f) Childlike Receptivity (Mk 10,13-16)

Jesus was indignant at his disciples who rebuked those who brought little children to him to be touched and blessed (10,13.16). He instructs the disciples to become childlike and to "receive the kingdom of God like a child" (10,14-15). *Childlike receptivity* is a necessary condition for having the gift of God's kingdom.

g) Detachment from Wealth (Mk 10,17-31)

When Jesus tells the rich man to sell his possessions and give the money to the poor and to follow him (10,21) in order "to inherit eternal life" (10,17), "he went away sorrowful" because he was unwilling to part with his "great possessions" (10,22). Undue *attachment to wealth* makes it more difficult for the rich to enter the kingdom of God than for a camel to pass through the eye of a needle (10,23-25). But Jesus promises the disciples, who "have left everything and followed" him, a *hundredfold* in this life and *eternal life* in the next (10,28-30).

1.2.3. Third Passion Prediction and Demands of Discipleship (Mk 10,32-45)

a) Third Passion Prediction (Mk 10,32-34)

On the road to Jerusalem, Jesus tells the Twelve about what is going to happen to him in the city. This is the third and most detailed passion prediction: "Behold, we are going up to Jerusalem; and the Son of man will be delivered to chief priests and scribes, and they will condemn him to death, and deliver him to the Gentiles; and they will mock him, and spit upon him, and scourge him, and kill him; and after three days he will rise" (10,33-34).

b) Servant-Leaders (Mk 10,35-45)

Jesus' detailed description of his imminent humiliations (being mocked, spat on, scourged), death and resurrection does not have any impact on the disciples. This is evident from the presumptuous request of James and John for *positions of power and privilege* in Jesus' kingdom (10,37) and the other ten disciples' envy and anger against the ambitious brothers (10,41). Even though Jesus predicts James' and John's martyrdom (symbolized by the "cup" of suffering and "baptism" of death) (10,38-39), he refuses to grant them positions of power ("to sit at my right hand or my left") (10,40). Jesus instructs his disciples that in the Christian community they should not, like the Gentiles, "rule over" others or "lord it over them" but rather they must be like a "*servant*" (*diakonos*) or a "*slave*" (*doulos*) ever *ready to serve* others (10,41-44). They must follow the example of *Jesus*, the *Son of Man*, the *servant-leader*, who "came not to be served but to serve and to give his life as a ransom for many" (10,45). They should be willing even to *sacrifice their lives* for the sake of others.

Unfortunately, there are only very few Church leaders who are Jesus-like servant-leaders whose goal in ministry is to serve others selflessly and generously, without counting the cost. Sadly, many Bishops and priests are like worldly leaders who are longing for wealth, power and prestige (name and fame)! However, Pope Francis is a beacon of light of self-giving love and self-sacrificing service of others.

1.2.4. Jesus' Healing of Blind Bartimaeus (Mk 10,46-52)

When the blind beggar Bartimaeus began to cry out, "Jesus, Son of David, have mercy on me" (10,47), many rebuked him and tried to shut him up but he kept on crying out all the louder, "Son of David, have mercy on me" (10,48). Bartimaeus addressing Jesus "*Son of David*" amounts to acknowledging him as the *royal Messiah*. When he is told that Jesus is calling him, he throws off his garment and springs up (with hope in his heart) and comes to Jesus (10,50). On being asked, "What do you want me to do for you?" the blind man replies, "My master (*Rabbouni*), that I may see again" (*hina anablepsô*) (10,51). His request implies that he had lost his sight and is now pleading to regain it. Acknowledging the blind man's faith, Jesus tells him, "Go, your faith has saved you" (*sesôken se* 10,52). Here "saving" seems to imply more than mere physical well-being. "And immediately he regained his sight (*aneblepsen*) and was following him on the way" (10,52). As a result of the recovery of his sight, the cured blind man's *faith in Jesus as the Messiah* is confirmed and he "follows" him.

Bartimaeus' "*following him*" means that he became a disciple of Jesus (cf. 1,17-18.20; 2,14; 10,21) and accompanied him "on the way" to Jerusalem. Thus *Bartimaeus* is an inspiring *example of true discipleship*.

1.3. Jesus, the Son of God's Passion (in Jerusalem) (Mk 11,1-16,8)

1.3.1. Jesus' Entry into Jerusalem, Temple-Cleansing and Teaching (Mk 11,1-12,44)

This Section starts with Jesus' *humble royal entry into Jerusalem* and his survey of the Temple (11,1-11), followed by the *cleansing of the Temple* (11,15-19) which is "sandwiched" between the cursing of the fig tree (11,12-14) and its drying up (11,20-25). The rest of the Section consists of Jesus' *authoritative teaching in the Temple* (11,27-12,44).

a) Humble Royal Entry into Jerusalem (Mk 11,1-10)

Jesus sends two of his disciples to fetch a *colt* from a neighbouring village (11,1-6) and he *rides on the donkey* (*not* on a warhorse) and enters Jerusalem as *a humble, peace-loving king* (11,7; cf. Zech. 9,9-10).

The crowds spread their garments and leafy branches on his path (Mk 11,8) and pay *royal homage*, crying out, "Hosanna! Blessed is he who comes in the name of the Lord! (11,9; cf. Ps 118,25-26). Their expectations are high that *Jesus*, the *kingly Messiah*, will soon restore David's kingdom: "Blessed is the coming kingdom of our father David!" (11,10;). But, like Peter (cf. 8,31-33), the crowds do not understand that Jesus will establish the kingdom of God not through armed conquest but through suffering and self-sacrifice.

b) The Triptych of the Cursing of the Barren Fig Tree, the Cleansing of the Temple and the Withering of the Tree (Mk 11,12-21)

From the artistic point of view, Mark has painted Jesus' *cleansing of the Temple* (11,15-19) as the *central panel* of a *triptych*, whose *first panel* is his *cursing* of the barren fig tree (11,12-14) and the *third panel* is its *withering* (11,15-21). It means that the cleansing of the Temple must be interpreted in the light of its neighbouring episodes.

> In one of Mark's famous sandwiching episodes, Jesus curses a fig tree, drives the merchants from the temple, and then returns the next day to find the fig tree withered (11, 12-25). While at first sight Jesus' actions may seem like an arbitrary tantrum against an innocent tree (Mark notes that figs were not in season), the intercalation shows something far more significant. In the Old Testament, unfaithful Israel is sometimes portrayed as a barren vine or fig tree (Mic. 7,1; Hos. 9,16; Isa. 5,1-7). For Mark, then,

> both the cursing [& withering] of the fig tree and the clearing of the temple represent Jesus' judgment of Israel. The Messiah symbolically acts against an unfaithful nation.[33]

When Jesus enters the Temple [the court of the Gentiles], he finds it like a market-place full of merchants, moneychangers and buyers, and he drives them all out of the area (11,15-16). This was a *prophetic action of protest* against the *desecration* of the *holy place of prayer for all the peoples* (both the Jews and the Gentiles).

As part of his prophetic teaching in the Temple, Jesus asks the merchants, moneychangers and others, "Is it not written, 'My house shall be a house of prayer for all the nations'? But you have made it a den of robbers ("bandits' stronghold": 11,17; cf. Is 56,7; Jer 7,11).[34]

The *withering* of the *fruitless fig tree* (11,20-21), which Jesus cursed on the day of the Temple cleansing (11,12-14), symbolizes the *demise of the Temple.* "Just as the fig tree withered and died because it did not bear fruit, so the Temple of Jerusalem will wither and die because it has not become a house of prayer for all the nations, Gentiles as well as Jews."[35]

The Jewish leaders (the chief priests, scribes and elders) question *Jesus' authority* to cleanse the Temple and to teach there, "By what authority are you doing these things, or who gave you authority to do them?" (11,28). Since they *pretend ignorance* to answer his counter-question about the origin of John's baptism (was it divine or human?), Jesus too declines to reply to their question about his authority (11,29-32). Thus Jesus not only *exposes the Jewish leaders' hypocrisy* but also *refuses to accept their presumptuous authority* to question him.

c) *The Parable of the Vineyard and the Wicked Tenants (Mk 12,1-12)*

When the owner of the vineyard sends his servants to the tenants to collect rent, some are beaten up and others are killed (12,1-5). Finally, when the owner's "*beloved son*" is sent to the tenants, they murder him and throw him out of the vineyard (12,6-8), for which the owner will "destroy the tenants, and give the vineyard to others" (12,9).

The *allegorical parable* of the *wicked tenants* shows that, just as *unfaithful leaders* of Israel had rejected, persecuted and killed God's *servants/messengers* (the *prophets*) over the centuries, the *Jewish leaders* will murder *Jesus, God's "beloved son"* (cf. 1,11; 9,7), the *heir* of the vineyard (12,6-8).

Realizing that "he had told the parable against them, they [the Jewish leaders] tried to arrest him" (12,12) but they could not because they were afraid of the crowd.

d) *Paying Taxes to Caesar (Mk 12,13-17)*

The hypocritical *Pharisees* and the pro-Roman *Herodians* try to trap Jesus first by flattering him (12,13-14) and then by asking him a *crafty question*, "*Is it lawful to pay taxes to Caesar or not?*" (12,14). If Jesus were to say "yes," the Pharisees would have branded him as being anti-Jewish, and if he were to say "no," the Herodians would have accused him as being anti-Caesar! Seeing through their wily and hypocritical plot to trap him, Jesus asks for a Roman coin (with the image and inscription of Emperor Caesar on it) (12,15-16) and declares: "*Render to Caesar the things that are Caesar's, and to God the things that are God's*" (12,17). His wise statement outwits the cunning Herodians and hypocritical Pharisees to their utter amazement (12,17)!

e) *Dispute with the Sadducees on the Resurrection (Mk 12,18-27)*

Now it is the turn of the *Sadducees* (who do not believe in the resurrection of the dead) to try and trap Jesus in his teachings (12,18). Citing the Mosaic law of levirate marriage (cf. Deut 25,5-10), they tell the story of a *woman* who was *married to seven brothers* one after the other (after each one's death) (12,19-22). And they question Jesus, "In the resurrection *whose wife* will she be? For the seven had her as wife" (12,23).

Jesus *authoritatively* tells the Sadducees that they are "*wrong*" (12,24.27) in their superficial interpretation of the resurrection of the dead since they "know neither the Scriptures nor the power of God" (12,24). He states that life after resurrection does not involve marriage: "For when they rise from the dead, they neither marry nor are given in marriage, but are like angels in heaven" (12,25). The risen life is not a resuscitated life but a spiritually transformed life beyond bodily/physical/sexual relationships. Jesus reminds the Sadducees of the burning bush revelation of God to Moses, "*I am* the God of Abraham, the God of Isaac and the God of Jacob" (cf. Ex 3,6). Jesus interprets it as, "He is not the God of the dead, but of the living" (Mk 12,27), which he understands as a reference to the resurrection of the dead. The God in whom Abraham, Isaac and Jacob believed and who manifested himself to Moses as "*I Am*" from the burning bush is the ever-present and eternal "God of the living" here on earth and hereafter. "The power of God" (12,24) transforms human beings through resurrection into ever-living spiritual beings "like angels in heaven" (12,25).

f) The Great Commandment of Love (Mk 12,28-34)

When one of the *scribes* asks Jesus the question: "Which *commandment* is the *first* of all?" (12,28), he states that whole-hearted "*love of God*" (cf. Deut 6,4) is the *first* commandment and large-hearted "*love of the neighbour*" (cf. Lev 19,18) is the *second* (Mk 12,29-31). Jesus places the "love of neighbour" *on a par* with the "love of God" or, rather, they are so *intrinsically interrelated* that one cannot exist without the other. And he concludes authoritatively: "There is no other commandment greater than these" (12,31). He *sums up* all the commandments of God in this *twofold commandment of love of God and neighbour.* Jesus assures the scribe who agrees with Jesus' teaching on divinehuman love (*agapê*): "You are not far from the kingdom of God" (12,34). Anyone who loves God and also neighbour is drawing near to the reign of God. *Love* is the straight *path* that leads *to God's kingdom.*

g) Question about the Messiah as the Son of David (Mk 12,35-37)

While teaching in the Temple, Jesus questions the scribes' understanding of the *Messiah* to be the "*son of David,*" since David himself, "inspired by the Holy Spirit," calls his son "*Lord*" (12,35-37; cf. Ps 110,1). Even though blind Bartimaeus had addressed Jesus as "son of David" (cf. 10,47-48), Jesus' puzzling question to the scribes implies that he is the "*Christ*" (*Christos*) and "Lord" (*Kyrios*) not because he is David's son but because he is *God's son* (cf. "my beloved Son": 1,11; 9,7).

h) The Widow's Offering (Mk 12,41-44)

After watching the rich putting large sums of money into the Temple treasury, Jesus praises a *poor widow's offering* of "two copper coins" as a generous and self-sacrificing act of *giving her all* (12,41-44). Jesus declares to his disciples that, whereas the wealthy have donated from their abundance, this widow "out of her poverty has put in *all what she had*, her whole living" (12,44). God does not look at the quantity of the offering but the quality of the giver. Jesus presents the *poor widow* as *prefiguring his own generous sacrifice of his life* and as an *ideal disciple* to be followed.

1.3.2. Jesus' Eschatological Discourse [on the Mount of Olives] (Mk 13,1-37)

When Jesus and his disciples come out of the Temple, one of them praises the beauty of the *Temple* building but Jesus predicts its *destruction* (13,1-2).

While sitting on the Mount of Olives (opposite the Temple), the disciples ask Jesus about the time of the Temple-destruction and its antecedent signs (13,3-4). But instead of answering their question directly, he gives a long *eschatological discourse* (13,5-37), which has three descriptive sections: a) "beginning of the sufferings" (13,5-13), b) "the great tribulation" (13,14-23), c)"triumph of the Son of Man" (13,24-27), followed by an "exhortation to confidence and vigilance" (13,28-37).[36]

> Jesus first warns the disciples not to be alarmed by *catastrophic events* common to the present age, which may be misconstrued as signs of the end: false messiahs will arise and deceive many; there will be wars, earthquakes, and famines. These are merely *precursor* events, like the birth pains of a woman in labour (13,5-9). Jesus seems to envision a significant time gap before the end: the gospel will be preached to all nations; believers will suffer great persecution and even betrayal by friends and family. The *climactic event* will be the "abomination of desolation," a phrase originally used of the desecration of the Temple by Antiochus

IV 'Epiphanes' (Dan 11,31-32)... Jesus says a similar idolatrous sacrilege will climax this great period of persecution. When his followers see this horrific event, they should flee Jerusalem, for the greatest persecution of all time will follow (13,14-23). Yet the outcome out of this great trial will be their deliverance: *the Son of Man will come on the clouds with great power and glory*, and his angels will gather his chosen ones from around the world (13,24-27).[37]

Since the exact *time* of this eschatological event of the *glorious coming of the Son of Man* is *known to no one* except to God the Father (13,32), Jesus instructs the disciples to be *faithful* like the devoted servants and be *watchful* like the alert doorkeeper ever ready to welcome the master of the house whenever he comes (13,33-37).

Jesus' disciples must be faithful to the end and always ready for his return. Jesus repeatedly tells them to be alert, keep watch, and be on their guard (13,5.9.23.33.34.35.37). The discourse thus continues *two key themes* in Mark's Gospel: *Israel's rejection and its consequences*, and the *need for faithfulness and self-sacrificial discipleship*. The suffering and trials which Jesus predicts for his disciples are those he is about to face. *His faithfulness* will serve as *an example.*[38]

© Jesus' ministry in Jerusalem [Mk 11-13] offers several *Christological insights*. First, he is *God's beloved Son* who *teaches and acts with authority* in Jerusalem's Temple. Second, he has come for a *harvest* that includes *Gentiles* as well as *Jews*, but those charged with the harvest have not been faithful. Third, *Jesus the Messiah* is *God's Son* rather than the son of David. Fourth, at a future time, the Son will return as the *glorious Son of Man* to gather his elect, but before this can occur, Jesus must tread the path of the *suffering Son of Man.*[39]

1.3.3. Jesus, the Son of God's Passion (in Jerusalem) (Mk 14,1-16,8)

Mk 14-16 consists of *seven Sections: a) Jesus' Anointing and the Last Supper (14,1-31); b) Jesus' Prayer, Betrayal and Arrest in Gethsemane (14,32-52); c) Jesus before the Sanhedrin and Peter's Denials (14,53-72); d) Jesus' before Pilate and the Mocking Soldiers (15,1-20); e) Jesus' Crucifixion and Death (15,20-41); f) Jesus' Burial by Joseph of Arimathea (15,42-47); g) Jesus' Empty Tomb and Resurrection (16,1-8).*

a) Jesus' Anointing and the Last Supper (Mk 14,1-31)

The *anointing of Jesus* by a woman (14,3-9) is "*sandwiched*" between the plot of the Pharisees and the scribes to arrest Jesus and kill him (14,1-2) and Judas' contract with the chief priests to betray him for money (14,10-11).

(i) Jesus' anointing (Mk 14,3-9)

The *anointing of Jesus' head* by an anonymous woman[40] with a very expensive perfume was a symbolic acknowledgement of his *royal Messianic identity* (cf. 11,7-10; 2 Kings 9,6). Jesus, however, interprets her anointing him as a preparation of his body for *burial* (14,7-9) since he is aware of his imminent passion (cf. 8,31; 9,31; 10,32-34).[41]

(ii) The Last Supper (Mk 14,12-31)

During the celebration of the Jewish Passover with his disciples (which they had carefully prepared: cf. 14,12-16), Jesus' *institution of the Eucharist* (14,22-25) is "*sandwiched*" between his predictions of Judas' betrayal (14,17-21) and the disciples' desertion and Peter's denials (14,26-31). Here there is a striking *contrast* between *Jesus' self-sacrificing death*, which is symbolized by his broken "body" and "blood of the covenant poured out for many" (14,22-24), and the *disciples' betrayal, desertion and denial*. All his disciples (like the sheep) will desert him when he (the Shepherd) will be struck (14,27; cf. Zech 13,7). But Jesus promises them, "after I am raised up, I will go before you to Galilee" (14,28). Thus the risen *Shepherd-Messiah* will gather them together in Galilee (cf. 16,7).

- Prediction of betrayal (14,17-21): During the Passover meal with the Twelve, Jesus predicts *Judas' betrayal*: "One of you will betray me, one who is eating with me" (14,18). It is heartbreaking for Jesus to realize that a close friend who enjoys table-fellowship with him ("one who is dipping bread into the dish with me" 14,20) is his treacherous betrayer! And he wishes that the betrayer had not been born (14,21)! By not revealing the betrayer's name, however, Jesus protects him from any harm by the other disciples. But Judas' heart is hardened and he refuses to repent of his plot to betray his master!

- Institution of the Lord's Supper (14,22-25): During the meal, having taken a loaf of bread and blessed it, Jesus *broke* it and *gave* it to the disciples, saying: "Take, this is *my body*" (14,22). The disciples are invited to share the *broken bread*, which highlights the *broken body of Jesus* to be *sacrificed*. Similarly, having taken a cup and given thanks (*eucharistêsas*) [to God], he *gave* it to them and said: "This is *my blood of the covenant*, poured out *for many* (*hyper pollôn*)" (12,23). The "blood of the covenant" reminds them of Ex 24,8 (where Moses sealed God's covenant with the people of Israel by sprinkling the *blood of the sacrificial animals* on them). The Hebrew expression "*for many*" means "*for all*," since the former alludes to Is 53,11-12 (the Servant of God who will make "many" righteous by suffering "for the sins of many"). Through these OT allusions, Jesus interprets his *death* as *a sacrifice for others/all.* In short, the *Lord's Supper* is primarily a *sacrificial meal.* But it may also point to the future *eschatological banquet* in the Kingdom of God (14,25).[42]

- Prediction of Peter's denial (14,26-31): After singing the hymns (psalms of praise), Jesus and the disciples go out to the Mount of Olives (14,26). Jesus tells them about their imminent desertion: "You will all fall away" (14,27) like the sheep that are scattered when the shepherd is stricken. But Peter claims: "Even though they all fall away, I will not" (14,29). Jesus tells him that he would deny him thrice before the cock crows twice that night, but he insists that, even if he must die with him, he would never deny him (14,30-31)!

b) Jesus' Prayer, Betrayal and Arrest in Gethsemane (Mk 14,32-52)

In the Garden of Gethsemane, Jesus takes Peter, James and John (the inner circle of the Twelve disciples), "and began to be greatly distressed and troubled" before them and he confides in them: "My soul is very sorrowful, even to death; remain here and watch" (14,33-34). And falling to the ground, he prays that the hour of his suffering and death may pass from him (14,35) and he pleads with his Father, "Abba, Father, all things are possible with you; remove this cup from me; yet not as I will but as you will" (14,36). Jesus' repeated agonizing prayer to the Father is to take away the cup of suffering but only if it is according to the Father's salvific will (14,36.39). But his disciples fail to watch and pray with him even for an hour but fall asleep and slumber (14,37-41)! Jesus, the suffering Son of Man and the beloved Son of God, willingly and unconditionally surrenders his life to accomplish the plan of his loving Father, namely, to save sinful humanity through his Son's sacrificial death.

In Gethsemane, there is a striking *contrast* between the praying Jesus and the sleeping disciples (14,37-41). Strengthened by his prayer to the Father, Jesus is ready to face his betrayer (14,42).

Judas (one of the Twelve) leads a crowd (armed with swords and clubs), sent by the Jewish leaders (chief priests, scribes and elders), and he addresses Jesus as "*Rabbi*" and *betrays him with a kiss* (14,43-45)! Jesus courageously confronts the armed arrest party by asking them: "Have you come out as against a robber, with swords and clubs to capture me? Day after day I was with you in the Temple teaching, and you did not seize me. But let the scriptures be fulfilled" (14,48-49). Voluntarily he lets himself be arrested to fulfil God's plan of salvation.[43]

As soon as Jesus is arrested, all the *disciples abandon* him and *flee* to save their lives (14,46-52). What a *contrast* between Christ who willingly accepts his passion and allows himself to be seized (14,49) and the disciples who desert their master (14,50) despite the earlier protestations of their unfailing loyalty to him (cf. 14,27-31)!

c) Jesus' Trial before the Sanhedrin and Peter's Denials (Mk 14,53-72)

Here *two trials* take place simultaneously, one of Jesus before the Jewish Sanhedrin (the Council of the chief priests, the elders and the scribes) presided over by the high priest (14,53-65) and the other of Peter in the courtyard of the high priest (before a servant-girl and the bystanders) (14,66-72).

Jesus is silent when false testimonies are made against him (14,55-61) but, when the high priest questions him about his identity ("Are you the Christ, the Son of the Blessed One?"), he declares unambiguously the truth ("I am; and you will see the Son of Man seated at the right hand of Power, and coming with the clouds of heaven") (14,61-62; cf. Dan 7,13). The whole Sanhedrin condemns him to death for blasphemy (14,63-64) because he affirmed his *identity* as "the Christ", "the Son of God" and "the Son of Man". These are the *three most important Messianic titles* frequently highlighted in Mark's Gospel ("*the Christ*": 1,1.11; 8,29; 9,41; 14,61; 15,32; "*the Son of God*": 1,1.11; 3,11; 5,7; 9,7; 15,39; "*the Son of Man*": 2,10.28; 8,31.38; 9,9.12.31; 10,33.45; 13,26; 14,21.41.62).

Whereas *Jesus declared* his *Messianic and divine identity* courageously before the highest Jewish Council, thrice *Peter denied* his *discipleship* and any association with Jesus before a maid-servant of the high priest and the bystanders (14,66-71)! Peter who had loudly and proudly professed his loyalty (14,29) and his readiness even to die with Jesus (14,31) proved himself to be a *coward* when questioned by a servant-girl and some onlookers about his being a disciple of Jesus! The only redeeming factor is that at the second cock-crow after his third denial Peter recalled Jesus' prediction of his denials (cf. 14,30) "and he broke down and *wept*" (14,72), which reveals his *repentance*.

d) Jesus before Pilate and the Mocking Soldiers (Mk 15,1-20)

In the Markan passion narrative, it is not only *Judas* (14,10.11.18.21.41.42) but also the *chief priests* (15,1.10) and Roman governor *Pilate* (15,15) who "*betrayed*" (*paredoken*) Jesus to others. When Pilate questions Jesus, "Are you *the king of the Jews*?", he gives an evasive answer, "You say so" (15,2), because the title has a political sense for the Roman governor but not for Jesus. Pilate is amazed at Jesus' silence when the chief priests brought many charges against him (15,4-5). Even though Pilate was aware "that it is out of envy that the chief priests had delivered him up" (15,10), instead of acquitting the blameless "king of the Jews", Pilate bargains with the chief priests and the crowd who cry for his crucifixion and he ends up appeasing them by releasing the murderer Barabbas and by delivering the innocent Jesus to be scourged and crucified (15,11-15). Thus the *Roman trial of Jesus* was *a travesty of justice*!

Now the whole battalion of *soldiers* gather in the praetorium and *mock* Jesus by making him wear a royal purple cloak and a crown of thorns, by kneeling and saluting him, "Hail, *King of the Jews!*" and by striking him on his head with a reed and spitting upon him (15,16-20). In this way, the sadist Roman *soldiers strip Jesus' human dignity* and inflict inhuman insult upon the whole of the vassal Israel.[44] After publicly disgracing the condemned "king of the Jews", the soldiers lead him out to be crucified (15,20).

e) Jesus' Crucifixion and Death (Mk 15,21-41)

On the way to "Golgotha" ("the place of the skull"), they compel a passer-by, *Simon of Cyrene*, to *carry the cross* of Jesus to the site of execution (15,21-22). On reaching there, they offer him wine mixed with myrrh (to drug him) but he refuses to drink it (15,23). They *crucify* "*the King of the Jews*" with two robbers, one on his right and the other on his left, and they divide his garments and cast lots for them (15,24-27; cf. Ps 22,19). The passers-by mock him, the chief priests and the scribes scoff at him, and they challenge him to save himself by coming down from the cross and thus manifest himself as the Messiah and the King of Israel (15,29-32). But the crucified Christ does *not* "*save himself*" by descending from the cross but *saves others* (like the criminals who were crucified alongside him) by dying on the cross.

Mark describes the *death* of Jesus in *apocalyptic* language (15,33-38). First of all, from noon ("the sixth hour") till three in the afternoon ("the ninth hour"), "there was *darkness* over the whole land" (15,33), indicating a divine judgement (cf. 13,24-25). Secondly, at Jesus' death "the *curtain of the Temple was torn open* in two, from top to bottom" (15,38: cf. the same Greek verb *skizein* at 1,10: "he [Jesus] saw the heavens *torn open*"). The tearing of the Temple-curtain, which separated the Holy Place from the Holy of Holies, symbolizes the divine disclosure of the direct access to God's presence due to the death of Jesus. Before Jesus died, he cried aloud, "*Eloi, Eloi, lama sabachthani?*" ("My God, my God, why have you forsaken me?" 15,34; cf. Ps 22,1) and with a loud cry "he breathed his last" (15,38). Seeing how he died, the *Gentile centurion confesses* his faith in Jesus as God's Son, "*Truly this man was son of God*" (*hyios theou*) (15,39).[45] This is the first time that a human being confesses Jesus as truly *human* ("this man") *and divine* ("God's Son").[46] Thus, Jesus' death is a revelation of his *human and divine identity*.

f) Jesus' Burial by Joseph of Arimathea (Mk 15,42-47)

On Friday evening, the day before the Sabbath, Joseph of Arimathea, a prominent member of the Sanhedrin, asked Pilate for the body of Jesus, which was granted to him after the centurion attested Jesus' death (15,42-45). According to the Jewish custom of burial, Joseph wraps Jesus' body in a linen shroud and lays it in a tomb hewn out of the rock and rolls a heavy stone against the door of the tomb (15,46). It is noteworthy that "a respected member of the Sanhedrin, who was also himself looking for the kingdom of God" (15,43), which Jesus had proclaimed (cf. 1,15), took courage to ask the Roman governor for the body of Jesus and to bury it in his own tomb, without any fear of pollution by the physical contact with the dead body and of adverse reaction from the Sanhedrin which had condemned Jesus to death (cf. 14,64). The death of Jesus liberates Joseph from all fear and enables him to experience in his heart the reign of God of justice, freedom and fellowship.

❖ ***Some features of Mark's passion narrative (Mk 14-15)***

The plotting of the chief priests and the scribes to arrest and kill Jesus (14,1-2) sets the tone to this section in which *Jesus is aware* not only of *his imminent suffering and death* but also of *his rejection.* When he is anointed with a precious perfume by a woman in Bethany, he interprets it as a preparation for his burial (14,3.8). During the Last Supper, he *foretells* his *betrayal* by Judas, *denial* by Peter and *desertion* by all his disciples (14,18.27.30). In Gethsemane, he is "greatly distressed and troubled" and "very *sorrowful*, even to death" (14,33-34) and *prays* repeatedly to the Father to remove the cup of suffering from him but he *surrenders* his will to that of the Father (14,35-36.39). In contrast to Jesus' persistent prayer and admirable faithfulness, the disciples fail to keep watch and pray with him (14,38-41). And when he is betrayed by Judas and arrested by the armed crowd (14,45-46), all the *disciples forsake* him and *flee* (14,50). Jesus' courageous declaration before the Sanhedrin that he is *the Messiah and the Son of God* and will be the glorified *Son of Man* in the future

(14,61-62), is contrasted with the scared *Simon Peter's triple denial* that he is a disciple of Jesus (14,66-71).

Not only Jesus' own disciples desert him but also his own people (the Jewish leaders and the crowds) *reject and disown* him and the Roman governor *condemns* him to death and the soldiers *mock* him.

> When he [Jesus] admits that he is "the Christ, the Son of the Blessed One," the high priest accuses him of blasphemy and the Sanhedrin calls for his execution. They mock and spit upon him; the guards beat him. At the trial before Pilate, the crowds which thronged to him for healing and free bread now cry out for his crucifixion. Pilate, the supposed administrator of Roman justice, turns a blind eye to Jesus' innocence and orders his crucifixion. The soldiers mock his kingship, beat him, and spit upon him.
>
> In the crucifixion scene, everyone present hurls abuse at Jesus. Passersby ridicule his claims; the religious leaders belittle him; even the crucified criminals heap insults on him.[47]

Finally, Jesus *dies* on the cross *in anguish*, feeling abandoned even by God, "My God, my God, why have you forsaken me?" (15,34). "And Jesus uttered a loud cry and breathed his last" (15,37). Even though his life looked like a failure and his death the final defeat, the manner of his dying manifested to the *Roman centurion* the *true identity of Jesus* because he confessed, "*This man* was truly *son of God*" (15,39).[48] "The cry of the centurion confirms again that Jesus' identity and mission are revealed not through power and conquest but sacrificial death."[49]

Mark's passion narrative challenges the readers (especially those persecuted for their faith in Jesus) and calls them to a decision. "Will they, like Jesus, face suffering and trials with faithfulness, or will they flee and deny him like the disciples? Will they respond to Jesus' suffering with recognition and faith, like the centurion, or with unbelief and rejection, like the religious leaders?"[50]

g) Jesus' Empty Tomb and Resurrection (Mk 16,1-8)

Mary Magdalene, Mary mother of Joses and James, and Salome, three of the devoted women who had followed Jesus in Galilee and ministered to him and accompanied him to Jerusalem and who were present at Calvary at his death and burial (cf. 15,40-41.47), came to the tomb with spices to anoint the body early in the morning on the next day of the Sabbath and found that the stone at the entrance to the tomb had been rolled away (16,1-4). To their utter amazement, they found a young man, dressed in a white robe (an angel?), sitting in the tomb (16,5). He reassured them and announced to them the *astounding news* that the man they were looking for, *Jesus of Nazareth who was crucified, has risen,* for which the empty tomb was the evidence (16,6)! He asked them to go and tell Peter and the other disciples, "he is going to Galilee; there they will see him, as he told you" (16,7; cf. 14,28). But it is surprising that the women fled from the tomb in fear and trembling, and "they said nothing to anyone" (16,8)!

This sudden ending of Mark's Gospel (16,8), without any narrative of the risen Jesus' appearance to anybody, is quite unexpected and puzzling! Mark seems to be asking the readers to *believe* that what Jesus had promised the disciples during the Last Supper (14,28) and what the "young man" in the empty tomb testified (16,6-7) had taken place, namely, that the crucified Jesus "has been raised" (êgerthê) and his disciples met him in Galilee.

1.x. Appendix: Later Additions (Shorter & Longer Endings of Mark) (Mk 16,9-20)

a) "The shorter ending" (immediately *after 16,8*) mentions: i) the women *reported* [which is a *correction* of *their silence* mentioned in 16,8!] what they were told at the tomb to inform Peter and other disciples and ii) the risen Jesus himself sent the disciples on the mission of "the sacred and imperishable proclamation of eternal salvation".

b) "The longer ending" of the Gospel of Mark (*16,9-20*) (probably based on John's and Luke's narratives of the risen Jesus' appearances to Mary Magdalene, to two (Emmaus) disciples and the eleven, and his ascension), is not found in any of the earliest and best manuscripts of Mark's Gospel. Furthermore, its vocabulary and style are quite different from the rest of the Gospel. Hence there is unanimous agreement among textual critics, Markan scholars and commentators that *16,9-20* is a *later addition.*[51]

The risen *Jesus' appearances to Mary Magdalene* and *two disciples* but the *other disciples' failure to believe* are reported in 16,9-13! Afterwards, he *appeared* to the *eleven disciples* and *reprimanded* them for their "*unbelief and hardness of heart*" (16,14) but he *commissioned* them: "Go into the whole world and preach the gospel to the whole creation" (16,15). *Faith* (followed by baptism) is stressed as a *condition for salvation* (16,16). Those who believe in Jesus' name are assured of performing miraculous signs like casting out demons, speaking in tongues, curing the sick, etc. (16,17-18). Finally, Jesus' ascension into heaven and the disciples' successful preaching mission everywhere (with the constant assistance of the ascended Lord) are reported in 16,19-20.

1.©. Mark's Good News of the Mysterious Messiah, the Suffering Son of Man and the Son of God

1.©.1. Markan Jesus' Titles[52]

a) The Christ (Messiah)

Although "Christ" (*Christos*) occurs only seven times in the Gospel of Mark (1,1; 8,29; 9,41; 12,35; 13,21; 14,61; 15,32), it is a *very important title* of Jesus because it is found in significant places in the plan of the Gospel. The very first verse of the Gospel starts by identifying Jesus as "*Jesus Christ*" (1,1), which stresses the fact that "Christ" has become part of Jesus' name.

Similarly, at the very end of the first part of the Gospel (1,15-8,30), when Jesus asks his disciples, "Who do you say that I am?", Peter confesses, "*You are the Christ*" (8,29). He might have understood "Christ" to be the *Davidic Messiah*, which was the major Jewish Messianic expectation at that time. This is supported by the blind Bartimaeus' cry, "Jesus, son of David, have mercy on me" (10,47-48). Also, the large Passover crowd welcomed Jesus to Jerusalem with cries of: "Hosanna! Blessed is he who comes in the name of the Lord! Blessed is the kingdom of our father David that is coming! Hosanna in the highest!" (11,9-10). The crowd took him to be the expected *Davidic king*. But Jesus does not fight and defeat Israel's enemies, the Romans, to establish a Davidic kingdom with its capital in Jerusalem. Then, what kind of a Messiah is Jesus?

While teaching in the Temple, Jesus asks, "How can the scribes say that the *Christ* is the *son of David?*" (12,35), since "David himself calls him Lord" (12,36-37; cf. Ps 110,1). It implies that Jesus considers himself as the Christ but not as a royal Messiah. He is more than David's son since David calls his son "*Lord*" (12,37).

This is made clear during Jesus' trial before the Sanhedrin, when the high priest asks Jesus, "Are you *the Christ*, *the Son* of the Blessed One?" (14,61), his reply is, "*I am*" but he immediately adds, "and you will see the Son of Man seated at the right hand of Power [God], and coming in the clouds of heaven" (14,62). His answer specifies that he is not only "*the Christ*" and "*the Son of God*" but also "*the Son of Man*" who will return in glory in the future (after his suffering, death and resurrection).

Finally, the chief priests and the scribes mocked the crucified Jesus saying, "Let the Christ, the King of Israel, come down now from the cross, that we may see and believe" (15,32). The fact that he refused to come down from the cross suggests that he does *not* claim to be the *royal Messiah* ("the Christ, the King of Israel") as the Jewish leaders (mis)interpreted him to be. Jesus is not a worldly royal Messiah but *the Son of God* and the *suffering "Son of Man"* (as we shall see below). In short, the Markan Christ is a *mysterious Messiah.*

b) The Suffering Son of Man

The enigmatic term "*the Son of Man*" occurs fourteen times in the Gospel of Mark.[53] It is found *only on Jesus' lips* and he always applies it to himself as a *self-designation.* Since he is never addressed or confessed as "the Son of Man," it is *not a confessional title* like "the Christ" and "the Son of God."

What does "*the Son of Man*" mean? The Aramaic *bar nasha* or the Hebrew *ben adam* ("son of man") normally means a "*human being*" (e.g., Ps 8,4).[54] "The divine voice that speaks to Ezekiel addresses him over ninety times as "son of man" (=

"human being"), a term that highlights the contrast between the heavenly message and the mortal recipient."[55] But Daniel has a vision of "one like a son of man who came with the clouds of heaven… and to him was given dominion and glory and kingdom…" (7,13-14). Here "*one like a son of man*" does not designate any human being but one who has a *mysterious origin* and is *glorified by God.*

> On several occasions in Mark, Jesus explicitly identifies himself with this messianic figure (Mark 8,38; 13,26-27; 14,62). Historically, Jesus probably preferred the title because it expressed his identity without the connotations of political and military insurrection which titles like Christ and Son of David carried in first-century Judaism. In Mark's narrative, the title ["*Son of Man*"] serves double duty, demonstrating *Jesus' true humanity* and revealing *his messianic authority and destiny.*[56]

> Jesus uses the term ["*Son of Man*"] in several ways within the Gospel: to highlight his *authority* (2,10.28); to refer to his *suffering, death and resurrection* (8,31; 9,9.13.31; 10,33; 14,21.41); and to point to his *glorious return* at the end of the ages (8,38; 13,26; 14,62) … During his earthly ministry, Jesus exercises authority to forgive sins and to heal on the Sabbath. When his ministry is completed, he must suffer, die, and rise so that he can return at the end of the ages to gather God's elect.[57]

In short, the Markan "Son of Man" is, on the one hand, human and will suffer and die as a *human being* but, on the other hand, he has *divine authority* to forgive sins even during his ministry and after his resurrection he will be seated at the right hand of God and at the end of time he will return as the judge with divine authority. Hence the Markan Jesus uses "*the Son of Man*" as his *self-designation* to manifest the *mystery* of his being *human* and *more than human.*

c) *The Son of God*

Mark starts his Gospel by identifying *Jesus* with "*God's Son*" (1,1) and during Jesus' baptism and transfiguration God the Father himself attests Jesus to be "*my Son, the beloved*" (1,11; 9,7). Demons repeatedly cry out: "you are the Holy One of God" (1,24); "you are the *Son of God*" (3,11); "Jesus, Son of the Most High God" (5,7) but Jesus silences them. In the parable of the vineyard and the wicked tenants, Jesus indirectly refers to himself as the "beloved son" (12,6) whom the tenants kill. During Jesus' trial before the Sanhedrin, the high priest asks him, "Are you the Christ, *the Son of the Blessed One?*" (14,61).

What does "*the Son of God*" mean in Mark's Gospel? Even though occasionally in the OT Israel (Hos 11,1), the king of Israel (Ps 2,7), the righteous person (Wis 2,16.18) and angels (Job 1,6) are called God's sons, Mark uses this title for Jesus to indicate his *unique filial relationship with God*, since he is *God's beloved Son* with whom he is well-pleased (Mk 1,11: "You are my Son, the beloved; in you I am delighted"). Jesus himself addresses God in prayer "*Abba*, Father" (14,36), which shows his filial intimacy with God. Jesus also exercises *divine authority* when he calms the stormy sea (4,39), casts out demons (5,8), cures the sick (2,3-12; 3,1-6; etc.), and raises the dead (5,35-43). Even though no human being recognized Jesus as the divine Son of God during his public ministry, after his death on the cross the *centurion acknowledges him* as "*God's Son*" (15,39). Hence the title "*the Son of God*" in Mark's Gospel designates *Jesus' unique divine Sonship.*

1.©.2. Markan Jesus's Identity

a) The Human Jesus

Mark's Jesus is *very human*, who *experiences and expresses* a variety of *emotions* like compassion (1,41; 6,34) and love (10,21), grief and anger (3,5), amazement (6,6) and indignation (10,14). At *Gethsemane*, he feels deeply *distressed and troubled*, extremely *sorrowful and anxious* at the thought of his imminent passion and death (14,32-36) but he *surrenders himself to God, the Father* (14,36). The Markan Jesus is a person to whom all human beings and especially the *Dalits* can easily relate because he has the same kind of human feelings and emotions as they have.[58] He too experiences *betrayals and denials* from his disciples and friends (14,43-45.66-72) and even *abandonment by God* (15,34).

b) Jesus' Supra-Human Authority

Even though Jesus is fully human, he manifests *supra-human authority* in his words and deeds. He displays *God's authority* in *teaching* as well as in working *miracles* of healing the sick and raising the dead, feeding the crowds, casting out demons and stilling the stormy sea. Like God, he even *forgives sins*. Hence the question about *his identity* naturally arises: "*Who* is this?" (4,41; 8,27).

c) Jesus' Divine Identity

While discussing the *title* "*the Son of God*" we have seen that Mark is convinced that Jesus is the *divine Son* who has a *unique filial relationship with God, the Father* (Mk 1,11; 9,7; 14,36).

© To conclude, the *titles* of Jesus "*the Messiah*," "*the Son of Man*" and "*the Son of God*" sum up important aspects of *Markan Christology*. They are not independent titles but they *interpret one another.* Jesus is the Messiah but not a Davidic Messiah because he is the *suffering Son of Man.* Similarly, Jesus, the Son of Man, is human but he shares in the *divine authority and nature of the Son of God.* It is the manner of Jesus' death on the cross that revealed to the centurion that the *human Jesus* was *God's Son.* Hence the Markan suffering "*Son of Man*" is a *bridge* between "the Messiah" and "the Son of God".

"In terms of *Christology,* the Gospel presents *Jesus* as the *Messiah*, the *Son of God*, whose destiny is the *fate* of the *Son of Man*, who must suffer, die, and rise from the dead if he is to return as a glorious and powerful figure at the end of the ages."[59]

Chapter 2

MATTHEW'S GOOD NEWS OF JESUS CHRIST

Matthew is dependent on Mark's Gospel in many ways (e.g., Jesus begins his ministry by proclaiming the kingdom of God/heaven in Galilee; he journeys from Galilee to Jerusalem; he is rejected by the Jewish leaders in Jerusalem and is handed over to Pilate who crucifies him as the king of the Jews. But in retelling Jesus' story, Matthew has made many changes. For instance, unlike Mark, Matthew starts the Gospel with the genealogy and birth of Jesus and ends with the risen Lord's appearances to the women and the disciples. Furthermore, at significant places in Matthew's Gospel Jesus delivers long major *discourses* (cf. Mt 5-7; 10; 13; 18; 23-25), which are alternated with *narratives* (cf. Mt 4,12-25; 8-9; 11-12; 13,53-17,27; 19-20).[60] Moreover, Matthew emphasizes Jesus' preaching (proclaiming) "*the good news of the kingdom*" (*to euangelion tou basileias*: Mt 4,23; 9,35; 24,14) of God.

Outline of Matthew's Gospel:

2.0. Introduction: Jesus Christ, the Son of David and the Son of God (Mt 1,1-4,11)

2.0.1. Infancy Narrative of Jesus (1,1-2,23)

2.0.2. Preparation for Jesus' Ministry (3,1-4,11)

2.1. Jesus, the Messiah and the Son of God, and His Mission of Preaching, Teaching and Healing, (in Galilee) (Mt 4,12-10,42)[61]

2.1.1. Beginning of the Galilean Ministry and Call of the Disciples (4,12-25) [Narrative]

2.1.2. The Sermon on the Mount (5,1-7,29) [Discourse]

2.1.3. Miracles of the Kingdom of God (8,1-9,38) [Narrative]

2.1.4. The Mission Discourse (10,1-42) [Discourse]

2.2. Jesus, the Suffering Son of Man, Teacher and Healer and Mixed Responses (from Galilee to Jerusalem) (Mt 11,1-20,34)

2.2.1. Rejection by this Generation but Acceptance by His Disciples (11,1-12,50) [Narrative]

2.2.2. Parables of the Kingdom of God (13,1-52) [Discourse]

2.2.3. Greater Rejection by the Jewish Leaders but Better Understanding by the Disciples (13,53-17,27) [Narrative]

2.2.4. Instructions on Community Life (18,1-35) [Discourse]

2.2.5. Teaching on the Way to Jerusalem (19,1-20,34) [Narrative]

2.3. Jesus, the Son of David and the Son of Man and His Rejection by the Leaders (in Jerusalem) (Mt 21,1-25,46)

2.3.1. Jesus' Confrontation with the Religious Leaders in Jerusalem (21,1-22,46) [Narrative]

2.3.2. Woes against the Scribes and Pharisees and Eschatological Discourse (23,1-25,46) [Discourse]

2.4. Jesus' Passion, Death and Resurrection (in Jerusalem) (26,1-28,20) [Narrative]

2.0. Introduction: Jesus Christ, the Son of David and the Son of God (Mt 1,1-4,11)

2.0.1. Infancy Narrative of Jesus (Mt 1,1-2,23)

a) Genealogy of Jesus Christ, the Son of David (Mt 1,1-17)

Matthew begins the Gospel with "the genealogy of Jesus Christ, the son of David, the son of Abraham" (1,1). It spans the whole history of Israel: fourteen generations each from Abraham to David, from David to the Babylonian exile, and from the exile to Jesus, the Christ (1,2-17). Since Joseph was a descendant of King David (cf. 1,6.16), Jesus was, *legally speaking*, "*Son of David*" (his descendant or successor), even though Joseph (the husband of Mary) was not Jesus' biological father (cf. 1,16.18.25) but only his foster father who adopted him as his son (cf. 1,18-25). The primary purpose of the genealogy is to show legally that Jesus is "*the Son of David*" (1,1.6.17).

b) Birth of Jesus, the Saviour and Emmanuel (Mt 1,18-25)

The angelic annunciation of the virginal conception of Jesus to Joseph in a dream assures him that his betrothed is not an adulteress "because that which is conceived in her is from the

Holy Spirit" (1,20; cf. also 1,18: "she was found having in her womb from the Holy Spirit"). The angel also tells Joseph to call Mary's son "Jesus" (*Iêsous,* the Greek form of "*Joshua*", which means, "Yahweh/God saves"), "for he will save his people from their sins" (1,21). The birth of Jesus, the *Saviour*, is seen as the fulfilment of Isaiah's prophecy about a virgin's conception and giving birth to a son whose name will be "*Emmanuel*" ("God-with-us") (1,22-23; cf. Is 7,14). Jesus is Saviour not only because he saves us from sins but also because he is "*Emmanuel*," God's saving presence with us ("I am with you always": Mt 28,20).

> The reader has learnt a great deal about Jesus in this opening chapter. Jesus is the son of David by Joseph his adoptive father, but he was conceived from the Holy Spirit. Therefore, he has a unique relationship to God, different from any other human being. His birth was the fulfilment of prophecy, and his mission (as made clear by the name given to him) is to save his people from their sins. Called Emmanuel, Jesus is the presence of God to his people (cf. also 18,20; 28,20).[62]

c) *The Wise Men's Visit to Jesus, the New-Born King of the Jews (Mt 2,1-12)*

After Jesus' birth, when the wise men from the East come to Jerusalem asking, "Where is the [new] born *king of the Jews*" (2,1-2), king Herod consults the chief priests and scribes and informs the Magi (wise men) that, according to the prophecy of Micah (5,2), *Bethlehem* is the place of birth of the Christ, the *new ruler of the kingdom of Israel* (Mt 2,4-6). And guided by a star, the wise men find the child Jesus with his mother Mary and they kneel and do obeisance to him and acknowledge Jesus' kingship by offering him gifts of gold, frankincense and myrrh (2,9-12).

While the gentile Magi rejoice in finding Jesus, the new "born king of the Jews," King Herod and all Jerusalem are deeply troubled by the news (2,3). The Magi's exemplary positive attitude to the new-born king is in striking contrast to the deceptive, hypocritical and violent reaction of King Herod to the birth of the Messianic king (cf. 2,7-8.13.16). Even though the chief priests and the scribes know from the Scripture that Bethlehem is the place of birth of the Messiah (2,5-6; cf. Mic 5,2), they are least interested in meeting him and paying their respects to him. All this forebodes the future negative response of the religious and political leaders to Jesus, the *Davidic Messiah*, "*the king of the Jews*" (cf. 27,37.41-42).

d) Flight of Jesus, God's Son, as a Refugee to Egypt (Mt 2,13-15)

Warned by an angel of the Lord about Herod's plot to murder the child Jesus, Joseph takes Jesus and Mary at night and flees to Egypt and remains there till the death of Herod to save the life of God's Son (2,13-15). This manifests not only Joseph's obedience and faithfulness to God (cf. also 1,24) but also the child Jesus' vulnerability. Like a *refugee* child, Jesus had to be carried by his parents to a foreign land to face an uncertain future.

e) Slaughter of the Infants in Herod's Attempt to Murder the Messianic King (Mt 2,16-18)

The cruel Herod's slaying of the innocent infants in his satanic attempt to assassinate the new-born Messianic king shows how inhuman power-crazy leaders (like Hitler) can become and eliminate innumerable innocent persons (like the Jews in the Holocaust)!

Are there not unscrupulous leaders in India who are ready to sacrifice the lives of ordinary people (e.g., the Dalits, Tribals, Muslims, Migrants) on the altar of power and vested interests often under the pretext of national security, economic development or majority religion? Any appeal to prophetic fulfilment (cf. 2,17-18) will not remove the pain of the victims of violence!

f) Return of God's Son from Egypt (Mt 2,19-23)

After the death of Herod, an angel of the Lord advises Joseph in a dream to take Jesus and Mary from Egypt back to the land of Israel and he follows faithfully the Lord's instructions. Their short stay in Egypt and return to their own country, we are told, fulfilled the prophecy, "Out of Egypt I have called my son" (2,15; cf. Hos 11,1), even though originally the text referred back to Ex 4,22 ("Israel is my first-born son"). It means that Jesus is not only "the Son of God" but also the representative of the people of Israel.

2.0.1. *© Twofold Purpose of the Matthean Infancy Narrative (Mt 1,18-2,23)*

(i) Fulfilment of Prophecies

Matthew narrates all the events of Jesus' infancy in such a way as to reveal to the reader that they occurred in *fulfilment of prophetic promises* made by God through his messengers/ prophets. Thus Jesus' birth from a virgin and in Bethlehem was prophesied by Isaiah (7,14; Mt 1,23) and Micah (5,2; Mt 2,6) respectively. Herod's cruel slaughter of infants in Bethlehem happened according to the prophecy of Jeremiah (31,15; Mt 2,17-18). Jesus' return from Egypt fulfilled the prophecy of Hosea (11,1; Mt 2,15). Joseph, Mary and Jesus settled in Nazareth to fulfil the words of the prophets: "He shall be called a Nazarene" (Mt 2,23; cf. Is 11,1; Jg 13,5.7).[63]

(ii) Revelation of Jesus Christ, the Son of David and the Son of God

The Matthean *infancy narrative manifests Jesus* primarily as the *promised "Son of David"* (Davidic Messiah: 1,1.6.17; cf. "king of the Jews": 2,1-6) and hints at his being the "*Son of God*" (2,15; cf. "conceived from the Holy Spirit": 1,18.20, and "*Emmanuel*", "God-with-us": 1,23).

2.0.2. Preparation for Jesus' Ministry (Mt 3,1-4,11)

After the infancy narrative, Matthew recounts *a) John the Baptist's Preaching (3,1-12), b) Jesus' Baptism (3,13-17)*, and *c) His Temptations (4,1-11).*

a) John the Baptist's Preaching (to Prepare the Way of the Mighty Messiah) (Mt 3,1-12)

John the Baptist appears in the Judean wilderness preaching *repentance* because of the imminent inauguration of the kingdom of God: "Repent, for the kingdom of heaven is at hand" (3,2). He cries out in the desert, "*Prepare the way* of the Lord, make his paths straight" (3,3). John baptizes the repentant crowds in the River Jordan (3,6) but he admonishes the presumptuous Pharisees and Sadducees ("brood of vipers") to bear fruit befitting true repentance lest they, like bad trees, be "cut down and thrown into the fire" (3,7-8.10). John tells the people: "I baptize you in water for repentance, but he who is coming after me is mightier than I, whose sandals I am not worthy to carry, he will baptize you in the Holy Spirit and fire"[64] (3,11). John preached repentance (*metanoia,* change of mind) to the sinners and baptised them in water (as a symbol of their conversion from sinful ways) to prepare them to receive the Spirit-filled *mighty Messiah*, who was about to come with an "axe" (3,10) and a "winnowing fork in his hand" (3,12), to *save* the repentant and to *judge* the unrepentant sinner.

b) The Baptism of Jesus, the Beloved Son of God (Mt 3,13-17)

As in the Gospel of Mark, Jesus comes from Galilee to John to be baptized in the Jordan (3,13-15). Immediately after his baptism, the Spirit of God descended from heaven and alighted on him and a heavenly voice declared his identity as *the beloved Son of God*: "This is my son, the beloved, in whom I am delighted" (3,17). Jesus is not only the Spirit-anointed Messiah (3,16) or the Messianic king (cf. Ps 2,7) but also God's beloved Son (3,17) with whom God is delighted. God's declaration of Jesus as "*my Son, the beloved*" at both the *baptism* (3,17) and the *transfiguration* (17,5) reveals that Jesus has a *unique filial relationship* with God the Father (beyond that of an anointed king or a chosen servant of God).

c) The Temptations of Jesus, the Son of God (Mt 4,1-11)

Jesus is led by the Spirit of God into the wilderness to be tempted/tested by the devil (4,1). Whereas Mark mentions only the fact of Jesus' temptations for forty days ("tempted by Satan" Mk 1,13), Matthew describes three kinds of temptations (4,1-11). First, when Jesus feels hungry after fasting for forty days and nights (4,2), the *tempter tests Jesus' divine Sonship*: "If you are the Son of God, command these stones to become loaves of bread" (4,3). The second temptation is also about his being God's Son: "If you are the Son of God, throw yourself down" (4,6) from the high pinnacle of the Temple in Jerusalem, thus testing God's providential care. The third temptation is about having *wealth and worldly glory* by worshipping the devil (4,8-9). Jesus *overcomes* all his temptations *by obeying God's word* as revealed in the sacred Scriptures (Deut 8,3; 6,16; 6,13; cited in Mt 4,4.7.10 respectively). Thus, unlike disobedient Israel during the wanderings in the wilderness, Jesus proves himself to be the *perfectly obedient Son of God.*

2.0.2.© Revelation of Jesus, the Messiah and Son of God in Mt 3,1-4,11

The purpose of John the Baptist's preaching was to prepare the hearts of the people to welcome the mighty *Messiah* (3,3.11-12). When Jesus was baptized, he was revealed as *God's beloved Son* ("my son, the beloved": 3,17). Jesus' *divine Sonship* was *tested* by Satan in the desert (3,3.6).

2.0.© Christology in Mt 1,1-4,11

In Mt 1,1-,4,11 *Jesus* is *introduced* as the *promised Davidic Messiah, Saviour, Emmanuel* and the *beloved Son of God.*

> The beginning of Matthew's Gospel presents readers with a *rich Christology*. Jesus the *Messiah* is the *son of David*, the son of Abraham. He is the legitimate *king of the Jews,* who will shepherd God's people, Israel. Conceived by the power of the Holy Spirit, he is the *beloved Son of God* who embodies the history of Israel and fulfils its prophetic scriptures. *Righteous and obedient to God's word*, he comes *to save* his people from their sins. He is *Emmanuel*, the one in whom God is present to his people.[65]

2.1. Jesus, the Messiah and the Son of God, and His Mission of Preaching, Teaching and Healing (in Galilee) (Mt 4,12-10,42)

In this Section of the Gospel, Jesus *proclaims* the presence of the *kingdom of heaven/God*, *teaches* the people and his disciples how to respond to the kingdom and manifests God's saving power through *healing* the sick. Thus Jesus, the *Messiah* and the *Son of God* is revealed as *preacher*, *teacher* and *healer* of the people.

2.1.1. Beginning of the Galilean Ministry and the Call of the Disciples (Mt 4,12-25) [Narrative]

a) The Beginning of Jesus' Galilean Ministry (Mt 4,12-16)
After John the Baptist's arrest by Herod, Jesus withdraws to Galilee and leaving Nazareth, goes and dwells in Capernaum in the "territory of Zebulun and Naphtali," "Galilee of the Gentiles" in fulfilment of Isaiah's prophecy (4,12-16; cf. Is 8,23-9,1). Jesus' dwelling there among a mixed population of Jews and Gentiles is interpreted as "a great light" seen by "the people sitting in the darkness" and "shadow of death" (4,16).

Here Jesus *inaugurates* his ministry by making a *programmatic proclamation* to the people (Jews and Gentiles): "*Repent*, for *the kingdom of heaven has come near*" (4,17).[66] The arrival of the *kingdom (rule/reign) of God* is the *central message* of *Jesus' preaching, teaching and healing*. The purpose of *Jesus' mission* (Messianic ministry) is *to establish God's reign on earth.*

b) The Call of the Disciples (Mt 4,18-22)
The call of the *four fishermen* to follow Jesus shows that he intends to associate his disciples with the project of establishing the reign of God on earth (4,19: "Follow me, and I will make you fishers of men"). The prompt and generous response of the *first disciples* (Simon Peter and Andrew, James and John) reveals their readiness to leave their occupation ("their nets" and "boat") and family ("their father") (4,20.22) for the sake of God's kingdom.

Summing up Jesus' initial ministry in Galilee (4,12-22), Matthew states: "And he went about all Galilee, *teaching* in their synagogues and *proclaiming the good news of the kingdom* and *healing* every disease and every infirmity among the people" (4,23). All that Jesus *said* (preaching and teaching) and *did* (especially healing the sick, demoniacs, epileptics, paralytics, etc.) revealed that *the reign of God* (in the form of holistic human wellbeing) was now here, which explains why great crowds (from Syria, Galilee, Decapolis, Jerusalem, Judea and beyond the Jordan) followed Jesus (4,24-25). "This points to the fact that there was no territory that did not need God's Messiah to come and heal them."[67]

2.1.2. The Sermon on the Mount (Mt 5-7) [Discourse]

Jesus' *Sermon on the Mount* functions as his *first discourse*, the *inaugural address of the kingdom of God* (5,1-7,29). Jesus' "going up on the mountain" (Mt 5,1) reminds the readers of Moses' on Mount Sinai (cf. Ex 19,3-6). Jesus' Sermon on the Mount is the *new Law* (Mt 5,17-20) which fulfils the old Law given by Moses on Sinai (Ex 20-23). Jesus' new Law will be summed up later as the commandment of *love of God and neighbour* (cf. Mt 22,37-40).

a) The Beatitudes (Mt 5,3-12) and the Metaphors of Salt and Light (5,13-16)

(i) The Beatitudes (Mt 5,3-12)

The *Beatitudes* announce the *blessings* of the *kingdom of God* (5,3-11). Thus, the poor in spirit, the mourners, the meek, the hungry and the thirsty, the merciful, the pure in heart, the peace-makers, the persecuted and the reviled are declared "*blessed*" *now* ("blessed *are* you…") because of the nearness/presence of God's kingdom ("for theirs *is* the kingdom of heaven": 5,3.10) and are assured of *rewards soon* ("for they *shall* …": 5,4-9).

While there are only *three* beatitudes in *Lk* (6,20-21), which deal with the economically poor and socially needy and broken people (the poor, the hungry and the mourners), there are *eight* beatitudes in *Mt* (5,3-10) and some of them are *spiritualized* in *Mt* (by adding "in spirit" to "the poor" in Mt 5,3, whereas Lk 6,20 says, "Blessed are the poor", and by specifying "for righteousness" in Mt 5,6.10, while Lk 6,21 simply states, "Blessed are those who hunger now"). Thus, Matthew has modified Jesus' original beatitudes of the socio-economically broken people (cf. Lk 6,20-21) into a long list of *Kingdom values/virtues* to be practised by the Christians. The *additional beatitude of the persecuted* applies especially to those Christians who were/are maltreated for their faith in Jesus (5,11-12). The *beatitudes in Mt* highlight the *right attitudes of the true disciples of Christ* (spiritual poverty, reliance on God, meekness/gentleness, longing for righteousness/justice, mercy/forgiveness and compassionate love, sincerity of heart, peaceful reconciliation, faithfulness when persecuted for justice and faith).

The *eight Beatitudes* are a *clarion call* for the Christians in our country *to live* the values of God's kingdom, the *Gospel values*, just as it was a challenging message to the Christian community in the first century.

(ii) The Metaphors of Salt and Light (Mt 5,13-16)

Immediately after the *beatitudes*, Jesus says to the disciples, "You are the *salt of the earth*" (5,13) and "You are the *light of the world*" (5,14). The metaphors of *salt* and *light* applied to the disciples mean that those who practice the *beatitudes* (5,14-16) have a *transformative and enlightening* effect on society.

Just as *salt* was/is used to preserve food (especially meat and fish) from rotting and to enhance flavour to the food, so those who live the beatitudes (e.g., a life of honesty and integrity) act as a preservative by protecting people from the evil of sin in the world (e.g., of corruption) and as a positive influence by the quality of Christian life (e.g., Christlike forgiveness by Graham Staines' wife, which inspires others to forgive). The 'salty' influence of the Christians in society is supposed to transform it into *a new social order* based on the Beatitudes and the rest of the Sermon on the Mount as Jesus himself was/is the embodiment of the Sermon. If that salt loses its quintessential quality of saltiness and becomes bland, it becomes worthless and hence has to be discarded by all.

Just as Jesus' life was "a great light" for the people living in darkness (Mt 4,16; cf. Is 42,6), he tells the disciples, "*You* are the *light* of the world", like "a city built upon a hill" which cannot be concealed (5,14). He goes on to say that their presence in the world must shine *like the light* (of a *burning lamp*) in the darkness so that seeing their *good deeds* people may glorify God the Father (5,15-16).

The *light of Christ shared* and *radiated by the Christians* must *dispel the darkness of evil* in today's world. This is symbolized by the *lighting* of the *candles of the faithful* from the *Paschal Candle* during the Easter Vigil service.

b) *Jesus' Fulfilment of the Law and the Prophets and His Authoritative Teaching (Mt 5,17-7,29)*

Jesus tells the Jewish people and the disciples, "Do not think that I have come to abolish *the law and the prophets*; I have *not come to abolish them* but *to fulfil* them" (5,17). But this fulfilment goes beyond the literal interpretation and external observance of the laws as done by the scribes and the Pharisees. Jesus looks at God's original purpose of the law and fulfils the *spirit of the law* and not the letter of the law. So Jesus warns his listeners that only those whose righteousness goes beyond that of the scribes and the Pharisees will enter the kingdom of God (5,20).

Jesus is the *authoritative interpreter* of *the Law and the Prophets*, as revealed in the *six antithetical statements*: "You have heard that *it was said... But I say* to you..." (5,21-22.27-28.31-32.33-34.38-39.43-44) in which Jesus contrasts his interpretation against the traditional understanding of the Law on important moral issues. Thus Jesus *forbids* not only murder but also *anger* (5,21-26), not only adultery and divorce but also *lust* (5,27-32), not only false swearing but also any *swearword* (5,33-37), not only retaliation within limits ("an eye for an eye and a tooth for a tooth") but also any *retaliation* (5,38-42). Jesus demands that his disciples must *love* not only their neighbours but also their *enemies* and *pray* for their *persecutors* so that they may be *sons/daughters of their Father* in heaven whose love is so inclusive and generous that "he makes his sun rise on the evil and the good, and sends rain on the just and the unjust" (5,43-45). *Jesus, the Son of God,* proposes *the Father* as *the ideal of perfection* towards which all the disciples are to strive: "You, therefore, must be perfect as your heavenly Father is perfect" (5,48).

Jesus also teaches the disciples to *shun* every form of *publicity* or *hypocrisy* while giving alms or praying or fasting (6,1-18). They are *not* to practise any form of *piety just for show* but only to please their heavenly Father. Jesus reveals to them the *secret of true holiness.* They are to be *detached* from earthly treasures (6,19-21) and riches (6,24) and they are *not to be anxious* about food or drink or clothing but *to trust*, like the birds of the air and the lilies of the field, in the *Father's loving care and providence* especially of those who "seek first his reign and his righteousness" (6,25-33).

Jesus *instructs* the disciples *not to judge* (condemn) others (7,1-5), *to pray perseveringly* ("ask..., seek..., knock...") (7,7-11), *to produce good fruits* (7,15-20), *to do the will of the Father* (7,21-23). Those who put into *practice* Jesus' Sermon on the Mount are like a *wise man* who builds his house on the strong foundation of solid rock (7,24-27).

Jesus' Sermon on the Mount had an amazing impact on his listeners, "the crowds were astonished at his teaching, for he taught them as one who had authority, and not as their scribes" (7,28-29). *Jesus' teaching* on the Kingdom of God is based on his *divine authority.*

2.1.3. Jesus' Miracles of the Kingdom of God (Mt 8,1-9,38) [Narrative]

Having presented Jesus as an authoritative teacher from God (Mt 5-7), now Matthew narrates *Jesus' mighty deeds of the Kingdom* (Mt 8-9), artistically arranged into *three groups of three miracles each: a) healing* the sick (a leper, a centurion's servant, Peter's mother-in-law & others) (8,1-17), *b)* calming a seismic storm in the sea, healing two demoniacs and a paralytic (8,23-9,1-8), *c)* raising a ruler's daughter to life and healing a woman with a haemorrhage, two blind men and a mute man (9,18-34). The above three sets of miracles are interspersed with two short *vocation stories* of would-be disciples and of Mathew (8,18-22; 9,9-13). The whole section ends with a *summary* of *Jesus' ministry of preaching, teaching and healing* that highlights his *compassion* for the crowds (9,35-38).

> Jesus' mighty deeds demonstrate that the one who proclaims the kingdom in word is also powerful in deed. Thus they further disclose the mystery of Jesus' person... Like the Sermon on the Mount, then, *Jesus' mighty deeds* are a Christological proclamation; they are *works of the Messiah* (see 11,2).[68]

a) Cleansing of a Leper, Healing of the Centurion's Servant, Peter's Mother-in-Law & Others (Mt 8,1-17)

(i) When a *leper* kneels before Jesus and pleads with him, "Lord, if you will, you can *cleanse me*" (8,2), Jesus *touches* him and makes him clean (8,3). Since leprosy was considered a contagious disease, nobody would touch him, which would also defile a person ritually. A leper had to live an isolated life away from the village without any human contact with his family members and neighbours. Hence Jesus' *touching the untouchable leper* and his reassuring words, "I will; *be cleansed*" (8,3) show his decision to *heal him physically and socially*. This is the reason why Jesus asks the cleansed leper to show himself to the priest for certification of his healing (8,4; cf. Lev 13,49) so that he can *re-join* his family, village and synagogue. Thus, Jesus shows himself both as a *healer of the sick* and as a *liberator of the outcast* and the *marginalized* (living on the margins of society) like the *Dalits*.[69]

(ii) While the Jewish leper's faith in Jesus is implicit in his request to heal him (8,2), the *Gentile Centurion's* humble and unique *faith* in the *power of Jesus' word to heal* his paralysed servant is revealed in his response: "Lord, I am not worthy to have you come under my roof; but only say the word, and my servant will be healed" (8,8). Just as the Centurion has human authority to command his soldiers and servants to do anything, he believes that Jesus has the *divine authority* to command the sickness to leave his servant (8,9). Jesus admires the quality of this Gentile's faith, for he tells his Jewish followers, "Not even in Israel have I found such faith" (8,10) and he says to the Centurion: "Go; be it done for you as you have *believed*" (8,13) and immediately his servant was *healed.*

(iii) Whereas in the previous two episodes Jesus cures the sick at the request of the leper and the centurion respectively, Jesus heals *Peter's mother-in-law* of fever on his own by touching her hand (8,14-15). His *healing touch* is the revelation of God's compassionate love for all, and especially for the suffering women.

Jesus' *casting out demons* from many possessed persons and *curing all the sick* people in the evening (8,16) fulfils the prophecy of Isaiah: "He took our infirmities and bore our diseases" (8,17; cf. Is 53,4). All the *healing miracles* manifest *Jesus' feeling of compassion* for the sick and *his desire to remove their suffering.*

- *The Radical Following of Jesus (Mt 8,19-22)*

A *scribe* says to Jesus, "Teacher, *I will follow you* wherever you go" (8,19). It shows his desire to become a disciple of Jesus.

But he tells his would-be follower that discipleship is quite demanding: "Foxes have holes, and the birds of the air have nests, but *the Son of man* has nowhere to lay his head" (8,20). Since he is an itinerant teacher, he has *no fixed abode*, no home, no permanent place of rest. His disciples must be ready to share his *radical way of life* involving a lot of daily *insecurity*.

When *one* of the *new disciples* says to Jesus, "Lord, let me *first go* and *bury my father*" (8,21), Jesus' shocking reply is: "Follow me and leave the dead to bury their own dead" (8,22). *Following Jesus* must be the *top priority* in the life of his disciples.

b) Calming of the Seismic (Stormy) Sea, Healing of Two Gadarene Demoniacs and a Paralytic (Mt 8,23-9,8)

(i) When the disciples were rowing across the Sea of Galilee, "there was a great *earthquake* (*seismos*) in the sea" (8,24). Matthew mentions *earthquakes* also at the time of *Jesus' dying* on the cross (27,51.54) and *rising* from the tomb (28,2). Since earthquake is one of the *signs* of the "*last days*" (cf. 24,7), its occurrence during Jesus' ministry, death and resurrection points to the beginning of the *eschatological era of salvation*.

When the boat is swamped by the seismic waves, the frightened *disciples* wake up the sleeping Jesus, saying, "Save, Lord; we are perishing" (8,25). This is an urgent prayer to rescue them from imminent death by drowning in the stormy sea but it also shows their *fear* and *lack of faith*, for Jesus asks them, "Why are you scared, O men of little faith?" (8,26). His question implies that there is no reason to be frightened when he is with them and when they have faith in him. When Jesus *calms the winds and the sea* (8,26), the disciples marvel about *his superhuman identity and authority*: "What sort of a man is this, that even the wind and the sea obey him?" (8,27).

(ii) When *two demoniacs* living among the tombs in the Gentile territory of the Gadarenes meet Jesus, the fierce demons cry out, "What have to do with us, *O Son of God*? Have you come here to torment us before time?" (8,29). Here the demons recognize *Jesus' divine identity* and are scared of him. Jesus *casts the demons out* and sends them into the herd of swine, which rushes down the precipice and perishes in the sea (cf. 8,30-33). This indicates that Jesus, *the Son of God,* has the *power to liberate* human beings from evil spirits. But it is surprising that when the Gadarenes meet Jesus, they ask him to leave their territory probably because of their loss of many swine (8,34)!

(iii) When some people bring to Jesus *a paralytic* lying on his bed and he sees their faith, he says to the paralysed man, "*Son, your sins are forgiven*" (9,2). Jesus does not specify whether the sins are forgiven by him or by God. The Jews believed that sins, which offend God, can be forgiven only by God. Hence some scribes judge Jesus to be blaspheming (9,3). Reading their thoughts, Jesus asks them, "Why do you think evil in your hearts?" (9,4). To show that Jesus, *the Son of man*, has *God-given authority* on earth *to forgive sins*, he tells the paralytic, "Rise, take up your bed and go home" (9,6). Healed of his physical and spiritual paralysis, he goes home (9,7). Seeing this, the people are filled with awe and they "glorify God for giving such authority to men" (9,8).

It should be noted that Jesus does not say, "I" or "the Son of God" but "*the Son of Man* has *authority* on earth *to forgive sins*" (9,6). Similarly, people glorify God not for granting Jesus authority to forgive sins but "to men" [in the plural] (9,8). Jesus, *the Son of man*, is *a representative of humans*, who is given the *divine authority to forgive sins*. Jesus will later confer this divine power on Peter, a representative of the disciples (cf. 16,19), and the risen Lord will impart it to all the disciples on Easter Sunday (cf. Jn 20,23). Thus, Jesus has given the divine authority to forgive sins not only to Peter but also to the community of the disciples (cf. also the prayer in the "Our Father": "Forgive us our debts [sins], as we also have forgiven our debtors" [sinners] (Mt 6,12).

- *The Call of Matthew, the Tax Collector, and Table Fellowship (Mt 9,9-13)*

The *vocation of Matthew* is narrated very briefly: "As Jesus passed on from there, he saw a man called Matthew sitting at the tax office; and he said to him, '*Follow me.*' And he rose and followed him" (9,9). Jesus calls *Matthew* as he is engaged in his work as *a tax collector*. Every Jewish tax collector was despised as a disloyal fellow by the Jews because he collaborated with the Roman rulers and was hated as *a sinner* because he usually exploited the people by charging them more than what was legally due. Jesus *chooses* such a *socially outcast and despised tax collector to be his disciple*. Although he must have been surprised at Jesus' calling to follow him, *Mathew's prompt and generous response* is truly inspiring.

Jesus' table fellowship with tax collectors and sinners in Matthew's house shocks the Pharisees (9,10-11). Jesus' answer to them is that it is *the sick*, not the healthy, who *need a physician*, and that he has come to call *the sinners*, not the righteous, because God desires mercy more than sacrifice (9,12-13). It means that Jesus is the *merciful Saviour of sinners*.

- *The Question about Not Fasting by Jesus' Disciples (Mt 9,14-17)*

The disciples of John the Baptist question Jesus *why his disciples* are *not fasting* (9,14). Jesus compares the latter to the *wedding guests* who are feasting with the bridegroom, implying that *Jesus* is the *Messianic bridegroom* (9,15), who has invited them to the joyful banquet during which the *new wine of God's kingdom* is served (9,17).

c) *Raising of the Ruler's Daughter to Life, Healing of the Bleeding Woman, Curing of Two Blind Men and a Dumb Man (Mt 9,18-34)*

(i) Matthew's abbreviated account of the Markan narrative of the *raising of a Synagogue ruler's daughter to life* (cf. Mk 5,21-24.35-43; Mt 9,18-19.23-26) stresses his *unshakable faith* in Jesus. Whereas in Mk the ruler comes to Jesus when she is "at the point of death" (5,23) and later the news of her death is brought to him by a messenger (5,36), in Mt the ruler says, "*My daughter has just died*, but come and *lay your hand* on her, and she *will live*" (9,18). Disregarding the Mosaic Law which forbids Jews to touch a defiling dead body, Jesus goes into the ruler's house and, after putting out all the mourners, *takes the dead girl by the hand* and she comes *alive* (Mt 9,25: êgerthê, which means, "she rose" or "she was raised up"). It indicates *Jesus' divine power to give life* even to the dead.

(ii) When Jesus is on the way to the ruler's house, a nameless *woman with a haemorrhage* (and hence regarded as ritually *unclean* according to the Mosaic Law [cf. Lev 15,25-30]) for twelve long years comes behind Jesus and touches the fringe of his garment with a prayer in her heart: "If I only touch his garment, I shall be made well" (9,20-21). Jesus' encouraging words reassure her and highlight *her faith*: "Take heart, daughter; your faith has made you well" (9,22).

(iii) *Two blind men* follow Jesus crying aloud: "Have mercy on us, Son of David" (9,27) and he asks them: "Do you *believe* that I can do this?" and they reply without any hesitation: "Yes, Lord" (9,28). It is noteworthy that they address Jesus as "*Son of David*" and "*Lord,*" which manifests their faith in Jesus, the merciful *Davidic Messiah* and the powerful *healer Lord*. Touching their eyes, he tells them: "According to *your faith* be it done to you" (9,29) and their eyes are immediately opened (9,30). Although Jesus tells them not to tell anyone about the miraculous cure, they spread his fame as a healer among the people in the whole district (9,30-31)! They are so grateful to him for giving them sight that they cannot remain silent but have to proclaim him to all the people.

(iv) When a *dumb demoniac* is brought to Jesus and he *casts out the demon*, the dumb man speaks (9,32-33), which reveals *Jesus' power over evil spirits*. This is recognized by the crowds who exclaim: "Never was anything like this seen in Israel" (9,34), but the unbelieving Pharisees accuse Jesus: "He casts out demons by the prince of demons" (9,34).

Whereas the sick and the suffering, the blind and the dumb, *believe* in Jesus and experience *healing* (a *sign of the presence of God's reign* among them), the obdurate Pharisees refuse to believe!

The *summary* statement of Jesus' going about all the cities and villages, *teaching* in the synagogues and *preaching* the *good news of the kingdom of God* and *healing all diseases*, manifests

Jesus' compassion (felt deep within himself) for the *harassed and helpless* people who are like *sheep without* a *shepherd* (9,35-36). And he asks his disciples to pray to God for sending more labourers into the harvest (9,37-38). This is also the urgent need of today.

2.1.4. The Mission Discourse (Mt 10,1-42)

Jesus' *mission discourse* (Mt 10), which is his second discourse in Mt, forms the *conclusion* of the first Section of Jesus' ministry (4,12-10,42). Like Jesus (cf. Mt 4-9), *the Twelve* are *to preach the Kingdom of God/heaven* and to manifest it through *healing*, and they will have to *face opposition* and *suffer persecution* (Mt 10). This shows that their mission is a continuation of Jesus' *mission of establishing God's reign.*

It may be noted that the mission discourse is meant not only for the *mission of the Twelve* apostles (10,1-15) but also for the *future mission of all the disciples* especially amid persecutions (10,16-42). Jesus speaks at *two levels*:

> In terms of the story, the *earthly Jesus* prepares his disciples for mission, but, in terms of the Matthean community, it is the *risen Lord* who instructs his church. Understood in this light, Jesus' missionary speech is an illustration of what it means to call him *Emmanuel*; the risen Lord is *present* to his church and continues to instruct it as once he instructed the Twelve.[70]

a) The Mission and Names of the Twelve Apostles (Mt 10,1-4)

Jesus calls to him the Twelve disciples and gives them authority to cast out the unclean spirits and to heal every disease and ailment (10,1). This *authority* of the Twelve *over demons and diseases* comes from Jesus.

The *Twelve apostles* symbolize the *twelve tribes* of Israel. The *names of the Twelve* are given starting with Simon called Peter. It is *a mixed group* of four fishermen (Simon Peter and his brother Andrew, James the son of Zebedee and his brother John), a tax collector (Matthew), a Cananaean (Simon) and six others (Philip and Bartholomew, Thomas, James [the son of Alphaeus] and Thaddaeus, and Judas Iscariot, the betrayer) (10,2-4). Although the members of the Twelve are from *different* backgrounds and occupations, there is unity in diversity because they are *united in their mission.*

b) The Commissioning of the Twelve (Mt 10,5-15)

Jesus instructs the Twelve not to go to the Gentiles or the Samaritans (10,5) but only to the Israelites (10,6). Just as Jesus has compassion on the crowds who are like "sheep without a shepherd" (cf. 9,36), he asks the Twelve to be compassionate shepherds of "the lost sheep of the house of Israel" (10,6). Just as Jesus went about all the Jewish villages and cities, preaching the good news of the kingdom and healing all the illnesses of the people (cf. 9,35), he sends the Twelve to preach the good news: "The kingdom of heaven is at hand" (10,7) and to "heal the sick, raise the dead, cleanse lepers, cast out demons" (10,8). In short, the *Twelve* are to do the *same ministry of preaching and healing as Jesus* did. They are to *proclaim the presence of God's kingdom* through word and deed. Like Jesus, they are to do all this *gratuitously* (10,8). Like Jesus, they are not to make any provision for themselves but to depend on the providence of God and the hospitality of the local people (10,9-13). However, if some refuse to receive them and listen to them, they are to symbolically "shake off the dust from their feet" (10,14) as they leave the unwelcoming house or town.

c) *Future Persecutions of the Twelve and Other Disciples (Mt 10,16-31)*

The further instructions that Jesus gives to the Twelve in 10,16-31 for their future mission in the midst of *persecutions* are applicable also to all the disciples in the future. Jesus sends them as "*sheep in the midst of wolves*" and so they have to "be wise as serpents and innocent as doves" (10,16), that is, they have to combine in their life and mission *serpent-like prudence* and *dove-like innocence.* Like Jesus, they will have to *suffer persecutions* by the Jews and Gentiles (10,17-18) and by their close relatives and neighbours (10,21-23) but the disciples should *not be anxious* because the Spirit of the Father will be guiding them in their mission (10,20). Like their teacher and master Jesus, the disciples and servants must be *willing to suffer* slander, persecution and even death (10,24-28). They are to *trust in God their Father* who protects them and cares for them (his children) (10,29-31).

d) *To Acknowledge Christ Courageously before Others (Mt 10,32-42)*

Jesus expects his disciples not to be afraid or ashamed to *acknowledge* him before others (10,32-33). This has to be done in word and deed even in conflict situations at home and outside. They have to be ready to *bear witness* to him even if it would mean carrying their *cross* and following him which may lead to losing their life for his sake (10,34-39). They are his representatives and are identified with him: "He who receives you receives me, and he who receives me receives him who sent me" (10,40).

Looking at Mt 10,32-33 from the *Christological* point of view, it reveals *Jesus' unique relationship with God as his Father* ("*my Father* who is in heaven").[71]

2.2. Jesus, the Suffering Son of Man, Teacher and Healer and Mixed Responses (from Galilee to Jerusalem) (Mt 11,1-20,34)

In this Section (Mt 11-20) Jesus continues his *mission of teaching and healing* to which there are *positive and negative reactions.*

> The *dual themes* which hold this section together are the responses, positive and negative, to Jesus' ministry. On the one hand, there is *increasing rejection* by and *animosity* from the *religious leaders.* On the other, there is *a degree of acceptance and understanding* on the part of the *disciples.*[72] But even the disciples find it difficult to understand Jesus as the *suffering Son of Man* (cf. their *negative reactions* to his *passion predictions* in Mt 16; 17; 20).

2.2.1. Jesus' Rejection by "this Generation" but Acceptance by His Disciples (Mt 11,1-12,50) [Narrative]

a) John Baptist's Doubt about Jesus' Messianic Identity (Mt 11,2-19)

The question of the Baptist from prison, who had earlier borne testimony to Jesus as the mighty Messianic Son of God (cf. 3,11-17), is puzzling to the readers: "Are you the one who was to come, or shall we look for another?" (11,3). Because the compassionate "deeds of Christ" (11,2) do not correspond to the Baptist's expectations of an end-time merciless Messianic judge of sinners (cf. 3,12), he begins to have doubts about Jesus' Messianic identity. Jesus' answer to John Baptist highlights the nature of his "*deeds*" (miracles and preaching) *in favour* of *the marginalized and the poor*: "the blind receive their sight and the lame walk, lepers are cleansed and the deaf hear, and the dead are raised, and the poor have the good news preached to them" (11,5). The poor and the outcasts are the privileged recipients of the kingdom of God. Jesus asks John "not to be scandalized" by him: "And blessed is he who takes no offence at me" (11,6).

> Jesus responds by defining his ministry as the great end-times restoration promised in Isaiah (35,4-6; 61,1) and then pronounces a blessing on those who do not "fall away on account of me" (11,4-6). The time for decision is now. With the coming of John, the forerunner, and Jesus the Messiah, the age of promise is giving way to the age of fulfilment (11,12-15). Jesus denounces "this generation" for rejecting both John's sombre call for repentance as well as his joyful announcement of the kingdom (11,16-19).[73]

b) Woes to the Unrepentant Cities (Mt 11,20-24)

Jesus also censures the *unrepentant cities* (Chorazin, Bethsaida, Capernaum), where his "mighty works" have been done, because their *response* to Jesus' ministry of proclamation of God's kingdom accompanied by many miracles has been *negative.* Since they refuse to repent and to be converted, they are doomed to destruction like the unrepentant cities of Tyre, Sidon and Sodom (11,20-24)!

c) Jesus' Praise of God the Father, the Revealer, and Invitation to the Exhausted to Rest (Mt 11,25-30)

Jesus praises the Father for his gracious will to reveal the hidden divine mystery to the little ones, the simple people, and not to the wise and the learned (11,25-26). Jesus gratefully acknowledges that all things have been entrusted to him by his Father. Just as the Father knows the Son most lovingly, Jesus claims to have a unique and intimate knowledge of the Father, and he enjoys the freedom to reveal it to anyone of his choice (11,27). So he invites the poor who are weary (with hard work) and the oppressed who are over-burdened (with many unjust laws and customs) to come to him and he assures them that he would give them *rest* (11,28). Compared to the rabbinic interpretations of the Mosaic Law, Jesus' "yoke/burden" (teaching on the *law of love of God and neighbour* cf. Mt 22,37-40) is easy/light for those who learn from him who is gentle and humble of heart (11,29-30; cf. 5,3-4). *Jesus' yoke/burden*, which is easy to carry, consists of the devoted filial love of the Father and the caring brotherly/sisterly love of the neighbour. This *way of Jesus-like love* (*agapê*) leads to *true rest* in Jesus.

d) Plucking the Grain of Wheat on the Sabbath (Mt 12,1-8)

The *controversy* between Jesus and the Pharisees on the interpretation of the *law of Sabbath* (12,1-8) illustrates the truth of Jesus' statement in 11,30 ("my yoke is easy and my burden is light"). While the Pharisees blame the hungry disciples for plucking some heads of grain and eating them while walking through the wheat fields on the Sabbath (12,1-2), Jesus justifies their action as lawful, just as the hungry David and his companions did not break the law when they entered the Temple and ate the bread of the Presence which only the priests had the right to eat (12,3-4; cf. Lev 14,5-9). While the Pharisees condemn the hungry disciples as *guilty* of breaking the Sabbath, the merciful Jesus declares them *innocent* (12,7). He also claims, "the Son of man is lord of the Sabbath" (12,8). It is noteworthy that Jesus says "the Son of man" (not "the Son of God") is "lord of the Sabbath," indicating thereby that the lordship of Jesus over the Sabbath is shared by all human beings, since "Sabbath is made for humans, not humans for Sabbath" (Mk 2,27). The welfare of human beings is God's original purpose of the Sabbath and its regulations.

e) *Healing of the Man with a Withered Hand on the Sabbath (Mt 12,9-14)*

Seeing a man with a paralysed hand and Jesus together at one place in the synagogue, the Pharisees try to trap him by asking him: "Is it lawful to heal on the Sabbath?" (12,10). Jesus tells them that if it is lawful to pull out a sheep that has fallen into a pit on a Sabbath, all the more is it permissible to *do good on the Sabbath* particularly to a helpless person (12,11-12). So he *heals* the man with the withered hand on the Sabbath (12,13). But the Pharisees go out and plot to kill Jesus (12,14).

f) *Jesus, the Beloved Servant of God (Mt 12,15-21)*

Even though Jesus has to withdraw from there to escape the Pharisees' evil designs, he heals all the sick among the crowds that follow him (12,15). Matthew interprets this as the fulfilment of God's prophecy in Isaiah 42,1-4 (the first Servant Song) which speaks of *God's chosen servant* whom God loves and who is filled with the Spirit of God. The *beloved Servant of God* will be gentle and caring towards the weak and the suffering, and in him the Gentiles will hope (12,17-21). "This humble and hidden liberative work of the anointed One was to continue until the end of the ages. It continues to do so even today."[74]

g) *Jesus and Beelzebul (Mt 12,22-32)*

When Jesus *heals a blind and dumb demoniac*, all the people are amazed and wonder whether he is the expected Son of David, the Messiah, but the unbelieving *Pharisees accuse* him of casting out demons by Beelzebul, the prince of demons (12,22-24). Jesus tells them that it is not by Satan, but by the Spirit of God, that he drives out devils, which manifests his victory over Satan and the liberating presence of God's rule (12,25-29). The Pharisees' obstinate opposition to the saving action of God's Spirit is an unforgivable "blasphemy against the Holy Spirit" (12,31-32). They are like "bad trees," producing rotten fruit and incapable of bearing good fruit (12,33). Jesus calls them "brood of vipers" (12,34), evil men with venomous mouths uttering blasphemous words against the Holy Spirit. He warns them that they will be condemned on the day of judgement (12,36-37).

h) Demand for a Sign and the Sign of Jonah (Mt 12,38-42)

When the scribes and the Pharisees ask Jesus for a prodigious sign that would vindicate his divine authority, he calls them "an evil and adulterous generation" and tells them: "no sign shall be given them except the *sign of the prophet Jonah*", namely, his *three-day stay in the belly of the whale* (cf. Jonah 1,17; 2,1.10), which prefigures *Jesus' burial and resurrection* (Mt 12,39-40). But Mt 12,41-42 refers to the Gentile *Ninevites' repentance at the preaching of Jonah* (cf. Jon 3,4-5) and the eagerness of the *queen of the south* to listen to the *wisdom of Solomon* (cf. 1 Kgs 10,1-10). Even though Jesus is "*greater*" than the prophet Jonah and the wise Solomon, "this generation" (the wilfully evil and hard-hearted scribes and Pharisees) refuse to listen to and believe in Jesus (the Spirit-anointed *prophet and king* of wisdom) and therefore they will be condemned by the people of Nineveh and the queen of Sheba on the day of judgement (Mt 12,41-42).

Jesus imparts important *lessons* in Mt 12,38-42:

(a) the uselessness of looking for spectacular signs (v 39); (b) Jonah's fate as a type of Jesus' resurrection (v. 40), a spectacular sign to believers after all; (c) the importance of preaching and repentance (v. 41); (d) that Gentiles are sometimes more receptive than Jews to God's messengers (vv. 41-42); (e) the importance of the quest for divine wisdom, in which women also share and sometimes excel (v 42); (f) that Jesus is greater than previous prophets and wise men (vv. 41.42) because he is the absolute revelation of the Father (11,27).[75]

i) Jesus' Family (Mt 12,46-50)

When someone in the crowd tells Jesus that his mother and brothers are waiting outside to speak to him (12,46), he asks a surprising question: "Who is my mother, and who are my brothers?" (12,47-48). Here he does not deny his natural family ties but points to an equally important *new relationship* with *his disciples*: "Here are my mother and my brothers! For whoever does the will of my Father in heaven is my brother, and sister, and mother" (12,49-50). *Doing the will of God, the Father,* is the *sine qua non* for anyone to have an intimate relationship with Jesus, the Son of God. "Our Father in heaven, ... your will be done..." (Mt 6,10) is the filial prayer that Jesus taught his disciples. This is what Mary, his mother, did when she said to God (at the time of the annunciation): "Let it be to me according to your word" (Lk 1,38), which reveals her readiness to do God's will wholeheartedly.

©Looking back at Mt 11-12, Jesus' *miracles, preaching and teaching* manifest him to be *the Christ* (11,2), *the Son of David* (12,23), *the Son of Man* (11,19; 12,8.32.40) and *the Son of the Father* (11,27). As a whole, the *disciples* respond to Jesus *positively*, but the *scribes* and the *Pharisees* react to him *negatively.*

2.2.2. Seven Parables of the Kingdom of God (Mt 13,1-53) [Discourse]

Mt 13 contains the third discourse consisting of *seven parables* that describe different dimensions of the kingdom/reign of God.

A parable is a story narrating a life-situation, which challenges the listener to look at his/her own life-situation and to take a decision affecting his/her life (e.g., Prophet Nathan's parable of the ewe lamb told to King David in 2 Sam 12,1-7). C. H. Dodd defines a parable as "a metaphor or simile drawn from nature or common life, arresting the hearer by its vividness or strangeness, and leaving the mind in sufficient doubt about its precise application to tease it into active thought."[76]

Jesus' parables are focussed on the *kingdom/reign of God*. Every parable of Jesus highlights mainly *one* aspect of the mystery of the kingdom (the *point of the parable*). However, Jesus (or probably the early Church) explains to the disciples (Christians) the *allegorical* meaning of the individual details of two of the parables.

a) Parable of the Sower (Mt 13,1-9.18-23)

As the sower sowed, some seeds fell along the footpath (which the birds ate up) or on rocky ground (which sprouted but were scorched by the sun) or among thistles (which choked the plants) but other seeds fell on good soil, which produced crops (hundred/sixty/thirtyfold) (13,3-9). The main message of the parable is that even though the kingdom of God is proclaimed to many, only some receive it, nurture it and allow it to produce fruit.

According to the *allegorical* interpretation of the parable of the sower, Jesus is the sower; the seed is the word (message) of the kingdom of God; the various types of soil on which the seeds fall represent the different kinds of people who react (negatively) or respond (positively) to the kingdom message; the bird who eats up the seed is the devil ("evil one") who snatches away the word of the kingdom from the heart of the hearer (cf. 13,18-23).

> His interpretation reveals that although people hear his proclamation of the kingdom, they do not accept it for a variety of reasons. Some hear without understanding. In others, the message never takes root, or worldly anxieties distract them. But those who hear the message of the kingdom with understanding bear a rich harvest. Therefore, although many have rejected Jesus' ministry, others have understood and will bear fruit.[77]

b) Parable of the Weeds among the Wheat (Mt 13,24-30.36.43)

The kingdom of God is compared to the *good seeds* (*wheat*) sown by a man in his field whose enemy sows *weeds* among the wheat (13,24-25). Lest the wheat is uprooted while removing the weeds, the farmer lets both grow together until the harvest, when the reapers will be told to gather the weeds first and burn them but to gather the wheat in his barn (13,29-30).

Jesus (or the early Church) explains to the disciples (Christians) the meaning of the parable of the weeds *allegorically*: "He who sows the good seed is the Son of man; the field is the world, and the good seed means the sons of the kingdom; the weeds are the sons of the evil one, and the enemy who sowed them is the devil; the harvest is the close of the age, and reapers are the angels" (13,38-39). Like the weeds which will be gathered and burnt with fire at the harvest time, the "evildoers" will be destroyed in the fiery furnace at the time of the last judgement (13,41-42), whereas "the just [righteous] will shine like the sun in the kingdom of their Father" (13,43). The kingdom of God on earth has both sinners and saints, who will be separated at the end of the world. Hence Christians are advised to be patient and tolerant till the end of time.

From the *Christological* point of view, it is noteworthy that "he who sows the good seed" and punishes "all evildoers" is "*the Son of Man*" (14,37.41). This can be understood at *two levels*: the *human* Jesus, "the Son of Man", sows the seed of the kingdom of God during his *ministry*, and the risen *glorified* Jesus, "the Son of Man," will judge/condemn the evildoers at the *end of the world* (cf. 24,30-31; 25,31-46).

> Like Jesus' missionary discourse, the parable discourse can be read on two levels. In terms of the story, Jesus is explaining what is happening in his earthly ministry. But in terms of the Matthean community, he is addressing the church living in the period of his resurrection. The members of the church are the children of the kingdom presently waiting for the Son of Man to separate good and evil and rescue them from their present circumstances... The readers of Matthew's Gospel know that he is the risen Lord, the Son of God, who will return at the close of the ages.[78]

c) Parables of the Mustard Seed and the Leaven (Mt 13,31-33)

In these parables, Jesus compares the *kingdom of God* to the *tiny mustard seed* and the *little leaven*. Like the smallest *mustard seed* sown in the field gradually grows into the greatest shrub, so the *kingdom of God* will slowly but surely *grow large* (13,31-32). Similarly, like the small amount of *leaven* which slowly transforms a large quantity of flour, the *reign of God* in the hearts of people will gradually *rejuvenate society* (13,31-33). The *disciples* who are radically transformed by the kingdom values will become a *leavening agent* of the society in which they live.

d) Parables of the Treasure and the Pearl (Mt 13,44-46)

The *kingdom of God* is like a precious *treasure* hidden in a field which one finds and gladly buys after selling all his possessions

(13,44). Similarly, God's kingdom is compared to a priceless *pearl* that a merchant of pearls finds and he procures it after selling all his other pearls (13,45-46). Both these parables emphasize the *inestimable value of God's kingdom* and the *need of sacrificing* everything else to receive this gift of God.

e) Parable of the Dragnet (Mt 13,47-50)

In this parable, the *kingdom of God* is compared to a *large net* thrown into the sea. When the net is full of fish, fishermen drag it to the shore and they *separate* the *good fish* from the *bad* and keep the good ones and throw away the bad. The message of this parable is the same as that of the wheat and the weeds. On the *day of judgement*, God's angels will *separate the good from the bad* and the Lord will invite the former to the fullness of life and condemn the latter to destruction. Even in the *Church* there were and are *good* Christians and *bad* ones who will be *separated* and *judged* on the last day!

© At the end of the parabolic discourse on the kingdom of God, Jesus asks his disciples if they have understood "all this" and their answer is an affirmative "yes" (13,51). This fulfils what Jesus assured them earlier: "To you it has been given to know the *secrets of the kingdom* of heaven..." (13,11). Jesus' parables *reveal* the mysteries of the kingdom to the *open-hearted disciples* but *conceal* them from the *hard-hearted humans* (cf. 13,13-15).

2.2.3. *Greater Rejection of Jesus by the Jewish Leaders but Better Understanding by the Disciples/Believers (Mt 13,54-17,27) [Narrative]*

a) Jesus' Rejection at Nazareth (Mt 13,54-58)

Having faced opposition from the Jewish leaders (the scribes and the Pharisees) to his miracles and teaching, Jesus goes to his native place and teaches in the synagogue. Even though at first the people of Nazareth seem to be amazed at his teaching, soon they become sceptical of his wisdom and miraculous powers: "Where did this man get this wisdom and these mighty works?" (13,54). They claim to know his humble origin (as the son of a carpenter and Mary) and his other family members (his brothers and sisters) of low social standing (13,55-56). *Familiarity breeds contempt* and it prevents his own people from believing in him. When they take offence at him, he tells them that a prophet is honoured everywhere except in his hometown and his own family (13,57). Because of their *unbelief*, Jesus does not perform many miracles there (13,58). In short, Jesus is *rejected by his own people of Nazareth.*

b) John the Baptist's Beheading by Herod (Mt 14,1-12)

On hearing about Jesus and his miraculous power, Herod Antipas wrongly concludes that Jesus is John the Baptist who has been raised from the dead (14,1-2). The narrative of the unjust imprisonment and brutal beheading of the Baptist by the unscrupulous Herod (to please the hate-filled Herodias) (cf.14,3-11) reminds the readers of the price true prophets have to pay if they dare to confront the wicked rulers of the people. It may also hint at Jesus' cruel death on the cross.

c) Feeding of the Five Thousand (Mt 14,13-21)

When Jesus comes to know about the cruel murder of John the Baptist, he withdraws with his disciples in a boat to a secluded place but large crowds reach there on foot before his arrival (14,13). He is moved with *compassion*[79] for the multitude and he *heals all the sick* persons among them (14,14).

In the evening the disciples ask Jesus to send the crowds away to their villages so that they can procure food for themselves (14,15). But Jesus asks the disciples to provide food for the hungry people (14,16). Taking the *disciples' five loaves and two fish*, he looks up to heaven and blesses God, breaks the bread and fish, and gives them to the disciples to distribute them to the crowds (14,17-19). After the people finish feasting (eating to the full), the disciples gather twelve baskets of leftover food (14,20), indicating the *abundance of food* supplied to the large multitude of five thousand men, besides women and children (14,21).

This *miraculous feeding of the hungry crowd* in the lonely place echoes *God's feeding the people of Israel* with manna and quails in the wilderness (cf. Exod 16; Num 11) and has many similarities with the *Last Supper* Jesus will later celebrate with his disciples (cf. 26,26-29). Both the feeding of the five thousand and the Last Supper are *anticipations of the Messianic banquet* during the reign of God.

d) Jesus' Walking on the Sea and Peter's Faltering Walk on the Water (Mt 14,22-33)

Matthew narrates two miracles of (a) Jesus' walking on the stormy sea and (b) his saving the scared Peter from drowning (14,22-27.28-33).

After asking his disciples to get into a boat and to go to the other side of the sea of Galilee and sending the people away, Jesus goes up to the mountain to pray alone at night (14,22-23). In the last quarter of the night, he comes *walking on the sea* to the storm-tossed disciples in the boat far away from the land. Mistaking him to be a ghost, they cry out in fear. Jesus reassures them: "Take heart, *I am*, don't be afraid" (14,25-27). Jesus here reveals *God's divine and saving power* operative in him.

Recognizing Jesus, *Peter* requests him: "Lord, if it is you, bid me come to you on the water" (14,28). Although he starts *walking on the water* confidently, seeing the strong wind he wavers in his faith and begins to sink, which makes him cry out in prayer: "*Lord, save me*" (14,29-30). It is striking that he addresses Jesus as "Lord" (14,28.30). The scared Peter is humble enough to cry for the Lord's help! Stretching out his hand, Jesus *saves him* from drowning, saying to him: "O man of *little faith*, why did you *doubt*?" (14,31), emphasizing the *need for unwavering faith in the Lord's saving power*. Jesus challenges Peter (the leader of the disciples) *to grow in faith*. This is equally applicable to many of the scared Church leaders facing stormy situations in the Church and the world today!

The moment Jesus gets into the boat, the wind ceases (14,32). Seeing his authority and power over the sea and the wind, the disciples fall on their knees before him (*prosekynêsan auto*), *confessing their faith* in him: "Truly you are *God's Son*" (*theou hyios*: 14,33). This is the first time that the disciples acknowledge him as "Son of God" even though the deeper meaning of it will be understood by them only after Jesus' resurrection. The disciples' confession of faith in the divine sonship of Jesus may reflect the later *faith of the Matthean community*.

When Jesus crosses over to the land of Gennesaret (south of Capernaum), the *people bring all the sick persons to him* so that they may touch the fringe of his garment. All of them who touch him are made well because they *believe* in *his healing power* (14,34-36).

e) *Tradition of the Elders and Cleanliness of the Heart (Mt 15,1-20)*

The *scribes and Pharisees* from Jerusalem *accuse* Jesus' *disciples* of transgressing "the tradition of the elders," since they *eat without washing their hands* (15,1-2). The oral traditions (later written down in the Mishnah) are scribal interpretations of OT laws, ending up in innumerable rules and regulations imposed on the people by the religious leaders, which often go against the original spirit of the commandments of God (cf. 15,3). For instance, God's commandment to honour the father and the mother (Ex 20,12) is negated by the practice of *qorbân* (declaring one's property or possession as dedicated to God and *offering* it as a *gift* to God). It nullifies God's law regarding one's obligation to help one's parents in need (15,4-6). Jesus calls such people "*hypocrites*", who honour God only with their lips and *not* in their deeds according to the just law of God (15,7-9). Ritual washing of hands before meals is only a human tradition, which must not be imposed on all as an obligation.

Jesus instructs the people: "Hear and understand: not what goes into the mouth defiles a man, but what comes out of the mouth, this defiles a man" (15,10-11). It is not what one eats but what comes out of one's heart that makes one impure. *No food* that is eaten defiles a person but the *heart's evil thoughts* pollute the person (15,16-20).

f) *The Canaanite Woman's Faith (Mt 15,21-28)*

When Jesus withdraws to the gentile region of Tyre and Sidon, a *Canaanite woman* pleads with him to *heal her daughter who is afflicted by demonic possession*: "Have mercy on me, O Lord, Son of David; my daughter is severely possessed by a demon" (15,21-22). Jesus' surprising silence to her prayer is a test of her faith. When he says that his mission is "only to the lost sheep of the house of Israel" (15,24), she kneels before him, saying: "Lord, help me" (15,25). His puzzling reply ("It is not fair to take the children's bread and throw it to the puppies":15,26) is *not* meant to be a *derogatory* remark because the Greek word (*kynaria*) does not mean "dogs" but "*puppies*" (which often lie under the dining table). Her quick and smart response ("Yes, Lord, but even the *puppies* eat the crumbs that fall from their masters' table": 15,27) confirms the benign interpretation. Jesus praises her faith and exorcises the demon then and there: "O woman, *great is your faith*! Be it done for you as you desire" (15,28). The *Canaanite woman* is an *excellent example* of *persevering prayer* with *unshakable faith*.

This *miraculous cure of a Canaanite woman's daughter* is a sign that the *reign of God* belongs not only to the Israelites but also to the Gentiles, in fact, to all who have faith in God. The *Gentile woman's great faith challenged Jesus to widen the horizon of his mission* beyond the borders of the Jews ("I was sent only to the lost sheep of the house of Israel": 15,24) to include the Gentiles. [Are we Christians/priests open-minded, like Jesus Christ, to be challenged by the profound faith of the followers of other religions?]

g) Feeding of the Four Thousand (Mt 15,29-39)

There are *many similarities* between the two narratives of the feeding of the four thousand in Mt 15,32-39 and Mk 8,1-10. *Jesus' compassion for the hungry crowd* (that has been with him for three days) is explicitly stated in both (Mk 8,2; Mt 15,32). In both Jesus asks his disciples: "*How many loaves have you?*" (Mk 8,5; Mt 15,34) and he uses the *disciples' seven loaves and a few small fish* to feed four thousand men ("besides women and children" who sit together to have a meal in common). Both mention Jesus' triple action of "*blessing*," "*breaking*" and "*giving*," symbolically pointing to Jesus' action during the *Last Supper*. At the end of the meal, the disciples gather *seven basketfuls of leftover food*. The number "*seven*" points back to the *disciples' "seven" loaves of bread* which they shared to feed the large crowd, indicating thereby that those are generous in feeding the hungry will be blessed abundantly.

Both Mark and Matthew narrate *two feedings* of large crowds (Mk 6,30-42; 8,1-10; Mt 14,13-21; 15,32-38) to emphasize the *compassion of Jesus* and to underscore the *priority of providing food to the hungry*, for which his *disciples* are asked *to share their food with the hungry* crowds (Jewish or Gentile) (Mk 6,37-38; 8,4-5; Mt 14,16-18; 15,33-34).

Instead of sharing their wealth with the poor, today many Christians (Bishops, Priests, Religious and Laity) live in luxury and spend crores of Rupees to build grandiose cathedrals and showy churches, pompous institutions and palatial houses even in a poor country like India, where millions in villages and slums have no houses to live in and have to go to bed with no food in their stomachs! Is not the *rich Church* in India a *scandal* and an "*anti-sacrament*" of the kingdom of God? When will the *rich Christian parishes* start *feeding the hungry* as the Sikh *gurudwaras* do? When will the *Indian Christians* become *like Jesus* who was *compassionate to the needy and the hungry*?

h) The Demand for a Sign by the Pharisees and Sadducees (Mt 16,1-12)

Just as the Pharisees and scribes had asked Jesus for a sign in 12,38-39, so now the Pharisees and the Sadducees (the priestly party in Jerusalem) come together to test Jesus by *asking for a sign from heaven* (16,1). He tells them that they know how to read the signs in the sky to predict the weather but *refuse to read the signs* of the times to understand how *God, working in and through Jesus, is actively saving* people through his *preaching and healing* (16,2-3). Therefore, Jesus refuses to perform any spectacular sign (wonder) to satisfy the "evil and adulterous generation" (especially the wicked and unfaithful leaders). The only sign that is given to them is "*the sign of Jonah*" (his coming out of the belly of a whale after three days, which symbolizes Jesus' resurrection three days after his death and burial: cf. Mt 12,39-40).

Jesus asks his disciples to be on their guard against "the *leaven* of the Pharisees and Sadducees" (16,6.11), which is their "teaching" (16,12). The disciples are not supposed to be influenced by the "*yeast*" of *Pharisaic teaching* but rather are to be transformed by the "*leaven*" of the reign of God (cf. 13,33).

i) Peter's Profession of Faith (Mt 16,13-20)

At Caesarea Philippi, Jesus asks his disciples, "Who do *people say* that *the Son of Man* is?" (16,13). The title "*the Son of Man*" has been used as a *self-designation by Jesus* quite frequently[80] but it does not have a univocal meaning in all instances; the *meaning varies* according to the context. Looking at its occurrences so far in Mt, sometimes it refers to Jesus, the *human being in solidarity* with others especially the poor (8,20) or the despised (11,19); at other times, it denotes him as the *sower of the good seed* (13,37), or as one having special *power to forgive sins* (9,6) or as the *Lord of the Sabbath* (12,8), or as the *eschatological judge* (10,23; 13,41). Hence *Jesus, as the 'Son of Man',* is a *human* being but with *superhuman powers*. In short, he is *a mysterious human being*.[81]

The disciples answer Jesus that *people* regard him as *John the Baptist* or *Elijah* or *Jeremiah* or *one of the prophets* (16,14). Then Jesus asks the *disciples*, "But who do *you* say that I am?" (16,15). It is clear that "I" in 16,15 is the same as "the Son of Man" in 16,13. Thus Jesus identifies himself as "the Son of Man". Simon *Peter's confession* "You are the Christ, the Son of the living God" (16,16) must be interpreted at *two levels*.[82] At the *historical* level of Simon's confession, the *two titles* ("*the Christ, the Son of the living God*)" are used almost *synonymously*. That is, Jesus is *the Messiah* (the anointed one), who is the adopted son like the *Davidic king* (cf. 2 Sam 7,14; Ps 2,7; 89,26-27) or like the people of *Israel* (Hos 2,23: "you are my people") who are called "sons of the living God" (Hos 1,10). But at the *post-resurrectional level*, the second title "*the Son of the living God*" in Peter's confession would have a deeper meaning, namely, Jesus is *the divine Son of God*.

j) Jesus' First Passion Prediction (Mt 16,21-28)

When Jesus tells the disciples that he "*must*" (*dei*) go to Jerusalem and *suffer* much and *be killed* and be *raised* (16,21), *Peter rebukes* him, "God forbid, Lord! It shall never happen to you" (16,22). This shows that even though Peter has just now confessed Jesus as the Messiah, he does *not understand* at all that he is a *suffering Messiah*. Peter, the rock/stone (16,18), is causing Jesus to stumble, tempting him like Satan (cf. 4,1-10)! Hence Jesus commands Peter: "Get behind me, *Satan*![83] You are a stumbling block to me; for you are not on the side of God, but of men" (16,23).

Realizing that Peter and the other disciples fail to grasp the need of suffering for the Messiah to fulfil God's salvific plan, Jesus tells them that every true follower of his must be willing to deny himself, *take up his cross* and *so doing,* be ready to lay down his life for Jesus' sake (16,24-25). It is only after his death and resurrection that Jesus, the Son of Man, will return in the glory of the Father as the eschatological judge who will repay all according to their deeds (16,27).

k) The Transfiguration of Jesus (Mt 17,1-13)

Six days after Simon Peter's confession of faith, Jesus takes Peter, James and John to a high mountain (17,1). "And he was *transfigured* before them, and his face shone like the sun, and his garments became white as light" (17,2), which means that he is transformed into a being of light, lighting up even his clothes. *Jesus' shining face and the brightness of his garments* point to the *divine* within and beyond his human form.

Seeing the vision of Moses and Elijah talking with the transfigured Jesus, Peter expresses his desire to build three booths for them to stay permanently on top of the high mountain (17,3-4)! He would like to confine the *divinehuman* Jesus to a man-made *tent* (*skênê*), oblivious of the fact that "he pitched his tent among us" (*eskênôsen en hêmin:* Jn 1,14)! Peter was ignorant of the truth that the incarnate Word of God was Jesus Christ dwelling among human beings (1,14.17).

The heavenly voice from the cloud (symbol of God's presence) declares: "This is *my Son, my beloved*, with whom I am well-pleased; listen to him" (Mt 17,5). These are the same words of God the Father at the time of Jesus' baptism in the Jordan (cf. 3,17). By directing the disciples to "*listen to him*" (17,5),

God is asking them to believe in Jesus' words especially about his imminent passion, death and resurrection (16,21; cf. also 17,12) and his instruction to carry their cross and follow him (16,24). *Jesus' transfiguration* is an anticipatory revelation of his risen glory, which would strengthen the disciples' faith in him.

l) The Healing of the Epileptic Boy (Mt 17,14-21)

When Jesus and the disciples come down from the mountain to the crowd, the father of a boy who is possessed by a demon of epilepsy comes to Jesus and kneels before him and pleads with him to pity his wretched son, whom the disciples were unable to cure (17,14-16). When the boy is brought to Jesus, he commands the demon to come out of the boy and he is healed immediately (17,17-18). When asked about the *reason for the disciples' inability to expel the demon*, Jesus tells them: "Because of *your little faith*" (17,19-20; cf. also 6,30; 8,26; 14,31). *Lack of trust* is the cause of their failure to cast out the evil spirit. If they have faith even as small as a mustard seed, they will be able to move even mountains (17,20), that is, accomplish impossible things. Jesus' ability to perform many miracles is due to his unshakable trust in the healing power of the Spirit of God working in and through him (cf. 12,28).

m) Jesus' Second Passion Prediction (Mt 17,22-23)

Now Jesus foretells again his death and resurrection but the *disciples* are deeply *distressed* (17,22-23) because they fail to see the passion as part of God's salvific plan. Whereas the first passion prediction caused Peter to protest (16,22), now the second one makes the disciples extremely *sad* because they (like most other human beings) see suffering primarily as a misfortune (17,23).

n) Payment of the Temple Tax (Mt 17,24-27)

Even though Jesus (the Son of God) was not obliged to pay the Temple tax ("half-shekel") (17,24-26), Jesus asks Peter to pay the tax (for both of them) so that nobody would be scandalized (17,27).

2.2.4. Instructions on Community Life (Mt 18,1-35) [Discourse]

This discourse deals basically with *discipleship* and *its demands* in the context of Christian living in the community.[84] Disciples are called to "*become like children*", simple and humble, to "enter the kingdom of God" (18,1-4). Since all the disciples are children of God, they are to receive them and relate to one another as Jesus himself did (18,5). Hence *scandalising "the little ones,"* causing them to stumble (to sin against God or others), is so serious that it would be better for the one who causes them to sin to drown oneself in the deep sea (18,6). The disciples are *not to despise* the "little ones" (18,10) nor allow them to *perish* (18,14), even if they sin, but they have to be brought back with love like a *good shepherd* does with the sheep that have gone *astray* (18,12-13). Jesus, the good shepherd, is asking the disciples to *be compassionate like him.*

Jesus also advises the disciples on how to practice *fraternal correction* personally or through mediation or the community (18,15-17). Whereas in 16,19 the power "to bind and loose" was granted to Peter, now the *power to forgive sins* is given to all the disciples (18,18). It is implied in the Lord's prayer (6,12: "*Forgive us* our sins as *we forgive* those who sin against us"). It means that God's children share in the forgiving power of God, their Father. Jesus also assures *his presence among the disciples* who are gathered in his name for prayer (in the family or community) (18,20: "I am there in their midst"; cf. also 28,20: "I am with you always").

To Peter's question about the *frequency of forgiveness* towards a sinful brother or sister ("how often... seven times?" (18,21), Jesus' answer is: "seventy times seven" (18,22), which means, *limitless* times, that is, *every time.*

Through the *parable of the unforgiving servant* (18,23-34) Jesus teaches the *absolute necessity of forgiving* others from our heart as God has forgiven us out of mercy and compassion (18,32-34). "The parable of the unforgiving servant illustrates that living in the kingdom means experiencing the immeasurable forgiveness of God and that those who belong to the kingdom reflect that forgiving nature in their relationships with others."[85]

Jesus' instructions to the disciples *not to scandalise* others but to *be compassionate and forgiving like Jesus* towards sinners (cf. Jesus' prayer from the cross: "Father, forgive them...") are very relevant for all the Christians in their individual and communitarian lives today. *Christlike forgiveness* is an *essential characteristic* of *Christian life and witness.* An unforgiving Christian is *not* a true Christian!

2.2.5. On the Way to Jerusalem (Mt 19,1-20,34) [Narrative]

a) Jesus' Teaching on Divorce (Mt 19,3-12)

When the Pharisees question Jesus about the *legality of divorce* (19,3), he says that Moses allowed divorce (cf. Deut 24,1-4) "because of your *hardness of heart*" (Mt 19,8). Divorce goes against the original intention of God who created human beings as male and female so that they "become one flesh" (19,5-6; cf. Gen 1,27; 2,24). Hence divorce, except on the ground of "unchastity" (*porneia* 19,9), separates what God has joined together (19,6) and it leads to adultery (19,9; cf. 5,32). Here Jesus claims to have the *authority to interpret God's original will* concerning marriage and declares *illegal* the Mosaic concession on *divorce*.

b) Jesus and the Rich Young Man (Mt 19,16-30)

When a young man asks Jesus: "Teacher, what good deed must I do, to have eternal life?" (19,16), Jesus tells him to keep the commandments (19,17-19). When he says, "All these I have observed; what do I still lack?" (19,20), Jesus invites him to *sell all his possessions* and *donate the money to the poor*, and then to come and *follow* him (19,21). This is the path to perfection but earthly possessions prove to be a stumbling block to him. Because of *his attachment* to his riches, he *goes away sad* (19,22).

Seeing the rich young man's sorrowful departure, Jesus surprises his disciples by his *puzzling statement*: "it is easier for a camel to go through the eye of a needle than for a rich man to enter the kingdom of God" (19,24). Salvation is God's gift and only God can help the rich to detach themselves from their wealth and use it to assist the underprivileged and the deprived (19,26). Just as Jesus left everything including his home ("where to lay his head": 8,20) to carry out the mission of establishing God's reign, the disciples who have left everything (family and possessions) to radically follow him "will receive a hundredfold and inherit eternal life" (19,27-29).

c) Parable of the Labourers in the Vineyard (Mt 20,1-16)

The kingdom of God is compared to a householder who goes out to the market place and invites five groups of labourers at different times of the day (from 6 in the morning till 5 in the evening) to work in his vineyard (20,1-7). At the end of the day, he gives *one denarius each to every worker* (20,8-10) at which the first labourers who toiled twelve hours ("who have borne the burden of the day and the scorching heat") grumble at the householder for paying the same wage even to the last labourers who "worked only one hour" (20,11-12). According to worldly standards, it is unfair and unjust to give equal wages to all, irrespective of the number of hours of work. But it is not due to their fault that the last labourers worked only one hour, for nobody hired them earlier (20,6-7)! They belonged to the helpless category of the "*unemployed*"! After being hired in the evening, they became "*underemployed*", since they got an opportunity to work only for an hour! So they must be paid an adequate wage that would sustain them and their families. God's generous sense of *social justice* is different from man's narrow quantitative justice! The values of the kingdom of God are radically different from those of the world.

Jesus teaches us through the *parable of the labourers* that *social injustice and inequality* will not be tolerated in the kingdom of God on earth, which Jesus came to establish. But the sense of *social justice* is *lacking* in many Christian families and parishes, and even in some Religious communities in India! This is *counter-witness* to Jesus and his kingdom values!

In this parable of the kingdom of God, there is also a striking *contrast* between "*the last*" and "*the first*." Thus "the last" are called "first" to receive their wages ("a denarius," the daily wage of a labourer) (20,8-9); when "the first" (who worked the whole day) come to collect their wages, they too get only "a denarius" (20,10), at which they grumble against the householder (20,11): "These last worked only one hour and you have made them equal to us…" (20,12). The employer's reply is: "I choose to give this last as I give to you" (20,14). The *final lesson* from the parable is: "So the *last* will be *first*, and the *first last*" (20,16).

d) Jesus' Third Passion Prediction (Mt 20,17-19)

To establish *God's reign of justice and equality*, Jesus has to suffer, die and be raised. On the way to Jerusalem, Jesus takes the Twelve aside and makes the most detailed prediction of his imminent passion, death and resurrection: "Behold, we are going up to Jerusalem; and the Son of man will be betrayed to the chief priests and scribes, and they will condemn him to death and will betray him to the Gentiles to be mocked and scourged and crucified, and he will be raised on the third day" (20,18-19). Jesus is quite conscious of what is going to happen to him in the capital city: "he will be betrayed" (*paradothêsetai*)[86] by Judas to the religious leaders (responsible for Jesus' condemnation), who, in turn, "will betray" (*paradôsousin*) him to the Gentiles (who will ridicule, mock and crucify him). Here there is a *double betrayal* of Jesus, one *by Judas* (one of his Twelve disciples) and the other *by the chief priests and the scribes* (the religious leaders of his people) (20,18-19). But "he will be raised" (*egerthêsetai*) on the third day" by God. Hence Jesus, the *suffering Son of Man*, will be *vindicated by God* and declared *victorious* even *over death* through his *resurrection* from the dead.

e) The Request of the Sons of Zebedee (Mt 20,20-28)

Just as the reactions of the disciples to the first two passion predictions were negative (cf. Peter's protest in 16,22; the disciples' sadness in 17,23), after the third prediction *James and John* (the sons of Zebedee) get their mother to plead for two prominent places ("one at your right hand and one at your left") in Jesus' kingdom: they want to reserve for themselves the chairs of the prime minister and deputy prime minister, as though Jesus would be a worldly Davidic king sitting on a throne in his kingdom (20,20-21)! James and John claim to be ready "to drink the cup" (of suffering) (20,22) to be *the greatest* in Jesus' kingdom.

The *indignation of the other disciples* at the two ambitious brothers indicates that all the disciples think only in worldly terms (20,24). But Jesus tells them that his kingdom is not quite like the kingdoms of the gentiles where the rulers dominate over the people (20,25). "It shall not be so among you, but whoever would be *great* among you must be your *servant*, and whoever would be *first* among you must be your *slave*" (20,26-27). *Humble service* with *selfless love* is the *sign of greatness* in Jesus' kingdom. Christian leadership consists in following the example of Christ, the *servant leader*, *the suffering Son of man*, who has come "not to be served but to serve, and to give his life as a ransom for many" (20,28).

I wonder how many of the present *leaders in the Church* in India and abroad are "*servant leaders*" *like Jesus or Pope Francis*! Even though Pope Francis avoids the title "Holy Father" and does not wish to be addressed as "your Holiness", *Cardinals* are still called "*princes of the Church*"[87] and some insist on being addressed as "*your Eminence*"! Similarly, many *Bishops* like to be called "*your Lordship*" by the Christians and priests! I wish there would be more Bishops like the simple Christlike *Bishop Saupain S.J.* of Daltonganj of happy memory, who used to *wear kurta and pyjama* and *a wooden cross* and to *visit poor families* and *share their modest meals* and even *sleep in their poor huts.*

He was *a true pastor* (*shepherd*) who had "*the smell of the sheep*" (as Pope Francis advised the Bishops and parish priests).

f) Jesus' Healing of Two Blind Men (Mt 20,29-34)

As Jesus leaves Jericho, followed by a large crowd, *two blind men* sitting by the roadside (probably begging), on hearing that Jesus is passing by, cry out, "Have mercy on us, Son of David!" (20,29-30; cf. also 9,27). Despite the crowd's attempt to silence them, they cry out all the louder (20,31). By addressing Jesus "*Son of David*" (20,30.31; cf. also 21,9) and later "*Lord*" (20,31.33), they manifest their faith in him as the *royal Messiah* who has power to heal their blindness (cf. 20,33: "Lord, let our eyes be opened"). Moved by compassion, Jesus touches their eyes and immediately they recover their sight and follow him (20,34).

It is an invitation to the disciples to open their *eyes of faith* and to follow Jesus to Jerusalem like the cured blind men, who had the *insight* into Jesus as the royal Messiah and the Lord.

> We could gain insights into the condition and also solutions to the social problems of our country if we cared enough to hear the voices of those who dwelt on the pavements of our megacities, i.e. the street dwellers. Though they have been socially impaired, their insights should by no measure [sic!] be considered inferior.[88]

2.2.©. From the *Christological* point of view, the long Section (Mt 11-20) presents Jesus as *teacher* and *healer* but *highlights Jesus' mission* as the *suffering* "*Son of Man*" (11,19; 12,8.32.40; 16,21-28; 17,22; 20,18-19.28).

Other aspects of Jesus' mission and identity are also mentioned in Mt 11-20, for example, "*the Christ*" (11,2), "*the Servant of God*" (12,15-21), "*the Son of David*" (12,23), "*the Son*" [of the Father] (11,27) and "*my beloved Son*" (17,5).

2.3. Jesus, the Son of David and the Son of Man and His Rejection by the Leaders (in Jerusalem) (Mt 21,1-25,46)

The third part of the Gospel of Matthew deals with *Jesus' confrontation with Israel's leaders in Jerusalem* and *their rejection of the Messiah*, which he had already predicted thrice (cf. 16,21; 17,9-11; 20,17-19).

2.3.1. Jesus the Messiah's Confrontation with the Religious Leaders in Jerusalem (Mt 21,1-22,46) [Narrative]

a) Jesus the Messianic King's Humble Entry into Jerusalem (Mt 21,1-11)[89]

Jesus *rides on an ass* and enters Jerusalem, which is explicitly stated to be in fulfilment of the prophecy: "Tell the daughter of Zion, Behold, your king is coming to you, *humble*, and *mounted on an ass*, on a colt, the foal of an ass" (21,4-5; cf. Zech 9,9).[90] By riding on the colt of an ass, Jesus manifests himself as a *humble Messianic king* to the crowds accompanying him to Jerusalem. They spread their garments and branches of trees on the road and hail him with shouts of joy "Hosanna to *the Son of David*" (21,9; cf. Ps 118,26),[91] which means that Jesus is their long-awaited *royal Messiah*. When the people of the city, agog with curiosity, ask: "Who is this?" (21,10), the crowds confess Jesus as the prophet from Nazareth: "This is *the prophet Jesus from Nazareth of Galilee*" (21,11). While many in the crowd identify Jesus as the *Davidic Messiah*, others acknowledge him as the *Galilean prophet*.[92]

b) *Jesus' Prophetic Cleansing of the Temple (Mt 21,12-17)*

After Jesus was acclaimed as "the Son of David" and "the prophet" by the crowds, he enters the Temple of God and *drives out all the sellers and buyers* of animals and pigeons and overturns the tables of the *money-changers* (21,12). He does this *prophetic act of protest* against the *traders* in the Temple because they have made the *house of God* ("my house") which is meant to be "*a house of prayer... a den of robbers*" (21,13; cf. Is 57,6; 60,7; Jer 7,11). With the collusion of thc pricstly class, the *Gentile Court of the Temple* was turned into a *bazaar* or a market place. Confronted by the desecration of the place of worship by the traders, *Jesus, the prophetic Messiah, cleanses the Temple* (cf. Zech 14,21).[93]

After the Temple-cleansing, *the blind and the lame* come to Jesus in the Temple and are *healed* by him (21,14), indicating the *inauguration of a new era of God's compassion.*

> The action of Jesus to heal the lame and the blind (v 14) was aimed to demonstrate the fact that God's temple was supposed to be principally a place of prayer and healing of people. Consequently, all who wanted to pray/be prayed over or needed healing were to be welcomed into the temple.[94]

But the *chief priests and the scribes* become *indignant* at Jesus for curing the cripple and the blind, and at the children for crying out in the Temple, "Hosanna to *the Son of David*!" (21,15). This shows the *hard-heartedness of the religious leaders* and *their antagonism* to Jesus.

c) *Jesus' Cursing of the Fruitless Fig Tree (Mt 21,18-22)*

While returning from Bethany to Jerusalem, the hungry Jesus *curses the fig tree* without any fruits and it *withers* immediately, which symbolizes the *fate* of the *barren Temple of Jerusalem* or *the unfruitful people of Israel.*

Since this episode takes place after Jesus' cleansing of the Temple, the cursing and withering of the fruitless fig tree may symbolize the *divine judgement* destroying *the Jerusalem Temple.*

> The Temple was epitomised by the green but fruitless fig tree (v 19). It was full of activities. It seemed to be flourishing like the tree full of leaves, but it was barren of fruits. The Temple produced no results out of its activities. It was neither creating faith nor critiquing nor questioning. At Jesus' word, "may no fruit ever come to you again", the tree withered at once (v 20). This demonstrated the judgement of the prophet of Nazareth.[95]

> Like the clearing of the temple, this is *a symbolic act of judgment.* Israel's rejection of her Messiah confirms that her religious life is barren and so she faces judgment (see Mic 7,1 which similarly portrays Israel as a barren fig tree).[96]

d) Jesus' Authority Questioned by the Religious Leaders (Mt 21,23-27)

While Jesus teaches in the Temple, the authoritarian chief priests and the elders of the people question his authority: "*By what authority* are you doing these things, and *who gave you this authority?*" (21,23). "These things" refer to his cleansing the Temple (21,12-13), his teaching and healing in the Temple (21,23-24). The religious leaders claim to have exclusive authority over the Temple. Jesus asks them a *counter-question* about the (divine or human) *origin of John's baptism* (21,24-25). Since the insincere and hypocritical Temple authorities refuse to answer his question by pretending ignorance ("We do not know"), he too declines to reply to their query about the source of his authority ("Neither will I tell you by what authority I do these things") (21,26-27).

e) *Parable of the Two Sons (Mt 21,28-32)*

Despite the initial negative response of the *first son* to his father's bidding to work in the vineyard, later he repents and *obeys his father*, whereas the *second son*, despite his preliminary consent, *does not* (21,28-30). The Jewish leaders' declaration that the first son did the will of the father, but not the second, is an implicit condemnation of themselves (21,31). For, unlike the tax collectors and prostitutes, they did not repent or believe the righteous John the Baptist, and so thcy arc cxcluded from the kingdom of God (21,31-32).

f) *Parable of the Wicked Tenants of the Vineyard (Mt 21,33-46)*

The parable of the *vineyard* and its *wicked tenants*, who ill-treat and kill the servants and the son of the owner, is a condemnation of the *religious leaders* who killed the prophets in the past and are now plotting to arrest and murder Jesus (21,33-41.45-46). It is to be noted that "*my son*," "*the son*" and "*the heir*" in the parable are implicit references to *Jesus, the Son of God* (21,37-39; cf. 3,17; 17,5).

> In this parable, the tenants-on-contract were metaphorically the religious elites (v. 33). Here Jesus was referring to himself as a son who was sent by the heavenly Father after many prophets of the past ages. The leaders of Israel had every time rejected the prophets and now they intended to kill God's Son, Jesus.[97]

Jesus tells "the chief priests and the Pharisees" that "the kingdom of God will be taken away from you and given to a nation producing fruits of it" (21,43). Unfaithful, greedy and murderous leaders will be excluded from the kingdom of God and it will be given to those who would be faithful tenants of the vineyard/kingdom of God.

g) Parable of the Wedding Banquet (Mt 22,1-14)

In this parable, the kingdom of God is compared to a *marriage feast for the king's son* (22,1-2) but the invitees, despite repeated requests, refuse to come (22,3-6). So the king sends his servants to the thoroughfares and crossroads to invite as many as possible, "both bad and good," to the wedding banquet (22,8-10).

Despite God's sending prophets after prophets to the chosen people of Israel to invite them to the *Messianic banquet*, they have proved themselves to be unworthy (22,8). Now the *invitation* is extended *to all* (cf. Is 25,6-10). Nobody is excluded except anyone who does not care to wear "*a wedding garment*" (available to all guests) for the wedding feast of the kingdom of God (22,11-14). Both the *invitation* and the *wedding garment* are *freely given* (by the banquet-giver/God) but the invitees must *respond positively* and *appropriately* to participate in the banquet (of the kingdom of God).

Looking at the parable from the *Christological point of view*, the *king's "son"* points to *Jesus, the Son of God,* who has inaugurated the kingdom of God (cf. 4,17).

This parable could also be applied to the *Eucharistic banquet* to which all Christians are invited but not all readily and wholeheartedly respond. Do all of us *wear* the *festal garment* of a *virtuous life* (a life of justice, love, service, etc.) when we celebrate the Eucharist? Do we *experience* the presence of Jesus, *the bridegroom*, while sitting at the Eucharistic table? Does our participation in the Eucharistic meal make a difference to our lives in the family, community and society?

h) The Question about Paying Taxes to Caesar (Mt 22,15-22)

The Pharisees and the Herodians try to trap Jesus by asking him a tricky question: "Is it lawful to pay taxes to Caesar?" (22,15-17). If he were to say "yes," he would antagonize the people of Israel who hated to pay the poll tax, but if he were to say "no," then he would be accused of inciting insurrection against the Romans. Being aware of their insincerity, hypocrisy and malice, Jesus asks them to show him the coin for paying the tax, and pointing to the image and inscription of thc Roman Empcror Caesar on the coin which they produce (22,18-20), Jesus tells them: "Render therefore to Caesar the things that are Caesar's and to God the things that are God's" (22,21). Since he does not fall into their trap, they leave him and go away (22,22).

i) The Question about the Resurrection (Mt 22,23-33)

Next, the Sadducees (who do not believe in the resurrection) pose a riddle regarding the levirate marriage (cf. Gen 38,8; Deut 25,5-6) and resurrection (Mt 22,23-24). A woman was married to seven brothers in succession, after each one's death (22,25-27). So the Sadducees' question to Jesus is: "In the resurrection, therefore, to which of the seven will she be wife?" (22,28). Their question is based on a wrong assumption that the resurrected life is merely a continuation of the earthly life, which Jesus denies. He tells them: "For in the resurrection they neither marry nor are given in marriage, but are like angels in heaven" (22,30). The risen life after death is a transformed life which transcends the limited relationships of human life on earth. The crowd is astonished at Jesus' wise teaching that has silenced the Sadducees (22,33-34).

j) The Question about the Great Commandment (Mt 22,34-40)

A Pharisee asks Jesus: "Teacher, which is the *great commandment in the law?*" (22,35). Jesus tells him that to *love God* is the greatest and the first commandment, and the second is to *love one's neighbour as one would oneself.* These two form the foundation of the law and the prophets (22,37-40; cf. Deut 6,5; Lev 19,18). "The citing of the two commandments of love from the *Torah* was aimed to place equal weight on both sides of the balance i.e. the human and the divine."[98] Hence all other laws and regulations must be interpreted in the light of the love of God and neighbour. *Love* is the *guiding star* on the journey of life.

k) Jesus' Question about the Christ being the Son of David and His Lord (Mt 22,41-46)

Now Jesus questions the Pharisees: "What do you think of the Christ? Whose son is he?" (22,41-42). When they answer him "the son of David" (22,42), he asks them if he is David's son, how can David call his son "my Lord"? (cf. Ps 110,1; Mt 22,44-45). The right reply to Jesus' puzzling question is that the Christ (Messiah) is not only the "*the son of David*" but also "*the Son of God*" (cf. 3,17; 4,3.6; 8,29; 17,5), which the Pharisees are ignorant of (22,46).

2.3.2. *Jesus' Warning and Woes against the Scribes and Pharisees (Mt 23,1-36)*

a) Jesus' Warning against the scribes and Pharisees (Mt 23,1-12)

Since the scribes (teachers of the Mosaic Law) and Pharisees (particular about the observance of the Mosaic precepts) occupy the seat of Moses (to teach and interpret the Law), Jesus tells his disciples and the crowd to distinguish what they say from what they do, "for they preach but do not practice" (23,1-3). Their deeds are hypocritical, merely for show ("to be seen by people"); they long for the places of honour; they love to be called "*rabbi*" (23,5-7).

Jesus tells the disciples: "But you are *not* to be called *rabbi*, for you have *one teacher* [*Jesus*], and you are all brothers [and sisters]" (23,8). Since *Christ* is their *only "master,"* they are *not* to be called "*masters*" (23,10). The disciples are *not* to call anyone "*father*," Jesus tells them, "for you have *one Father* in heaven" (23,9). In short, since *all the disciples* are the *children of God the Father,* and therefore *brothers and sisters of Jesus* and one another, all have *equal dignity*. Christologically, *Jesus*, the incarnate Son of God, is our Elder *Brother* and *Teacher*.[99]

b) Jesus' Woes against the Scribes and Pharisees (Mt 23,13-36)

This section consists of *seven woes* (*denunciations*) against the *scribes* and the *Pharisees*, who are accused of being "*hypocrites*" (23,13.15.16.23.25.27.29), "*blind guides/fools*" (23,16.17.19.24.26), "*whitewashed tombs*" (23,27), and "*serpents/ brood of vipers*" (23,33). *Jesus' scathing attacks* on the *hypocritical religious leaders* and *inauthentic teachers* manifest him as a *courageous prophet* who is ready *to challenge* them without fear or favour.

Are there no courageous Christlike Christians to critique the numerous hypocritical leaders (cf. 23,25-28) in the Church today? Why are there so few prophetical lay leaders (like Christ) to challenge the scandalous priests and bishops of today? What are they afraid of? Marginalization and persecution by the authoritarian clergy? All the prophets and Jesus were persecuted and/or killed by the so-called religious leaders of their time (cf. 23,33-34)!

c) Jesus' Lament over Jerusalem (Mt 23,37-39)

After the severe criticism of the scribes and the Pharisees, Jesus laments over Jerusalem: "O Jerusalem, Jerusalem, killing the prophets and stoning those who are sent to you! How often would I have gathered your children together as a hen gathers her brood under her wings, and you would not (come)!" (23,37). This simile of a *mother hen* harbouring chicks under her wings suggests Jesus' longing to gather the people of Jerusalem under his loving and caring protection (cf. Is 31,5; Deut 32,11; Ps 36,7). But because they refuse to be sheltered by God's love manifested in and through Jesus, he predicts: "Behold! Your house is forsaken and desolate" (23,38), which may be an allusion to the destruction of Jerusalem by the Romans in 70 AD.[100] Because Jerusalem ("city of peace") refused to recognize the Prince of peace and has decided to do away with him, the city is abandoned and is destined to be destroyed!

2.3.3. Jesus' Eschatological Discourse (Mt 24,1-25,46)

In this discourse, Jesus speaks about the *destruction of the Temple/Jerusalem* and his *final coming as the Son of Man* but it is difficult to distinguish between the two. Matthew seems to interpret the first episode as a *foreshadowing* of the events in the last days to come. "The imminent destruction of Jerusalem and its Temple becomes a metaphor for the final judgement at the close of the age, a warning and encouragement to the disciples to be constantly in a state of preparedness for the coming of the Son of Man."[101]

a) Prophecy of the Destruction of the Temple (Mt 24,1-2)

After the prediction of the destruction of Jerusalem (23,38), Jesus foretells the utter devastation of the Temple: "Truly, I say to you, there will not be left here one stone upon another, that will not be thrown down" (24,2). The magnificent Temple built by Herod the Great will be reduced to rubble because of the rejection of Jesus by its leaders (the chief priests and the elders, the scribes and the Pharisees) (cf. Mt 21-23).

b) Trials and Tribulations after the Destruction of the Temple and before the Parousia of the Son of Man (Mt 24,3-28)

After Jesus predicts the destruction of the Temple (24,2), the disciples ask him: "When will this be, and what will be the sign of your coming and the close of the age?" (24,3). They want to know (a) the time of the Temple's demolition, and (b) the sign related to his final "coming" (*parousia*).

Without answering the two questions separately or successively, Jesus' discourse deals with both the destruction of Jerusalem/Temple and the coming of the Son of Man without making a clear distinction between the two events.

The events described in 24,15-25 seem to refer primarily to the *destruction of Jerusalem and the desecration of the Temple* ("abomination of desolation": 24,15; cf. Daniel 9,27; 11,31; 12,11). When it happens, the disciples are advised to flee from Judea to the mountains to escape the great tribulation (24,16.21.34).

Jesus predicts *a period of trials and tribulations* between the destruction of the Temple and the final coming (*parousia*) of the Son of Man. During this difficult time, there will be false messiahs and pseudo-prophets, wars between nations, famines and earthquakes, hatred and persecution of the disciples, but the gospel of the Kingdom of God will be preached to all nations (24,4-14; cf. also 24,26-28).

c) *The Final Coming of the Son of Man in Glory (Mt 24,29-31.36-51)*

Jesus talks about the *final glorious coming of the Son of Man* ("coming on the clouds of heaven with power and great glory") accompanied by his angels (to "gather his elect") (24,30-31), which will be preceded by *cosmic convulsions* (darkening of the sun and the moon, falling of the stars, quaking of the powers of heaven: cf. 24,29). But no one (neither the angels nor *the Son*) but only *the Father* knows about "that day and the hour" (the exact time) of the *parousia* of the Son of Man (24,36).

The disciples/believers are advised to *be always watchful* (24,37-43). They are to be ever alert to welcome *the Son of Man* whenever he comes: "Therefore you also must be ready, for the Son of Man is coming at an hour you do not expect" (24,44). They are to be like the *faithful and wise servant* (whom the master has put in charge of feeding his household) who does his duty of selfless service, and not like the unfaithful and selfish servant, who makes merry with drunkards and ill-treats his fellow servants. The faithful servant will be rewarded abundantly but the unfaithful one will be punished severely when their master will suddenly arrive at an unexpected time (24,45-51).

This parable is relevant for all Christians but particularly for all the *leaders* in the Christian community (i.e., bishops, parish priests, rectors, etc.) who are appointed to serve Christ's household as *servant-leaders*.

Jesus is presented here as the *glorious Son of Man*, the *just master*, the *final judge*, who will reward or punish all according to their deeds (cf. also 25,31-51).

d) Parable of the Wise and Foolish Maidens (Mt 25,1-13)

The kingdom of God is compared to a wedding feast. *Ten maidens* with their lamps are waiting to welcome the bridegroom (25,1). While the *foolish five* have taken only their lamps, the *wise five* have brought along flasks of oil as well (25,2-4). Due to the delay in the coming of the bridegroom, all of them fall asleep; at the sudden announcement of the arrival of the bridegroom at midnight, all of them get up and trim their lamps but the foolish maidens cannot light their lamps because they have no oil (25,5-8)! So when they are away to buy oil from the dealers, the bridegroom arrives and enters the wedding hall accompanied by the wise maidens with the lit lamps, and the door is shut (25,10). When the foolish maidens come and knock at the door, saying: "Lord, Lord, open to us," the bridegroom's reply is: "I do not know you" (25,11-12).

In this allegorical parable, *Jesus, the Son of Man*, is *the bridegroom* (cf. 9,15; 22,1-14); the *wise maidens* represent the *committed faithful* who are ready to welcome the Son of Man and the *foolish ones* stand for those who are *unprepared* to take part in the *wedding feast of the Kingdom*. Jesus reminds all the believers: "*Watch* therefore, for you know neither the day nor the hour" (25,13; cf. 24,44). All are to "*be prepared*" to welcome the Son of Man at all times.

e) Parable of the Talents (Mt 25,14-30)

Before going on a long journey, a man calls his *servants* and entrusts his property to them, to one he gives *five talents*, to another *two* and another *one*, according to each one's ability (25,14-15). Whereas the first two servants trade with the talents and double them, the third servant buries it in the ground (25,16-18). When the master returns, he asks every servant for an account (25,19). He *congratulates* the first two hardworking, responsible servants who have gained five or two more talents, saying: "*Well done, good and faithful servant*; you have been faithful over a little, I will set you over much; enter into the joy of your master" (25,21.23). But the master *punishes* the lazy and irresponsible servant, who *buried* the one talent, by taking it away from him and by casting him out into the outer darkness (20,24-30). The *kingdom of God* is his *gift* to us but it is also a *task* to be done faithfully and generously, without which we cannot share in "the joy of the master" or enter into "eternal life" (cf. 25,34.46). God has given us many talents (abilities and qualities) and he expects us to make diligent use of them in the service of the kingdom of God.

f) The Last Judgement (Mt 25,31-46)

When *the Son of Man* comes *in his glory* with his angels and sits on his glorious *royal throne* before all the peoples, he will *judge* them based on their *deeds of caring love and service of the needy* (e.g., the hungry, thirsty, naked, sick, prisoners and strangers). Only those who have lived a *life of loving service* will be judged *worthy to inherit God's kingdom*, for the king will say to them: "Come, O blessed of my Father, inherit the kingdom prepared for you from the foundation of the world" (25,34). Whatever *act of love and compassion is done to the least of the brothers and sisters* is regarded as *done to the Lord himself*, for he *identifies* himself with each one of them (25,35-40: "*you did it to me*"). But those who *lived a selfish life*, unconcerned about the plight of the least ones (e.g., the hungry, thirsty, strangers, naked, sick, imprisoned), will be *condemned to eternal punishment* (25,41-46). *No selfish person is fit to share in God's eternal life of love.*

Only those who *live as loving and caring children of God* here on earth will be found worthy to enjoy the fullness of life and eternal bliss with God. Without passing the *test of selfless love*, no one can get a *passport to the heavenly life of love. Love expressed in deeds* to the needy in this life is *the only key* that *can open the door to eternal life.*

2.4. Jesus' Passion, Death and Resurrection (in Jerusalem) (Mt 26,1-28,20)

Even though Mt 26-28 forms *one literary unit* (*narrative*), *thematically* it consists of *two subunits*: 1) *Jesus' passion-death* (betrayal, denial, trials before the Jewish Sanhedrin and Roman governor, crucifixion, death and burial) (26,1-27,66); 2) *Jesus' resurrection* ending with the great commission (28,1-20).

2.4.1. Jesus' Passion and Death (Mt 26,1-27,66)

It should be noted that Mathew's description of Jesus' passion and death (Mt 26-27) is mostly dependent on Mk 14-15 but with some expansions and developments. In the words of Benedict T. Viviano:

> In the story of the Passion, chaps. 26-27, Matthew follows closely his *one source, Mark* (Q has no passion narrative). His several *expansions*, at the Last Supper, the arrest, the fate of Judas, at the trial before Pilate (the bloody cry, Pilate's wife's dream, the handwashing), the cosmic portents at the death of Jesus, generally flow from Mark's narrative logic... Matthew develops *three main themes* that he found in his source: *Christology* (especially through prophetic knowledge and fulfilment), a *polemical emphasis* on the responsibility of the Jewish leaders

> and their supporters, and a series of *moral examples*, primarily that of Jesus...[102]

a) *The Secret Plot to Kill Jesus (Mt 26,1-5)*

Two days before the Passover, Jesus is prophetically aware of his imminent betrayal and death on the cross and he tells the disciples: "the Son of Man *is delivered up to be crucified*" (26,2),[103] as part of the providential plan of God. As in his earlier passion predictions (17,12.22; 20,18), now also he refers to himself as "*the Son of Man*," indicating his solidarity with the suffering human beings. He is going to suffer and die on the cross as *a representative of suffering humanity.*

The *Jewish authorities* (the chief priests and the elders) gather together secretly in the palace of the high priest Caiaphas[104] and plot to arrest Jesus stealthily and kill him quietly, preferably after the Passover (26,4-5). They are afraid to do it publicly during the Passover feast, lest it should cause a riot among the *ordinary people* who regard Jesus as *the royal Messiah and the prophet from Nazareth* (cf. 21,9-11). The *hypocritical religious leaders* are ready to commit the *heinous crime of murdering the Messiah secretly* to protect their vested interests!

b) *Anticipatory Anointing of Jesus' Body for Burial (Mt 26,6-13)*

When Jesus reclines at table in the house of Simon the leper in Bethany, a woman brings an alabaster jar of *very expensive perfume* and *pours it on his head* (26,6-7).[105] This is a symbolic action revealing her generous love for him. But the disciples are angry with her for the useless "waste" of the precious perfume instead of selling it for a large sum and giving it to the poor (26,8-9).[106] But Jesus defends her by telling them: "Why do you trouble the woman? For she has done a *beautiful thing (ergon kalon) for me*... In *pouring the ointment on my body* she has done it to *prepare me for burial*" (26,10.12). By *pouring* the perfume "*on his head*" (26,7), it would naturally fall "*on his body*" (26,12), which is interpreted by Jesus as *a prophetic act* "*preparing him for burial*" (26,12). Her *loving act of anointing his body for burial*, Jesus tells them, will be told in memory of her wherever the gospel of Jesus' Paschal mystery will be preached in the whole world (26,13).

c) Judas' Contract to Betray Jesus (Mt 26,14-15)

Judas Iscariot, one of the Twelve, takes the initiative to go to the chief priests and asks them: "What are you willing to give me (*moi dounai*) and I will *betray* him to you? (*hymin paradôsô auton*)" (26,14-15). And they pay him *thirty pieces of silver* and from that moment he keeps looking for an opportunity to betray him (26,15-16). Thus, one of the core group of the disciples of Jesus (the Twelve) becomes his betrayer because of his greed for money (cf. Zech 11,12). The *greedy Judas' betrayal* of his master (26,15) is a striking *contrast* with the *generous woman's anointing* of Jesus with a very costly ointment (cf. 26,7)!

d) Jesus' Passover with the Disciples and Prediction of Betrayal (Mt 26,17-25)

Jesus, knowing that *his time* ("my time," *ho kairos mou,* the significant moment preordained by God) is *at hand* (26,18), sends his disciples to prepare the Passover in a house (probably of a disciple) in Jerusalem, which they faithfully do (26,17-19).[107] Jesus is aware of the arrival of his *kairos,* the beginning of "*the hour*" *of his passion* (cf. 26,45), and therefore this Passover is a very special one for Jesus and his disciples.

As Jesus is reclining for the Passover meal with the Twelve disciples, he tells them: "Truly, I say to you, *one of you will betray me*" (26,21). The distressed disciples ask Jesus in turn: "Is it I, Lord?" (26,22). His reply ("He who has dipped his hand in the dish with me will betray me": 26,23) shows that Jesus knows exactly who his traitor is. The *hypocritical Judas* too dares to ask Jesus: "*Is it I, Rabbi?*" and Jesus' reply is: "*you* have said so" (*sy eipas*) (22,25),[108] and he stresses *Judas' responsibility for the betrayal* (cf. 26,24: "The Son of Man goes as it is written of him, but *woe* to the man by whom the Son of Man is betrayed!"). Jesus knows for certain not only the identity of the betrayer but also *his betrayal* as the *fulfilment of the Scriptures* (26,24; cf. Ps 41,9; Zech 11,12).

e) Institution of the Eucharist (Mt 26,26-29)

During the celebration of the *Jewish Passover* with his Twelve disciples (cf. 26,17.19.20), *Jesus institutes the Eucharist*: "Now as they were eating, Jesus took *bread*, and blessed, and broke it, and gave it to his disciples saying: 'Take, eat; this is *my body*'" (26,26). The "bread" that Jesus "took" from the Passover table was the "unleavened bread" (cf. *matzo,* bread of "affliction" and of "freedom,"[109] eaten by the Jewish ancestors on the night of the exodus from the slavery in Egypt: Ex 12,8.15-20). Jesus "*blessed*" (*eulogêsas,* that is, recited the prayer of blessing over the bread) and "*broke* it and gave it," identifying it with his "*body*" that was *going to be broken* during his passion and death. "And he took a *cup*, and when he had *given thanks* (*eucharistêsas*, from which derives "Eucharist") he gave it to them, saying, 'Drink of it, all of you; for this is *my blood of the covenant*, which is poured out for many for the forgiveness of sins'" (26,27). "*Blood*" is the symbol of *life* and "my blood of the covenant" recalls the blood of the first (Passover) covenant between God and His people (cf. Ex 24,8) and points forward to the *new covenant* to be established by Jesus' "blood" ("*my blood*") that will be shed on the cross ("poured out for many [all]"). Mt 26,27 adds the phrase "for the forgiveness of sins" to Mk 14,25 to underline that the Eucharist is also a *sacrifice* for the pardon and redemption of sinners. The Eucharist is *Jesus' sacrificial self-gift* (symbolised by his "*body*" to be broken and "*blood*" to be shed) for the salvation of all. "*Body*" and "*blood*" stand for the *totality of Jesus*; "*eating*" and "*drinking*" point to the Eucharist being a *meal* that has to be assimilated so that Jesus may become one with the disciples who receive him. In short, the *Eucharist* is both a *meal* and a *sacrifice*, or rather a *sacrificial meal.*

f) Prediction of the Disciples' Desertion and Peter's Denial (Mt 26,30-35)

On the way from the Last Supper room to the Mount of Olives (26,30), Jesus tells the disciples that they would all be "*scandalized*" (stumble and fall) because of him that night like the *sheep* that are *scattered* when their shepherd is stricken (26,31; cf. Zech 13,7). But he assures them that, after his resurrection, he will *gather* them all in Galilee ("But after I am raised up, I will go before you to Galilee": 26,32; cf. 28,7.10).

Peter, however, responds: "Even though all stumble and fall, I will *never* stumble and fall" (26,33).[110] But Jesus tells him: "Truly, I say to you, *this very night*, before the cock crows, you will *deny me three times*" (26,34). Still, Peter is cocksure of his faithfulness, for he boasts: "Even if I must die with you, I will not deny you" (26,35). It is said that pride goes before a fall!

We know that despite his loud protestations of loyalty, Peter denied Jesus thrice (cf. 26,69-75)!

g) Jesus' Prayer in Gethsemane (Mt 26,36-46)

Jesus goes to Gethsemane with his disciples to pray (26,36). He reveals his *utter anguish and deep distress* to Peter, James and John (the same three disciples who had witnessed his transfiguration: 17,1-8) and confides in them: "My soul is very sorrowful, even to death; remain here and keep awake with me" (26,38). Falling on his face, he prays to the Father three times to spare him the *cup of suffering and death*: "My Father, if it is possible, let this cup pass from me; nevertheless, not as I will, but as you will" (26,39). He *surrenders his will* in total filial obedience *to his Father's will.* (This is what Jesus had taught his disciples in the "Our Father": "Your will be done": 6,10). Strengthened by the prayer to his Father and ready to drink the cup of suffering, Jesus wakes up his sleeping disciples to witness his imminent betrayal, saying: "Behold, the hour is at hand, and the Son of Man is betrayed into the hands of sinners. Rise, let us be going; see, my betrayer is at hand" (26,45-46). Jesus is fully aware that "the hour" of his suffering as "*the Son of Man*" has arrived. Here Jesus reveals his *infused knowledge* of what is going to happen to him and his *human submission* to his Father's will regarding his passion beginning with his betrayal.

h) Judas' Kiss of Betrayal, Jesus' Arrest and the Disciples' Desertion (Mt 26,27-56)

Matthew depends on Mk 14,43-50 for the description of the betrayal and arrest of Jesus. *One* of the *two additions in Mt* is Jesus' question to Judas when he addresses him "Hail, Rabbi!" and betrays him with a kiss: "Friend, why are you here?" (26,49-

50). Jesus addresses *his betrayer as "friend"*! It shows that Jesus still *loves* him, even though he has betrayed his friendship and has turned out to be a deceitful disciple and a greedy agent of his arrest (26,47-50). The *second* Matthean addition is *Jesus' reprimand* to the disciple [Peter] who cut off the ear of the slave of the high priest:[111] "Put your sword back into its place; for all who take the sword will perish by the sword. Do you think that I cannot appeal to my Father, and he will at once send me more than twelve legions of angels? But how then should the scriptures be fulfilled, that it must be so?" (26,52-54). It reveals Jesus' strong *opposition to violence* which breeds violence and his total trust in his Father even after his arrest and his determination to fulfil the Scriptures in and through his sufferings (cf. also 26,56). Calmly Jesus confronts the armed crowds by asking them: "Have you come out as against a robber, with swords and clubs to capture me?" (26,55), even though he has frequently been in the Temple teaching the people. Willingly he *accepts his arrest as God's will* foretold in the Scriptures, but seeing that Jesus does *not resist* his capture, *all the disciples desert* him and *flee* (26,56).

i) Jesus before the Sanhedrin (Mt 26,57-68)

Jesus is taken to a night session of the Sanhedrin (the council of chief priests, scribes and elders) presided over by Caiaphas, the high priest (26,57). Despite many testimonies against Jesus, nothing substantial could be found to condemn him to the death penalty (26,59-60). Then two false witnesses accuse him of having said: "I can destroy the temple of God" (26,61). Jesus had indeed foretold the destruction of the Temple (24,2) but he had not claimed to destroy it himself. The high priest asks him to answer the allegation but Jesus remains silent (26,62-63). Finally,

Caiaphas asks him to respond to his next question by putting Jesus under divine oath: "I adjure you by the living God, tell us if you are *the Christ, the Son of God*" (26,63). Jesus' answer "*You have said so*" (26,64) implies that Caiaphas is responsible for taking him to be the (political) Messiah and Son of God. But Jesus identifies himself as the eschatological *judge*, "*the Son of Man* seated at the right hand of Power [God], and coming on the clouds of heaven" (26,64; cf. Dan 7,13). Now the high priest accuses Jesus of *blasphemy* and the Sanhedrin condemns him to death for it (26,65-66; cf. Lev 24,10). Then they mock him as the Christ by spitting on his face and by slapping him (26,67-68).

Christologically it is noteworthy that Jesus is *condemned to death* for his being *the Christ*, *the Son of Man* and *the Son of God.*

j) Peter's Triple Denial of Jesus (Mt 26,69-75)

While seated in the courtyard of the high priest, Peter is questioned thrice by two maids and the bystanders about his being a disciple of Jesus and of having been "with Jesus," but *thrice* he *denies* it by saying or swearing, "I do not know what you mean" or "I do not know the man" (26,69-74). Peter, the leader of the Twelve, *denies Jesus by denying his discipleship* and even any *association* with him! Immediately after the third denial, the *cock crows* and he recalls Jesus' prediction of his denials, and he goes out and *weeps bitterly* (26,75). Through the triple denial, the proud Peter has become the *repentant Peter.*

k) Judas' Suicide (Mt 27,3-10)[112]

When Judas comes to know the Sanhedrin's decision to put Jesus to death (27,1), he feels *guilty* of the grave sin of "*betraying innocent blood*." He brings the thirty pieces of silver to the chief priests and the elders and flings them down in the Temple and, in despair, he goes away and *hangs himself* (27,3-5). They take the "blood money" and buy the potter's field, later called "the field of blood," to bury strangers (27,6-8). Judas "repented" (remorsefully) of his sin of betraying innocent Jesus (27,3) but failed to seek forgiveness from the merciful Lord and so ended up in committing suicide (27,5)!

l) Jesus' Trial before Pilate (Mt 27,11-26)[113]

The religious leaders who condemned Jesus to death for blasphemy (26,65-66) must have accused him of treason by claiming to be "the king" of Israel when they handed him over to the Roman governor. Hence Pilate's question to Jesus: "*Are you the king of the Jews?*" to which he replies: "*You have said so*" (27,11). Jesus puts the responsibility for his answer on the questioner (cf. 26,25.64). But when the chief priests and the elders bring many false charges against him, he refuses to defend himself to the great astonishment of the governor (27,12-14).

Even though Pilate knows that Jesus has been delivered to him by the chief priests and the elders "out of envy" (27,18) and that he is a "*righteous*" man (as attested by Pilate's wife: 27,19) who has done no evil (27,23), he asks the people to *choose* between the "notorious prisoner called *Barabbas*" and "*Jesus* called *the Christ*" (27,15-17.23). But the chief priests and the elders persuade the people to ask for the release of Barabbas and the crucifixion of Jesus, the Christ (27,20-23). Seeing the futility of bargaining with the blood-thirsty people, Pilate *washes his hands* as a symbolic gesture to show that he is not responsible for Jesus' death: "I am innocent of this man's blood" (27,24). All the people cry out: "His blood be upon us and upon our children!" (27,25). Under pressure from the shouting crowd,

Pilate *sets free the bandit Barabbas* and *condemns the innocent Jesus* to be scourged and crucified (27,26), thus committing flagrant acts of injustice.

After the terrible scourging, the Roman *soldiers* take Jesus to the praetorium, strip him and put a scarlet robe upon him, a crown of thorns upon his head and a reed in his right hand, and kneeling before him, they *insult* him by saying "*Hail, King of the Jews!*" and by spitting on his face and by striking him on the head. After the inhuman humiliation, they remove the purple robe and put his clothes back on him and lead him away to be crucified (27,27-31).

Like the earlier Jewish trial, the *Roman trial* too is *a mockery of justice*, because a robber-murderer is freed but an innocent and righteous person is scourged and crucified!

Sometimes such terrible trials take place in Indian courts even today! Often the criminals go scot-free but the innocent remain behind bars for years or for life! Many innocent persons are lynched by fanatical mobs on suspicion of cow slaughter! It is not unheard of for undertrials to be summarily executed by the police in fake "encounters" in some States in India!

m) Jesus' Crucifixion (Mt 27,32-44)

Seeing that the scourged Jesus may collapse on the way, the soldiers compel a stranger, a certain Simon of Cyrene, to carry the cross on his behalf (27,32). On reaching Golgotha ("the place of a skull"), just outside the city of Jerusalem, the soldiers give Jesus a drink of wine mixed with bitter gall, but after tasting it, he refuses to drink it, probably desiring to be conscious of his sufferings to the end (27,33-34). After crucifying him, they display the charge against him above his head: "This is *Jesus the*

King of the Jews" and they cast lots for his clothes (27,35-37).[114] Then they crucify two bandits, one on his right and the other on his left (27,38) as if Jesus was one among the criminals.

Now the passers-by, the chief priests, scribes and elders, *mock Jesus* as "*the Son of God*" and "*the King of Israel*" and challenge him to *come down from the cross* and even the robbers *revile* him from the cross (27,39-44). But Jesus refuses to save himself by coming down from the cross so that he can save sinners through his suffering and death on the cross.

n) Jesus' Death on the Cross (Mt 27,45-56)

Matthew does not describe the details of the death of Jesus but reports some *extraordinary phenomena surrounding his death.* There was *darkness* all over the land from noon until three in the afternoon (27,45). Towards the end of that dark period, "Jesus cried with a loud voice: "*My God, my God, why have you forsaken me?*"" (27,46). These are the opening words of Ps 22, the *agonizing cry of the righteous* person praying for divine deliverance from his deep distress (22,1-2.19-21), who is later vindicated by God for which he will praise Him (cf. Ps 22,22-31). Therefore, the *crucified Jesus cries out in anguish but not in despair.* It indicates *his trust* that God will eventually *vindicate* him. With this *trust* and *hope* in his heart, "Jesus cried again with a loud voice and *yielded up his spirit*" (Mt 27,50).

At the death of Jesus on the cross, the *curtain of the Temple* sanctuary is suddenly *torn in two*, from top to bottom; the *earth* is *shaken* and the *rocks* are *split*; the *tombs* are *opened* and many *bodies of the saints* are *raised* (27,51-53). Seeing the awe-inspiring *earthquake* and *other astounding events* associated with the *death of Jesus*, the *Roman centurion* confesses: "*Truly this one was God's Son*" (27,54). God the Father had proclaimed Jesus as "*my Son*" at his baptism and transfiguration (3,17; 17,5), and Peter, representing the Twelve, had confessed Jesus as "the *Son of the living God*" (16,16).

The *earthquake* and the *centurion's confession of faith* in the *crucified Jesus as the Son of God* indicate that *his death* is an *eschatological* and *soteriological event*, that is, *God's final saving action* in the human history of salvation.

o) Jesus' Burial (Mt 27,57-61)

In the evening *Joseph of Arimathea*, a rich disciple of Jesus goes to Pilate and gets permission to bury Jesus. Joseph takes down his body from the cross, wraps it in a linen shroud and lays it in his new tomb, hewn in the rock, and closes its entrance by rolling a heavy stone against it (27,57-60).

Mary Magdalene and *Mary the mother of James and Joseph* (two of the many women "who had followed Jesus from Galilee, ministering to him") witnessed not only his death on the cross (cf. 27,55-56) but also his burial.

p) The Guard at the Tomb of Jesus (Mt 27,62-66)

The chief priests and the Pharisees remember Jesus' prediction of his resurrection after three days and so they go to Pilate with the request to make his sepulchre secure lest his disciples should steal his body and spread the rumour that he has risen from the dead (27,62-64). But Pilate tells them to do the needful by themselves (27,65). "So they went and made the sepulchre secure by sealing the stone and setting a guard" (27,66).

Shockingly, the *wicked chief priests and the hypocritical Pharisees* describe the *innocent Jesus* as "*the impostor*" (*ho planos*: 27,63) and *his disciples* as *liars* and *agents of "fraud"* (*planê:* 27,64). In fact, on the day of Jesus' resurrection, the unscrupulous chief priests will bribe the guards to spread the blatant lie that Jesus' body was stolen from the sealed tomb by his disciples when the guards were asleep (cf. 28,4.11-15)! But even the most corrupt priests cannot bribe God to cover up the truth!

2.4.2. Jesus' Resurrection (Mt 28,1-20)

Even though nobody was a witness to the actual resurrection of Jesus, some of his disciples (women and men) saw the risen Jesus. It is from their experiences of him and their testimonies, more than from the fact of the empty tomb, that we know the truth of the resurrection of the Lord. "The resurrection is God's vindication of Jesus' obedient death. The puny efforts of the chief priests and Pharisees to secure the tomb, of course, cannot prevent the Resurrection from taking place!"[115]

a) *Jesus' Resurrection, His Appearance to the two Marys and their Mission (Mt 28,1-10)*

Mary Magdalene and the other Mary, who had witnessed the death and burial of Jesus, come to his tomb before dawn on Sunday and experience a great earthquake because of the descent of an angel from heaven and his rolling back the stone (from the entrance of the tomb) (28,1-2). Seeing the angel's appearance like lightning and his garment white as snow, the guards get terrified. But the angel tells the women not to be afraid, since they are looking for the crucified Jesus, and he reveals to them: "He is not here, for he has risen, as he said. Come, see the place where he lay" (28,3-6). After showing them the empty tomb, he tells them to go quickly to the disciples and announce the good news of Jesus' resurrection and ask them to go to Galilee where they will see him (28,7). As they run "with fear and great joy" to tell this astounding news to the disciples, the risen Jesus meets them and greets them, and they hold his feet and worship him (28,8-9). Then Jesus tells them: "Do not be afraid; go and tell my brethren to go to Galilee, and there they will meet me" (28,10).[116]

Here the risen Lord himself *sends his women disciples on a mission to the Eleven*. Hence the *two female disciples* are the risen Lord's "*apostles to the apostles*". It is only if they listen to their testimony and follow the Lord's instruction will the Eleven be able to meet the risen Lord (cf. 28,16).

b) *The Report of the Guard (Mt 28,11-15)*

When the chief priests hear the report of the guards regarding what had happened at the tomb of Jesus on that Sunday morning, they in consultation with the elders bribe the guards to spread the false news that while they were asleep at night, the disciples stole the body of Jesus from the tomb (28,11-15). The dishonest and hard-hearted leaders will go to any extent to prevent the people from knowing the truth of Jesus' resurrection!

Even today many corrupt and power-crazy leaders (political and even religious) bribe the police to file false FIRs and hire witnesses to bear false testimony in the Indian courts! Truth and justice are sacrificed at the unholy altar of power and greed!

c) *Jesus' Appearance to the Eleven Disciples in Galilee and Their "Discipling" Mission (Mt 28,16-20)*

Following the risen Jesus' instruction, given through his women disciples (the two Marys), the Eleven disciples go to Galilee

(28,16). There they have a transformative experience of the risen Lord who entrusts them with a new "*discipling*" mission (28,17-20).

Seeing Jesus, the disciples who recognize him fall prostrate before him (*prosekynêsan:* "worshipped") but some doubt! (18,17). The risen Lord tells them: "*All authority* in heaven and on earth has been given to me" [by God] (28,18). Already during his ministry, Jesus had manifested his divine authority in his teaching (7,29), healing the sick (8,9), casting out demons (1,1), forgiving sinners (9,6.8), and cleansing the Temple (21,23-24.27). Now God has given him *universal authority as the risen Lord, the Son of God and the Son of Man* in glory (cf. 26,64).

With this *universal authority* (28,18) the *risen Lord sends his disciples* on a *worldwide mission*: "*Go,* therefore and '*disciple*' *(mathêteusate) all the nations (panta ta ethnê), baptizing* them *into the name* of the Father and of the Son and of the Holy Spirit, *teaching* them to keep all that I have commanded you" (28,19).[117] The *primary purpose* of the *disciples' mission* is to "*disciple all the nations*", that is, to lead all peoples of the earth to become true disciples of Jesus, for which they are *initiated* by "*baptizing*" them in the *name* of the Triune God of love ("the Father, the Son and the Holy Spirit") and by "*teaching*" (instructing) them to follow Jesus' commandments of love (of God and neighbour: cf. Mt 22,34-40).

> The power embedded in this authority [Mt 28,18] was to be used for harnessing *true discipleship* (v 19). Jesus *commissioned his disciples* to work towards *creating a community of transnational solidarity and committed discipleship* of all those who after hearing the gospel's message would affirmatively respond to it (v 19).[118]

During Jesus' ministry, Jesus sent his disciples only "to the lost sheep of the house of Israel" and not to "the Gentiles" or "the Samaritans" (10,5-6). But now the risen Lord sends them to "*all the nations*" (Gentiles) "*to disciple*" them all. The disciples are to do this by *teaching* and *baptizing* them. They are to teach them whatever Jesus has commanded them to do (e.g., in his discourses in Mt 5-7; 13; 18; 23-25). Like Jesus, they are to teach both by deed and by word. Only those who practice what they teach will have any credibility. Only such authentic teachers will inspire others to become disciples of Jesus.

"*Baptizing*" means "immersing," just as when Jesus was baptized in the Jordan, he was "immersed" into the river water.[119] "*Name*" stands for the person that is revealed, the Triune God manifested as the Father, the Son and the Holy Spirit. Hence "*baptizing into the name* of the Father and of the Son and of the Holy Spirit" signifies *immersing into the life-stream of the Holy Trinity* as a result of which the believers in Jesus, the Son of God, *become children of God, sharing in the very life of love of the Triune God.* In short, they become *members of God's family.*

The risen Lord assures his *permanent presence* with the disciples till the end of the world: "Behold! *I am with you* all the days till the end of the age" (28,20). This ongoing presence of the risen Lord reminds us of "*Emmanuel*" ("God-with-us": 1,23; cf. Is 7,14) and of Jesus' earlier promise to the disciples: "where two or three are gathered in my name, there *I am in the midst of them*" (18,20). The *"discipling" mission* of the Christian Church can be accomplished only in the *power of the ever-present risen Christ* (28,18-20).

2.©. Matthew's Good News of the Davidic Messiah, the Son of Man and the Son of God

2.©.1. Matthean Jesus' Titles[120]

The *most important titles* to designate Jesus in Matthew's Gospel are "*the Son of David,*" "*the Son of Man,*" and "*the Son of God,*" to which may be added "*Emmanuel.*"[121]

a) The Son of David[122]

It is to be noted that Matthew begins his Gospel with "the book of the genealogy of *Jesus Christ, the Son of David,* the son of Abraham" (1,1). By the time this Gospel was written, the term "Christ" had become part of the name/identity of "Jesus" (1,1.18). Already the genealogy mentions "*Christ*" (*Christos*) as a *title* meaning the "anointed one" (Messiah) (1,16.17). Hence Matthew firmly believes that *Jesus* is *Israel's long-expected Messiah* because he is identified as "*the Son of David,*" that is, Jesus is the *promised Davidic* or *royal Messiah* (1,1). To support the Davidic origin of Jesus, *Joseph* (the foster father of Jesus) is shown as *a descendant of David* in the genealogy (1,6-16).

Joseph is explicitly addressed as "*son of David*" by the angel of the Lord when he asks him to take the pregnant Mary as his wife (1,20).

> Although Jesus was conceived through the power of God's Spirit, Matthew insists that *Jesus* is the *royal descendant of David* since Joseph adopted him into David's royal lineage [1,20-24]. Jesus the Messiah, then, is a royal descendant of David who was born in David's city of Bethlehem, as the prophet foretold [2,1-6].[123]

The title "*Son of David,*" is applied to Jesus *nine times* in Mt (1,1; 9,27; 12,23; 15,22; 20,30.31; 21,9.15; 22,42). Even though the title had strong political connotations and the crowds of Jesus' time welcome him to the royal city of Jerusalem with shouts of "Hosanna to the Son of David!" (21,9), Matthew interprets him, not as a "triumphant and victorious" warrior king like David, but as a *humble king*: "Behold, *your king* is coming to you, *humble, and mounted on an ass*" (21,5; cf. Zech 9,9).

Jesus is a *compassionate* "*Son of David*" who *hears the cries* of the blind, the dumb and the lame (Mt 9,27; 12,22-23; 20,30-31; 21,14-15) and of others in deep distress like the Canaanite woman (15,22; cf. also 11,4-5).

> The Davidic Messiah of Israel comes as the one who takes the infirmities of his people upon himself (8,17). He is a servant who proclaims justice to the nations (12,18-21). He does not enter the royal city of Jerusalem as a powerful warrior but as a *humble and meek king* (21,5). Consequently, it is *people of little social status* (*the blind, a Canaanite woman, the children of Jerusalem*), rather than Israel's leaders, who *recognize Jesus* as *the son of David*.[124]

Right at the beginning of his public ministry, Jesus proclaims "*the kingdom of God*" (Mt 4,23) and he teaches it in the Sermon on the Mount (Mt 5-7); especially in the eight Beatitudes, he indicates who are called to participate in God's kingdom (5,3-10). He tells the disciples to pray for the coming of the kingdom of God (6,10). Jesus explains to the crowds the various dimensions of the kingdom through seven parables (Mt 13).

Jesus is *greater* than David's son, *Solomon*, (whose *wisdom* the queen of Sheba came to hear), for Jesus says: "Behold, something greater than Solomon is here" (12,42). Jesus' *mission and ministry* are not only to the *Israelites* but also to the *Gentiles*, as is clear from Jesus' healing of the Centurion's servant (8,5-13), his casting out the demon from the Canaanite woman's daughter in the Gentile region of Tyre and Sidon (15,21-28), his feeding the crowd of four thousand (15,32-39) including Gentiles who "glorified the God of Israel" (15,31).

Jesus, the *Messiah* (*anointed* by the Holy Spirit at the time of his baptism in the Jordan: 3,16) is *not* just an *adopted Son of God* like David but *God's beloved Son* ("my Son, the beloved, with whom I am well-pleased": 3,17; 17,5).

b) The Son of Man

Jesus uses the designation "*the Son of Man*" to refer to *(i) himself as self-designation*, *(ii)* his *suffering-death-resurrection*, and *(iii)* his *second coming* (*parousia*).

(i) Self-designation

Jesus never calls himself "the Son of David," or "the Son of God" but frequently he refers to himself in the third person as "the Son of Man".[125] For instance, Jesus says: "The Son of Man has nowhere to lay his head" (8,20), for he has no house of his own. Unlike the ascetic John the Baptist, "the Son of Man came eating and drinking" (11,19). Although others speak against him (12,32), he is the sower of the good seed of God's word (13,37). But unlike other humans, he has the authority to forgive sins (9,6) and he is the Lord of the Sabbath (12,8). He describes himself as a self-sacrificing servant: "The Son of Man has come not to be served but to serve, and to give his life as a ransom for many" (20,28). (All the disciples are invited to do the same.)

(ii) Suffering-death-resurrection of the Son of Man

Most of the time when Jesus makes predictions to his disciples about his suffering, death and resurrection, he refers to himself as "the Son of Man" (17,9.12.22; 20,18; 26,2.24.45). In short,

Jesus, *the Son of Man, suffers* as a representative of suffering humanity and *dies* for others and is vindicated by God by raising him from death to new immortal life. (His disciples also are expected to participate in the Paschal mystery by carrying their cross for the sake of others.)

(iii) Second coming (parousia) of the Son of Man

When Jesus speaks of his *final coming (parousia)* in his glory, he uses the title "the Son of Man" (24,27.30.37.39.44; 25,31; 26,64). The *glorious Son of Man* will return at the end of the ages to gather the elect and judge the nations.

(Since the time of the *parousia* is not known, the disciples are to be ever vigilant. Amid future suffering and persecution of Christians, the hope of *parousia* of the Son of Man will encourage them to persevere in their faith commitment and mission of loving service.)

c) The Son of God

Although Jesus himself never says explicitly: "I am the Son of God," he frequently but obliquely refers to himself as "*the Son*" (11,27.27.27.36; 22,2; 24,36; 28,19) and very often he speaks of God as "*my Father*" (7,21; 10,32.33; 11,27; 12,50; 15,13; 16,17; 18,10.19.35). Furthermore, God the *Father* attests during Jesus' *baptism*: "You are *my beloved Son*" (3,7), and during his *transfiguration*: "This is *my beloved Son*" (17,5).

> He [Jesus] not only spoke like 'the Son' but also acted like 'the Son' in knowing and revealing the truth about God, in changing the divine law, in forgiving sins, in being the one through whom others could become children of God, and in acting with total obedience as the agent of God's final kingdom… Jesus came across as expressing a unique filial consciousness and as laying

> claim to *a unique filial relationship with the God* whom he addressed as '*Abba*'.[126]

After Jesus' calming the stormy sea, the *disciples* worship him (*prosekynêsan autô*, "knelt/did reverence to him"), saying: "Truly you are *God's Son*" (*theou hyios ei*:14,33). At Caesarea Philippi *Peter* confesses: "You are the Christ, the Son of the living God" (16,16). Immediately after Jesus' death on the cross and seeing the earthquake, the *centurion* says: "Truly this one was *God's Son*" (*alêthôs theou hyios ên houtos*: 27,54).[127]

Devil/Satan tempts Jesus in the wilderness by saying: "If you are the Son of God…" (4,3.6) and later he addresses Jesus as "Son of God" (8,29). The *passers-by* deride the crucified Jesus, saying, "If you are the Son of God, come down from the cross" (27,40). Likewise, the *chief priests*, the *scribes* and the *elders* mock him for allegedly saying: "I am the Son of God" (27,43).

On the one hand, God the Father, the disciples and the Gentile centurion declare that Jesus is the Son of God; on the other hand, Satan (the leader of the demons) and the Jewish leaders tempt and challenge Jesus to miraculously prove his divine identity and filial relationship with God. But, instead of coming down from the cross, Jesus manifests himself as the *obedient Son of God* who accomplishes his Father's will in suffering (cf. 26,39.42) and even in death (cf. 27,50).

d) Emmanuel ("God-with-us")

Matthew mentions Jesus as *Emmanuel* ("God-with-us") at the time of the annunciation. He interprets the virginal conception of Jesus as the fulfilment of the prophecy: "Behold, a virgin shall conceive and bear a son, and his name shall be called *Emmanuel*" (which means "God with us") (Is 7,14; Mt 1,23).

God became present in a unique way not only in the *birth of Jesus* but continued to be present *during his ministry* of *preaching, teaching, healing and forgiving.* During the Sermon on the Mount, Jesus tells the crowd and the disciples: "You have heard that it was said . . . but *I say to you* . . ." (5,21-22.27-28.31-32.33-34.38-39.43-44). The OT prophets used to say: "Thus says the Lord", but Jesus says: "*I say* to you." It means that the *words of Jesus* are the *words of God.* Like God, Jesus *forgives* sins (9,2) and *knows* the thoughts and intentions of others (9,4; 12,25; 22,18). Jesus *promises his disciples* that wherever they gather in his name, he *is present in their midst* (18,20).

And at the very end of the Gospel, the *risen Jesus assures* his disciples of his *permanent presence* with them till the end of the world (28,20: "And behold! *I am with you all the days till the end of the age*"). In short, the *divinehuman Jesus* is *Emmanuel* ("God-with-us") now and forever. Hence we can *experience him* (his loving and saving presence) *everywhere* and *every day* of our lives.[128]

2.©.2. Matthean Jesus' Identity

Jesus in Mathew's Gospel is *human* and *divine.* He is both the *human Davidic Messiah* ("Son of David") and the *divine Son of God* ("the Son of God", "the beloved Son" of the Father). Because he is not only the *suffering* "Son of Man" (as the representative of suffering humanity) but also the *glorious* "Son of Man" (who will come to *judge* the nations with *divine authority*), he is a *divinehuman person.* Even though *human*, he has *divine authority* to teach and interpret the Law of Moses, to forgive sinners, to cast out demons, and to raise the dead to life. He is "God-with-us" (*Emmanuel*).

Chapter 3

LUKE'S GOOD NEWS OF JESUS CHRIST

Instead of using the noun "*goodnews*" (*euangelion*) as Mark does, Luke employs the verb "*to goodnews*" (*euangelizein*) in his Gospel. For instance, after announcing to old Zachariah: "your wife will bear a son, and you shall call his name John. And you will have joy and gladness, and many will rejoice at his birth" (1,13-14), angel Gabriel tells the disbelieving Zachariah: "I was sent to speak to you and *to goodnews* (*euangelisasthai*) *to you* these things" (1,19). Again, the angel of the Lord who appeared at night to the shepherds in Bethlehem tells them: "I *goodnews* (*euangelizomai*) *to you* a great joy...; for *to you is born this day* in the city of David *a Saviour*, who is Christ the Lord" (2,10-11). Thus, the *births* of *John*, the precursor, and of *Jesus*, the Saviour, are "*goodnewsed*" by angels to old Zachariah and the poor shepherds respectively.

After reading Is 61;1-2 ("The Spirit of the Lord is upon me because he has anointed me *to goodnews (euangelisasthai) to the poor* ...) (Lk 4,18), Jesus announces to all in the synagogue at Nazareth: "Today this scripture has been fulfilled in your hearing" (4,21). From now onwards, Jesus feels an inner urge "*to goodnews* (*euangelisasthai*) the kingdom of God" (4,43) to all. He goes through cities and villages "*goodnewsing* (*euangelizomenos*) *the kingdom of God*" (8,1; 9,6), or "the kingdom of God *is goodnewsed*" (*hê basileia tou theou euangelizetai:* 16,16). His "teaching in the Temple" is part of this '*goodnewsing*'" (20,1). In fact, the Lukan *Jesus' mission* consists in "*goodnewsing*" through his life, words and deeds, to all the people, especially the poor, the sick, the marginalized and the oppressed. It means that *Jesus Christ is "the good news"* because *his entire life* is *the revelation of the reign of God.*

Outline of Luke's Gospel:[129]

- **Preface (1,1-4)**

3.0. Introduction: Birth of Jesus, the Saviour, Fulfilment of God's Promises (1,5-2,52)

3.1. Preparation for the Public Ministry of Jesus, the Christ, the Son of God (3,1-4,13)

3.2. Galilean Ministry of Jesus, the Prophetic Messiah, the Suffering Son of Man and the Son of God (4,14-9,50)

3.3. Jesus' Journey to Jerusalem and Following Christ's Way (9,51-19,46)

3.4. Jesus' Teaching in the Temple in Jerusalem (19,47-21,38)

3.5. Jesus' Passion, Death and Resurrection in Jerusalem (22,1-24,53).

- **Preface (Lk 1,1-4)**

The Gospel of Luke begins with a *preface* by the author (Lk 1,1-4). He states: 1) there are many *others* who "have undertaken to *compile a narrative*" about Jesus Christ (e.g., Mark and Matthew) (Lk 1,1); 2) from the beginning there were "*eyewitnesses and proclaimers of the word*" (e.g., his family members like his mother Mary and his disciples who had experienced Jesus, seen his deeds and heard his words especially during his ministry and who proclaimed them to others after his resurrection) (1,2); 3) after having examined all things carefully, it seemed good to Luke also "*to write an orderly account*" (1,3); 4) its *purpose* is "that you may come *to know the truth…*" (1,4).[130] This "*truth*" about Jesus Christ is not only *historical* but also *theological*, as will be made clear in the course of the narrative. He interprets the identity and meaning of Jesus keeping in mind the *Gentile context* of his readers. For instance, instead of the Hebrew *Rabbi*, the Greek title *Epistata* (Master) is used to address Jesus (Lk 5,5; 8,44.45; 9,33.49; 17,13).

3.0. Introduction: Birth of Jesus, the Saviour, Fulfilment of God's Promises (Lk 1,5-2,52)

This *introduction* (1,5-2,52) is sometimes called "*Birth of the Saviour*" [131] or "*Dawn of God's Fulfilment of Promise.*[132] "The *central theme* of the birth narrative is the *arrival of God's salvation* and the *fulfilment of his promises* to Israel."[133] This is evident from the *announcements* (by angel Gabriel and the other angels), *dialogues* (between Gabriel and Zechariah, Gabriel and Mary), *songs of praise* (by Elizabeth and Mary) and *prophecies* (by Zechariah and Simeon).

The *human characters* involved in the birth narrative (Zechariah and Elizabeth, Mary and Joseph, the Shepherds,

Simeon and Anna) "represent the *faithful remnant* of the people of God, *waiting expectantly for the fulfilment of the promises* God has made to them."[134]

> *Related themes* include *Jesus as the Messiah* from David's line, *John the Baptist* as the Elijah-like *forerunner* of the Messiah, the central role of the *Holy Spirit* in the *age of salvation*, the *gospel* as *good news* especially for the lowly, poor, and oppressed, and *salvation* for the Gentiles as well as the Jews.[135]
>
> *Two structural features* help to carry these themes forward. The *first* is the *dual accounts of the births of Jesus and John*. The two stories are intertwined, with *parallel announcements* by the angel Gabriel and similar accounts of *their birth, circumcision, and naming*. Mary's visit to her relative Elizabeth further connects the stories (1,39-56). The narrator's purpose is twofold, both to link Jesus and John as co-agents of God's salvation and specially to distinguish their status and roles. While *John* will be "*a prophet of the Most High*" (1,76), *Jesus* is "*Son of the Most High*" (1,32). John's birth to a barren woman is miraculous, but Jesus' birth to a virgin is unique and unprecedented. John's role is to *prepare the way for the Lord* (1,17), but *Jesus* is that *Lord - the Saviour*, who is *Christ the Lord* (2,11). ...
>
> A *second structural feature* of the birth narrative is the series of birth narrative *hymns, or songs of praise*, offered up by Spirit-filled characters in the drama... Mary, Zechariah, Simeon, and the angelic chorus break into Spirit-inspired *celebration of God's salvation. Mary* glorifies the Lord for exalting the lowly and humbling the proud (1,46-55). *Zechariah* praises God for raising the Saviour from David's line (1,67-79). The old prophet *Simeon* predicts that this Messiah will bring salvation to the Gentiles as well as to the Jews (2,29-32).[136]

The angel (messenger) Gabriel *foretells* the birth of John to his old father Zachariah (1,5-25) and the birth of Jesus to his virgin mother Mary (1,26-38). These *two parallel angelic annunciations* form a *diptych*.[137] This is followed by the joyful meeting of the two pregnant women who sing *songs of praise* (1,39-56). Like the above annunciation diptych, the narratives of the *births* of *John the Baptist* (1,57-80) and of *Jesus* (2,1-21) form *another diptych*. Finally, the presentation of the *child Jesus in the Temple* (2,22-40) and the *boy Jesus' stay in the Temple* (2,41-52) form a concluding Christological *diptych*.

3.0.1. Annunciations of the Births of John the Baptist and Jesus, the Son of God (Lk 1,5-56)

a) Annunciation of the Birth of John the Baptist (Lk 1,5-25)

A righteous priest Zechariah, husband of Elizabeth, was offering incense to the Lord in the Temple in Jerusalem (1,5-10). The angel Gabriel appeared to him and told him that his wife (although barren and advanced in years) would bear him a son and he should call his name John (1,11-13). The angel assured him that John would be filled with the Holy Spirit and would be a great prophet like Elijah, who would prepare the people for the coming of the Lord (1,14-17). But since the prospect of them becoming parents at such an advanced age seemed laughable, he responded with scepticism, which resulted in him being rendered speechless (1,18-20). However, after his return home, his wife Elizabeth conceived and she praised the Lord for taking away her "reproach among men," the shame or disgrace of having been barren (1,24-25).[138]

b) Annunciation of the Birth of Jesus, the Son of God (Lk 1,26-38)

Six months after the conception of John by Elizabeth, God sent his messenger, angel Gabriel, to Nazareth in Galilee to the virgin Mary, betrothed to Joseph of the house of David, and he greeted her: "Hail, O favoured one, the Lord is with you!"

(1,26-28). Seeing that she is greatly troubled by his greeting, he reassures her not to be afraid because she has found favour with God (1,29-30). "And behold! You will conceive in your womb and bear a *son*, and you shall call his *name Jesus*. He will be great, and will be called Son of the Most High; and the Lord God will give him the throne of his father David, and he will reign over the house of Jacob forever, and of his kingdom, there will be no end" (12,31-32). The angel promises her that her son would be great because he is *Son of God* ("Son of the Most High") and he would be a *Davidic king*, who would reign over the house of Jacob forever, according to God's promise to David (1,33; cf. 2 Sam 7,12-16). Like Zechariah, Mary asks the angel for explanation of how she would conceive, since she has no sexual relationship with her fiancé: "How shall this be, since I do not know a man (husband)?" (*epei andra ou ginôskô*:1,34). Gabriel informs her that her conception will be through the divine power of the Spirit of God: "*Holy Spirit* will come upon you, and power of [the] Most High will overshadow you, and therefore the *holy* one to be born will be called *Son of God*" (1,35).[139] This means that it is not through sexual intercourse but through the divine intervention of the Holy Spirit that child Jesus will be conceived in the womb of the virgin Mary. To show that "with God, nothing will be impossible" (1,37), the angel tells her that her barren kinswoman Elizabeth in her old age has also conceived a son (1,36). Now Mary consents humbly and wholeheartedly to God's plan revealed to her: "Behold the handmaid of the Lord! Let it be to me according to your word" (1,38).[140] With her free *fiat* she conceives God's Son in her womb.

c) *Mary's Visitation of Elizabeth (Lk 1,39-45)*

Having been told by Gabriel that old Elizabeth is in her sixth month of pregnancy (1,36), Mary goes "with haste" to visit her pregnant relative in Zechariah's house in Judah and to care for her in her need (1,39; cf. 1,56). On hearing Mary's greeting, Elizabeth is filled with the Holy Spirit and exclaims with a loud cry (1,41): "Blessed are you among women, and blessed is the fruit of your womb!" (1,42). Mary is the most blessed woman because she has believed the Lord's (God's) word (1,45) and, as a result, has become the "mother of the Lord" Jesus (1,43).[141] Even the six-month-old baby in Elizabeth's womb "leaped for joy" at the presence of Jesus in his mother's womb (1,41-44), signifying that Elizabeth's child (John) has joyfully recognized Mary's child (Jesus) as *the Messiah*. God's promises have already begun to be fulfilled in John and Jesus.

d) *Mary's Song of Praise (Magnificat) (Lk 1,46-55)*

Mary sings the praises of the Lord and rejoices in God, her Saviour, for the great things he has done for her and for the people from generation to generation (1,46-50). There is a radical reversal of the proud/mighty and the lowly/powerless, the rich and the hungry in God's preferential liberative action (1,51-53).

> Mary's canticle is thoroughly "theological," focussing on the mighty acts of the Saviour God who is already effecting a reversal of fortunes. Although she does not understand all that happens, Mary recognizes that the action of God in her life is the first stage in the fulfilment of the promises made to Abraham and his descendants.[142]

3.0.2. *Births of John the Baptist and Jesus, the Christ, the Saviour (Lk 1,57-2,21)*

a) Birth and Naming of John the Baptist (Lk 1,57-66)

According to the prediction of the angel Gabriel, Elizabeth gives birth to a son to the great joy of her relatives and neighbours (1,57-58). On the day of circumcision, both Elizabeth and Zechariah insist that the *child's name* must be "*John*" (which means "Yahweh is gracious"), acknowledging God's favour to them, and at that very moment Zachariah regains his speech and blesses God (1,59-64).

b) Prophecy of Zechariah (Benedictus) (Lk 1,67-80)

Filled with the Holy Spirit, in his prophetic canticle, Zechariah praises the God of Israel for raising up a *Davidic saviour* who will deliver the people of Israel from their enemies according to the promises made to Abraham (1,68-75). He foresees his son John as the prophet of God, called to prepare the way of the Lord by helping the people to recognize the light of the Saviour (1,76-79).

c) Birth of Jesus in a Stable in Bethlehem (Lk 2,1-7)

Joseph and Mary had to go to Bethlehem, the city of David, to be enrolled (in the census decreed by the Roman Emperor Caesar Augustus) (2,1-5). "And while they were there, the time came for her to be delivered. And she gave birth to her first-born son and wrapped him in swaddling clothes, and laid him in a manger, because there was *no place* (*topos*) for them in the *guest-room*" (*katalyma*: 2,6-7)[143] of the *house* (cf. Mt 1,11: *oikia*). Since the "guest-room" was overcrowded, when Mary's labour pain began, she was moved to the adjacent *stable* where she "gave birth to her firstborn son" (2,7) whom she wrapped in *swaddling clothes* and laid in a *manger* (feeding place of the stable), which are *symbols of poverty* in which Jesus, the Saviour, was born.

d) *Angel's Good News of the Saviour's Birth to the Shepherds (Lk 2,8-20)*

An angel of the Lord appears to the shepherds, keeping watch over their flock out in the field in Bethlehem at night (2,8-9) and announces to them: "I *goodnews to you* (*euangelizomai hymin*) *a great joy* (*charan megalên*) which will be for all the people; for *to you* is *born today* in the city of David a *Saviour*, who is *Christ* the *Lord*" (2,10-11).[144] In short, the *goodnews* of *great joy* is the *birth of the Saviour* who is *Christ* and *Lord.*

> The confluence of these *three titles* (Saviour, Messiah, Lord) is the *Christological climax* of the infancy narrative... The language of the angel's announcement indicates that the one who is the *Saviour* is both *Messiah* and *Lord*... While "Messiah" indicates the specifically Jewish nature of Jesus' salvific role, "Lord" anticipates the royal enthronement of the Messiah and describes how believers view the crucified Messiah in the light of the resurrection.[145]

The *birth of Jesus* in Bethlehem is the *dawn of salvation* "*for all the people*" (2,10). But the "*goodnews*" is given not to the rich and the powerful but to *the poor and marginalized shepherds*. It shows God's *preferential option for the poor*. The *sign* for them *to recognize the Saviour* is: "you will find *a babe wrapped in swaddling clothes and lying in a manger*" (2,12). "Possibly the bands made of ordinary or used cloth, and manger – a place of animal food – were the two realities of the life of poor shepherds which connected them directly with their future Saviour."[146]

Now a heavenly host of *angels* praises God, saying: "*Glory* to God in the highest, and on earth *peace* among men with whom he is pleased" (2,14). Paradoxically, *Jesus in the manger* reveals God's *glory* (*doxa*) in heaven and *peace* (*eirênê*) on earth among human beings of God's delight (*eudokia*). The lowly shepherds are the representatives of the poor people in whom God takes delight.

Immediately after the angels' departure, the *poor shepherds* go "with haste" at night to Bethlehem *searching for the Saviour* and they *find* "Mary and Joseph, and the *babe lying in a manger*" (2,16). They make known to all what the angel had told them about the child (2,17-18). The simple shepherds become the *first witnesses of the Saviour* and they return "glorifying and praising God" (2,20). And Mary keeps all these things in her heart, meditating on their meaning (2,19; cf. also 2,51). This is Luke's implicit invitation to the readers to pray over the mysteries of the Saviour's birth and its revelation to the shepherds in order to fathom their salvific significance.

e) Circumcision and Naming of Child Jesus (Lk 2,21)

According to the Jewish custom, Mary's new-born son is *circumcised* on the eighth day and is given the name "*Jesus*" (which means "*Yahweh saves*"), following angel Gabriel's instruction to Mary at the time of the annunciation (2,21; cf. 1,31). Jesus' circumcision indicates that he is a member of God's chosen people and his name "*Jesus*" means that he is the *Saviour*.

3.0.3. *Presentation of the Child Jesus in the Temple and the Boy Jesus' Stay in the Temple (Lk 2,22-52)*

a) Presentation of the Child Jesus in the Temple (Lk 2,22-35.36-38.39-40)

Forty days after the birth of Jesus, the law-abiding Joseph and Mary bring him (the firstborn son) to the Temple *to present him and to consecrate him to the Lord* according to the law of Moses (Lk 2,22.27; cf. Ex 13,2.12; 34,19) and *to offer a sacrifice* of two turtledoves or pigeons ("the offering of the poor") for the purification of his mother (Lk 2,22-24; cf. Lev 12,2-8).

Simeon, a "righteous and devout" old man, who was "looking for the consolation of Israel" (awaiting God's saving action) and to whom the Holy Spirit had revealed that he would not die before seeing "the Lord's Christ" (God's Messiah), comes into the Temple, inspired by the Spirit, at the time of Jesus' presentation and, taking up the child in his arms, blesses/praises God (2,25-28). Since he has met the long-awaited Saviour, he is now ready to die in peace: "for my eyes have seen *your salvation* which you have prepared in the presence of *all the peoples*, a light for revelation to the *Gentiles* and for the glory to your people *Israel*" (2,29-32). Simeon recognizes and proclaims *Jesus* as the *universal Saviour "of all the peoples"* (*light to the Gentiles* and *glory of Israel*). Joseph and Mary marvel at Simeon's revelatory words about Jesus (2,33). Simeon prophesies that the child will cause *division* in Israel and will be "*a sign* that is *spoken against*" (2,34). He predicts that the people's *rejection of Jesus* will cause great anguish to his mother Mary and the sword of sorrow will pierce her heart (2,35). This is a Lukan hint at *Jesus' future passion and death.*

Now *Anna*, a very old widow and a prophetess, who prays, fasts and worships long hours in the Temple, comes up at the hour of Jesus' presentation in the Temple and thanks God for the *Saviour* and speaks about him to all those longing for redemption (2,36-38). Like Simeon, she too *recognizes Jesus*, the *redeemer*, and *bears witness* to him.

After the presentation of Jesus in the Jerusalem Temple, the Holy Family returns to Nazareth, where "the child grew and became strong, filled with wisdom" and "the favour of God" (2,39-40). As a *human child*, Jesus grows not only in physical size and strength but also in *wisdom* (mental and spiritual maturity) under the constant influence of *God's favour* (*charis*) (cf. also 2,52).

b) Episode of the 'Lost and Found' Boy Jesus in the Temple (Lk 2,41-51.52)

When Jesus was twelve years old, he went with his parents to Jerusalem to celebrate the feast of Passover (2,41-42). At the end of the feast, Joseph and Mary returned to Nazareth but Jesus stayed back in Jerusalem without informing his parents. After a day's journey, they searched for him among their relatives and acquaintances, and, on not finding him, they returned to Jerusalem seeking him (2,43-45). After three days of anxious search, they found him in the Temple sitting among the teachers and listening to them and questioning them. All were amazed at his great understanding and wise answers (2,46-47). His mother asked him: "*Son, why* (*ti*) did you treat us so? Behold, your father and I have been looking for you anxiously" (2,48). This shows their agonizing search for him for three long days. Instead of directly answering her question ("*why?*"), Jesus questions them in turn: "*Why* is it that (*ti hoti*) you were seeking me? Did you not know that *I must be (dei)* in *my Father's house?*" (2,49). This is the *Christological climax* of the Temple episode, since it points to *Jesus' consciousness of God* being *his Father* and the Temple (the house of God) being the privileged place of his Father's presence. As *the Son of God* he *must be* in *his Father's house*. His divine filial relationship with God the Father takes priority over his human bond with his parents, which they fail to understand (2,50). Already at the age of twelve, Jesus has an awareness of *a unique Father-Son relationship with God.*

Jesus, however, went down with his parents to Nazareth, and "was *obedient* to them" (Mary and Joseph); and "his mother kept all these things in her heart" (2,51). She kept prayerfully pondering, trying to understand the meaning of his questions to them and of his continuous obedience to them. How is *Jesus* the *(human) son of Mary* (2,48) the *(divine) Son of God* the Father (2,49)? Only prayerful meditation will reveal the *divinehuman mystery of his person.*

As at the end of Jesus' presentation in the Temple (cf. 2,40), so the episode of his stay in the Temple ends with the summary statement about his *growth* "in *wisdom and stature*, and in *favour with God and men*" (2,52). In his home at Nazareth he *grew physically, mentally, spiritually and socially* as an ideal *integrated* person, pleasing both to God and neighbours.

3.0.©. To *sum up* the *Christology of the Lukan infancy narrative* (1,5-2,52), the *humandivine Jesus* is the *promised Messiah* of Israel, the *royal descendant of David*, the *Son of God* and the *Saviour* of *the Jews* and *the Gentiles.*

3.1. Preparation for the Public Ministry of Jesus, the Christ, the Son of God (Lk 3,1-4,13)

As part of the preparation for launching Jesus' ministry, Luke gives enough information about the *context of Jesus' times*, which included the *socio-political* and *economic* life of those times (3,1-20). With this context as the background Luke *introduced Jesus* by showing, on the one hand, *his relationship to God* (3,21-38), and on the other, *his encounter with the actual realities of human life* (4,1-12).[147]

Lk 3,1-4,13 consists of *four subsections:* 1) John the *Baptist's Preaching* (3,1-20), 2) *Baptism* of Jesus (3,21-22), 3) *Genealogy* of Jesus (3,23-38), and 4) *Temptations* of Jesus (4,1-13).

3.1.1. John the Baptist's Preaching: Prepare the Way of the Messiah (Lk 3,1-20)

Like prophet Jeremiah (Jer 1,1), John, the son of Zechariah, receives the word of God in the wilderness and he preaches "*a baptism of repentance for the forgiveness of sins*" to the people of the Jordan region (3,2-3). This fulfils Isaiah's prophecy: "The voice of the one crying in the wilderness: *Prepare the way of the Lord*, make his path straight... and the crooked shall be made straight, and the rough ways shall be made smooth; and *all flesh shall see the salvation of God*" (3,4-6; cf. Is 40,3-5).[148]

> John was very clear about his role to "*Prepare the way of the Lord*" (v 4). He had to deal with human situations, which had become stone like (rigid), crooked and rough (vv 4-5); but despite all these hardships in the way of the Lord (Jesus), John still had the sure hope of *all the people* experiencing *God's salvation* (v 6). The *universality of salvation in Christ* is stressed here.[149]

Like a true and courageous prophet, John challenges the sinners to repent of their wicked ways (3,7) and exhorts all the multitudes (who come to him to be baptized) to "bear fruits that befit repentance" (3,7-8). To their question, "what shall we do?" John tells them to share their clothes and food with those who have none (3,10-11). Similarly, he advises the tax collectors and the soldiers to act with justice and righteousness (3,12-14). All are exhorted to change their selfish and unjust ways of life through a radical conversion of heart that is manifested in concrete deeds of charity and integrity.

When all the people wonder whether John could perhaps be the expected Messiah, he tells them all that he is only a slave who "baptizes with water" and who is unworthy even to unfasten the sandal strap of the *mighty Messiah* who "will baptize you in Holy Spirit and fire" (3,15-16).[150] "John is inferior to Jesus. John uses the purifying agent of water; Jesus will use the superior purifying and refining agents of the Holy Spirit and fire."[151] This is the "good news" about Jesus, the Messiah, that John the Baptist was preaching to the people (3,18).

3.1.2. Baptism of Jesus, the Son of God (Lk 3,21-22)

When Jesus was praying after being baptized in the river Jordan, "the heaven was opened, and the Holy Spirit descended upon him in bodily form, as a (female) dove (*hôs peristeran*), and a voice came from heaven, 'You are my Son, the beloved; in you I am delighted'" (3,21-22).

Theologically Jesus' baptism is very significant in many ways. First of all, *Jesus' baptism with the people* shows *his solidarity* with them and *his submission to God's plan* (as preached by John the Baptist) (3,6.16). Secondly, it is during *Jesus' prayer* that the heavenly *theophany* takes place (3,21-22). Thirdly, the *opening of heaven* indicates that a *divine revelation* is about to take place (cf. Ezek 1,1; Is 64,1). Fourthly, the *Holy Spirit* comes down upon Jesus in bodily form *as a female dove* (*hôs peristeran*).[152] The Holy Spirit descends upon Jesus as a mother-dove comes down upon her new-born (to protect it under her wings or to feed it). Fifthly, the heavenly voice (of the Father) declares Jesus' *divine Sonship*. He is the Father's beloved Son with whom he is fully pleased ("you are *my Son,*[153] *the beloved*; in you I am delighted") (Lk 3,22; cf. also 9,35). Finally, it is to be noted that the *mystery of the Holy Trinity* (the Father, the Son and the Holy Spirit) is manifested, as it were, in a nutshell in 3,22.

3.1.3. Genealogy of Jesus from Adam, Son of God (Lk 3,23-38)

Whereas Matthew's "genealogy of Jesus" begins with Abraham and finishes with Joseph his foster father (Mt 1,1-16), Luke's genealogy starts with Joseph and goes back to "Adam (son) of God" (3,23-38) through David and Abraham. Thus Luke seeks to highlight that Jesus is not just the Messiah of the Jews but "*the Saviour of all humanity*."[154] Jesus has come *to save all children of Adam*, i.e. all human beings (irrespective of race or nationality).

3.1.4. Temptations of Jesus, the Son of God (Lk 4,1-13)

Jesus, on whom the Holy Spirit had descended and whom God the Father had declared as his "beloved Son" (3,22), is "full of the Holy Spirit" and is "led by the Spirit" into the desert for forty days and is "tempted/tested by the devil" (4,1-2). It shows that the Holy Spirit, who is constantly present in Jesus, the Son of God, is the one who leads him to the wilderness and enables him to fast for forty days and be victorious over the tempter (devil).

The *three temptations/tests* are about Jesus' being "*the Son of God*" (4,3.9) and his having (worldly) "*power*" (4,6) and "*glory*" (4,6). When he is hungry after fasting for forty days, the devil *tests him*: "If you are *the Son of God*, command this stone to become bread" (4,3). The tempter asks the hungry Jesus to use his divine power as "the Son of God" to change miraculously a stone into bread. But Jesus overcomes the temptation by citing Deut 8,3a: "It is written, 'Man shall not live by bread alone'" (Lk 4,4), which shows the power of the Word of God (cf. Deut 8,3b; Mt 4,4). The second temptation (in Lk) is to gain political position and power and the glory of "all the kingdoms of the world" by worshiping the devil (instead of God), for he says to Jesus: "To you I will give all this *power* and their *glory*... If you, then, will *worship me*, it shall all be yours" (Lk 4,5-7). Jesus' answer is: "It is written, 'You shall worship the Lord your God, and him only shall you serve'" (4,8; cf. Deut 6,13). Now the devil takes Jesus to the pinnacle of the Temple in Jerusalem and asks him: "If you are *the Son of God*, throw yourself down from here" (4,9), and he quotes Scripture (Ps 91,11-12) to support his devious temptation to presumption (Lk 4,10-11)! His deceptive argument is that if Jesus is "the Son of God" (as God has declared, cf. 3,22), God will protect him from any injury by ordering his angels to guard his Son from any harm. Jesus overcomes the wily temptation by appealing to God's word: "You shall not put the Lord your God to the test" (Lk 4,12; cf. Deut 6,16). Unlike Adam, "son of God" (3,38), Jesus, "the Son of God", shows his fidelity to God, his Father, through his wholehearted obedience to his will (cf. 22,42).

The *three tests* that *Jesus, the Son of God,* had to go through show his *solidarity* with all human beings who are *tempted* to amass *riches*, attain *power* and gain *glory*. But the *Spirit-filled Jesus* was *victorious* over the evil spirit and his temptations.

3.2. Galilean Ministry of Jesus, the Prophetic Messiah, the Suffering Son of Man and the Son of God (Lk 4,14-9,50)

Jesus' ministry in Galilee, often identified as his 'period of popularity,' is covered in Luke 4,14-9,50. Here Jesus proclaims the message of the kingdom of God, calls disciples and performs miracles demonstrating his kingdom authority. His popularity grows and grows. As in the other Synoptics, opposition begins here, with the religious leaders challenging Jesus' claim to forgive sins (5,21-26), his association with sinners (5,27-32; 7,36-50), his failure to fast (5,33-39), and his apparent Sabbath violations (6,1-11).[155]

3.2.1. Jesus' Inaugural Mission Manifesto and His Rejection at Nazareth (Lk 4,14-30)

Empowered by the Holy Spirit, Jesus begins his public ministry in Galilee by teaching in the synagogues; and the news spreads in all the surrounding territory (4,14-15).

Jesus comes to his hometown "Nazareth, where he had been brought up" (4,16), and goes to the synagogue, as usual, on a Sabbath. When he stands up to read, he is given the book (scroll) of the prophet Isaiah and he opens it and finds Is 61 and reads aloud Is 61,1-2a:

> "The *Spirit of the Lord* is upon me,
> because he has *anointed me*
> *to [be/bring] goodnews* (*euangelisasthai*) to the poor.
> He has *sent me (apestalken me)*

to proclaim (kêryxai) liberty (aphesin) to the captives
and *recovery of sight (anablepsin)* to the blind,
to send (aposteilai) the oppressed *in liberty (en aphesin)* [cf. Is 58,6e LXX],
to proclaim (kêryxai) the acceptable year of the Lord"[156] [cf. Is 61,2a LXX].

Jesus deliberately chooses to read the first verse (Is 61,1), adds the phrase "*to send the oppressed in liberty*" (taken from Is 58,6e) and concludes by reading the first part of the second verse (Is 61,2a).[157] Lk 4,18-19 highlights *Jesus' liberative mission*, following the example of *God* who *liberated the oppressed people of Israel* in Egypt (cf. Ex 3,7-10).

The *purpose* of the *anointing* of Jesus by "the Spirit of the Lord" (God) is "*to* [be/bring] *goodnews* (*euangelisasthai* [verb]) to *the poor*" (Lk 4,18 does *not* say "*to preach* [*kêrussein*] good news"). He is the "*anointed one*" (*Messiah*, *Christ*) *to be/bring glad tidings* to the *destitute*, which he does through his words and deeds in favour of them. (He is *not* just a *preacher* of *good news* to them; rather, he is personally the *good news*; *his life* is the revelation of the *good news* to the poor). At the same time, Lk 4,18-19 is Jesus' *Nazareth Manifesto*, his *mission statement* introducing the *scope* and *content* of his *God-given mission*.

The socially and economically "*poor*" (*ptôchoi*) are exemplified by the "*captives*" (prisoners), the "*blind*" (handicapped), the "*oppressed*" (downtrodden). The "*good news*" to the "poor" is illustrated by the "*release*" of the captives, "*sight*" for the blind, and "*liberty*" (freedom) for the oppressed (cf. 7,22). God has sent Jesus "to proclaim the acceptable year of the Lord" (4,19), which refers to *the Jubilee Year*.[158]

When "the eyes of all in the synagogue are fixed on him," Jesus declares: "Today this scripture has been fulfilled in your hearing" (4,21). Here Jesus clearly announces the fact that the *Messianic era of liberation* foretold by the prophet Isaiah has commenced.

Since Jesus announces *deliverance* for the poor and the oppressed, *the people of Nazareth welcome his message of freedom.* All the people in the synagogue initially *respond favourably* to his *inaugural liberative mission statement* ("*all spoke well of him*, and *wondered* at the gracious words which proceeded out of his mouth; and they said: 'Is not this Joseph's son?'") (4,22). They are particularly *astonished* because they have known him for years as an ordinary *carpenter's son* and yet now he speaks of himself as *God's chosen prophet* and the *fulfilment of his promise*!

So Jesus' townspeople are tempted to ask him to perform miracles "in your own country" (as "you did at Capernaum" Lk 4,23) to prove his prophetic credentials. Jesus tells them: "Truly, I say to you, no prophet is acceptable in his own country" (4,24). Jesus reminds them that God sent the prophet Elijah only to a Gentile widow during the time of a great famine and only the Gentile Naman was cleansed of leprosy by the prophet Elisha (4,25-27).

> Jesus shocks his audience by pointing out that in the past, God favoured Gentiles like the widow of Zarephath and Naman the Syrian. They, not Israel, were the recipients of God's grace. Enraged, the townspeople drive Jesus out of town and attempt to throw him off a cliff. Jesus walks through the crowd and escapes [4,25-30].[159]

The Spirit-anointed *Jesus* (*the Messiah*), who proclaimed the *liberative mission of salvation* is *misunderstood* and *rejected* by *his own people of Nazareth.*

Jesus' inaugural mission manifesto indicates what is going to unfold in the rest of the Gospel and *his rejection at Nazareth* foreshadows his future rejection by his own people Israel.

3.2.2. Jesus' Prophetic Messianic Ministry in Galilee (Lk 4,31-9,50)

Despite his rejection by the people of Nazareth, Jesus carries on his *prophetic Messianic ministry in Galilee.* He casts out demons (4,31-37), cures the sick (4,38-41), and brings the good news of God's kingdom (4,42-44); he calls fishermen to be his disciples (5,1-11), cleanses a leper (5,12-16), heals a paralytic (5,17-26), and calls a tax collector to follow him (5,27-32); he restores the withered hand of a man (6,6-11), chooses the Twelve apostles (6,12-16), and proclaims the good news of the reign of God (6,17-49); he heals a centurion's dying servant (7,1-10), and raises to life a widow's dead son at Nain (7,11-17). Jesus clarifies the nature of his messianic identity (7,18-35), forgives a sinful woman (7,36-50), tells the parables of the seed (8,4-15) and the lighted lamp (8,16-18); he calms a storm (8,22-25), exorcises a Gerasene demoniac (8,26-39), heals a bleeding woman and raises Jairus' daughter to life (8,40-56), and he sends the Twelve on a mission (9,1-6). Jesus feeds the five thousand (9,10-17), predicts his passion-death-resurrection (9,21-27); and after his transfiguration (9,28-36), he heals a boy with an unclean spirit (9,37-43), and foretells his passion and death a second time (9,44-45).

a) Liberator of the Demon-Possessed and the Physically Sick (Lk 4,31-44)

Jesus *frees* those who are *oppressed by the evil spirits and sicknesses*, and *makes them whole*, through the *power of his word* (manifest in his preaching and teaching, healing and exorcising) (4,31-41).

While *teaching* the people *with authority* in the synagogue at Capernaum on a Sabbath (4,31-32), Jesus *liberates a man from the evil spirit* with a rebuke and command: "Be silent, and come out of him!" (4,33.35). Surprisingly, the unclean spirit cries out: "I know who you are, the Holy One of God" (4,34). Was the demon trying to flatter "Jesus of Nazareth" by calling him "*the Holy One of God*" so that he would not cast him out from the possessed person? The people are amazed at *Jesus' authority over the evil spirits*: "What is this *word*? For with authority and power, he commands the unclean spirits, and they come out" (4,36). Jesus, "the Holy One of God" has power over the unclean spirits because he is "*the Son of God*" (cf. 4,41).

Jesus *heals Simon Peter's mother-in-law* suffering from high fever by "*rebuking the fever*" (4,38-39). The immediate effect of Jesus' rebuke is that the fever (that had the power to confine her to bed) "left her" (4,39). Jesus' word healed her from her physical sickness, which enabled her to get up and serve them (4,39).

At sunset, Jesus lays his hands on all those suffering from *various sicknesses* (who are brought to him) and he *cures* them all (4,40). He also *casts out demons* and "*rebukes* them" for crying out: "You are *the Son of God!*" (4,41).

Even though at sunrise Jesus goes to a lonely place, the people seek him and try to keep him from leaving them (4,42). But Jesus tells them: "I *must* [bring] *goodnews the kingdom of God* (*euangelisasthai me dei tên basileian tou theou*) to other cities also; for I was *sent* for this purpose" (4,43). Jesus feels an inner urgency or necessity (*dei*) to proclaim the reign of God through his word and deed to as many people as he can because he is constantly conscious of his God-given mission. "And he was proclaiming (ên kêrussôn) [the kingdom of God] in the synagogues of Judea" (4,44).

b) Call of the First Disciples (Four Fishermen to be Fishers of Men) (Lk 5,1-11)

After teaching the crowd on the lakeshore (5,3), Jesus asks Simon with his companions (who had caught no fish the whole night) to put out into the deep and let down the nets (5,4). When they do so because he asks them, the resulting catch is so huge that the nets are stretched to breaking point and they have to take the help of their partners in the other boat to haul it safely in (5,5-7). All of them are astonished at the miraculous catch of fish (5,9-10), and Simon falls at Jesus' knees, pleading: "Depart from me, for I am a sinful man, O Lord" (5,8). The miracle makes Simon confess himself to be a *sinful human being* and acknowledge Jesus as "*Lord*". But Jesus tells him: "Do not be afraid; from now on *you will be catching human beings alive*" (*anthrôpous esê zôgrôn:* 5,10). This is an important moment in Simon's life for he is called to catch human beings (instead of fish). So Simon, the *fisherman*, becomes a *fisher of men*. But unlike the purpose of catching fish is to kill them (and sell them or eat them), the reason for catching humans alive is to help them to live a new life. And so, after bringing their boats to the shore, "they *left everything and followed him*" (5,11). Here Simon, James and John (the sons of Zebedee) abandon their boats, nets and fish, to follow Jesus, the Lord. Their *response* to Jesus is *immediate*, *total* and *whole-hearted*.

c) *Cleansing of an Untouchable Leper (Lk 5,12-16)*

A *leper* falls on his face and with faith in his heart beseeches Jesus: "Lord, if you will, you can make me clean" (5,12). Stretching out his hand, Jesus *touches* the leper, saying: "I will; be clean" and immediately he is cleansed of his leprosy (5,13). The leper is an "unclean" outcaste, an "untouchable," and therefore forbidden to associate with others or to participate in any worship in the synagogue or the Temple. Every leper (regarded as a *social outcast*) had to live in isolation away from home and society. No Jew would ever dare to touch a leper for fear not only of contagion but also of becoming ritually unclean. But Jesus deliberately *touches him* to *heal him holistically.*[160]

To reinstate the leper into the Jewish community, Jesus asks him to go and show himself to the temple priest to attest to the people that he is no more leprous and unclean (5,14). Thus Jesus frees him not only from physical illness but also from socio-religious isolation and thus gives him back his human dignity. The news of the leper's healing spreads far and wide and great multitudes flock to Jesus "to hear him and to be healed of their infirmities" (5,15). "But he withdrew to the wilderness and prayed" (5,16) because intimate communion with God in prayer is for Jesus as important as his preaching and healing ministry to the people.

d) *Healing and Forgiving a Paralytic (Lk 5,17-26)*

When Jesus was teaching the crowd, some men were trying to bring a bedridden paralytic before him but, unable to do so, they went up on the roof, removed some tiles and let him down in front of Jesus (5,17-19). Seeing their faith, he says to the paralytic: "Man, your sins are forgiven you" (5,20). The scribes and the Pharisees blame Jesus (in their hearts) of blaspheming because he forgave the paralytic since only God can forgive sins (5,21-22). To show them that God has given "the Son of Man" "authority on earth to forgive sins," Jesus tells the paralytic: "Rise, take up your bed and go home" (5,24). Immediately he goes home carrying his bed and "glorifying God" (5,25). Filled with awe, all the people too "glorify God" for Jesus' saving acts of *healing* the paralytic and *forgiving* his sins (5,26). Jesus the *Son of Man's power to forgive sins* is confirmed by his healing the paralysed man. Jesus enables him to start *a new life* of physical and spiritual freedom.

e) *Call of Levi (a Tax Collector) and Jesus' Table Fellowship with Sinners (Lk 5,27-32)*

Jesus *calls Levi*, a *tax collector*, despised by the Jews as a Roman collaborator and as a sinner, *to be his disciple* ("Follow me": 5,27); and his immediate response is wholehearted for he leaves everything and follows him (5,28). To celebrate his new life, Levi throws a grand party in his house for Jesus and his disciples and invites his friends ("a large company of tax collectors and others") to the banquet (5,29). But the self-righteous Pharisees and scribes murmur against (find fault with) Jesus and his disciples for eating and drinking with "tax collectors and sinners" (5,30). Jesus justifies his *table fellowship with sinners* because they represent the sick (i.e. the ones who truly need a physician) (5,31). Jesus tells them: "I have not *come to call* the righteous, but *sinners to repentance*" (5,32). The *compassionate Jesus' mission* consists in inviting sinners to a *conversion of heart and true repentance* (*metanoia*).

f) Jesus, the Messianic Bridegroom (Lk 5,33-39)

When *Jesus' disciples* (unlike those of John the Baptist and the Pharisees) are accused of *not fasting* but feasting ("eating and drinking"), he compares them to the *bridegroom's guests* eating, drinking and making merry with him during the wedding feast (5,33-34). In the OT "bridegroom" is a figure of God who loves his people as a bride (e.g., Is 62,5; Jer 2,2).[161] Here Jesus likens himself to the *Messianic bridegroom* at whose presence the guests (the disciples) rejoice by feasting. He gives them "*new wine*" to drink to cheer their hearts (5,37-38), which symbolizes the *gospel.*[162]

g) Jesus, the Son of Man, the Lord of the Sabbath (Lk 6,1-5)

When the Pharisees blame Jesus' disciples of breaking the Sabbath law (which prohibits doing any work) by plucking some heads of grain (from the fields), rubbing them in their hands and eating them, he reminds them of what David and his companions did when they were hungry, for they entered the Temple and ate the holy "bread of the Presence" (bread offered to God, which only the priests were allowed to eat) (6,3-4; cf. 1 Sam 21,1-6). It means that all religious laws are meant for the welfare of humans. Jesus insists: "The Son of man is lord of the Sabbath" (6,5). Jesus, "the Son of man" is not only God's eschatological agent but also the representative of all men and women, and therefore they too, like Jesus, have the right to interpret the Sabbath laws for their wellbeing (cf. 6,9).[163]

h) Healing on the Sabbath (Lk 6,6-11)

On another Sabbath, seeing a man with a withered hand in the synagogue (6,6), Jesus asks the scribes and the Pharisees: "Is it lawful on the Sabbath to do good…?" (6,9). By healing the man by asking him to stretch out his hand (6,10), Jesus shows that "Jesus and his disciples are not bound by Sabbath regulations when it is a question of doing good to people or saving a person's life. Jesus, the Son of Man, enunciates the principle of compassion."[164] But the critical scribes and the legalistic Pharisees are furious at Jesus' curing the handicapped man on the Sabbath (6,7.11).

i) *Selection of Twelve Apostles (Lk 6,12-16)*

After spending the whole night alone on the mountain in prayerful communion with God, Jesus calls his disciples together and handpicks twelve of them to be his "apostles" (6,12-16). The "Twelve" symbolically represent the twelve tribes of Israel and the reconstituted people of God (the new Israel). These "Apostles" will be sent by Jesus to continue his mission of "proclaiming the reign of God" and of "healing" the sick and casting out demons (cf. 9,1-2).

The Twelve Apostles are a *heterogeneous group*: four Galilean fishermen (Simon Peter, Andrew, James and John), a tax collector (Matthew), a zealot (Simon), an opportunist (Judas Iscariot), one with a Greek name (Philip), and four others (Bartholomew, Thomas 'the twin', James the son of Alphaeus and Judas the son of James).[165] Jesus' choice of such a diverse group points to his intention to train leaders to build *a new community of disciples from all walks of life.*

j) *Sermon on the Plain (Lk 6,17-49)*

Accompanied by the Twelve, Jesus comes down from the mountain to the plain to minister to the great multitude of people from Jerusalem and all Judea, even from the coastal areas of Tyre and Sidon, who are gathered there to hear him and to touch him to be healed of all their diseases (6,17.19). After curing all the sick and those who are troubled with unclean spirits (6,18-19), Jesus looks at *his disciples* and pronounces the following *blessings* on them:

> "Blessed [are you] the poor, for yours is the kingdom of God.
> Blessed [are you] who hunger now, for you shall be satisfied.
> Blessed [are you] who weep now, for you shall laugh" (6,20-21).

Unlike in Mt 5,3-10, here in Lk 6,20-21 Jesus directly addresses his *disciples* "[*you*] *poor*" [materially poor cf. Lk 4,18], "[*you*] who *hunger* now," and "[*you*] who *weep* now" and declares them "*blessed*," not because of their present poverty, hunger or sorrow, but because God's kingdom *belongs to them* ("*yours is the kingdom of God*") (6,20)[166] and because their existing sad situation will be reversed ("you *shall be satisfied*", "you *shall laugh*") (6,21). There is a clear *contrast* between their present situation "now" and their future "blessings". The *poor* are the special recipients of the "good news" of Jesus (cf. 4,18).

The next beatitude of those who are *hated, excluded, insulted and/or defamed* for the sake of Jesus, "the Son of Man," did not apply to the actual situation of the disciples listening to Jesus at that time but to their future condition and those of the future believers who will come to be persecuted for their faith (6,22). "Rejoice in *that day* and leap for joy, for behold, your reward is great in heaven" (6,23). Those who suffer hatred and persecution for the sake of Jesus are asked to '*rejoice*' because they are *assured of a great heavenly reward*, a glorious vindication by God (as in the case of the crucified-risen Lord). This is true of all the Christian martyrs from the first century till the twenty-first (e.g., the riot victims of Kandhamal in Orissa in 2008). All modern prophets and martyrs (e.g., St. Oscar Romero of San Salvador,

Blessed Sr. Rani Maria F.C.C., Fr. A. T. Thomas S.J., Dr. Graham Staines) had to face ill-treatment and even cruel death for their faithfulness to their prophetic and liberative mission.

The four "*woes*" in 6,24-26 form a clear *contrast* (both in structure and content) to the four "*blessings*" (beatitudes) in 6,20-23. "Woes" are pronounced against those who are (selfishly) "rich," "fully satisfied now," "laugh now," and "spoken well of" (flattered); their present condition will be *reversed* in the future (6,24-26: they "shall hunger," "shall mourn and weep"). Unlike the "poor" to whom "the kingdom of God" belongs (cf. 6,20), the uncaring "rich" will have no share in the blessings of God's kingdom (6,24; cf. 16,19-30: the parable of the Rich Man and Lazarus).

What Jesus said in 6,27-39 was meant not only for the disciples who listened to him (6,27a: "I say to you that hear") but also for the would-be disciples in the future: "*Love* your *enemies*, do *good* to those who *hate* you; *bless* those who *curse* you, *pray* for those who *abuse* you" (6,27-28). This is *a new radical ethic of love* for Jesus' disciples. This is summed up in the "Golden Rule": "Do to others as you would have them do to you" (6,31).

> The demand for this kind of love arises from the *identity* of the *people of God*. To love only those who love you would reflect no more than the standards of the *people of the world* (6,32-34). *God's children* must live to a *higher standard*, reflecting the *nature of their Father*, who loves even those who are ungrateful and wicked (6,35).[167]

The disciples are asked to be *loving and compassionate like God the Father*: "Be merciful even as your Father is merciful" (6,36). They are not to judge or condemn others; they are to pardon the debts of others (6,37), and they are to be generous in giving, and much more will be given to them by God their Father (6,38). Jesus asks the rich disciples to share their possessions with the needy ones and even with their enemies.

Those *hypocritical disciples* who *blame* their brothers and sisters for small failures but do not acknowledge their own gross failures are more blind, like those having a *log* in their eye, than those having a *speck* in their eye (6,39-42).

Just as a *good tree* does not produce bad fruit nor a *bad tree* good fruit, so a good man naturally does good and an evil man, evil (6,43-45). What one does and speaks reveals the treasure of one's heart. So Jesus demands from his disciples a *radical conversion of heart* so that they always *produce good fruits* befitting their discipleship.

To be genuine disciples of Jesus, it is not enough to call him 'Lord, Lord,' but it is necessary to *do* what he teaches (6,46-47). Those who live according to his teaching are like a well-built house with a strong foundation on rock, whereas those who do not are like a house without a foundation, which is sure to collapse in the event of a flood (6,48-49). The disciples have to be like Jesus, who practices what he teaches by loving and giving without counting the cost. *Jesus* is the *'gold standard' of Christian life and conduct.*

k) Healing of a Centurion's Slave (Lk 7,1-10)

A *Gentile centurion* (a Roman army officer having charge over 100 soldiers) but large-hearted enough to build a Jewish synagogue at Capernaum sends some elders of the Jews to Jesus to request him to come and heal his slave who is critically ill (7,1-5). As Jesus is about to reach to the man's house, he humbly sends word through his friends: "*Lord, … I am not worthy* to have you come under my roof; therefore, I did not presume to come to you. But say the word, and let my slave be healed" (7,6-7). This army officer knows well how his soldiers and slaves obey his orders and hence has absolute faith in the power of the authoritative word (7,8). Jesus tells the multitude: "I tell you, *not even in Israel have I found such faith*" (7,9). And because of his genuine and great faith, his slave is saved from mortal sickness and is made fully well (7,10). Here Jesus *admires the deep faith of a Gentile* (compared to the shallow faith of Israel) and readily responds to his request to heal his slave by working a miracle, revealing thereby that he is *the Saviour* not only of the Jews but also *of the Gentiles.*

l) Raising of the Widow's Son at Nain (Lk 7,11-17)

Jesus is moved to compassion when he sees a *weeping widow* of Nain, accompanying her only son's body for burial, and he consoles her in her sorrow by telling her: "Do not weep" (7,11-13). Unasked for by the desolate mother, Jesus touches the bier and tells the dead man: "Young man, I say to you, *arise*" (7,14). When the dead man sits up and starts speaking, Jesus gives him to his mother (7,15) and gives her *a new life of hope.* Witnessing the awe-inspiring miracle, the people glorify God, saying: "A great prophet has arisen among us!" and "God has visited his people!" (7,16). The people, who are eye-witnesses of Jesus' raising the widow's son to life, spread the good news to all in Judea and the surrounding region (7,17).

m) Response to John the Baptist's Messengers (Lk 7,18-35)

John the Baptist, who had told the people about the imminent arrival of the Messiah (3,16-17) and who had baptized Jesus

(3,21-22), *begins to doubt*, after hearing about Jesus' ministry, if he is truly the expected Messiah or not. And so the Baptist sends two of his disciples to ask Jesus: "*Are you he who is to come, or are we to wait for another?*" (7,19-20). Jesus answers them:

> "Go and tell John what you have seen and heard:
> the blind see, the lame walk, lepers are cleansed,
> and the deaf hear, the dead are raised up, the poor are evangelized (*euangelizontai: "goodnewsed"*).
> And blessed is he who is not scandalized by me" (7,22-23).

Jesus tells John not to judge him by his own expectation of a mighty and judging Messiah (cf. 3,16-17) but to be open to his way of being *a compassionate Messiah* by bringing the *good news to the poor* and by *doing miracles* on behalf of *the helpless and the marginalized* (the blind and the deaf, the lame and the lepers, etc.).

After the departure of the disciples of *John the Baptist*, Jesus praises him as one who is "*more than a prophet*," since he is the chosen messenger sent by God to prepare his way, and as the *greatest human being* born of women (7,26-28). But many (e.g., the scribes and the Pharisees) refuse to listen to John's preaching and allege his ascetical ways to be signs of his being possessed (7,30-33), just as they accuse Jesus, the Son of Man, of being "a glutton and a drunkard, a friend of tax collectors and sinners" (7,34) because of his table-fellowship with them (cf. 5,30).

n) Forgiveness of a Sinful Woman (Lk 7,36-50)

When Jesus was reclining for a meal in Simon the Pharisee's house, *a sinful woman* of the city wets his feet with her tears, wipes them with her hair, kisses them and anoints them with an ointment (7,36-38). Since Jesus does not object to her touching him, Simon presumes that he is ignorant of her being a sinner and hence concludes that he could not be a prophet (7,39). Reading Simon's thoughts (which shows that Jesus is a prophet), he tells the Pharisee the *parable of a creditor* who forgave one debtor five hundred denarii and another fifty (7,41). Then Jesus asks him: "Now which of them will love him more?" (7,42). And Simon's answer is: "The one, I suppose, to whom he forgave more" (7,43).

Now Jesus *contrasts Simon's negative actions* (of giving him no water to wash his feet, no kiss of welcome, and no anointing of his head with oil) with the *woman's loving actions* (wetting his feet with her tears and wiping them with her hair, kissing his feet and anointing them with ointment) (7,44-46). Therefore, Jesus declares that her many sins have been forgiven (*apheôntai*), which is manifested in her actions of great love (7,47). It is not because of her love that her sins are forgiven but because of *her faith*: "Your faith has saved you; go in peace" (7,50). However, the other guests at table question among themselves: "Who is this, who even forgives sins?" (7,49). Jesus' forgiveness of sin makes them wonder about his identity. Just as God's compassionate love welcomes and pardons sinners unconditionally (cf. the parable of the prodigal son: Lk 15,11-24), *the compassionate Jesus accepts and forgives the sinful woman unconditionally* and thus manifests that he is *the Son of the loving God*. Forgiveness is the greatest gratuitous gift of God to the repentant sinner. Therefore, a forgiven sinner (like the "woman of the city") "loves more" than others (7,42).

o) Women Disciples of Jesus (Lk 8,1-3)

When Jesus goes through cities and villages, "preaching and bringing the good news of the kingdom of God," the Twelve are with him, and some *women disciples* (Mary Magdalene, Joanna and Susanna and other women) *accompany Jesus*. They not only *travel with* him and the Twelve but also *minister* to them out of their means or family resources (8,1-3).

Jesus journeys through the villages and towns, *proclaiming (kêryssôn) and bringing the good news (euangelizomenos) of the reign of God* (8,1). His travelling band consists of not only "the Twelve" but "also some women." These *women disciples* have personally experienced the power of God's reign manifest in Jesus because he healed them of "evil spirits and infirmities." Hence "*the reign of God*" is *proclaimed by Jesus' word* (preaching) and is *embodied* by his band of *male and female disciples* (the Twelve and the women).

Some of these *women disciples* are singled out: *Mary Magdalene* (who had been liberated from seven demons), *Joanna* (wife of Chuza, Herod Antipas's steward, a person of high position and possessions), and *Susanna*. At the time of Jesus, it was unheard of that women would leave their homes or husbands and journey with a rabbi. But these women disciples and many others not only *accompany Jesus* but also *provide for the needs* of Jesus and the Twelve (8,2-3).

p) Parable of the Seed and Its Allegorical Interpretation (Lk 8,4-15)

Most of the translators and commentators call this parable "the parable of the sower" but the evangelist's *emphasis* is not on the sower but the *seed* (*ho sporos*: 8,5). Surprisingly, the sower sows only *four seeds* (Lk 8,5-8: please note the *singular* "*seed*" *(sporon)* at 8,5 and the *singular* "*another*" *(heteron)* at 8,6.7.8). *One seed* falls on the *footpath* and it is eaten by the birds, a *second seed* falls on the *rock* and it grows but withers away, a *third seed* falls among *thorns* with which it grew but is choked by them, and the *fourth seed* falls on *good soil*, which grows and yields a hundredfold (8,5-8).[168]

Jesus asks his audience to listen carefully to the parable, ponder over its meaning and apply it to their life: "He who has ears to hear, let him hear" (8,8). Each one must ask oneself *what kind of soil* one is and *how* one *receives the seed of God's reign* and *how* one *cooperates* with it.

But Jesus' disciples fail to understand the meaning of the parable (Lk 8,9). So he interprets it for the disciples (and later Christian community) so that they may "know the secrets of the kingdom of God" (8,10). Whereas the *point of Jesus' original "parable of the seed"* was "*the reign/kingdom of God*" (8,10), now in *its allegorical interpretation*, the *seed* is identified with the *word of God* (8,11), and the *various kinds of soil* are understood as representing the *different types of persons differentiated by the fate of the seed* (8,12-15). Some persons hear the word of God but let the devil take it away from their hearts and, as a result, they do not believe and hence are not saved (8,12). Some others receive the word of God with joy and believe it for a while but they fall away at the time of temptation (8,13). Some others allow the word of God to grow with the thorns and they are chocked by anxieties, riches and pleasures of life (8,14). Finally, the best recipients of the word of God are "those who, hearing the word, hold it fast in an honest and good heart, and bring forth fruit with patience" (8,15), that is, the genuine disciples respond to God's word with generosity and perseverance. To sum up, the Lukan allegorical interpretation of the parable underlines the *diverse ways of hearing the word of God* and the *different results* in terms of the fruit that is produced, ranging from zero to hundredfold.[169]

q) Lighted Lamp on a Stand (Lk 8,16-18)

Now Jesus uses the *metaphor* of a *lighted lamp* to refer to those who have heard and welcomed God's word whole-heartedly (8,16-18). The *word of God* is like the *light* and the *disciple* has to be like the *burning lamp on a stand* so that others may see the *light of revelation* (8,16). If *God's word* is *light*, every *enlightened disciple* is to be a *lighted lamp* for others.

r) Jesus' Mother and Brothers (Lk 8,19-21)

Jesus' mother and brothers come seeking to meet him but could not reach him because of the large crowd (8,19). On being informed about their waiting outside (8,20), Jesus tells the people: "*My mother and brothers* are those who *hear the word of God and do it*" (8,21). Jesus' mother Mary is the one who hears God's word, ponders on it in her heart and acts on it (cf. 1,38; 2,19.51). Christian disciples become members of Jesus' family not by birth nor by blood relationship but by hearing (welcoming) the word of God, acting on it and living by it. "*Hearing*" the word of God and "*doing*" (following) are both necessary to establish a *true relationship with Jesus*.

s) Calming the Storm to Save the Disciples from Drowning (Lk 8,22-25)

When Jesus was asleep in the boat which his disciples were rowing across the lake of Galilee, there arose *a great storm* and they were in danger of getting drowned (8,22-23). So they woke him up, saying: "Master, Master, we are *perishing*!" (8,24). He *saves* them by "*rebuking*" the mighty wind and the raging waves

(8,24).[170] Afterwards Jesus asks his disciples: "Where is your faith?" (8,25). After having witnessed so many of his miracles till now, they were expected to have some faith in him. They *marvel at his real identity*, for they ask one another: "*Who* then *is this*, that he commands even wind and water, and they obey him?" (8,25). This is a Christological question that every reader is invited to ask himself or herself and find an answer in the light of the rest of the Gospel.

t) *Transformative Healing of a Gerasene Demoniac (Lk 8,26-39)*

As soon as Jesus and the disciples cross the lake of Galilee and land in the country of the Gerasenes, *a demoniac* crosses their path. His condition was both terrifying (for he had broken the chains and fetters with which he had been bound) and pitiable (for he was living alone in the desert and naked among the tombs). But on seeing Jesus, he falls down before him and cries out: "What have you to do with me, Jesus, Son of the Most High God? I beseech you, do not torment me" (8,28). The evil spirit within the demoniac recognizes Jesus' divine identity but he commands the unclean spirit to come out of the man (8,29). Jesus allows the legion of demons to enter the herd of swine (unclean animals; cf. Lev 11,7; Deut 14,8), which rush down the steep bank and get drowned in the sea (8,30-33).

In this awesome *exorcism* of a demoniac, *Jesus restores a human being to the wholeness of life and a human community.* This is clear from the *contrasts* between *his life before* and *after the miracle*:

> "outside the city (8,27) inside the city (8,39); living in the tombs (8,27) living in a house (8,27.39); unclothed (8,27) clothed (8,35); demented (8,27) of sound mind (8,35); living in the desert

> (8,29) living in a house (8,39). These contrasts involve *transfers* from *destructive insolation* to a *nurturing human community*, transfers which Luke identifies as '*being saved*' (8,36) and which are effected *by Jesus*, '*the Son of the Most High*' (8,28)."[171]

It is note-worthy that the Lukan understanding of *salvation* is not simply the salvation of souls but *holistic liberation* from all evils and divisive forces and *integral transformation* of body, mind and spirit of human beings, enabling them to live in a harmonious community. In short, Jesus restores the *wholeness of life* to the demoniac.

Now the liberated demoniac expresses his desire to follow Jesus ("the man... begged that he might be with him [Jesus]": 8,38) but Jesus tells him: "Return to your home, and declare *how much God has done for you*" (8,39). He becomes Jesus' witness and emissary, "proclaiming throughout the whole city *how much Jesus had done for him*" (8,39). He gratefully acknowledges and loudly testifies to his fellow Gentiles *how much God in Jesus has done for him*. A liberated person's genuine testimony is the best witness to Jesus, the Saviour.

u) Healing of a Bleeding Woman and Raising of Jairus' Daughter to Life (Lk 8,40-56)

While the last two miracles were done for men (Jewish disciples and a Gentile demoniac), now Jesus performs *a pair of miracles* in favour of *two women*.

Jairus, a ruler of the synagogue, comes to Jesus and, falling at his feet, appeals to him to come to his house and cure his *daughter who is critically ill* (8,41-42).

As Jesus is on the way to Jairus' house, a woman who was bleeding for twelve long years comes through the crowd with *great faith* in her heart and *touches* him from behind and she is immediately *healed* of her haemorrhage (8,43-44). Realizing that healing power has gone forth from him (8,46), Jesus asks: "Who touched me?" (8,45). The woman declares publicly that it was she who touched him and, as a result, she was instantly and completely cured. "Here the faith of the wretched woman, who was considered perpetually unclean and untouchable, drew out the healing power from Jesus (vv. 45-47)."[172] This truth is confirmed by Jesus when he says to her: "Daughter, *your faith has saved you* (*sesôken se*); go in peace" (8,48). It is to be noted that Jesus affectionately addresses her "*daughter*" and *praises her firm faith* which prompted her to touch him to be *saved/ made whole.*

On hearing that the ruler's daughter is already dead (8,49), Jesus tells him: "Do not fear; *only believe*, and *she will be well/ saved* (*sôthêsetai*)" (8,50). For Jesus, *faith* is the only requirement for anybody *to be saved*, even for a dead person to be brought back to life. *Restoring life* is part of the *saving mission* of Jesus. Jesus felt the urgent need to let a young girl (of twelve years) live. So he goes to the ruler's house and, without bothering about getting polluted by touching a dead body (cf. Num 19,11), Jesus takes the girl by the hand, tells her: "Child (*hê pais*), arise (*egeire*)" (8,54), and her spirit returns to her and she gets up at once, and Jesus instructs her parents to give her food to eat (8,55). Jesus' action of lifting up the girl by the hand and his words to her ("Child, get up") and to her parents (to feed her) show *his genuine compassion and concern for the girl child* who needs nourishment to live and to grow up. While the parents are amazed at the miraculous gift of life to their dead daughter, Jesus asks them not to make it public (8,56). He accomplishes his life-giving mission, not for publicity but to please the Father of life.

v) Christlike Mission of the Twelve (Lk 9,1-6)

The *mission of the Twelve* disciples is a personal *participation in the mission of Jesus' proclamation of the reign of God* through preaching, teaching, exorcisms, healings and raising the dead (cf. Lk 4,18-8,56). Hence Jesus sends them out to proclaim the reign of God and he shares with them his power and authority to cast out demons and to cure diseases (9,1-2). In short, the Twelve are to continue his mission of preaching and healing. Since theirs is a *Christlike mission*, the Twelve should take *no provisions* for the mission but are to depend, like Jesus, on the providence of God and the generosity of the people to whom they are sent (9,3-4). Just as there are mixed (positive or negative) responses to Jesus, some will receive the disciples, while others will reject them (9,5).

Following Jesus' mission to "goodnews the kingdom of God" (4,13: *euangelisasthai tên basileian tou theou*), the Twelve go through the villages, "goodnewsing (*euangelizomenoi*) and healing (*therapeuontes*) everywhere" (9,6).

"*Goodnewsing*" means not only "preaching (*kêrussein*) the gospel (*euangelion,* goodnews)" through words (proclaiming the kingdom of God) but also bringing the "goodnews" of God's reign to others through their life-witness and deeds such as healing. Through their peaching, healing and life-testimony, they have to assist the people to experience the presence of the reign of God in their lives, just as Jesus has been doing it in his Galilean ministry (cf. 4,18-8,56).

w) *Revelations of Jesus and Diverse Responses to His Galilean Ministry (Lk 9,7-50)*

All the episodes and responses in this subsection are to be interpreted from the perspective of the *cross*. The fate of John the Baptist (his beheading by Herod Antipas: 9,9) casts a shadow on Jesus' ministry. Herod's question about Jesus' identity: "*who is this?*" (9,9) is an echo of similar questions put by the scribes and the Pharisees (cf. 5,21; 7,49) and the disciples (cf. 8,25), and it is a hint at Jesus' question to his disciples: "But *who do you say that I am?*" (9,20). Peter answers that Jesus is "*the Christ of God*" (9,20). But Jesus refers to himself as the *suffering "Son of Man*" (9,22), and God the Father declares: "This is *my Son, the Chosen one*" (9,35). Therefore, the subsection (9,7-50) is the *Christological climax* of the entire Section (4,14-9,50).

(i) *Feeding of the five thousand (Lk 9,10-17)*

On their return from their mission, the apostles recount to Jesus all that they had done; and Jesus and the disciples withdraw to Bethsaida (9,10). But when the crowds come to him, he welcomes them and speaks to them about the reign of God and cures all those who need healing (9,11). *Proclaiming God's reign* and *healing the sick sum up Jesus' Galilean ministry.*

Now towards evening, the Twelve request Jesus to send the crowd away to the villages and hamlets so that they may find food and lodge (9,12). But he tells them: "You give them something to eat" (9,13). *Feeding the hungry is an integral part of their mission.* But since they have only "five loaves and two fish" they feel completely helpless to feed a large crowd of five thousand (9,13-14). Yet Jesus asks his disciples to make the people recline (for a meal) in groups of fifty, which they do (9,14-15). Now Jesus, "*taking*" the five loaves and two fish of the disciples and looking up to heaven (in a prayer of thanksgiving), "*blessed* and *broke* them, and *gave* them to the disciples to set before the crowd" (9,16). These actions of Jesus correspond to those in the Lukan narrative of the *institution of the Eucharist* (cf. 22,19).

In this *miraculous feeding* of the five thousand, both *Jesus and the disciples* play *significant roles*. On the one hand, Jesus asks the disciples to share their food with the hungry crowd, and he multiplies the five loaves and the two fish with his prayer and blessing and gives them to be distributed to the people. On the other hand, it is the disciples who make the crowd recline for a meal, give their meagre provisions to Jesus for his blessing, and serve them to the reclining people. And after all of them are satisfied, the disciples gather up twelve baskets of leftover pieces of bread and fish (9,17). In this miracle, the Twelve collaborate with Jesus, indicating their willingness to share in his *mission of feeding the hungry*, just as they were ready to be sent on his mission of preaching and healing.

(ii) *Peter's declaration of faith in Jesus as "the Christ of God" and Jesus' prediction of the suffering "Son of Man" (Lk 9,18-27)*

After Jesus' prayer, he asks the disciples about the people's understanding of who he is: "Who do the *people* say that I am?" (9,18) and they answer: "John the Baptist," or "Elijah" or "one of the old prophets" (9,19; cf. also 9,7-8). Now he asks them a personal question about his identity: "Who do *you* say that I am?" As the spokesperson of the disciples, Simon Peter answers: "*the Christ of God*" (9,20). Peter declares the disciples' *faith in Jesus* as "the anointed one of God", the long-expected Jewish *Messiah*.

But Jesus forbids the disciples from divulging his being the Messiah to anyone (9,21), for "*the Son of Man must suffer* many things, and be *rejected* by the elders and chief priests and scribes, and be *killed*, and on the third day *be raised*" (9,22). The *suffering* of the *Messiah*, the *Son of Man*, is a necessity (cf. *dei*, "must") according to God's salvific plan, which, however, cannot be understood by any of his disciples now before his resurrection, and hence Jesus' ban on their revealing his Messianic identity to others, since it would be misunderstood by them.

However, Jesus tells all that *carrying their cross daily and following him* is a *necessary condition* for being his *true disciples* and for their *salvation* (9,23-25). Christians are the *followers of the crucified Christ*. "Christ dies on the Cross of Calvary, and left Christianity as a glorious heritage."[173]

(iii) *Transfiguration of Jesus and the Father's declaration as His Son (Lk 9,28-36)*

A week after Jesus' prediction of his imminent suffering, death and resurrection, he takes with him Peter, John and James and goes up the mountain to pray (9,28). And while praying, his whole appearance changes and his raiment becomes dazzling white (9,29). Now Moses and Elijah appear in glory and speak with Jesus about his "departure" (*exodos*) to be accomplished in Jerusalem (9,30-31). His "*exodus*" refers to his *death-resurrection-ascension* (departure from this world to God).

> Only Luke mentions that the topic of Jesus' conversation with Moses and Elijah is his "departure" (*exodos*), which he was going to fulfil in Jerusalem (9: 31). The term "departure" probably refers to the whole event of Jesus' death, resurrection, and ascension, and calls to mind the exodus from Egypt, God's great act of deliverance in the Old Testament. Through suffering, Jesus the

> Messiah will lead God's people to salvation through a new and greater "exodus".[174]

It is surprising that during the transfiguration of Jesus, his chosen disciples (Peter, James and John) fall asleep! They wake up only when Moses and Elijah are about to part from Jesus! Then Peter says to Jesus: "Master, it is well that we are here; let us make three booths, one for you and one for Moses and one for Elijah" (9,33), and Luke comments: "without knowing what he was saying"! This shows that Peter is ignorant of the real meaning of the transfiguration.

However, the merciful God allows Peter, James and John to experience his presence by overshadowing them with a cloud, although they are afraid to enter it (9,34). Now God the Father reveals the identity of Jesus to them: "This is *my Son*, the Chosen one" and he tells them: "*listen to him*" (9,35). He asks them to pay careful attention to His Beloved Son's words especially about his impending passion-death-resurrection (cf. 9,22.44) and about the need of following him carrying their own crosses (cf. 9,23-24). It is only by following the way of the cross, they will one day be able to understand the meaning of the mystery of the cross.

(iv) *Healing of a boy with an unclean spirit (Lk 9,37-43)*

A father of an only child possessed by an unclean spirit pleads with Jesus to have mercy on him and to cure him (9,37-40). This was a case where the disciples themselves had failed. Jesus rebukes the unclean spirit and casts it out of the boy and gives the healed boy back to his father (9,42). And all are astounded at the greatness of God revealed in Jesus' power (9,43).

(v) *Second passion prediction and the disciples' lack of understanding (9,43-50)*

While all are marvelling at Jesus' power manifested in his miraculous deeds (9,43), Jesus tells the disciples of his *powerlessness* to be seen *in his imminent passion*: "Let these words sink into your ears, the Son of Man is going to be betrayed into the hands of men" (9,44). But the *disciples fail to understand* this passion prediction, for its meaning is concealed from them (9,45) till after his resurrection (cf. 24,13-27).

Immediately after Jesus' second passion prediction, the disciples argue about who is the *greatest* (most powerful) among them (9,46), which shows their lack of understanding of Jesus' powerlessness in his suffering and death. Putting a *child* (an embodiment of powerlessness) in their midst, he tells them: "he who is *least* among you all is the *greatest*" (9,48). This is a very difficult lesson to learn for all the disciples of Jesus of all times and places.

(vi) *Instruction to the disciples to be inclusive (Lk 9,49-50)*

John is shocked to see a man (who does not belong to the group of the Twelve disciples) casting out demons in Jesus' name and so they forbid him (9,49). Like Joshua, who wanted Moses to forbid Eldad and Medad from prophesying in the camp because he thought that possessing the Spirit and prophesying were the exclusive privileges of the seventy elders who were present in the tent (Num 11,25-28), John is narrow-minded in his thinking that exorcism is the exclusive power granted only to the Twelve. Just as Moses tells Joshua that he would like all people to be Spirit-inspired prophets (Num 11,29), Jesus asks John and the Twelve not to be narrow-minded and exclusive but to be large-hearted and inclusive: "Do not forbid him; for he who is not against you is for you" (9,50).

3.2.© *Progressive Revelation of Jesus' Identity (the Prophetic Messiah, the Suffering Son of Man and the Son of God) (Lk 4,14-9,50)*

> By the conclusion of Jesus' Galilean ministry, there is little doubt about *his identity* and the nature of his messianic ministry. He is the *Spirit-anointed Messiah*, a *prophetic Messiah*, the *Messiah of God*, the *Son of God*. *His messianic ministry* entails preaching the good news of the Gospel to the poor, curing the sick, freeing those bound by Satan, restoring sight to the blind, forgiving sins, and calling sinners to repentance.[175]

Already in his *Nazareth Manifesto* (declaration), Jesus reveals himself as the Spirit-anointed *prophetic Messiah*[176] who brings good news to the poor and liberty to the oppressed (Lk 4,18-19.21).

Jesus' answer to John the Baptist's question about his *Messianic identity* ("Are you the one who is to come?": 7,19-20) shows that his *miraculous deeds* (curing the sick like the blind, the deaf, the lame and the lepers, feeding the hungry, casting out demons and raising the dead) and the *evangelization of the poor (ptôchoi euangelizontai: the poor are goodnewsed)* manifest him to be *promised Messiah* (7,21-22).

Also, the *Christological titles* or designations in 4,14-9,50 reveal Jesus' *identity*. Simon Peter, a leper and the centurion address him as "*Lord*" (5,8.12; 7,6);[177] Peter, John and the disciples call him "*Master*" (8,24.45; 9,33.49). Peter confesses him as "*the Christ of God*" (9,20). Jesus refers to himself as "*the Son of Man*" (5,24; 6,5) and especially the *suffering Son of Man* (9,22.44). The demons declare him as "*the Holy One of God*"

(4,34), "*the Son of God*" (4,41) and "*Son of the Most High God*" (8,28). During Jesus' transfiguration, God the Father proclaims him to be "*my Son, my Chosen one*" (9,35).

The disciples and others (who believe in him) normally address Jesus as *Lord* or *Master*, but Jesus prefers to refer to himself as *the (suffering) Son of Man*. The demons recognize him as *the Son of God* and God the Father declares him as *his Beloved Son*. Even though Jesus' identity is gradually revealed during his Galilean ministry, no human being can grasp the *mystery* of Jesus's *humandivine identity* (not only as of the promised *prophetic Messiah* but also the *suffering Son of Man* and the *divine Son of God*) before his death-resurrection.[178]

• ***Positive and Negative Responses to Jesus (Lk 4,14-9,50)***

The *responses* to Jesus in Lk 4,14-9,50 are *mixed*. On the one hand, *people* acknowledge the authority and power of Jesus' word (4,32.36) and they glorify God for Jesus' liberative words and miraculous deeds (5,26). Great crowds come to Jesus to hear him and to be healed of their illnesses (6,17-19) and they recognize him as *a great prophet* of God (7,16-17; 9,19). Because of Jesus' miracles, his *disciples* and even Herod wonder and ask: "*Who then is this?*" (8,25; 9,9). When Jesus asks the disciples: "Who do you say that I am?" *Peter* answers "*the Christ of God*" (9,20). On the other hand, *the scribes and the Pharisees oppose* Jesus for forgiving sins (5,21; 7,48-49), his table fellowship with sinners (5,30), his healing the sick on the Sabbath (6,6-11), and they doubt his being a true prophet (7,39). In short, while the *responses* of *the people and the disciples* to Jesus are *mostly positive*, the *reactions* of the *Jewish leaders* are *negative*.

3.3. Jesus' Journey to Jerusalem and Disciples' Following Christ's Way (Lk 9,51-19,46)

Luke's *travel narrative* begins with a significant statement about *Jesus' resolute journey to Jerusalem*: "When the days drew near for him to be taken up, *he set his face to go to Jerusalem*" (9,51), indicating his indomitable determination to do God's will even if he has to face much opposition, persecution and even death. The *purpose* of Jesus' journey is *to fulfil God's salvific plan* by accomplishing his "exodus" in Jerusalem (9,31) through his suffering, death and resurrection (cf. 9,22.44). "The travel narrative in Luke is not a straight-line journey to Jerusalem but an expression of Jesus' heightened resolve to reach his Jerusalem goal."[179]

On the way to Jerusalem, Jesus *teaches his disciples* the *meaning of his way* (cf. Acts 9,2; 18,16; 24,22, where the community of his disciples is called "*the Way*") by instructing them on the *requirements* of following his way (*Christ's Way).*[180] "Luke's 'journey narrative' paints a captivating portrait of Jesus, the faithful and resolute Son (9,35), who in word and deed *teaches the way* that leads to life with God."[181] An *important theme* of his teaching in this section is *discipleship.* In the presence of his disciples, he proclaims the *kingdom of God* to the people through *parables* and *miracles* and he confronts the hypocritical Pharisees and scribes and challenges them to change their life of duplicity.

Lk 9,51-19,46 may be divided into the following ***eight subsections*** according to their *themes*, as shown below:[182]

1. ***Nature and Demands of Discipleship (9,51-11,13)***

2. ***Growing Opposition to Jesus by the Pharisees and Scribes (11,14-54)***
3. ***Disciples' Readiness for the Coming Crisis (12,1-13,21)***
4. ***Demands of the Kingdom and Cost of Discipleship (13,22-14,35)***
5. ***The Parables of the Lost Sheep, Lost Coin and Lost Son (15,1-32)***
6. ***Teaching on Discipleship through Parables and Warnings (16,1-17,10)***
7. ***The Coming of the Kingdom of God and the Son of Man and the Responses of the Disciples (17,11-18,30)***
8. ***Jesus' Final Approach to Jerusalem (18,31-19,46)***

3.3.1. Nature and Demands of Discipleship (Lk 9,51-11,13)

a) Samaritans' Rejection of Jesus and His Teaching on Non-Retaliation (Lk 9,51-56)

Even though the Jews would normally avoid passing through the land of the Samaritans (of mixed blood) on the way to Jerusalem, Jesus would like to reach out to them. But the people of a Samaritan village refused to receive him "because his face was set toward Jerusalem" (9,53), the rival city to Mount Gerizim with its temple where the Samaritans worshipped. His overzealous disciples James and John are outraged at the Samaritan refusal of hospitality and their hostility to Jesus and they want to retaliate by calling down "fire from heaven to consume them" (9,54) as Elijah did (cf. 2 Kings 1,10.12). Jesus rebukes them for their intolerance (9,55), and moves on patiently to another Samaritan village (9,56), just as, when he faced rejection by his own people at Nazareth (4,24-29), he quietly went on to other places (4,30-31.42-44). Through his word and example, Jesus *teaches* his disciples *not to retaliate* (cf. 6,27-29.35) but to be *tolerant* like him in the face of opposition and rejection.

b) The Cost of Unconditional Discipleship (Lk 9,57-62)

As Jesus is *on the way (en tê hodô:* 9,57*)* to Jerusalem, fully focussed and determined to realize God's salvific plan to bring about God's reign, a man volunteers to become his disciple ("I will follow you wherever you go": 9,57). Jesus tells him that *following* him is going to be quite *costly*, since, unlike beasts or birds which have holes or nests to rest at night, "the Son of Man has nowhere to lay his head" (9,58). The disciple has to be ready to share the uncomfortable and insecure life of Jesus without a home.

Jesus calls another man to "follow" him but he puts a *condition*: "Lord, let me first go and bury my father" (9,59). Probably his father was very old and he would like to wait till his father's death and burial. He is not willing to follow Jesus *unconditionally*. He does not see the urgency and priority of going to "proclaim the kingdom of God" (9,60).

Like the first would-be disciple, a third man offers himself to follow Jesus but, like the second man, he will do it provided he is allowed to bid farewell to his parents, brothers and sisters: "I will follow you, Lord; but let me first say farewell to those at my home" (9,61). Jesus demands an *unconditional* following and an *uncompromising singleness of purpose* in his service of the reign of God, like a focussed farmer who wants to plough straight furrows in his field for sowing the seeds: "No one who put his hand to the plough and looks back is fit for the kingdom of God" (9,62).

The three would-be disciples of Jesus are challenged to consider the *costly and unconditional character of discipleship* for the sake of the kingdom of God, just as Jesus himself is totally committed to and completely focussed on establishing God's reign on earth without counting the cost. Anyone who is not willing to be like Jesus is not worthy to be his disciple.

c) *The Scope and Success of the Mission of the Seventy(-Two) Disciples (Lk 10,1-24)*

The *purpose* of the mission of the seventy(-two)[183] is to prepare the way for the coming of Jesus to specific towns and villages (10,1). It does not, however, mean that they are sent only to give the message of his imminent coming but they are to "heal the sick" and proclaim that "the kingdom of God has come near to you" (10,9). Their curing the sick in Jesus' name shows that salvation is at hand because the Messiah will be in their midst to establish God's reign among them. In short, their preaching and healing *manifest the reign of God*. Jesus even identifies himself with his missionary disciples: "He who hears you hears me" (9,16).

The mission of the seventy(-two) has been *successful* since they report to Jesus: "even the demons are subject to us in your name" (10,17.20). The seventy(-two) share in the same *authority* of Jesus (10,19) which he has over the demons (8,26-39), which he gave also to the Twelve (9,1-2).[184] The evil forces are overcome not only in the ministry of Jesus and the Twelve but also in that of the seventy(-two) (9,17-19). "The success of the seventy(-two) points to the joyful results ahead of those who join in mission as true disciples. In this respect, the mission of the seventy(-two) prefigures the mission to the Gentiles of the primitive Church."[185]

Those who have participated in the liberative mission of Jesus return with *joy* because of their victory over the demons (10,17). But Jesus tells them that there is a greater reason to rejoice because their "names are written in heaven" (10,20) as citizens of God's kingdom. Jesus too rejoices in the Holy Spirit because God the Father has revealed "these things… to babes" (10,21). "In the Lukan context, the references are to the nature of God's kingdom, the union of Jesus' disciples with him in mission, and Jesus' relationship with God."[186] Their unique relationship is spelt out as that of "the Son" and "the Father", who have a deep, loving, mutual knowledge, which is revealed by Jesus, the Son, to the disciples ("babes," the little ones who approach him with open minds and hearts) (10,22). Jesus declares his chosen disciples *blessed* because of the special grace of experiencing ("seeing" and "hearing") the *divine mystery of the Father-Son relationship*: "Blessed are the eyes which see what you see! For I tell you many prophets and kings desired to see what you see, and did not see it, and to hear what you hear, and did not hear it" (9,23-24). This revealed relationship between Jesus (the Son) and God (the Father) (cf. 3,22; 9,35) is the *foundation of Christology and Christian mission.*

d) Parable of the Good Samaritan (Lk 10,25-37)

A lawyer (a teacher of religious law) asks Jesus a question to put him to the test: "Teacher, *what shall I do to inherit eternal life?*" (10,25). Jesus asks him a counter-question: "What is written in the law [of Moses]?" (10,26). The lawyer answers by citing Deut 6,5 and Lev 19,18, which command people to *love God wholeheartedly* and to *love one's neighbour as oneself* (10,27). And Jesus tells him: "You have answered right; do this, and you will live" (10,28). In short, if you do *love God and neighbour*, you will share in God's eternal life.

Now the lawyer asks Jesus a second question: "And *who is my neighbour?*" (10,29). In reply, Jesus elaborates his particular view of *"neighbour"* through the *Parable of the Good Samaritan.* (10,30-37). A man on the way from Jerusalem to Jericho is beaten, stripped and robbed by bandits and is left half-dead on the road (10,30). A priest and a Levite (two Temple functionaries), on seeing him lying mortally wounded on the road, "passed by on the other side" (10,31-32). These law-observant people do not bother to do anything for the dying/dead fellow Jew perhaps because they are afraid of becoming ritually polluted by touching a dead man (cf. Num 19,10-13). But when a Samaritan (a pariah, an outcast to the Jews) sees the wounded and dying Jew, "he has compassion" on him. He bandages his wounds, takes him on his beast to an inn, tends to him and pays the innkeeper for looking after him till he is fully well (10,33-35). "Which of these three, do you think," Jesus asks the lawyer, "proved neighbour to the man who fell among bandits?" (10,36). Instead of saying straightaway "the Samaritan," the lawyer grudgingly admits: "The one who showed mercy on him" (10,37). What a *striking contrast* between the *uncaring priestly class* and the *compassionate Samaritan! Only the Good Samaritans* who love in deed those in need will "*inherit eternal life*" (cf. 10,25).

e) Martha and Mary: Jesus' Women Disciples (Lk 10,38-42)

After welcoming Jesus in her house, *Martha* is busy preparing a meal, while her sister *Mary* "*sitting at the Lord's feet, listens to his word*" (*logos*, teaching: 10,38-39), which is typical of *a true disciple* (cf. 8,35). Here both Martha and Mary are presented as *women disciples of Jesus*, because while Martha receives him in her home and gets ready a meal for him, her sister sits at his feet and listens to him. But Martha complains to Jesus about Mary: "Lord, do you not care that my sister has left me to serve alone? Tell her to help me" (10,40). But Jesus tells Martha that she is over-anxious and worried about many things (like getting ready many dishes) (10,41), "but there is need of one thing (*henos de estin cheira*); Mary has chosen the good portion, which shall not be taken away from her" (10,42); that is, the one thing necessary for all disciples is to *listen to his "word"* (*logos* 10,39; cf. 8,4-21). Here Jesus does not deny the role of service in the life of disciples (cf. 22,26-27) but highlights the importance of *listening* to him attentively. *Serving* him should not be a substitute for spending time with the Lord in *listening* to him, without which *discipleship* cannot grow. Here Jesus defends the *rights of a woman disciple* (like that of a male disciple) *to sit at Jesus' feet and learn his teaching.* Jesus regards *all his disciples* as *equal.*

f) Teaching about Prayer (Lk 11,1-13)

Jesus regarded *prayer* as *an integral part of his life and ministry* (3,21; 5,16; 6,12; 9,28-29). One day at the end of his prayer, one of the disciples requests him: "*Lord, teach us to pray...*" (11,1). He instructs them to address God as "*Father*" (*Abba* in Aramaic) whenever they pray (11,2), just as he himself did during his prayers (10,21; cf. Mk 14,36).

> Jesus' constant use of *Abba* to address God in prayer indicates his unique, intimate, divine *filial* relationship with the Father. So by asking his disciples to address God as "Father"..., he is inviting them to enter into the *loving filial relationship with God* whom he endearingly calls *Abba* (which may be translated as "*Papa*" or "*Daddy*" in English).[187]

As God's children, with childlike trust, we pray to the Father so that his "*name*" ("Father") may be "*hallowed*" (sanctified) through us and that His "*kingdom come*" (that the "reign" of God the Father may become a manifest reality in this world) (11,2). We also pray to our Father for "*our daily bread*" (our everyday sustenance) (11,4) and for "*forgiveness of our sins*" (11,5).

> Since God is our loving Father, we can depend upon him for 'our daily bread' (Lk 11,3), for the bread for the morrow, for all our material and spiritual needs and especially for the bread of life of the eschatological banquet. Since he has allowed his only begotten Son to die on the cross for our sins, we can, though we are sinners, throw ourselves into his loving hands, saying, "Abba, forgive us our sins" (Lk 11,4), knowing that he will surely pardon us, for he knows the weakness and helplessness of his little ones. And when we are about to stumble in temptation, he will lift us up like an affectionate mother watching the unsteady steps of her little child learning to walk. We can be sure that our loving Father will not let us "succumb to temptation" (Lk 11,4), especially the great temptation of apostasy, of falling away from him. Thus we see that '*Abba*' as an address to God *lights up*, like the current that passes through the filament of an electric bulb, *all the petitions of the Lord's Prayer.*[188]

The *parable* of the *Friend at Midnight* (11,5-8) insists on the necessity of *perseverance in prayer* and it implies that the man has *full trust* in his friend to respond positively to his request for help. "Go on asking, and it will be given to you; go on seeking, and you will find; go on knocking, and it will be opened to you" (11,9). If human parents know how to give good gifts to their children (11,11-12), will not the heavenly Father shower on his children the gift of the Holy Spirit if they ask for it (11,13) in prayer?

3.3.2. Growing Opposition to Jesus by the Pharisees and Scribes (Lk 11,14-54)

a) Jesus and Beelzebul (Lk 11,14-23)

When Jesus casts out a demon from a dumb man, some marvel at the miracle but others accuse him of doing it through the power of Satan, "Beelzebul, the prince of demons" (11,14-15), that is, they try to demonize Jesus' work of liberation. Jesus tells them that it is by the power ("finger") of God that he expels demons (the evil forces), which is a sign of the powerful presence of the reign of God (11,20) who rescues enslaved people (cf. Ex 8,15). In short, *Jesus' exorcism manifests his divine liberative power and godly victory over the evil one* (11,21-22).

b) Demand for a Sign and Jesus' Response (Lk 11,29-36)

Jesus' miracles like exorcism manifest his divine power to those who are open-hearted (cf. 11,14). So the demand for "a sign from heaven" (an extraordinary miracle, 11,16) by "an evil generation" points to their hardness of heart, and therefore "no sign shall be given except the sign of Jonah" (11,29). "For as Jonah became a sign to the men of Nineveh, so will the Son of Man be to this generation" (11,30). *Jonah's sign* is his *preaching the word of God*, as a result of which the people of Nineveh (a Gentile city) repented of their sins, turned from their evil ways and so received divine forgiveness (cf. Jon 3,1-10). The proclamation of the reign of God through the words (preaching) and the deeds (miracles) by Jesus, the Son of Man, is the sign to "this generation" of the people of God but it refuses to listen to the one who is "greater than Jonah" and so it (the unrepentant sinful group) will be condemned by the Ninevites on the day of judgement (11,32). Likewise, the queen of Sheba, a Gentile who came from a distant land to listen to King Solomon's wisdom (cf. 1 Kg 10,1-11), will convict the present unbelieving generation on the last day for their refusal to listen to God's word of wisdom spoken by Jesus, who is much "greater than Solomon" (11,31).

Jesus does not have to give another "sign" because he is like a burning "*lamp*" put on a stand so that all can "see the light" (11,33). But to be able to see the light and one's body in that light, one's eye must be healthy; if not, one's entire body will be shrouded in darkness despite the light of the lamp (11,34-36). In other words, *one's heart must be pure* to be able *to see the light of Jesus* and *to live in his light*. Those who demand "*signs*" from Jesus or *misinterpret* his miracles like the exorcisms (attributing them to Satan) have *unhealthy eyes* (*impure hearts*).

In 11,29-36 Jesus reveals himself as *the Son of Man, a prophet greater than Jonah* and *a man wiser than Solomon* and a *burning lamp* giving light to all.

c) Prophetic Denunciation of the Pharisees and Scribes (Lk 11,37-54)

A Pharisee who invited Jesus to dine with him was amazed at his failure to wash before the meal (11,37-38). Jesus said to him: "Now you Pharisees cleanse the *outside* of the cup and of the dish, but *the inside of you* (*to esôthen hymôn*) is full of *greed/extortion and wickedness.* You fools! Did not he who made the outside make the inside also?" (11,39-40). Nobody will eat or drink from a plate or cup that is clean outside but is dirty inside! *Interior purification* of the heart is more important than exterior washing of the hands because God who created both (the exterior body and the interior heart) looks especially into the heart. "Give as alms *the things inside* (*ta enonta*)" (11,41): *food* (inside the plate) and *love* (inside the heart), that is, give food to the hungry with love in the heart. Then "all things (*panta*) are clean/pure (*kathara*) for you" (11,41). Love in the heart makes everything pure.

In the *three "woes"* against the *Pharisees* ("Woe to you Pharisees!": 11,42-44) Jesus the prophet *rebukes* them for 1) *neglecting "justice and the love for God"* while meticulously observing minor prescriptions of the law (like "ritual washing of hands"), 2) being *vain-glorious* ("loving the best seat in the synagogues and salutations in the market place"), and 3) being *hypocrites* (like unseen covered graves).

In the next *three "woes"* against the *scribes* ("Woe to you lawyers also!": 11,46-52) Jesus the prophet *reprimands* them for 1) "loading men with burdens hard to bear" (11,46) by imposing the heavy laws on the people but without practicing them, 2) "building the tombs of the prophets whom your fathers killed" (11,47), since the scribes too commit the same crimes of persecuting and killing the "prophets and apostles" who speak to them in God's name (11,47-49), and 3) "taking away the key of knowledge" (11,52) by claiming to be the sole interpreters of the Scriptures (without, however, living according to the divine revelation in them) and by preventing others from appropriating it.[189]

"As he went away from there, the scribes and the Pharisees began to try hard to provoke him to speak on many things, lying in wait for him, to *trap* him in something that he might say" (11,53-54). This shows the *growing opposition and mounting hostility to Jesus* by *the scribes and the Pharisees.*

3.3.3. Disciples' Readiness for the Coming Crisis (Lk 12,1-13,21)

Some of the *teachings of Jesus* in Lk 12 apply to the *time of Jesus* (12,1-3.13-14.49-59) but others to the *time of the Church* (12,4-12.15-24.35-48). By combining the two times Luke sees a *continuity of the crisis* in the *two periods.*

a) Prophetical Boldness against Pharisaic Hypocrisy and Courageous Confession of Christ during Persecution (Lk 12,1-12)

Jesus warns his disciples: "Beware of the *leaven of the Pharisees*, which is *hypocrisy*" (12,1). The hypocritical Pharisees try to cover up their corruption like a *grave* that covers a rotting body (cf. 11,44). The disciples must be careful not to be affected by the *yeast* of hypocrisy (the hidden corruption of religious leaders), lest they too are exposed: "Nothing is covered up that will not be revealed, or hidden that will not be known" (12,2). Here Jesus insists that his disciples must be courageously *honest* and *transparent* in their life and ministry.

Now Jesus addresses his disciples lovingly as "*my friends*" (12,4) and, looking to the future time of persecution, he asks them *not to be afraid* of those who threaten them with death: "do not fear those who kill the body" (13,4) but *trust in God* who does not forget but takes care of even the small sparrows (12,6): "Fear not; you are of more value than many sparrows" (12,7).

During the time of *persecution*, the disciples will have to *confess Christ courageously* by *bearing witness* to Jesus, the Son of Man (12,8). They are asked not to be anxious about how they are to defend themselves or what they are to say during the judicial process when they are brought before Jewish synagogues or Gentile courts ("rulers and authorities") (12,11), "for the Holy Spirit will teach you in that very hour what you ought to say" (12,12). They will be guided by the Holy Spirit especially in the context of trial and persecution (cf. 21,12-15).

b) Parable of the Rich Fool (Lk 12,13-21)

In the context of someone in the crowd asking Jesus to settle the dispute on inheritance between him and his brother (12,13), he warns the people to be wary of *greed*: "Take care, and beware of all covetousness; for a man's life does not consist in the abundance of his possessions" (12,15). Often greed is the cause of the corruption of one's priorities, for it makes one believe that the worth of one's life depends on the amount of wealth one accumulates. The *parable of the rich fool* (12,16-21) illustrates the *futility and folly* of amassing wealth for the selfish purposes of eating, drinking and making merry for many years (12,18-19), without giving a thought to the transitory nature of life: "God said to him, 'Fool! This night your soul is required of you; and those things you have prepared, whose will they be?" (12,20). The lesson from the parable is: "So is he who lays up treasure for himself, and is not rich toward God" (12,21). *Selfish hoarding of riches* for one's security and enjoyment ("treasure for himself") is of no avail when confronted with sudden death. Everyone must answer the basic question: "What is life all about?" Each one must find the real meaning of life by being "rich toward God" (by *acknowledging God* as the Creator of all and *sharing one's wealth with the needy* children of God (cf. 12,33).

The number of billionaires in India is on the increase, while those who live below the poverty line are increasing year by year. This is illustrated by the following episodes and reports:

> On August 8, 2020, Mukesh Ambani became the fourth richest man in the world. The same day, a laborer in Madhya Pradesh who had lost his job after the coronavirus-induced lockdown killed himself and his three daughters by tying the girls to his waist and jumping into a well.
>
> This is a tale of two Indias and the broadening economic inequality between them.
>
> In the last five months during the coronavirus pandemic, Mukesh Ambani, Asia's richest man and the chairman of the Reliance group, amassed over $48 billion in net worth, according to the Bloomberg Billionaires Index. His net worth has doubled to over $80 billion in just the past year.
>
> At the same time, the International Labour Organization (ILO) estimated that nearly 400 million workers in India's informal economy are at risk of falling deeper into poverty. According to the Centre for Monitoring Indian Economy, over 18.9 million salaried people lost their jobs since April 2020 - 5 million in July alone.[190]

c) Disciples' Trust in God's Providential Care (Lk 12,22-34)

Jesus tells his disciples *not* to be *anxious* about *food* or *clothing* (12,22-23) but to *trust in* the *God* who *feeds* the *birds* of the air and *clothes* the *lilies* of the field (12,24-29), for "your Father knows that you need them" (12,30). Since the disciples are the children of God the Father, he cares for them and provides for their necessities of life. They are advised to "*seek his kingdom*" (12,31), to focus their attention on the reign of God, and they are assured that all the rest will be taken care of by the loving Father. Since "it has pleased the Father to give you the kingdom" (12,32), the disciples ("the little flock") are advised not to worry. This should not be interpreted as "*opium of religion*" or "*pie in the sky after you die*"! The Christian community has the responsibility to take care of the needs of the poor members.

Instead of spending crores of rupees on building big cathedrals, Christian parishes and dioceses must be concerned about and care for the malnourished children and the unemployed youth, the sick and the abandoned. The rich disciples must sell their earthly possessions (often amassed through the sweat of the poorly paid workers!) and help the needy brothers and sisters, without which the wealthy cannot have the incorruptible heavenly "treasure" (12,33). "For where your treasure is, there will your heart be also" (12,34). While on earth, they are to direct constantly their heart's attention heavenward for the spiritual blessings of God's reign.

d) Parable of the Vigilant Servants (Lk 12,35-48)

Like the *watchful servants* "waiting for their master to return from the wedding celebrations" (12,36), the *disciples* must *be ready* ("let your loins be girded and your lamps burning" (12,35) *to receive the Son of Man* at his second coming ("You also must be ready; for the Son of Man is coming at an *unexpected hour*") (12,40). But the *roles* of the servants and the master in the parable are surprisingly *reversed*, for he makes the *vigilant servants sit at the table* and *he serves them* instead of their serving him (12,37-38; cf. 22,27: "I am among you as one who serves")!

Any servant whom the master appoints as *a wise steward* over his household is expected to be *faithful* in fulfilling his responsibility of *serving others* according to the *master's will* (12,42-44). If he does not, and rather he ill-treats those under his care, he will be punished severely when the master returns (12,45-48). "The story concludes that the higher the status, the higher the responsibility that goes with it (v.48)."[191] This must be remembered by those Church leaders (e.g., Bishops and parish priests) who are expected to know the will of the Lord but are negligent or unfaithful in their duty of serving the community today.

e) *Jesus and the Fire of the Holy Spirit (Lk 12,49-50)*

Jesus makes two parallel statements about his mission:

> "I came *to cast fire* upon the earth; how I wish it were already kindled!" (12,49).
>
> "I have a *baptism to be baptized with*; and how I am constrained until it is accomplished!" (12,50).

The *purpose of Jesus' mission* is "*to cast fire* upon the earth" (12,49a) but it is *not yet* "kindled" (12,49b). Jesus has "*a baptism to be baptized with*" (12,50a); for its "accomplishment" he is "*constrained*" (12,50b) so that his mission of "casting fire on earth will be completed". What do "*baptism*" and "*fire*" stand for or what do they symbolize? Here "baptism" does *not* refer to Jesus' *baptism in water* by John the Baptist (cf. 2,21) but to *another baptism (in suffering)* (cf. Mk 10,38-39). John the Baptist associates "*fire*" with *the Holy Spirit* ("he [Jesus] will *baptize* you in *Holy Spirit and fire*": Lk 3,16)[192] and *judgement* ("but the chaff he will *burn* with unquenchable *fire*": 3,17), but in Acts Luke uses "*fire*" ("tongues as of *fire*") as a symbol of the *Holy Spirit* given to the disciples at Pentecost (Acts 2,3-4). In short, Lk 12,49-50 may be *paraphrased* as follows: Jesus will be able *to kindle the fire of the Holy Spirit* in the human hearts *only after his baptism in suffering* through his passion and death on the cross.

f) *Jesus and Division in the Family (Lk 12,51-53)*

Jesus makes a paradoxical statement to the disciples about *peace* and *division*: "Do you think that I have come to give peace on earth? No, I tell you, but rather division" (12,51). This seems to contradict the angels' song after the birth of Jesus: "Glory to God in the highest, and on earth *peace* among humans of goodwill" (2,14).[193]

There may be *divisions* among the members of the family (between father and son, mother and daughter, mother-in-law and daughter-in-law, and *vice versa*) (12,52-53). Jesus' message may cause tension and division among family members, depending on whether they are "humans of goodwill" (pleasing to God) or not. Some family members who welcome Jesus and his message and become his disciples may be opposed by others in the family, which may result in division, as it sometimes happens in India today. Hence *Jesus* is *not the cause of the division* in the family; it is the result of the *positive or negative* responses of the different family members to him and his message. "Peace will not be obtained at any cost, esp. at the cost of compromising God's word. Yet even in non-peaceful situations, the Lucan Jesus calls for forgiveness and reconciliation (e.g., 9,51-56) and love of enemies (6,27-36)."[194]

g) Reading the Weather and Interpreting the Signs of the Present Time (Lk 12,54-56)

Jesus admits the crowd's capacity to *discern* (to observe and interpret correctly) *the signs of changing weather* (e.g., "a cloud rising in the west" [the Mediterranean Sea] resulting in rain or "the south wind blowing" [from the desert] leading to scorching heat) (12,54-55). But Jesus criticizes the hypocritical crowd's unwillingness to *discern* the salvific significance of "the present time": "You hypocrites! You know how to interpret the appearance of earth and sky; but how is it that you do not know how to *interpret the present time?*" (*ton kairon toutôn:* 12,56).

Correct *discernment* of this *kairos* (the opportune time) by reading the signs of salvation present in the person and ministry of Jesus is necessary for their redemption.

h) Exhortations to Repentance (Lk 13,1-9)

(i) *Need of repentance for all (Lk 13,1-5)*

Jesus exhorts the people on the urgent *need of repentance* by citing two recent occurrences: 1) the Galileans (zealot protestors?) whose blood Pilate shed, and 2) the Jerusalemites who died accidentally in the collapse of a tower in Siloam. Jesus tells the audience that those persons (murdered by Pilate or killed in an accident) were not worse sinners than others in Galilee or Jerusalem; however, he insists: "but unless you *repent* you will all likewise *perish*" (13,3.5). *Repentance* is the *necessary condition for salvation.*

(ii) *Parable of the barren fig tree (Lk 13,6-9)*

The owner of a vineyard planted a *fig tree* but, after it grew up, it produced *no fruit* at all for three years.[195] So he orders the vinedresser to *cut the barren tree* down (13,6-7). But the vinedresser suggests waiting for another year so that he could dig and put manure around it to see if it would yield fruit or not (13,8-9). The barren tree is given *another chance to bear fruits.* This shows the divine patience and compassion towards sinners but also the need for their repentance and "bearing fruits" of genuine repentance in their life (cf. 3,8-14).

i) *Healing of a Bent Woman on a Sabbath (Lk 13,10-17)*

As Jesus teaches in a synagogue on a Sabbath, he notices a *bent woman* unable to straighten herself (because of a disability for eighteen years) and he lays his hands on her and frees her of her long infirmity (13,10-13). But the *ruler of the synagogue* is *angry* with him for *healing her on the Sabbath* (13,14). Jesus exposes the hypocrisy of his adversaries by questioning them: "Hypocrites! Does not each of you on the Sabbath untie his ox or his ass from the manger, and lead it away to water it? And ought not this woman, a daughter of Abraham whom Satan bound for eighteen years, be loosed from this bond on the Sabbath day?" (13,15-16). Doing deeds of compassion is not only compatible with Sabbath law but also a moral obligation. Jesus has freed a "woman, a daughter of Abraham" from the crippling power of Satan on a Sabbath, for which the cured woman praises God (13,13) and the people rejoice (13,17). This healing points to the *liberative nature of the kingdom of God.*

j) *Parables of the Mustard Seed and the Leaven (Lk 13,18-21)*

Jesus asks the people: "What is the *kingdom of God* like? And to what shall I compare it?" (13,18). "It is like a *grain of mustard seed...*" (13,19). "It is like *leaven...*" (13,21). Both these parables highlight the *growth* and *spreading* of *God's kingdom* because of its *inherent power.* Because of the *inner vital energy* of the *mustard seed* it gradually *grows* into *a tree* and because of the *transforming power* of the *yeast* the *whole flour* is *leavened* (13,19.21). The *kingdom of God* will *slowly but steadily grow great* so that diverse human beings ("like the birds of the air") will find refuge in it ("make nests in its branches"). This hints at the *universality* of God's kingdom. Likewise, just as the *yeast hidden* in the flour will *leaven* the "*whole*" (*holon*) of it, the *reign of God* will slowly but surely *transform* the *whole of society* according to the kingdom values.

3.3.4. *Demands of the Kingdom and Cost of Discipleship (Lk 13,22-14,35)*

a) Entering the Kingdom of God through the Narrow Door (Lk 13,22-30)

Someone asks Jesus, "Lord, will those who are saved be few?" (13,23). The emphasis in Jesus' answer to the question is not on "how many?" but on "who?" and "how?": "*Strive to enter* through the *narrow door*" (13,24a). They must "*continue to struggle*" (*agônizesthe*) through constant self-denial to enter through the narrow passage to salvation, just as those who are obese must reduce their fat through strenuous exercise to be able to pass through a narrow door. Without constant struggle (denial of self), "they will not be able" (13,24b) to enter God's kingdom.

Now using the *allegory* of the *master of the house locking the door* from inside, Jesus stresses the necessity and urgency of responding to his message of salvation here and now, for once the door is closed, it will not be opened again, even if they keep on knocking at the door and saying, "Lord/master, open to us" (13,25-26; cf. Mt 25,11). Even if Jesus the master's contemporaries claim to have eaten and drunk in his presence and to have heard him teach, his answer to them will be: "I do not know where you come from" (13,26-27; cf. Mt 25,12). Those who listen to the message of salvation must *respond* to it *positively and promptly* through their faith-commitment in order to be saved.

Jesus' concluding statement is a *proverbial saying of reversal* of places in the age to come: "And behold, some are *last* who *will be first*, and some are *first* who *will be last*" (13,30).

> The saying is an isolated logion of general application. It may mean here that those who regard themselves as oppressed and hopeless will gain entry to the kingdom, while those who think that they alone are worthy will be excluded (cf. 1,51-53). It is possible that the saying contrasts the Jews, who were first to hear the gospel, with the Gentiles.[196]

b) Jesus' Journey towards and Lament over Jerusalem (Lk 13,31-35)

Warned by some Pharisees of Herod's plan to kill him (13,31), Jesus tells them that he is not scared of that "fox" and he is determined to continue his ministry of casting out demons and of performing cures for a short time (13,32) and then in Jerusalem, he will meet his *prophetic destiny of death* (13,33). Here Jesus understands himself as a *courageous prophet* ready to lay down his life for the fulfilment of his mission.

Jesus' *lament over Jerusalem* reveals his *heart's compassion, loving care and protection*, for his people: "O Jerusalem, Jerusalem, killing the prophets and stoning those who are sent to you! How often would I have gathered your children together *as a hen* gathers her brood under her wings, and you would not! Behold, your house is forsaken" (13,34-35). Even though the Temple and the city will be abandoned by God and destroyed by the Romans (cf. 21,20.24), Jesus hopes to hear their words of welcome: "Blessed is he who comes in the name of the Lord" (13,35; cf. 19,38), pointing to his people's final conversion of heart in the future.

c) Healing of a Man with Dropsy on a Sabbath (Lk 14,1-6)

One Sabbath, as Jesus was going to the house of the ruler of the Pharisees (probably a member of the Sanhedrin), he meets a sick man suffering from dropsy (14,1-2). Jesus asks the critical ("watching") scribes and Pharisees: "Is it lawful to heal on the Sabbath or not?" (14,3). While they are silent, he cures the sick man (14,4). Then he asks the hypocritical Pharisees if on a Sabbath day they would not pull out of the well their own son or ox that has fallen into it (14,5). But they could not answer him (14,6). By healing the sick man, Jesus manifests himself as the "Lord of the Sabbath" (cf. 6,5) and advocates works of compassion even on the Sabbath.

d) Not to Seek Places of Honour and to Invite the Poor and the Handicapped (Lk 14,7-14)

Noticing how the guests rush to choose the first couches to recline for dinner, Jesus tells them, when they are invited for a wedding feast, not to seek the places of honour but to recline at the last place, and the host may honour them by asking them to go up higher (14,7-8.10). "For everyone who exalts himself will be humbled, and he who humbles himself will be exalted" (14,11). God always exalts the humble (cf. 1,52).

Now turning to the host who invited Jesus to the dinner, he advises him not to invite the rich (e.g., wealthy relatives and friends, rich neighbours) for his banquet, lest they repay him by inviting him in turn, but to *invite the poor and the handicapped* (e.g., the maimed, the lame, the blind), who cannot return the favour. "And you will be *blessed* because they cannot repay you. You will be repaid at the *resurrection of the righteous*" (14,14). God will bless the generous persons and reward them abundantly on the day of the resurrection of the righteous (where the "righteous" are those who have shared food with the hungry, the poor and the disadvantaged) (14,13; cf. Mt 25,34-35).

e) *Parable of the Great Banquet (Lk 14,15-24)*

When one of the fellow-guests, reclining with him for dinner, says: "Blessed is he who shall eat bread in the kingdom of God" (14,15), Jesus narrates the parable of the "*Great Banquet*" to which many are invited (14,16). When the householder sends his servant to remind the guests to come for the banquet that is already ready, all of them give some *excuse* or other for not coming (new "field" or "five yoke of oxen" or new "wife") (14,17-20). *Attachment to possessions or pleasure* prevents them from participating in the "great banquet".

Insulted by the invitees, the angry householder sends his servant to "the streets and lanes of the city" (14,21) and to "the highways and hedges" (14,23) to *invite* "the poor and maimed and blind and lame" (14,21), that is, *the poor and the disadvantaged, the last and the least in society*, to the banquet hall until it is full (14,21-23). Finally, Jesus tells the *audience*: "For I tell *you* (*hymin*) none of those men who were invited shall taste my banquet" (14,24).[197] All are invited to the (eschatological) *banquet in the kingdom of God* but *the poor and the marginalized* respond to the invitation positively and hence are "*blessed*" (cf. 14,15).

f) *Cost of Discipleship (Lk 14,25-35)*

Jesus tells the accompanying crowds that they can be his disciples only if they are willing to renounce their attachments to their family members (father and mother, wife and children, brothers and sisters) and their own life, and be willing to carry their cross and follow him (14,25-27).[198] Christian *discipleship* is very *costly* since it demands *renunciation*, *self-denial* and *readiness to suffer* for the sake of Christ and his mission. "So, therefore, whoever of you does not *renounce all that he has* cannot be my disciple" (14,33).[199] The high cost of discipleship is compared to that of building a tower or of waging a war, and hence proper *discernment* is necessary for its success or victory (14,28-32).

Just as *tasteless salt* is useless and is thrown out, so *Christ-less disciple* is worthless and is cast out (14,34-35). What makes *Christian discipleship* meaningful for humanity is *its Christlike seasoning quality* in society. Jesus invites us to reflect on it: "Those who have ears to hear, let them hear" (14,35). Does my daily Christian life make any difference to others?

Christian discipleship is indeed very *demanding* since it necessarily involves radical *renunciation* and relentless *readiness to follow Christ* without counting the cost. Jesus asks his disciples to *be like him* who is ready to sacrifice everything and even his own life to accomplish his mission.

3.3.5. The Parables of the Lost Sheep, Lost Coin and Lost Son (Lk 15,1-32)

The *three parables in Lk 15* have *three common refrains*: *losing* (vv. 4.4.6: sheep, vv. 8.9: coin, vv. 24.32: son), *finding* (vv. 4.5.6: sheep; vv. 8.9.9: coin; vv. 24.32: son), and *rejoicing* (vv. 5.6.7; vv. 9.10; vv. 23.24.32). They highlight the theme of *God's unconditional love and unlimited compassion for sinners.*

While many "tax collectors and sinners" (the excluded and despised ones in Jewish society) "draw near to hear" Jesus (to listen to him), the Pharisees and the scribes (religious leaders and teachers) "grumble" against him for "receiving [welcoming] sinners and eating with them" (sharing fellowship meal with them) (15,1-2). This is the immediate *context* of Jesus telling these three parables.[200]

The first two parables (*lost sheep* and *lost coin*) are short and parallel to each other, but the third one is longer, two-pronged (*lost son and lost brother*) and climactic.

a) Parable of the Lost Sheep (Lk 15,3-7)

While grazing a herd of hundred sheep, if one were to stray and be lost, the shepherd (owner) will leave the ninety-nine in the wilderness and will keep on searching until he finds the *lost sheep* and he will *carry it* on his shoulders and, on reaching home, will invite his friends and neighbours to *rejoice* with him (15,4-6). Jesus highlights the point of the parable: "Just so, I tell you, there will be more *joy in heaven* over one sinner who repents than over ninety-nine righteous persons who need no repentance" (15,7). It reveals *God's limitless love and compassion for the sinner* (which is manifested in Jesus' table fellowship with sinners: 15,2). It is the personal experience of Jesus' unconditional compassionate love that leads the sinner to true *repentance and conversion* of heart.

b) Parable of the Lost Coin (Lk 15,8-10)

The parallel *female parable* too stresses the woman's diligent search for the *lost coin* (*drachma*, a day's wage for a labourer) by lighting a lamp and sweeping the whole house until she finds it, and she too *rejoices* with her friends and neighbours over the *lost* and *found* coin (15,8-9). The meaning of the parable is: "Just so, I tell you, there is *joy* before the angels of God over one sinner who repents" (15,10). God and the angels *rejoice* over the *repentance and conversion* of every sinner.

c) Parable of the Lost Son and Lost Brother (Lk 15,11-32)

The first part of the parable describes the younger son getting his share of inheritance from the father, the son's loose living far away from home, his pitiable condition during the famine and his repentance and return to his father (15,11-24) and the second part deals with the elder son's angry and resentful reaction to the father's generous and joyful welcome given to the prodigal son (15,25-32).

At the request of his younger son, the father divides his property and gives the youngster his share, and he goes abroad and squanders all his property in loose living (15,11-13). Faced with a severe famine in that country, he is employed to feed a herd of swine but without even enough food for him to eat (15,14-16). Having experienced this misery for many days, he comes to his senses (becomes aware of his inhuman condition),[201] and decides to return to his father and plead for his forgiveness: "I will arise and go to my father, and I will say to him, 'Father, I have sinned against heaven and before you; I am no longer worthy to be called your son; treat me as one of your hired servants'" (15,18-19). The father, seeing his son from a distance, is moved with *compassion* and *runs* to meet him, *embraces* him and *kisses* him (15,20). Before his son could complete his confession (15,21), the father tells his servants: "Bring quickly the best robe and put it on him, and put a ring on his hand and shoes on his feet; and bring the fatted calf and kill it, and let us eat and make merry; for this my son was dead and he is alive again; he was *lost* and is *found*" (15,22-24). The *loving and compassionate father* throws a grand party to welcome back his *lost and found son.*

As all are *making merry* with music and dance, the *elder son* returns from the field and, on finding out the reason for the feasting, refuses to go in, but his father comes out and pleads with him to join the celebration (15,25-28). However, the *angry, self-righteous* son accuses his father of not rewarding him for his loyal service and filial obedience for long but of being partial to his dissolute younger son ("when this son of yours came, who has devoured your living with harlots, you killed for him the fatted calf!") (15,29-30). But the father tries to pacify his agitated son: "Son, you are always with me, and all that is mine is yours. It was fitting to *make merry and be glad*, for *your brother* was dead and is alive; he was *lost* and is *found*" (15,31-32). We are not told whether the elder son relented or not!

This parable portrays the *prodigality of the father's (God's) unlimited love and unconditional compassion for the lost son* (*the sinner*), which is reflected in Jesus' compassionate love and forgiving mercy for sinful men and women. This is contrasted with the self-righteous attitude of the Pharisees and the scribes (represented by the elder son) (cf. 15,1-2.28-30). But it is also inspiring to see the father's patient and persuasive attempt to reconcile the angry elder son with the repentant younger son and to renew their brotherly and loving relationship.

The following are some of the theological, soteriological (concerning salvation) and ecclesial *insights* from the *three Lukan parables*:

> The insights these stories contain and reveal concerning the nature of God and his unconditional love, how he actively searches for the lost children, the acceptance and affirmation of the repentant sinners, the impact of salvation on the relationship of persons (brother/sister to brother/sister), and the wholeness that unconditional love bestows on those who will receive it are nowhere found in as effectively compelling a form as in Luke 15.[202]

3.3.6. *Jesus' Teaching on Discipleship through Parables and Warnings (Lk 16,1-17,10)*

a) Parable of the Shrewd Steward (Lk 16,1-17)[203]

A rich man calls the steward of his estate and questions him about reports of squandering his goods and tells him that his stewardship is going to be taken away from him and hence to submit the final account (16,1-2). He wonders what to do after the loss of stewardship: "I am not strong enough to dig, and I am ashamed to beg" (16,3). Finally, he decides to curry favour with the master's debtors by reducing a hundred measures of oil to fifty and a hundred measures of wheat to eighty (16,4-7). Surprisingly, the master praises the *shrewdness of the steward* (16,8a).[204]

Now Jesus conveys to the disciples the lessons to be learnt from the parable of the shrewd steward: "for the sons of this world are shrewder in dealing with their own generation than the sons of light. And I tell you, make friends for yourselves utilizing the unrighteous mammon, so that when it fails they may receive you into the eternal habitations" (16,8b-9). The disciples, the sons of light, are advised to make responsible and prudent use of mammon (worldly wealth) by giving alms to the poor and the needy (cf. 12,33). Today riches are accumulated by many through unjust and exploitative means! If the well-to-do are selfishly attached to their wealth and refuse to share it with the underprivileged, they will forfeit eternal life (16,9; cf. 16,19-31).

The riches of this earth and the wealth of this world belong to God, the Creator, and all his children have the right to a just share in it. The rich are only the *stewards* of this common inheritance from God. If they are unfaithful custodians and dishonest usurpers of the world's wealth, they deprive the poor and marginalized of their rightful share. If the rich are attached to their money and possessions, they worship the idol of mammon (money/riches) (cf. 16,10-12). "No one can serve two masters… You cannot serve God and mammon" (16,13). Single-minded service of God (without any attachment to riches) is a characteristic of the true disciple. The capitalists of today, like the Pharisees of Jesus' time, who are "lovers of money," may scoff at this radical teaching of Jesus on the right use of riches (16,14). The idol of mammon, the greedy and selfish accumulation of worldly wealth that is exalted among men, is "an abomination [a detestable thing like an idol] in the sight of God" (16,15).[205]

Only those who share their wealth generously with the poor and the needy will be pleasing to God. "The good news" of "the kingdom of God" is preached to all, but only those who are ready to enter it "violently" (by doing self-sacrificing deeds in favour of the poor here on earth) (16,16) will be welcomed "into the eternal habitations" (16,9). Selfless love in action is the only key that can open the door to eternal life.

b) Parable of the Rich Man and Lazarus (Lk 16,19-31)

A very wealthy (nameless) man, clothed in costly purple, feasts daily and sumptuously, whereas a very poor man named Lazarus, a destitute beggar whose body is full of sores, lies hungry at the rich man's gate, craving for the crumbs that may fall from the rich man's table (16,19-21). The poor man dies and is escorted by the angels to Abraham's bosom, and the rich man also dies and is buried (16,22). Now the poor man, reclining at Abraham's bosom, is feasting at the banquet of the kingdom of God (cf. 13,28-29), while the wealthy man, thrown into the flames of Hades, is suffering terrible thirst. Seeing Lazarus in the bosom of Abraham, the thirsty rich man begs Abraham to send Lazarus to Hades to cool his scorched tongue with a drop of water (16,23-24). But Abraham reminds him: "Son, remember that you in your life received good things, and Lazarus in like manner evil things; but now he is comforted here, and you are in anguish" (16,25). Death has caused an irrevocable *reversal* in their conditions. It is impossible to cross from one side of the great chasm to the other (16,26). One's decisions and deeds on earth determine one's destiny forever after death!

The rich man requests Abraham to send Lazarus to the former's family of five brothers to warn them to mend their ways before it is too late but Abraham replies that, if they decline to listen to God's word (spoken through Moses and the prophets) and refuse to respond to the crying needs of their poor neighbours, they would not listen to the warning of even a resuscitated man (16,27-31). Their hard-hearted sins of omission (like the heartless indifference of their brother to the poor Lazarus) will condemn them also to the fire of hell!

c) Warnings and Instructions to the Disciples (Lk 17,1-10)

Jesus *warns* the disciples (especially the Christian *leaders*) sternly against being "stumbling blocks" (*skandala*, stones that cause others to stumble): the tempter should be tied to a millstone and drowned in the sea rather than tempt his brothers and sisters to sin (17,1-2). Woe to the bishops and priests who are scandals in the Church today! Woe to those in responsible positions in religion or society who seduce or abuse women or children!

Jesus also *instructs* his disciples to *rebuke* their brothers and sisters if they *sin* and to *forgive* them *repeatedly* if they *repent*

(17,3-4; cf. 11,4). *The gentle rebuke of sinners* and *generous forgiveness of penitents* are equally important Christian duties. But nobody has the right to rebuke others unless one loves them, and everybody must be ready to forgive others many times.

When the apostles ask the Lord to increase their *faith*, he tells them: "If you had faith as a grain of mustard seed, you could say to this mulberry tree, 'Be uprooted and planted in the sea,' and it would obey you" (17,5-6). Since the mulberry tree is very large with many roots it is quite difficult to uproot it and impossible to plant it in the sea! But Jesus assures his disciples that, if they have *faith as small as a mustard seed*, they would be *able to do* even *impossible things*, or rather, God in whom they trust will do them.

Now Jesus asks his disciples to have the *ideal attitude of a devoted and dutiful servant* who does all that his master asks him to do (e.g., ploughing the field, keeping the sheep, cooking the meal and serving it) (17,7-9). "So you also, when you have done all that is commanded you, say, 'We are unworthy servants; we have only done what was our duty'" (17,10). The *devoted servant finds joy in doing the will of the master.*

3.3.7. The Coming of the Reign/Kingdom of God and the Son of Man and the Responses of the Disciples (Lk 17,11-18,30)

a) Gratitude and Faith of a Healed Samaritan Leper (Lk 17,11-19)

On the way to Jerusalem, Jesus enters a village between Galilee and Samaria (probably on their common border); and ten lepers, who "stand at a distance" (because they are considered as unclean and untouchable), cry out in a loud voice: "Jesus, master, have mercy on us" (17,11-13). Seeing the ten outcast lepers with compassionate eyes, he tells them: "Go and show yourselves to the priests" (17,14), so that they could be examined and declared ritually clean by the priests; and on their way, all of them are cleansed. Now, one of them, *a Samaritan*, seeing that he is healed, returns to Jesus, falls at his feet, thanks him and praises God for the miraculous cure (17,15-16). Jesus asks him: "Were not ten cleansed? Where are the [other] nine?" (17,17). Jesus is surprised that only a "*foreigner*" has come back to give glory to God (17,18).[206] Jesus tells him: "Rise and go your way; *your faith* has *saved you* (*sesôken se*)" (17,19). The ten lepers' prayer for a cure and their obedience to Jesus' command to show themselves to the priests indicate that they have faith in his healing ability, and so they are cured of their leprosy miraculously. But Jesus' words to the healed Samaritan ("*your faith* has *saved you*") reveal that something more than physical healing is implied. The believing and grateful Samaritan has experienced God's "*salvation*" more fully than the others. *Physical healing* is a *symbol* of *integral salvation* of body, mind and spirit. The *message of salvation* is: "Jesus is the one who *saves* from disease and restores to the human concourse. In him, disciples find the *fullness of human wholeness*."[207] It means that Jesus is a *holistic Saviour*.

b) The Inner Reality of the Reign/Kingdom of God and the Sudden Second Coming of the Son of Man (Lk 17,20-37)

Being asked by the Pharisees about the *time* ("when") of the coming of God's kingdom, Jesus tells them, "the reign of God does not come with signs to be observed [from outside] (*meta paratêseôs*)" (17,20) "for behold, the reign of God *is within you*" (*entos hymôn estin:* 20,21). God's kingdom/reign is *not* an *external reality* observable from the outside but it is an *inner reality* (already present) which can be experienced in one's heart.

Now Jesus explains to his disciples the *sudden second coming of the Son of Man:* "For as the lightning flashes and lights up the sky from one side to the other, so will the Son of Man be in his day" (17,24). Like the *unpredictable lightning*, the exact time of the final arrival of the Son of Man is unknowable. However, Jesus tells the disciples that it will happen only after his passion and death (17,25).

"Jesus' references to Noah and Lot serve to illustrate the *suddenness* of the revelation of the Son of Man [17,26-30]."[208] Hence the disciples are advised to *be ever ready*, like Noah or Lot (and not like their contemporaries who were destroyed by flood or fire), to receive the glorified Son of Man (17,26-30) by renouncing their attachments to possessions and persons (17,31-35).

Jesus' reply to the disciples' question about the *place* ("Where, Lord?") of the appearance of the Son of Man is enigmatic: "Where the body is, there the vultures will gather together" (17,37). Just as the gathering of the birds of prey points to the place of the corpse, so wherever the Son of Man appears, there the final judgement will take place. Jesus refuses to give a precise answer about the location of the final judgement.

In short, what is stressed in 17,22-37 is *not* the *time* and *place* but the *certainty* and *suddenness* of the *Son of Man's second coming*, for which *all the disciples* must *always be ready.*

c) *Parable of the Persistent Widow and the Unjust Judge (Lk 18,1-8)*

The *purpose* of this parable is clearly stated: "that they ought always to pray and not lose heart" (18,1). The widow who keeps going again and again to the unrighteous judge saying: "Vindicate me against my adversary" (18,2-3) is an excellent example of *persistent prayer* despite delay in God's response. Jesus assures the disciples who persevere in prayer: "And will not God vindicate his elect, who cry to him day and night? Will he delay long over them? I tell you, he will vindicate them speedily" (18,7-8). But God's "speedy" vindication may seem to be a very long time to those who have been experiencing injustice for long and praying for help day and night! God will certainly grant justice to his chosen ones in distress at the proper time. But they need a lot of faith to persevere in prayer before the final coming of the Son of Man (18,8). Those who face discrimination and suffer persecution must pray repeatedly to the Father not to put them to the test (cf. 11,4) lest they should falter in their faith!

d) *Parable of the Pharisee and the Tax Collector (Lk 18,9-14)*

A Pharisee and a tax collector go to the Temple to pray. Whereas the self-righteous and proud *Pharisee* praises himself, during his prayer, for his virtuous life (e.g., fasting and giving tithes) and despises others as sinners (18,9-12), the *tax collector* (a social outcast) stands at the door of the Temple (acknowledging his unworthiness to enter the presence of the all-holy God), beats his breast (as a sign of sorrow for his sins) and humbly pleads for forgiveness: "God, be merciful to me a sinner" (18,13). Jesus declares that the tax collector won God's approval, but not the Pharisee (18,14). God sees the heart and exalts the one who humbles himself and humbles the one who exalts himself (18,14; cf. 1,52; 14,11).

e) The Little Children and the Kingdom of God (Lk 18,15-17)

When the disciples rebuke those who bring their little children to Jesus to be blessed by him (18,15), he welcomes the children and tells the disciples: "Let the children come to me, and do not hinder them; for to such belongs the kingdom of God" (18,16). *Theirs is the kingdom of God* because they (children) know how to receive it as a *gift from God*. Hence Jesus instructs his disciples to accept the gift (of God's kingdom) *as a child* does: "Truly, I say to you, whoever does not receive the kingdom of God like a child shall not enter it" (18,17). A *childlike* attitude enables the disciple to enter into the kingdom. In the words of Robert J. Karris, "disciples should approach God as a child does: with spontaneity, a spirit of dependence, a sense of wonderment, with no plaques of achievement. The doors of the kingdom do not swing open to those who comport themselves differently."[209]

f) The Rich Ruler's Attachment and the Disciples' Detachment (Lk 18,18-30)

To the rich ruler, who asked Jesus the question: "what shall I do to inherit eternal life" (18,18), Jesus' answer is to keep the commandments (18,20). When Jesus hears that the ruler has observed all the commandments from his youth, he tells him what more he should do: "Sell all that you have and distribute it to the poor, and you will have treasure in heaven; and come, follow me" (18,22). On hearing this, he becomes *sad* because he finds it difficult to renounce his possessions in favour of the poor to follow Jesus (18,23). *Inordinate attachment to riches* is the *greatest obstacle* to enter the kingdom of God (18,24). A wealthy fat man's attempt to enter the narrow gate of God's kingdom is like a camel's futile effort to go through the eye of a needle! (18,25). But Jesus assures Peter and the other disciples who have left their homes, near and dear ones, and followed him that they would receive abundant recompense in this life and eternal life in the next (18,28-30).

Like the first disciples of Jesus, many missionaries over the centuries have left their families and friends, relatives and neighbours, and, while evangelising millions in Asia, Africa and Latin America, found new friends, brothers and sisters in the Lord Jesus. Many of them have also won the crown of martyrdom.

3.3.8. Jesus' Final Approach to Jerusalem (Lk 18,31-19,46)

a) Another Prediction of Jesus' Passion-Resurrection (Lk 18,31-34)

Now Jesus reveals to the Twelve disciples that the *purpose* of "*going up to Jerusalem*" is *to accomplish* "everything that is written about the Son of Man by the prophets" (18,31). Jesus is quite aware and determined to realize the *divine plan of salvation* through his suffering, death and resurrection. "For he will be delivered to the Gentiles and will be mocked and shamefully treated and spit upon, and they will scourge him and kill him, and on the third day he will rise" (18,32-33). Unlike the first passion-prediction, which is rather general (cf. 9,22: "suffer many things," "be rejected" by the Jewish leaders, "be killed"), this one spells out many *details* of the passion (like handing over to the *Gentiles, mocking, insulting, spitting, scourging*). The reference to "the Gentiles" points to Pilate and the Roman soldiers. There is also a difference in the way Jesus' *resurrection* is mentioned in the two passion-predictions: while "*to be raised*" (*egerthênai*) hints at *God's action* (9,22), "*he will rise*" (*anastêsetai*) refers to *Jesus' own action* (18,33).

The Evangelist emphasizes the Twelve's *total failure to grasp* Jesus' detailed prediction of his passion-death-resurrection: "But they *understood none* of these things; this saying *was hid from them*, and they *did not grasp* what was said" (18,34). Luke attributes their complete lack of understanding of the saying to a divine action of "*hiding*" it from them (18,34; cf. also 19,42; 24,16)! The Evangelist seems to excuse the disciples' inability to fathom Jesus' Paschal mystery because they had *no idea* of a *"suffering" Messiah* until after it would be explained to them by the risen Lord (cf. 24,25-27.32.44-46).

Even today many Christians are unable to understand the salvific significance of Jesus' suffering until they experience a lot of suffering in their own lives. Only those who carry the cross can recognize the Crucified; only those who identify the Crucified can embrace the risen Lord. They will also discover the crucified/risen Lord in the crucified/raised people of today.

b) Healing of a Blind Beggar near Jericho (Lk 18,35-43)

As Jesus approaches Jericho with a crowd accompanying him, a blind man is begging by the roadside (18,35-36). Coming to know that Jesus of Nazareth is passing by, the blind beggar keeps on crying out: "Jesus, Son of David, have mercy on me" (18,37-39). His addressing Jesus as "*Son of David*" and his insistent pleading for compassion are clear expressions of his faith in the *royal Messiah*. Jesus asks him: "What do you want me to do for you?" and he replies: "Lord, *that I may see again* (*hina anablepsô*) (18,41). His prayer means that he longs to regain his lost sight. Jesus' word of healing is: "See again (*anablepson*); *your faith has saved you* (*sesôken se*)" (18,42). Jesus restores his sight and attributes it to his faith.

Here the miraculous sudden recovery of the blind man's physical sight is an experience of "salvation." Luke has a *holistic/ integral* understanding of *salvation* (total wellbeing of body, mind and spirit). This is confirmed by the fact that as soon as the man regained his sight, he started "following" and "continued to follow" (êkolouthei) Jesus, "glorifying God" (*doxazôn ton theon*), together with the people giving praise to God (18,43). Following Jesus and glorifying God are the manifestations of the *healed man's deep faith and true discipleship*. Through a personal encounter with Jesus, the Saviour, a blind beggar has not only recovered his *physical sight* but also gained *insight of faith* which has made him *a genuine and witnessing disciple* of Jesus.

c) Jesus and Zacchaeus, the Tax Collector (Lk 19,1-10)

As Jesus passes through Jericho, a short man Zacchaeus, a chief tax collector, runs ahead of the crowd and climbs on a sycamore tree to be able to see Jesus (19,1-4). But Jesus surprises him by looking up, by calling him by name, and by asking him to come down quickly, because he feels the *inner urge to be his guest* for a day ("for I *must [dei]stay* in your house today": 19,5). "So he made haste and came down, and received him joyfully" (19,6). While many murmur against Jesus' staying with "*a sinner*" (a tax collector) and eating with him, Zacchaeus openly confesses his *conversion of heart* by declaring: "Behold, Lord, the half of my goods I give to the poor; and if I have defrauded anyone of anything, I restore it fourfold" (19,8). Jesus' loving gestures, words and actions have touched the sinful man and transformed him into a just and generous person. *His experience of the Saviour* results in *justice to the exploited* and *generosity to the poor*. Because of Jesus' initiative to invite himself to Zacchaeus' house and his joyful acceptance, his whole household experiences salvation. In Jesus' own words, "Today *salvation* has come to this house, since he also is a son of Abraham. For *the Son of Man* came *to seek and to save the lost*" (19,9-10). By offering warm hospitality to Jesus, Zacchaeus has proven himself to be "a (true) son of Abraham" who welcomed the "three men" and served them as his guests (cf. Gen 18,1-8). The mission of Jesus, the Son of Man, the Good Shepherd, consists in tirelessly *seeking the lost* sheep and lovingly *saving* the sinners (19,10).

d) Parable of the Ten Pounds (Lk 19,11-27)

As Jesus approaches Jerusalem, he tells the parable of the Ten Pounds to those (people and disciples) who think or expect "*the kingdom of God*... to *appear immediately*" (19,11). Before setting out for a distant country "to receive for himself *kingship*" (*labein heautô basileian:* 19,12), a nobleman calls ten of his servants and gives them a *pound*[210] each and tells them: "*Trade with these until I come*" (19,13). On his return *as king*, he calls his servants to give him an account of their gains by trading with the money. The first servant says: "Lord, your pound has yielded ten pounds" (19,16). The king congratulates him for the good work and gives him authority over ten cities because of his faithfulness (19,17). Likewise, the second servant who made five pounds by trading is given charge of five cities (19,18). But the third servant, who did nothing with the pound because of his fear of the master, is severely scolded and pitilessly punished by taking away his pound and giving it to the one who has ten pounds (19,20-26).

This part of the parable stresses the responsibility of taking risks in utilizing the endowments entrusted to each, knowing that an exacting account will be demanded by the master when he returns as king (19,15-26). The *kingdom of God* is both a *gift* and a *task*. Humans must welcome it and work for its growth. The faithful servants of the kingdom will be rewarded but the kingdom will be taken away from the faithless ones.

There is another group of citizens who *hate the king* and *revolt* against him saying: "We do not want this man to reign over us" (19,14). They are the *religious leaders* who have a negative and aggressive attitude to Jesus, the king, which will be highlighted in the rest of the Gospel (cf. 19,47; 20,1.19; 22,2.52; 23,10.35). On his return, the king punishes his enemies severely: "But as for these enemies of mine, who did not want me to reign over them, bring them here and slay them before me" (19,27). "The imagery of destruction for those who refused to accept the king shows that accepting God's rule over oneself is a moment of great and grave decision. Unfortunately, some decided against the life that the kingship of Jesus brings."[211]

e) The Messianic King's Entry into Jerusalem (Lk 19,28-40)

On his way up to Jerusalem, as Jesus approaches the Mount of Olives, he sends two of his disciples to a close-by village to untie a tethered colt and bring it to him (19,28-32). When they are questioned by the owner, their answer (as Jesus had instructed them) is: "The Lord has need of it" (19,33-34). They bring it to Jesus, "and throwing their garments on the colt they set Jesus upon it. As he rides along, they spread their garments on the road" (19,35-36). They do these things as a sign of respect to *Jesus the king* (cf. 2 Kings 9,13). Now the whole multitude praises God loudly and joyfully for all the mighty works (miracles) they have seen, and they hail *Jesus as the king of peace*: "Blessed is the *King* who comes in the name of the Lord! *Peace* in heaven and glory in the highest!" (19,38). Jesus, riding on a colt (not a warrior horse) and entering Jerusalem (the city of peace), is publicly proclaimed by his disciples as "the long-expected *prince of peace* or the *messianic ruler*" (cf. Zech 9,9; Ps 118,26).[212]

Whereas at Jesus' birth a multitude of angels proclaimed: "Glory to God in the highest and on earth peace among men" (2,14), now a multitude of disciples declare: "in heaven peace and glory in the highest!" (19,38).[213] "To speak of *peace in heaven* is unusual; *contrast* 2,14 where the effect of the *Messiah's birth* is *peace on earth* among men, i.e. salvation."[214] Whereas "in the highest" and "on earth" in 2,14 are contrasted, in 19,38 the parallel expressions "in heaven" and "in the highest" refer to the same abode of God, and the words "peace" (God's gift of salvation) and "glory" (God's saving presence) are presented as parallel gifts from God, which are brought to us by Jesus, "the King who comes in the name of the Lord" (19,38; cf. 13,35). Jesus, the Messianic king, who comes as God's representative, offers *God's gifts of heavenly peace and glory* to those who welcome him in faith. Thus the disciples' proclamation is *a faith affirmation* of the *salvific mission* of Jesus, the *Messianic king of peace.*

When some of the Pharisees in the crowd protest against the disciples' public proclamation of Jesus' kingship and ask him to rebuke them (19,39), his puzzling reply is: "I tell you, if these were silent, the very stones would cry out" (19,40). It means that everything is right out in the open now. The time for concealment is over.

f) Jesus' Weeping over Jerusalem (Lk 19,41-44)

When Jesus approaches the city of Jerusalem, he weeps over it and its inhabitants (19,41), saying: "Would that even today you knew the things that make for peace!" (19,42). Since they refuse to believe in God's messenger of peace, their city with all its residents will be destroyed "because you did not know the time of your visitation" (19,43-44). "The city, whose name means peace, does not recognize the visitation of Jesus, God's agent for peace (see 13,34-35)."[215] Jesus' lament over Jerusalem manifests his love for God's people and his sorrow for the impending destruction of the city with all its inhabitants (which took place in 70 CE).

g) Jesus' Cleansing of the Temple (Lk 19,45-46)

Jesus enters the Jerusalem Temple and, in a bout of righteous fury, attacks the unabashed commercialism going on in the precincts: "It is written, 'My house shall be a house of prayer'; but you have made it a den of robbers" (19,46; cf. Is 56,7 and Jer 7,11). The traders, with the connivance of the money-loving religious leaders, had defiled the holy place of prayer and communion with God by turning it into a mammon-worshipping robbers' den. By purging the traders from the Temple, Jesus, *the Son of God*, takes possession of *his Father's house* (cf. 2,49: "my Father's house").

3.3.© Christology of *Lk 9,51-19,46:*

The journey section enhances Luke's Christology in several ways. First, it presents *Jesus* as a *prophetic Messiah* who proceeds to Jerusalem with a profound awareness of his messianic destiny

(9,51; 13,31-35; 18,31-34) and unique relationship to God (10,21-22). Second, it portrays Jesus as the *preacher of the kingdom* who understands his unique role in God's plan (10,23-24; 11,29-32) and summons Israel to repentance because the kingdom is at hand (13,1-9). Third, it depicts Jesus as the *compassionate Messiah* who calls sinners to repentance and brings salvation to those in need (13,10-17; 15,1-32; 17,11-19; 18,35-43). Fourth, it represents Jesus as *faithful to Moses and the prophets* (10,25-28; 16,16-17.29; 18,18-23). Finally, it points to the Messiah's destiny as the *Son of Man* who will return suddenly and unexpectedly to gather the elect (17,22-37).[216]

Here it must be added that Jesus' entry into Jerusalem and his cleansing of the Temple manifest Jesus as the *Messianic king* (19,38) and *the Son of God,* his Father (19,46; cf. 2,49).

3.4. Jesus' Teaching in the Temple in Jerusalem (Lk 19,47-21,38)

Now onwards Jesus *teaches daily in the Temple* (19,47; 21,37-38).[217] Even though the religious leaders (priests, scribes and elders) seek to destroy/kill him (19,47), they cannot do it because *the people are with him* and *listen to his teaching eagerly* (19,48: "for all the people hung upon his lips"; cf. also 21,38: "And all the people used to rise early in the morning to come to him in the temple to hear him"). Thus there is a striking contrast between the *negative* response of the *leaders* and the *positive* response of the *people* to Jesus' teaching in the Temple.

Earlier there have been many controversies between Jesus and mainly the Pharisees primarily about his ministry to the sick and needy, but in this Section (19,47-21,38) the *controversies* take place *in the Temple* and with the chief priests, scribes, Sadducees and elders, and they deal mainly with *Jesus' authority* and *identity* (as a *teacher*, *prophet*, the *Son of God*, the *Son of David*, the *Lord*, and the *Son of Man*).

3.4.1. Questions about Jesus' Authority and Identity (Lk 20,1-47)

a) Question about Jesus' Authority to Teach and Preach (Lk 20,1-8)

While "*teaching*" (*didaskontos*) the people in the Temple and "*goodnewsing*" (*euangelizomenou*) the gospel, Jesus is questioned about his *authority as teacher and preacher* by the chief priests, scribes (teachers of the law) and the elders (leaders of the people) (20,1): "Tell us by what authority you do these things, or who gave you this authority?" (20,2). The religious leaders claim the exclusive authority to teach the people in the Temple and they sense Jesus' authority as a threat to their competence and position of authority! Since they refuse to answer Jesus' counter-question to them about the origin of John's baptism: "Did the baptism of John come from heaven, or was it of human origin?" (20,4.5-7), he declines to reply to their query about his authority: "Neither will I tell you by what authority I am doing these things" (20,8). But the Christological significance of this controversy is clear: If the prophetic authority of John the Baptist to preach, teach and baptize comes from God (cf. 3,2-14), *a fortiori* Jesus' authority (as "the Son of God") to teach in the Temple ("the house of God") is derived from God (the Father).[218]

b) Parable of the Vineyard and the Wicked Tenants (Lk 20,9-19)

Using the Biblical imagery of the vineyard (cf. Is 5,1-7), Jesus tells the people the parabolic allegory of the vineyard planted by the owner and let it out to tenants. But the latter repeatedly ill-treat and beat the servants sent by the owner to collect the agreed-upon rent (a portion of the grapes). Finally, his "beloved son," "the heir," is sent to the tenants but they cast him out and kill him. Therefore, the tenants are killed and the vineyard is given to others (21,9-16).

According to the *allegorical interpretation* of the parable, the owner (*God*) of the *vineyard* (the people of Israel), entrusts it to the *tenants* (the religious leaders), to whom are sent the *servants* (the prophets), who are ill-treated and persecuted, and finally the *beloved son* (Jesus), who is killed by the wicked tenants. The *climax* of the story is the *killing of the "beloved son" and "heir"* (Jesus, the Son of God), for which the wicked tenants (those responsible for Jesus' crucifixion) are destroyed and the vineyard given to "*others*".

Christologically, the parable/allegory points to *Jesus* as more than the prophets and as the *beloved Son of God,* who has *a unique loving and filial relationship with God* and hence he has *God's authority*.

Jesus' citation of Ps 118,22 ("The very stone which the builders rejected has become the head of the corner") points to the leaders' rejection of Jesus ending in his crucifixion and indicates God's vindication of Jesus through his resurrection and his salvific role as the *cornerstone* of *God's new edifice* (the new people of God) (20,17).

Realizing that Jesus had told the parable of the tenants against the chief priests and the scribes, they "tried to lay hands on him" but could not because "they feared the people" (20,19). This shows the growing opposition of the religious leaders to Jesus, who is loved by the people.

c) *Question about Paying Taxes to Caesar (Lk 20,20-26)*

Now the Jewish leaders *send spies to trap Jesus* in his words and, pretending to be sincere (20,20-21), they ask him: "Is it lawful for us to give tax to Caesar or not?" (20,22). Their question puts Jesus in a dilemma: a negative reply would land him in trouble with the Roman governor; a positive answer would displease the Jewish people, especially the zealots! Perceiving their craftiness, Jesus tells them to show him a Roman coin (*denarius*) and asks them: "Whose image and inscription has it?" and they answer "Caesar's" (20,23-24). Jesus tells them: "Then give back to Caesar the things that are Caesar's, and to God the things that are God's" (20,25). *Jesus' wisdom outsmarts the spies* and *silences* them (20,26).

d) *Question about the Resurrection and Marriage (Lk 20,27-40)*

The Sadducees, who deny the resurrection of the dead, present Jesus the teacher with a hypothetical case of a woman/widow who was successively married to seven brothers (all of whom died childless) according to the levirate (brother-in-law) marriage law of Moses (Deut 25,5-6), after which the woman also died (20,27-32). Jesus is asked the question: "In the resurrection, therefore, whose wife will the woman be?" (20,33). Jesus contrasts the *present life* in this world ("of this age"), when people "marry and are given in marriage," with the *resurrected life* after death ("that age"), when people "neither marry nor are given in marriage, for they cannot die anymore" because they are the risen sons and daughters of God (20,34-36). Therefore, marriage and remarriage are irrelevant for the risen persons who share in God's fullness of life and plenitude of bliss.

Jesus tells the Sadducees that the Lord God, who revealed himself to Moses as "I am the God of your father, the God of Abraham and the God of Isaac and the God of Jacob" (Ex 3,6.15-16), "is not God of the dead, but of the living; for all live to him" (20,37-38). That is, the Patriarchs (Abraham, Isaac and Jacob) had died long ago but now they live a new life with God. Hearing this, the scribes (the teachers of the law, who believe in the resurrection) appreciate and approve Jesus' wise answer: "Teacher, you have spoken well" (20,39), which has also silenced the Sadducees (20,40). Jesus' resurrection from the dead will substantiate his claim that God is the one who vindicates the just through the resurrection to new life (cf. 24,27.32.45-46).

e) Jesus' Question about the Christ as the Son of David (Lk 20,41-44)

After answering all the questions of his opponents (the chief priests, the scribes and the Sadducees), Jesus poses a question to them: "How can they say that the Christ is David's son?" (20,41), since David himself calls him "Lord" (20,42; cf. Ps 110,1: "The Lord said to *my Lord*, Sit at my right hand…"). If David calls *Christ* his "*Lord*", *how* can he be *his son*? (20,44). But the religious leaders are at a loss to answer Jesus' puzzling question!

The purpose of Jesus' question is not to deny the Messiah's Davidic descent and kingship (cf. 1,32-33; 18,38-39) but to correct the popular notion of a warrior Messiah like David who would be victorious over the enemies and would lead the people of God to political freedom. Jesus, *the Messiah*, is both *David's son* (cf. genealogy in 3,23-31) and *his Lord* because he is the *Son of God* (1,35; 4,3.9.41;8,28;22,70), who is, therefore, *greater than David.*

f) Jesus' Warning to the Disciples to Beware of the Scribes (Lk 20,45-47)

In the presence of the people, Jesus tells the disciples: "*Beware of the scribes*" for their showy dress and life-style, insatiable thirst for public salutations and places of honour, hypocritical long prayers and unscrupulous devouring of widows' possessions (see similar denunciations of the Pharisees and the scribes in 11,37-54). Jesus condemns them for their unbecoming, unjust and hypocritical life and practices (cf. also 12,1: "*Beware* of the *leaven* of the Pharisees, which is *hypocrisy*").

Like the scribes and the Pharisees of Jesus' time (cf. 20,45-47), many of the political and religious leaders in our country and some even in the Church today are guilty of hypocrisy, injustice, corruption, etc. and so they deserve to be denounced! But are there Christlike courageous prophets to do it today and risk their lives like St. Oscar Romero of San Salvador?

g) The Poor Widow's Offering (Lk 21,1-4)

Watching the wealthy putting precious coins into the Temple treasury, Jesus notices a poor widow putting in two copper coins (*lepta*), worth less than a penny (21,1-2), and declares: "Truly I tell you, this destitute widow has put in more than all of them [the wealthy]; for they all contributed out their surplus, but she out of her want put in all that she had" (21,3-4). Jesus praises the *poor widow* for her *self-sacrificing generosity of giving* her "*all*", which is more valuable in the eyes of God than the large sums donated by the well-to-do. As St. Mother Teresa of Calcutta used to say: "We must give until it hurts us". *Self-sacrificing love* does not count the cost, as Jesus himself has taught us by laying down his life for us.

3.4.2. Jesus' Prophetic Discourse (Lk 21,5-38)

Lk 21,5-38 deals with *the destruction of the Temple and Jerusalem, the coming of the Son of Man*, and *the Parable of the Fig Tree and the coming of the Kingdom of God.* [219]

Lukan ("Winding Staircase") Plan of 21,5-38:

a): Jesus' prediction of the destruction of the Temple and warning to the people (21,5-9)

b): Terrible signs and persecutions before the coming of the Son of Man (21,10-19)

a'): Jesus' prediction of the siege and destruction of Jerusalem (21,20-24)

b'): Cosmic signs and the coming of the Son of Man with power and glory (21,25-28)

c): Parable of the Fig Tree and the coming of the Kingdom of God (21,29-33)

b"): Exhortation to watch for the coming of the Son of Man (21,34-36)

a"): Jesus' teaching in the Temple and the people's eagerness to listen (21,37-38).

It must be noted that the text (21,5-38) is developed in such a way that the *predictions* on the *destruction of the Temple & Jerusalem* and the *coming of the Son of Man alternate.*

a): Jesus' prediction of the destruction of the Temple and warning to the people (21,5-9)

When some people comment on the splendour of the Temple "adorned with beautiful stones and votive offerings" (21,5), Jesus *predicts* its *destruction*: "the days will come when there shall not be left here one stone upon another that will not be thrown down" (21,6). The demolition seems to be the punishment for the desecration of the Temple by the traders by turning "the house of prayer" into "a den of robbers" (cf. 19,46) and for the crime of murdering the Messiah by the religious leaders ("the chief priests and the scribes and the leaders of the people sought to destroy him") (19,47; cf. 23,18-25).

When the people request Jesus to reveal to them the time of the Temple's destruction and any sign indicating its imminence (21,7), he tells them about the arrival of false messiahs: "many will come in my name, saying, 'I am he!' and, 'The time is at hand!' (21,8) but he instructs them not to believe or follow them. There will also be "wars and tumults," "but the end will not be at once" (21,9). This may hint at the First Jewish Revolt (66-70 CE against the Romans before the destruction of the Temple in 70 CE).

b): Terrible signs and persecutions before the coming of the Son of Man (Lk 21,10-19)

Some of the *signs* before the coming of the Son of Man will be wars and natural calamities like earthquakes, famines and pestilences (21,10-11). But before all these things will happen, the followers of Christ will be hated, persecuted, imprisoned and even killed by foes, friends and family members, but they are exhorted to persevere as his faithful witnesses under timely divine guidance and protection (21,12-19).

a'): Jesus' prediction of the siege and destruction of Jerusalem (Lk 21,20-24)

Now Jesus predicts the destruction of Jerusalem: "But when you see Jerusalem surrounded by armies, then know that its devastation has come near" (21,20). This refers to the Roman siege of the city of Jerusalem. When the people see this, those in Judea must flee to the mountains, those out in the country must not enter the city and those in the city must try to depart as quickly as possible (20,21-22). It will be a terrible time for pregnant women and mothers of suckling children (21,23). "Jerusalem will be trodden down by the Gentiles" (21,24) and its inhabitants will be killed or taken captives and dispersed among nations.

b'): Cosmic signs and the coming of the Son of Man with power and glory (Lk 21,25-28)

There will be *cosmic "signs"* ("in the sun, moon and stars", "the roar and fury of the sea"), at which people will "faint with fear and with foreboding" of the apocalyptic events about to take place in the world (21,25-26). "And then they will see *the Son of Man coming in a cloud with power and great glory*" (21,27). His victorious and glorious return, however, is not a frightening event but one full of hope for the faithful disciples "because your redemption is near" (21,28). "This verse bursts with a message of confidence and hope for disciples. In contrast to the cowardly action of other men and women (vv. 26-27), faithful disciples stand erect with heads held high to greet their faithful judge, Jesus, Son of Man."[220]

c): Parable of the Fig Tree and the coming of God's Kingdom (Lk 21,29-33)

Jesus asks the people to look at the *fig tree.* As soon as they see the *new shoots* on it, they know that the *summer is near* (21,29-30). "So also, when you see these things taking place, you know that the *kingdom of God is near*" (21,31). Now, what do "these things" refer to? They denote all that Jesus has said so far about the destruction of the Temple and Jerusalem and about the cosmic signs occurring before and at the coming of the Son of Man in 21,5-28. When Jesus' predictions come true (like the new shoots of trees at the start of summer), they announce the *imminence of the kingdom of God* (20,31).

Now Jesus makes a solemn statement: "Truly, I say to you, *this generation* will not pass away until all will have taken place. Heaven and earth will pass away, but my words will not pass away" (21,32-33). He is certain that all his predictions will be fulfilled. He also assures "this generation" (the people of his time) that the devastation of the Temple and Jerusalem (which they will witness) will be the beginning of the fulfilment of his prediction and the foreshadowing of the cosmic signs at the final coming of the Son of Man in glory.[221]

b"): Exhortation to be watchful for the sudden coming of the Son of Man (Lk 21,34-36)

Since the *final coming of the Son of Man* will be *sudden and unexpected* for all the inhabitants of the earth, Jesus' hearers and especially his followers are advised to be ever *vigilant* and prepared for the day (21,34-35). He exhorts them: "watch at all times, praying that you may have the strength to escape all these things that will take place, and stand before the Son of Man" (21,36). "*Watch and pray*" constantly is the right way to be ready to receive the Son of Man whenever he will come to judge the world.

a"): Jesus' teaching in the Temple and the people's eagerness to listen (Lk 21,37-38).

Luke *concludes* this Section (Lk 19,47-21,38) by explicitly stating: "Every day he was *teaching in the temple*" (21,37; cf. 19,47). Daily he taught in the Temple (by day) but he spent the nights (in prayer) on the mount of Olives (21,37). "And early in the morning, all the people came to him in the temple to hear him" (21,38). This shows that, unlike the Temple authorities who were deadly against Jesus, *all the people* were *very eager to listen* to him.

© Looking at *21,5-38 from the Christological perspective, Jesus* rightly reads the signs of the times and *prophetically predicts the destruction of the Temple and Jerusalem.* Their devastation by the Romans (70 CE) will be not only the *fulfilment* of Jesus' prediction but also a *foreshadowing* of the *final judgement* at the end of the world.[222] Besides, *Jesus discerns God's plan* of the *consummation of the Kingdom of God* at the *glorious coming of the Son of Man.*

3.4.©. Conclusion: Christology of Lk 19,47-21,38

Luke's exposition of Jesus' Jerusalem ministry presents a kaleidoscope of *Christological images* that are rooted in his messianic theology. Jesus comes to Jerusalem as its *promised Messiah* to bring God's eschatological gift of peace (19,42). As Messiah, he takes possession of his Father's house, the Temple, and there he teaches Israel with an authority that threatens the leadership of the chief priests, scribes, and elders, who will eventually hand him over to the Romans. Aware that he is the *beloved Son* whom the Father has sent, Jesus knows that Israel will reject him. But he proceeds with his *prophetic mission* because the final redemption of Israel can only occur when the Messiah returns as the *glorious Son of Man.* Before this can take place, however, *the Messiah must suffer and die.*[223]

3.5. Jesus' Passion, Death and Resurrection in Jerusalem (Lk 22,1-24,53)

The narrative of *Jesus' Passion, Death and Resurrection* in Jerusalem is the *climax* of the Lukan story of Jesus.

3.5.1. Plot to Betray Jesus (Lk 22,1-6)

Luke starts Jesus' Passion with the plot to betray him. As the feast of the Passover was fast approaching, the chief priests and the scribes were looking for a way to eliminate Jesus secretly (for fear of the people). *Judas Iscariot, one of the Twelve*, under the influence of Satan, went off to the plotting chief priests and the captains of the temple guards and conferred with them how to betray him to them (22,1-4). Overjoyed by this Satanic offer, they agreed to give Judas money, and from then on he was looking for a favourable opportunity to betray him without the people's knowledge (22,5-6). Thus one of Jesus' close disciples becomes his betrayer for a paltry sum of money!

3.5.2. The Last Supper (Lk 22,7-38)

a) Preparation for the Passover (Lk 22,7-13)

On the day of the Unleavened Bread (Nisan 14), on which the Passover lamb had to be sacrificed, Jesus sent Peter and John to prepare the Passover in "the guest room" ("a large upper room furnished" with couches for reclining), for which Jesus seemed to have contacted the master of the house previously and made arrangements secretly. There Peter and John (the two servant-leaders) prepared the paschal meal (22,7-13).

b) The Institution of the Lord's Supper at Passover (Lk 22,14-20)

When "the hour" comes for the Passover celebration, Jesus reclines with his apostles and tells them that he has longed earnestly to eat this *Passover meal* with them before his suffering, for he will not eat it "until it is fulfilled in the kingdom of God" (22,14-16), that is, in the eschatological banquet of God's kingdom (cf. 13,29). Jesus is aware of his imminent passion and expresses his intense desire to share this last Passover meal with his disciples.

Now Jesus takes a cup of wine (probably the first cup of the Passover celebration) and, after giving thanks to God for the fruit of the vine, he tells his disciples: "Take this, and divide it among yourselves" (22,17). This act of *sharing the same cup of wine* is not only a sign of their *fellowship* but also a pledge of their sharing in the *eschatological banquet* in God's kingdom (22,18). It is to be noted that in 22,16.18.30 Jesus expands the idea of "the kingdom of God" to include the eschatological heavenly kingdom (beyond the earthly kingdom).

Now taking a *loaf of bread*, and having given thanks, Jesus *breaks* it and *gives* it to them, saying: "This is my body, which is given for you. Do this in remembrance of me" (22,19).[224] Thus the "*broken bread*" is "*my body*" (*to sôma mou*) which stands for the whole person of Jesus. "Jesus now provides not bread but himself for his own. This is the meaning of the Gk *sôma*, which does not mean the mere human body, but one's entire life, the whole human being."[225] Jesus' broken "body" (himself) "is given on behalf of you" (*hyper hymôn didomenon*), that is, given in *sacrifice* for the salvation of the disciples. Then Jesus tells them: "Do this in *my remembrance*" (*eis emên anamnêsin:* 22,19). It does not simply mean to repeat ritually what he did to remember him (that is, just to recall him and his action to memory) but to *relive* it by sacrificing themselves for others, just as Jesus does it on the cross to save them.

At the end of the meal, Jesus takes the cup and says: "This cup which is poured out for you is the new covenant in my blood" (22,20). The *cup of wine* that is "*poured out*" on behalf of the disciples stands for the *new covenant* established *in his blood,* shed on the cross. "For Luke, the cup... symbolizes the new covenant, in the sense that the new covenant is brought into being by what it signifies, namely the sacrificial death of Jesus."[226]

In short, the *Lord's Supper* (the Eucharist) is both a *meal of communion* and *sacrifice of the new covenant*, which *unites the disciples with God and with one another through Jesus.*

c) Prediction of Betrayal (Lk 22,21-23)

Unlike Mark who places the prediction of the betrayal before the institution of the Lord's Supper (Mk 14,18-21), Luke puts it immediately after it (22,21-23). Jesus tells the disciples that the hand of his betrayer is with him on the table, hinting at the betrayal of friendship in table fellowship (22,21). Jesus interprets the betrayal as foreseen by God or as part of the plan of God but he holds the betrayer responsible for it ("For the Son of Man goes as it has been determined [by God]; but woe to that man by whom he is betrayed!": 22,22). Since Jesus has not divulged the betrayer's name, the disciples began to ask one another who among them would do such a terrible thing (22,23).

The presence of the betrayer at the Lord's Supper is a warning to the future disciples about the real possibility of betrayal despite their having participated in the Eucharist! Any Christian can become a betrayer!

d) Disciples' Dispute about Greatness (Lk 22,24-30)

Despite Jesus' frequent instructions on being watchful, faithful and responsible "servants" (cf. 12,35-48; 17,7-10; 19,11-27), the disciples still argue about who is *the greatest* among them

(22,24). They are ambitious and self-centred like leaders in the world! Jesus tells them that they are not to be like the kings of the Gentiles who lord it over them, but their greatness and leadership must consist in excelling in the service of others like Jesus himself who is a *servant-leader*: "I am among you as one who serves" (22,25-27).

Those who have been faithful and steadfast companions of Jesus in his trials during his public ministry will be bequeathed by the Lord a share in his royal authority ("sit on thrones judging the twelve tribes of Israel," symbolizing the new people of Israel) and table-fellowship in the eschatological banquet of his kingdom (22,28-30). Jesus does not promise them worldly authority and kingly power in the Church but the *spiritual authority* of *servant-leaders* like *Pope Francis.*

e) Prediction of Simon Peter's Temptations and Denials (Lk 22,31-34)

Jesus tells Simon that Satan wants to sift him (and other disciples)[227] like wheat but Jesus has prayed for Peter that his faith (in Jesus as "the Christ of God": cf. 9,20) may not fail; and after his conversion, he is asked to strengthen his brothers (in their faith) (22,31-32). It is a hint that Simon will fall into Satan's temptation, but because of Jesus' prayer for him, he will repent and will then help his fellow disciples in their weaknesses. But Peter proudly proclaims that he is prepared to suffer and die with him: "Lord, I am ready to go with you to prison and death" (22,33). Jesus replies: "I tell you, Peter, the cock will not crow today [tonight] until you deny thrice that you know me" (22,34).[228] Pride goes before Peter's fall! This is the sad story of many Church leaders even today!

3.5.3. Jesus' Prayer, Betrayal, Arrest, Denial and Trial before the Sanhedrin (Lk 22,39-71)

a) Prayer of Jesus on the Mount of Olives (Lk 22,39-46)

From the Last Supper room, Jesus goes, followed by his disciples, to the Mount of Olives (22,39). *(a)* There he asks them to *pray lest they enter into temptation*; *(b)* he moves away from them, kneels and prays: *(c)* "***Father, if you will, take this cup away from me; yet not my will but yours be done***." *(b')* Rising from prayer and returning to the disciples, he finds them sleeping, *(a')* and asks them to *pray lest they enter into temptation* (22,40-42.45-46).[229] In these five verses "*pray/prayer*" occurs four times but whereas *Jesus prays to do the Father's will*, the disciples fail to pray (they fall asleep)! The agonizing Jesus prays to the Father to *remove the cup of suffering* from him if it is according to his will; if not, the obedient *Jesus surrenders his will to the Father's will*. He is ready and willing to suffer and die if such is the Father's plan for the salvation of humankind. Without prayer, the disciples are sure to fall into the temptation of denial and apostasy. Here the *praying Jesus* is *contrasted* with the *sleeping disciples*!

b) Betrayal and Arrest of Jesus (Lk 22,47-53)

Judas, "one of the Twelve," one of the specially chosen disciples, leads the arrest-party and draws near to kiss Jesus, who asks him: "Judas, would you *betray* the Son of Man with a *kiss*?" (22,47-48). A sign of friendship becomes a sign of betrayal!

When another disciple (Simon Peter) strikes the high priest's slave with a sword and cuts off his right ear, Jesus stops him from further violence and touches the slave's ear and heals him (22,49-51). This miraculous healing of an enemy manifests

Jesus' *non-violent way* of resistance and his *compassion* without frontiers.

But Jesus also *confronts courageously the armed arrest party* (of chief priests, captains of the Temple guard and elders), and rebukes them: "Have you come out as against a robber, with swords and clubs? When I was with you day after day in the temple, you did not lay hands on me. But this is your hour, and the power of darkness" (22,52-53). Jesus, the preacher of peace and teacher of God's reign *allows himself to be arrested* by the agents of violence and powers of evil.

In this first scene of the Passion, the *faithful and compassionate Jesus* is *contrasted* with the heartless and hypocritical betrayer (*Judas*), the impulsive and violent disciple (*Simon Peter*) and the power-hungry and unscrupulous leaders of the people (*the chief priests and the elders*).

c) Peter's Denials of Jesus (Lk 22,54-62)

As the arrested Jesus is led to the house of the high priest (Annas), Peter follows him at a distance and he joins the crowd sitting around the fire in the middle of the courtyard. When he is questioned thrice (by a maid and two men) about his association with Jesus as a disciple, *Peter denies any knowledge of him* (22,54-60). Peter, who had proudly declared his readiness to suffer and die with Jesus (cf. 22,33), now publicly and insistently denies ever having known him! At his third denial, the cock crows, and the Lord looks at Peter and he recalls Jesus' prediction of his triple denial, and he goes out and weeps bitterly (22,60-62). Jesus' compassionate look transforms Peter into a repentant disciple.

Immediately after Jesus' prophetic prediction of Peter's denials has come true, the guards ridicule Jesus by blindfolding him, beating him and telling him: "Prophesy! Who is it that struck you?" (22,63-64). They continue to revile him for long (probably the whole night) (22,65).

d) Jesus' Trial before the Sanhedrin (Lk 22,66-71)

The next day morning Jesus is led to the Sanhedrin (the assembly of the elders of the people, the chief priests and the scribes) and he is asked: "If you are the *Christ*, tell us" (22,66-67). Since they are unwilling to believe, Jesus refuses to answer their question about his being the Messiah but he tells them about his imminent vindication as the Son of Man: "But from now on the *Son of Man* will be seated at the right hand of the power of God" (22,67-69). Thus the exalted Son of Man will share in the authority and power of almighty God. Their final question is: "Are you the *Son of God*, then?" And, instead of giving a straight answer "I am" or "I am not," his indirect and ambiguous answer is: "You say that I am." (22,70), that is, their question implies that he is the Son of God, with which he agrees. The Sanhedrin interprets Jesus' reply as a blasphemous affirmation of his divine Sonship and so concludes that there is no need for any further testimony or evidence for his condemnation (22,71).

It is noteworthy that, in the trial before the Sanhedrin, there is *a progressive revelation of Jesus' identity*: (a) the promised/expected *Messiah*, (b) the exalted *Son of Man* at the right hand of God, and (c) the divine *Son of God*. These *Christological titles* reflect the early Church's confessions of faith in Jesus (cf. Acts 2,32-35; 7,56; 9,20).

3.5.4. Jesus' Trials before Pilate and Herod, Crucifixion, Death and Burial (Lk 23,1-56)

a) Jesus' Trials before Pilate and Herod (Lk 23,1-25)

The Jewish leaders bring Jesus before Pilate (the Roman governor) and falsely accuse him of *three crimes*: a) "perverting our nation" (misleading the Jewish people), b) "forbidding us to give tribute to Caesar" (opposing payment of tax to the Roman emperor), and c) "saying that he is Christ, a king" (claiming to be Messianic king) (23,1-2). So Pilate questions him: "Are you the king of the Jews?" And Jesus gives an indirect affirmative answer: "You say so" (which means, "it is you who say so") (23,3). After examining Jesus, when Pilate declares Jesus' innocence: "I find no crime in this man" (23,4), the chief priests and the scribes persist in their accusation of his stirring up the people by his teaching all through Judea starting from Galilee (23,5).

Hearing that Jesus is a Galilean, Pilate sends him to Herod (since Galilee is under his jurisdiction) for a second trial but Jesus keeps complete silence and refuses to answer any of Herod's questions, even though the chief priests and the scribes keep on accusing him (23,6-10). Frustrated by Jesus' silence, Herod, together with his guards, mocks him, ridicules him by putting on a royal robe and sends him back to Pilate (23,11). Jesus' silence before Herod reminds us of the silent suffering of the Servant of God (cf. Is 53,7).

Now calling together the chief priests, the rulers and the people, Pilate publicly declares to them that neither he nor Herod has found Jesus guilty of any charge/crime deserving a death sentence. But, instead of immediately releasing the innocent Jesus, Pilate tries to placate his adamant accusers by scourging him (23,13-16).

Despite Pilate's repeated attempts to release the righteous Jesus, the crowds keep on crying out for freeing the imprisoned Barabbas (an insurrectionist and a murderer) and for crucifying Jesus, and finally, Pilate yields to their demands by releasing the criminal Barabbas and by delivering the blameless Jesus to be crucified (23,17-25)! Thus, the *trials* of Jesus before Herod and Pilate are *a mockery and travesty of justice!*

Even today many powerful hard-core criminals (with political connections) go scot-free but several righteous poor persons, who are falsely accused, are unjustly imprisoned for years and even condemned to death by the present Pilates in some of the Indian courts!

b) Crucifixion of Jesus (Lk 23,26-43)

On the way to the place of crucifixion (Calvary), the soldiers force a foreigner (Simon of Cyrene), coming in from the fields, to carry Jesus' cross behind him (23,26). A great wailing crowd of people and women beating their breasts, follow him (23,27). But turning to the weeping women, Jesus tries to comfort them: "Daughters of Jerusalem, do not weep for me but weep for yourselves and for your children. For behold, the days are coming when they will say, 'Blessed are the barren, and the wombs that never bore, and the breasts that never gave suck!'" (23,28-29). The great suffering of the innocent Jesus is not as bad as the terrible plight of women and children when Jerusalem will be destroyed by the Romans in the near future (cf. 21,20-24, especially 21,23). "For if they do this when the wood is green, what will happen when it is dry?" (23,31). This is Jesus' final appeal to the Jerusalemites to repent and his timely warning of the drastic consequences of their refusal to repent. If the innocent and life-giving Jesus ("the green wood) is destroyed, what will be the fate of the unrepentant Jerusalem ("the dry wood")?

When they reach the place of execution called "the Skull" (Calvary), the soldiers crucify Jesus and two criminals, one on his right and the other on his left (23,32-33). Thus, Jesus' prediction about himself is fulfilled: "And he was reckoned with transgressors" (22,37). And, like the innocent *suffering Servant of God* (cf. Is 53,12), Jesus prays from the cross for his executioners: "*Father, forgive them*, for they do not know what they do" (Lk 23,34). Even on the cross Jesus practises his teaching on the forgiveness of enemies (cf. 6,27-28; 17,4). This has inspired many Christians and martyrs (like deacon Stephen in Acts 7,60) to pray for those who persecute and even kill them.

While the people stand by and watch Jesus on the cross, the *rulers* (leaders of the people) *mock* him, saying: "He saved others; let him save himself, if he is the Christ of God, his Chosen One!" (23,35). But Jesus, *the Saviour, refuses to "save himself"* (cf. 9,35: "to save his life") by coming down from the cross. Similarly, seeing the inscription over Jesus: "This is the King of the Jews" (23,38), the *soldiers scoff* at him, saying: "If you are the King of the Jews, save yourself!" (23,36-37). Even one of the criminals crucified next to him says disparagingly: "Are you not the Christ? Save yourself and us!" (23,39). Thus, *Jesus is sneered at as a false Messiah* by the Jewish leaders and also as a convicted criminal and *jeered at as a bogus Jewish king* by the Roman soldiers. Their *responses* to Jesus are *all negative*. It must be noted, however, that all their taunting titles for Jesus (e.g., "*the Christ*," "*the King of the Jews*") are *true* for those who believe in him (cf. 9,20; 19,38)! Even though the crucified Jesus suffers extreme humiliation, even though he is repeatedly goaded to "save himself," he does not come down from the cross because it is not his Father's will (cf. 22,42). His will is to *"save" the sinners* through the Son of Man's suffering, death and resurrection (as is evident from Jesus' Passion predictions in 9,22; 18,33).

In contrast to all the negative responses (23,35-39), the *"good" criminal* has a *positive faith response* (23,40-42). He *confesses* that, unlike the crucified criminals who have done evil deeds, *Jesus* is completely *innocent*: "this man has done nothing wrong" (23,41; cf. also the centurion's confession at 23,47) and he *prays* to him with faith in his heart: "*Jesus, remember me* when *you come into your kingdom*" (23,42). Jesus assures him: "Truly, I say to you, *today you will be with me in Paradise*" (23,43). The crucified Jesus not only forgives the repentant sinner but also promises him free access to "Paradise". The *kingdom* that he establishes through his death on the cross is a *new Paradise*, a new "garden of Eden" (cf. Gen 2,8-9) where all (including repentant sinners) can enjoy the fruits of "the tree of life" with Jesus, (the new Adam).

c) Death of Jesus (Lk 23,44-49)

From the sixth hour (noon) till the ninth hour (3.00 P.M.) the whole land was plunged in darkness "due to the sun's eclipse" (*tou hêliou eklipontos*) and the curtain of the Temple sanctuary (*tou naou*) (which prevented the people from entering "the holy of holies") was torn (in two) down the middle (*meson*) (23,44-45), which indicates that now, with Jesus' death on the cross, all have free and direct access to God. And crying with a loud voice, Jesus said: "Father, into your hands I entrust my spirit" (23,46; cf. Ps 31,6). With these words of *total trust*, he *surrenders his life to the Father* and breathes his last (23,46). Jesus' death on the cross is a trusting surrender of his life to the loving Father. Seeing such a self-surrendering death, the centurion glorifies God, saying: "Indeed this man was righteous!" (23,47). This public *declaration of the crucified man's innocence by a Gentile centurion* is *an expression of his faith in Jesus*, hinting at the *universal meaning of his death*. All the multitudes, seeing what had happened, "returned home beating their breasts" (23,48), a symbol of sorrow and repentance for what was done to Jesus. While all his acquaintances stand at a distance from the crucified Jesus, *his women followers* from Galilee "*see*" (*horôsai*) him from *close quarters* (23,49).

d) Burial of Jesus (Lk 23,50-56)

Now Joseph of Arimathea, a member of the Sanhedrin, "a good and righteous man," who did not consent to the Sanhedrin's condemnation of Jesus, goes to Pilate and asks for his body. He takes it down from the cross and wraps it in a linen shroud and lays it in a new rock-hewn tomb (23,50-53).

3.5.5. Jesus' Resurrection, Appearances and Ascension (Lk 24,1-53)

a) Jesus' Resurrection Announced by Angels and Women Disciples (Lk 24,1-12)

The women disciples (Mary Magdalen, Joanna, Mary the mother of James and others: cf. 24,10) who had witnessed Jesus' death and burial, come to his tomb (with the prepared spices) early at dawn on the first day of the week (Sunday) but they find the tombstone rolled away and nobody inside the tomb (24,1-3). While they are perplexed, suddenly two men in dazzling clothes ("angels": 24,23) stand by them and ask them: "Why are you seeking the living one among the dead?" (24,4) and they remind the women about Jesus' predictions about his passion, crucifixion and resurrection on the third day (24,6-8).

Even though the *enlightened women disciples*, returning from the empty tomb, *announce the good news of Jesus' resurrection* to the Eleven and all the others, they do not believe them, since the women's words seem to them "like nonsense" (*hôsei lêros*) (24,9-11)! The *male leaders* of the community *refuse to believe in the Easter gospel (good news) proclaimed by the faithful women disciples* (cf. 24,22-23)! *Peter*, however, rushes to the tomb and finds the linen cloths lying by themselves but returns home "wondering what had happened" (24,12.24), that is to say, even *the leader of the Twelve fails to understand that Jesus has risen*!

b) Jesus' Appearance to the Emmaus Disciples (Lk 24,13-35)

Now Luke narrates the moving story of how the (risen) Jesus (appearing as an unknown visitor) walks with two sad and depressed disciples (Cleopas and his companion) returning from Jerusalem to their village Emmaus and dialogues with them on the way and how they recognize him "in the breaking of the bread" and they go back to the Eleven in Jerusalem that very night with the good news of the resurrection of the Lord (24,13-35).

The two disciples were disappointed because Jesus' death on the cross had shattered their hopes (24,21) and so they abandoned the way of discipleship and were going back home frustrated! The risen Jesus accompanies them on the way, listening attentively to their sad story of how "Jesus of Nazareth," "a mighty prophet in deed and word," on whom they had pinned their hope of the Messianic restoration of Israel, was "condemned to death and crucified," and how they found it difficult to believe the women disciples' tale of their "vision of angels" who told them that Jesus "was alive" (24,15-24)! It reveals the risen Jesus' loving compassion for his desperate disciples. He challenges them to open their hearts so that they may believe what all the prophets had predicted about the Messiah (24,25): "Was it not necessary that the Christ should suffer these things and enter into his glory?" (24,26). His interpretation of Christ's passion and death as the fulfilment of God's promises in the sacred Scriptures helps the dejected disciples to believe in the suffering and risen Messiah (24,27.32; cf. also 24,44-46).

As the party drew near to Emmaus in the evening, those two disciples invited Jesus to stop over with them for the night (24,28-29), and while sitting at table with them "he *took* the bread and *blessed*, and *broke* it and *gave* it to them, and at that instant their eyes were opened and they recognized him" (24,30). The risen Jesus' four actions ("taking," "blessing," "breaking," and "giving") reminded them of what Jesus had done at the time of the institution of the Eucharist during the Last Supper (cf. 22,19). During their table-fellowship with a stranger "*in the breaking of the bread*" (24,31.35) the *disciples' eyes of faith are opened to recognize the risen Jesus.* Their encounter with the risen Lord transforms them and fills them with new energy to return to Jerusalem at night itself and to share their joyful Easter experience (24,32.35) with the Eleven and other disciples, who have their own stories to tell: "The Lord is risen indeed, and has appeared to Simon" (24,34). The risen Jesus' special love for the sad Simon, who denied him thrice, is part of the good news of Easter for all the repentant sinners of all times.

> The account of the Emmaus disciples is Luke's most important contribution to the Gospel resurrection narratives, confirming that the death and resurrection of the Christ is the fulfilment of God's purpose in salvation history.[230]

c) Jesus' Appearance to the Disciples (Lk 24,36-49)

It is surprising that, when the risen Jesus stands in the midst of the disciples and wishes them "peace," they are frightened mistaking him to be a spirit (24,36-37). But the risen Lord gently calms their fears by showing them his (pierced) hands and feet, by inviting them to touch him (and verify that he is not a spirit), and by eating a piece of broiled fish before them (24,38-43). The risen Jesus reveals himself to be *fully human* even after his resurrection and dispels his disciples' doubts.

Now the risen Lord reminds the disciples about his passion predictions and explains to them that his suffering and resurrection from the dead are all in fulfilment of the Scriptures (24,44-46; cf. also 24,25-27). Then he commissions his disciples/witnesses to "*preach repentance for the forgiveness of sins*" (*metanoia eis aphesin hamartiôn*) in his name to all nations (24,47-48; cf. Acts 3,15-16).[231] But he also asks them to stay on in Jerusalem till he sends "the promise of the Father" (the Holy Spirit) upon them (24,49; cf. Joel 2,28-29; Acts 1,4-5.8; 2,4.17-18.38) to empower them to accomplish their mission. It is only in the power of the Spirit, they can be true *witnesses* to Jesus (cf. Acts 1,8) and effective *proclaimers* of the good news of salvation in and through him to all the peoples (*universal salvation*) (cf. Acts 1,8; 26,23).

d) Jesus' Ascension into Heaven (Lk 24,50-53)

After giving his final instructions to the disciples, the risen Jesus leads them out as far as Bethany and, lifting his hands, he *blesses* them, and while blessing them, he parts from them and is *taken up into heaven* (24,50-51). After having completed his mission on earth, the risen Lord blesses his disciples and departs from them to return to his Father in heaven.

The ascending *Jesus' blessing* filled the disciples' hearts with heavenly happiness and so "they returned to Jerusalem with great *joy* and they were continually in the *temple* blessing God" (24,52-53). They praise and thank God for what he has done for them through Jesus. It is noteworthy that Luke's Gospel begins and ends in the *Temple* (1,9; 24,53) and with great *joy* (1,14; 2,10; 24,52).[232]

3.©. Luke's Good News of the Prophetic Messiah, the Son of Man, the Son of God and the Saviour

"Like the many sides of a diamond, *Luke's portrait of Jesus* is *multifaceted*, and *many titles* are used for him."[233]

3.©.1. A Great Prophet

Like all great prophets starting from Moses, Jesus is sent by God to *proclaim the word of God* and is empowered to *perform miracles*. When he raises the widow's son from the dead, the people exclaim: "*A great prophet* has arisen among us!" (7,16). When Jesus asks his disciples: "Who do people say that I am?", one of their answers is: "one of the old prophets has risen" (9,19). The Emmaus disciples acknowledge him as "*a prophet mighty in deed and word*" (24,19). In the light of Jesus' experience of rejection by his people at Nazareth, he says that "no prophet is acceptable in his own country" (4,24) and on his way to Jerusalem he asserts that "no prophet can die outside Jerusalem!" (13,33).

3.©.2. The Suffering Messiah

Jesus is more than a great and powerful prophet, for he is *the Messiah (Christ)*, the anointed one, sent by God. Peter, the representative of the Twelve, declares Jesus to be "*the Christ of God*" (9,20). Even though the disciples acknowledge Jesus as the Messiah, they find it very difficult to understand him as *the suffering Messiah*, and therefore Jesus has to tell them repeatedly during his public ministry about his *passion* (cf. 9,22.44; 13,32-34; 17,25; 18,32-34) and even after his resurrection that the *Christ had to suffer* in fulfilment of what had been spoken by the prophets and written in the Scriptures (24,26.46). In short, Christ's suffering was per God's plan of saving the sinful humankind.

> The startling revelation to which Luke's narrative builds is that God's salvation is accomplished not only through a suffering prophet but through the *suffering Messiah*. This is the main theme of the Emmaus resurrection account. Though the two disciples already recognize Jesus as a great prophet (24,19), Jesus opens their eyes to Scripture, showing them that *the Christ had to suffer* (24,25-27). This is repeated to all of the disciples in the following episode (24,46) and serves as a repeated refrain in Acts (3,18; 17,3; 26,23). The *Messiah* fulfils the role of the *suffering Servant* of Isaiah 53, bringing salvation to his people.[234]

3.©.3. The Son of Man

Jesus was reluctant to admit during his public ministry that he was the Messiah because of its political connotation, but very often he referred to himself as "*the Son of Man*".[235] This title has *many meanings* depending on the context: a) *a self-designation of Jesus* (5,24; 6,5.22; 7,34; 9,58; 11,30; 12,8.10; 19,10; 22,22.48), b) a *suffering human being* in the *passion-predictions* (9,22.44; 18,31; 24,7), c) a *glorious being* at his *final coming* (*parousia*) (9,26; 12,40; 17,24.26.30; 18,8; 21,27.36; 22,69). As "*the Son of Man*" Jesus *identifies* himself with *every human being* (*a member of the human race*) and *shares in his/her sufferings*; and when he is raised, *humanity shares in his resurrection*; and when he comes in glory as the "Son of Man" at the *parousia*, he (the *humandivine Son of Man*) will *judge* all humans. Hence the *Lukan "Son of Man"* is a *bridge* between the *human Messiah* and the *divine Son of God.*

3.©.4. The Son of God

Jesus is *more than the Messiah* because he is the *Son of God* ("*Son* of the Most High") as announced by the angel Gabriel to Mary for he is conceived through the power of the Holy Spirit (1,32.35). Immediately after Jesus' baptism and at his transfiguration, God the Father declares that Jesus is his *beloved Son* (4,22; 9,35). Sometimes Jesus calls God "*my Father*" (11,22) and in prayer, he addresses Him "Father" (*Pater* [which is the Greek equivalent of the Aramaic *Abba*]: 11,21; 22,42; 23,46). "*The Father*" and "*the Son*" have *unique, mutual, intimate knowledge of each other* (11,22), which no one else can claim to have. Not only demons cry out: "You are the Son of God!" (4,41; 8,28) but also when the Sanhedrin asks Jesus: "Are you the Son of God?" he indirectly accepts that he is the *divine Son of God*: "You say that I am" (22,70).

It is to be noted that Jesus, the *divinehuman* ("Son of God/ Man") person, has a *unique relationship with God the Father,* which is manifested by his *prayer life*. He prays after his baptism (3,21), after healing a leprous man (5,16), before choosing the Twelve (6,12), alone (in the presence of the disciples) (9,18), at the transfiguration (9,28), before teaching the disciples to pray (11,1); he prays for Peter (during the Last Supper) (22,32) and his own murderers (from the cross) (23,34), for himself (during the agony in the garden and just before breathing his last) (22,41-42; 23,46).

3.©.5. The Saviour

Precisely because Jesus is the human Messiah, the suffering Son of Man and the divine Son of God, he is *the Saviour* (2,11).

> [T]he messianic Son of God is *the Saviour* of his people. Anointed with the Spirit of God, he brings salvation to his people by preaching the good news to the poor, freeing those under Satan's bondage, curing the sick, calling sinners to repentance, and suffering upon the cross.[236]

It is clear from the above that the Lukan understanding of *salvation* is not simply *redemption* of the soul but the *integral* (physical, psychological, socio-cultural, moral and spiritual) *liberation of the whole person and of the people* (1,69.71.77; 19,9).

Even though the *salvation* Jesus offers is *for all*, it is specially for *the poor and the oppressed* (4,16-22; 6,20-21; 7,22), *sinners and tax collectors* (15,11-32; 18,9-14; 19,1-10; 23,39-43), *the outcasts* (7,36-50) and *women* (7,12-15.36-50; 8,43-48; 13,10-17), *Samaritans* (9,52-56; 10,29-37; 17,11-19) and *Gentiles* (2,32; 3,6.8; 4,25-27).

3.©.6. The Lord

Even though the "Lord" (*kyrios*) is primarily a post-resurrectional title for Jesus (e.g., Acts 1,6.21; 2,36), it is often used for Jesus already during his earthly life (e.g., Lk 1,43; 2,11; 5,12; 7,6.18).

> Finally, the Messiah is *the Lord*, the one who exercises divine prerogatives because he is enthroned at God's right hand. Since this *enthronement as Lord* only occurs after Jesus' resurrection and ascension, properly speaking it is not part of the Gospel story of Jesus. But the Lukan narrator introduces the term "Lord" in narrative comments (10,1) and even puts it on the lips of certain characters before Jesus' resurrection (1,43). In doing so, he points to the *unity of the earthly Jesus and the risen Christ*. Jesus did not become the Messiah and Lord by virtue of his resurrection; he was already *Messiah* and *Lord* at his *birth*.[237]

3.©.7. To sum up, the Lukan Jesus is a *great Prophet*, the *suffering Messiah*, the *humandivine Son of Man*, the *divine Son of God*, the *Saviour* and the *Lord*.

> Though Jesus' status as a prophet is important, it is exceeded by his role as Messiah. This is evident already in the birth narrative. While John the Baptist is a great prophet, Jesus is the Messiah and the Son of God (1,32-33). He is the "Saviour . . . Christ the Lord" (2,11). These *four important titles -- Messiah (Christ), Son of God, Saviour, and Lord* -- are closely linked, all portraying Jesus as God's agent of deliverance, the fulfilment of God's saving purpose.[238]

Chapter 4

JOHN'S GOOD NEWS OF JESUS CHRIST

The Fourth Gospel is written based on the *testimony* of the *Beloved Disciple* (Jn 21,24; cf. 13,23.25; 21,20) with a *Christocentric* (Christ-centred) *purpose*: to persuade the readers to *believe* in Jesus, "*the Christ*" and "*the Son of God*," and to *deepen the believers' faith* in him and to enable them to "*have [eternal] life* in his name" (20,31). The *immediate theological scope* of the Gospel is to manifest Jesus as *the Messiah and the divine Son of God* and the *final spiritual aim* is to lead the believers to attain (eternal) *life* in its fullness (cf. 3,16; 10,10), to share in the divine life of the Father and the Son (cf. 5,26).[239]

The overall *outline* of John's Gospel is simple: **INTRODUCTION (Jn 1)**, **Part I**: **JESUS' SIGNS *(PATH OF FAITH)* (Jn 2-12)**, **Part II**: **JESUS' HOUR *(PATH OF LOVE)* (Jn 11-20)**, **CONCLUSION (20,30-31)** and **Epilogue (Jn 21)**. ***FAITH*** and ***LOVE*** are the responses to **Jesus' SIGNS** and **Jesus' HOUR** in **Part I** and **Part II** respectively. The two Major **Parts I** and **II** may be subdivided into **five Sections (Jn 2-4; 5-10; 11-12; 13-17; 18-20)**. [**Jn 11-12** is a "**Bridge-Section**" which concludes **Part I** and introduces **Part II.**][240]

The following **main aspects** of the **mystery** of the **person and mission of Jesus** are highlighted in the development of the **Sections** of the Gospel of John:[241]

4.0. Introduction: Jesus, the Life-giving Word/Son of God and the Messiah (Jn 1)

4.1. Jesus, the Universal Messiah (Jn 2-4)

4.2. Jesus, the Coworker/Son of God (Jn 5-10)

4.3. Jesus, the Loving Life-Giver (Jn 11-12)

4.4. Jesus the Lover's Last Testament (Jn 13-17)

4.5. Jesus' Paschal Mystery (Jn 18-20)

4.* Conclusion: Jesus, the Messiah, Son of God and Life-Giver (Jn 20,30-31)

4.6. Jesus, the Caring Risen Lord (Jn 21).

4.0. Jesus, the Life-Giving Word/Son of God and the Messiah (Jn 1)

Jn 1,1-51 consists of *two units*: ***1) Prologue,*** a hymn to the (incarnate = enfleshed) Word of God *(1,1-18)*, and ***2) Prelude*** *(1,19-51),* which consists of *a) the Baptist's Testimony* to Jesus (1,19-34) and *b) the Disciples' Messianic Discovery* (1,35-51).

4.0.1. Prologue: Creative, Revelatory, Life-giving, Incarnate Word/Son of God (Jn 1,1-18)[242]

The Word (*Logos*) [of God] existed in the beginning, even before the creation of the cosmos, and was personally related to God and was *divine* in nature (1,1-2). The Word is what God is but the divine Word is also *distinct* from God, the Father (cf. 1,1-2.14.18).

It is *through* the Word of God that everything is created (1,3.10; cf. Gen 1,1-24) but *life* is created *in* the Word (1,4a). Each living creature is formed *within* the Word (as in a womb). This highlights the *life-giving role* of the Word of God and stresses how *precious life* is in the eyes of God. Every living being (animal, bird, fish, plant, etc.) is a shining *light* (revelation of God) to human beings (1,4b-5). By contemplating the myriad forms of life on earth, humans have been and are still drawing near to God, their Creator. The mystery of the Life of God is manifested to the mystics in the mystery of life on earth.

Like the light of dawn that dispels the darkness on the face of the earth, the Word of God has been "the true light that enlightens every human being" (1,9). Even though the divine Word was in the world of humanity, they did not recognize the Word (1,10). "He (*Logos*) came to his own but his own did not receive him" (1,11). This is the sad (his)story of the rejection of God's Word by human beings. But there is a silver lining around the dark clouds of history. "But to all who received him [*Logos*, the Word], he *gave them power to become children of God [tekna theou genesthai]*, to those believing in his name, who were *born... from God* (*ek theou egennêthêsan:* 1,12-13). The Word of God empowers *all the believers in the divine Word* "*to become God's children*" (1,12).[243]

To facilitate this *divinization* of the believers, "the *Word became flesh* (*sarx*) and pitched his tent (*eskênôsen*) among us" (1,14; cf. Ex 40,34-38: God's dwelling with his people in a tent). The *incarnation of the Word of God* manifests the mystery of the divine *solidarity* with the *weak and mortal humanity* ("*flesh*"). The *enfleshed Word* (Jesus) manifested his "glory as of a *unique* one (*monogenês*) [Son] from the Father" (1,14). The saving presence ("glory") of the incarnate Son among human beings has revealed the Father "full of grace and truth" (merciful love and faithfulness) (1,14). If the Mosaic Law was God's gift to the people of Israel, the greatest grace of God's revelation to humanity came through Jesus Christ (1,17) because, while "no one has ever seen God [cf. 5,17; 6,47], a unique God (*monogenês theos*), the one who is in the bosom of the Father, has made him known (*exêgêseto*)" (1,18; cf. 14,9). "If God has been manifesting himself through his Word spoken through Moses and other prophets of Israel, sages and saints of other religions, *the Father's self-revelation* has reached its *climax* in the *incarnate Son of God.*"[244]

4.0.1.© To sum up, the Prologue begins with the pre-existent divine Word of God (1,1-2) through whom all things came into existence (1,3) and in whom all life (1,4) came into being. This Word is the true light of revelation that enlightens every human being (1,9) and who empowers believers in him (the *Logos*) to become children of God (1,12-13). This divine, creative, revelatory and regenerative Word became an ordinary, mortal human being [Jesus], and in his human life, passion and death he manifested his saving presence as of a unique Son fully reflecting the Father's steadfast love and faithfulness (1,14.17). In short, the Prologue proclaims *the pre-existent, divine, creative, life-giving, revelatory, incarnate and regenerative Word.*

4.0.2. Prelude: Jesus, the Messiah and the Son of God (Jn 1,19-51)

The *Prelude* contains many *Christological titles:* "the Lamb of God" (1,29.36), "the Son of God" (1,34.49), "Rabbi/Teacher" (1,38.49), "the Messiah/Christ" (1,41), "the King of Israel" (1,49), "the Son of Man" (1,51).

a) *The Baptist's Testimony to Jesus, the Hidden Messiah, the Lamb of God and the Son of God (Jn 1,19-34)*

John the Baptist denies that he is the Christ (1,20) but confesses *Jesus* as *the hidden Messiah* (1,26) and acknowledges his superiority and pre-existence (1,30-31). His repeated denials of being the long-awaited Messiah (1,20) or his precursor Elijah (1,21; cf. Mal 4,5) or the promised Moses-like prophet of the final times (1,21; cf. Deut 18,18) indirectly point to Jesus as the Messiah (cf. 1,41) and the final prophet (cf. 1,45).[245]

In Jn 1,21 John the Baptist was explicitly asked: "Are you *the prophet*? (*ho prophêtês ei sy?*)" and his unambiguous answer was "*No*" (*ou).* John the Baptist states that his mission/ministry of water-baptism is *to reveal Jesus, the Messiah*, to Israel (1,26-27.31) and *to bear witness* to him as *the Lamb of God* (1,29.36) and *the Son of God* (1,34).

John Baptist proclaimed Jesus as "*the Lamb of God* who *takes away the sin* of the world" (1,29). But what did the title *mean* for the Baptist and the Evangelist? The *Baptist* meant *Jesus* to be the *conquering Apocalyptic Lamb* (leader) who destroys sin/evil ("takes away the sin") by eliminating the sinner/evil-doer (cf. 3,36; 1 Jn 3,5.8; Rev 7,17; 17,14). But in the post-resurrectional period, the *Evangelist* understood *Jesus* to be the *suffering Servant of God* ("like a lamb that is led to the slaughter": Is 53,7) who "bears the sin of many" (Is 53,12) and thus "takes away the sin of the world" (Jn 1,29) through his suffering and death (cf. Is 53,1-12). Furthermore, for the Evangelist and the Johannine community, "the Lamb of God" meant the *Paschal Lamb*, since Jesus was condemned to death on "the day of preparation for the Passover… about the sixth hour" (19,14; cf. Ex 12,6) when the paschal lamb was killed in the Temple, and since the crucified Jesus' bones, like those of the paschal lamb, were not broken (Jn 19,33.36; Ex 12,46). Jesus, the *suffering Servant* and the *Paschal Lamb*, "takes away *the sin* of the world" (1,29), *the sin of the unbelief* of humanity (16,9; 12,37-38; Is 53,1) through his passion and death on the cross.

John the *Baptist bore witness* to *Jesus* also as "*the Son of God*" because the Baptist saw the Holy Spirit descend as a dove from heaven and remain on Jesus during his baptism in the Jordan and because God, who sent him to baptize in water, revealed to him that the *Spirit-filled* Jesus is "the Son of God" (1,32-34). This title for the Baptist would have meant that Jesus was the *expected Messiah* since he was anointed by the Spirit of God (cf. 1,49; 11,27; cf. Is 11,2; 61,1), whereas for the Evangelist and his Christian community in the post-Easter era the title had a deeper meaning, namely, that Jesus was the *divine Son of God* (cf. 20,31).

© In short, John the Baptist's testimony revealed Jesus as the *hidden Messiah, the Lamb of God* and *the Son of God.*

b) Disciples' Messianic Discovery (Jn 1,35-51)

On hearing the Baptist's revelatory statement "Behold, the Lamb of God!", two of his disciples start to "follow" (walk behind) Jesus. He turns and sees them following him and asks them: "*What do you seek?*" and they disclose their heart's desire to know where he stays: "Rabbi, *where do you remain?*" and he invites them to go with him and find it out for themselves: "*Come* and *you will see*" (1,35-39). It is an *invitation* ("come") and a *promise* ("you will see"). By going with him and remaining with him that day (that is, through a personal experience of Jesus), Andrew and his companion *discover* him to be the long-expected *Messiah,* and Andrew announces their *Messianic discovery* to his brother Simon: "We have discovered (*heurêkamen*) the Messiah" and he leads him to Jesus (1,40-42).

On the following day, Jesus takes the initiative to find and call *Philip*: "*Follow me*" (1,43), to which he responds readily. He finds his friend Nathanael and proclaims the discovery (*heurêkamen*) of "Jesus *from Nazareth*" (*apo Nazaret*) to be the final prophet about whom Moses and the prophets had written (1,45; Deut 18,15.18). But *Nathanael* exclaims: "*From Nazareth* (*ek Nazaret*)! *Can he be any good?* (*dynatai ti agathon einai?* 1,46).[246] Nathanael has doubts whether Jesus is a "*good*" *prophet* or a "*false*" one who "leads the people astray" (7,12; cf. also 7,47.52) since many false prophets had arisen from Galilee, but Philip gently invites his doubting friend to "come and see" (find out) for himself (1,46).

When Jesus sees *Nathanael* coming to him, he tells him: "Behold, truly an Israelite, in whom there is no guile!" (1,47). Nathanael is surprised at Jesus' prophetic, intuitive knowledge of him, for he asks him, "Whence do you know me?" (1,48). *Jesus' 'tele-vision'* of Nathanael under the fig tree (1,48) makes him realize that Jesus knows him through and through and it helps him to open his eyes of faith and to declare: "Rabbi, you are *the Son of God*! You are *the King of Israel*!" (1,49). Here Nathanael confesses him as the *royal Messiah*, the anointed king who is the adopted Son of God (cf. 2 Sam 7,14: "my son"; Ps 2,6-7: "my king… my son"). Jesus assures him of a *greater faith-vision* in the future: "you will see greater things than these" (1,50).

Jesus promises a future heavenly vision to Nathanael and all disciples/believers: "You [plural] will see the heaven opened and the angels of God ascending and descending upon the

Son of Man" (1,51). Although "the angels of God ascending and descending" is a reference to Jacob's dream at Bethel (Gen 28,12-13), here "*the Son of Man*" replaces "the ladder" in Jacob's dream, hinting that the human Jesus with a mysterious origin ("the Son of Man") will be the *medium of God's presence and revelation* to human beings (as will be seen in the rest of the Gospel).

©To sum up the Christology of 1,35-51, the disciples discover *Jesus* to be the expected *Messiah*, the *final prophet*,[247] the kingly *Son of God* and the revelatory *Son of Man*.

4.1. Jesus, the Universal Messiah (Jn 2-4)[248]

Jesus the Messiah has already been introduced in Jn 1 (especially in 1,19-51), as we have seen above.

In Jn 2-4 Jesus manifests himself as the *Messiah of all peoples*.[249] In his first round of journey from Cana to Cana (via Capernaum, Jerusalem, Judean countryside, Samaria), Jesus meets different individuals and groups (*Jews, Samaritans* and *Gentiles*) in the whole of Israel and reveals himself to them in and through miraculous signs and prophetic actions, dialogues and discourses. Jn 2-4 is enclosed between the *two Cana signs* done in favour of a *Jewish* family (2,1-11) and a *Gentile* family (4,46-54) respectively.

Jn 2-4 consists of ***six Episodes***: *1) First Cana Sign: Changing of Water into Wine* (2,1-12); *2) Temple-Cleansing and the Jews at Jerusalem* (2,13-25); *3) Nicodemus and Birth from Above & Eternal Life* (3,1-21); *4) John the Baptist and the Messiah & Eternal Life* (3,22-4:3); *5) Samaritan Woman, Living Water & True Worship* (4,1-42); *6) Second Cana Sign: Healing of the Official's Son* (4,43-54).[250]

4.1.1. Jesus, the Messianic Bridegroom (Jn 2,1-12: First Cana Sign) [251]

Jesus and his disciples are invited to a marriage at Cana in Galilee (2,1-2). When the wine runs short during the celebration, Jesus' mother requests him to save the 'have-nots' (the family of the bridegroom) from the embarrassing situation of 'having no wine' (2,3) to serve the wedding guests. Although Jesus feels his "hour" (the divinely determined time of his passion-death-resurrection) "has not yet come" (2,4; 7,30; 8,20; cf.12,23.27; 13,1; 17,1) the plight of the 'have-nots' and the faith of the "woman" (his mother) persuade him to anticipate his "hour" and to provide an abundance of quality wine by changing miraculously about 500-700 litres of water into wine (2,6-10). Thus, he inaugurates the *Messianic era* with an abundance of wine (and grain) according to Jewish Messianic expectations based on prophetic predictions (cf. Hos 2,22; Joel 3,18; Amos 9,13; Is 36,17; Jer 31,12; cf. also Gen 49,11-12). Jesus' gift of the best wine in abundance at the end (Jn 2,10) is a Messianic sign and an eschatological symbol of the dawn of God's *new age of salvation*.

The *lack of wine* during the wedding feast (2,3) symbolizes the *penury* of the human predicament. Jesus hears God's call through his mother's request to act in favour of those who "have no wine" to celebrate life. His generous supply of "the good wine" reveals "his glory" (saving presence 2,11). He manifests himself as *the Messiah* by responding positively and effectively to a negative and hopeless human situation.

Even though it was the duty of the bridegroom to supply wine to the wedding guests, it was not he but Jesus who provided them plenty of good wine (2,9-10), thereby hinting at Jesus being the Messianic bridegroom (cf. 3,29). In and through this "*sign*" (a miracle that points to Jesus as the Messiah cf. 6,14; 7,31; 20,30-31) in the context of a marriage feast (which has Messianic overtones cf. Jn 3,29; Mt 9,15; 25,10; Mk 2,19), *Jesus* manifests himself as the *Messianic bridegroom* to whom his disciples commit themselves (like a bride cf. 3,29) by entering into a covenantal relationship in faith (2,11: "his disciples believed in[to] him" [*episteusan eis auton*]).[252]

4.1.2. Jesus, the Messianic Prophet and the Son of God (Jn 2,13-25: Temple-Cleansing)[253]

Jesus goes up to Jerusalem for the Jewish Passover feast and he is appalled to find sellers of sacrificial animals (oxen, sheep and pigeons) and money changers in the Temple (in the Court of Gentiles), turning it into a marketplace, thus preventing the Gentiles from praying there (2,13-14). Seeing this as a desecration, Jesus makes a whip of cords and drives them all out in a fit of rage (2,15-16). This is a courageous *prophetic protest* against the Jewish authorities' profanation of the sacred Temple for commercial gain. This *prophetic purification* of the Temple has *Messianic* overtones, for it fulfils the prophecy of Zechariah: "And there shall no longer be traders in the house of the Lord of hosts on that day" (Zech 14,21). Thus, the Temple-cleansing manifests Jesus as *the Messianic prophet.*

Jesus' reference to the Temple as "*my Father's house*" (2,16; cf. also 14,2) is a hint that *God* is *his Father* and hence he is *the Son of God.* Therefore, the cleansing of the Temple is more than a prophetic act; it is an *authoritative act of God's Son.* His burning zeal for his Father's house, which drives him to do the Temple-cleansing, will eventually lead him to the cross (cf. the *future* tense in "Zeal for thy house *will consume* me" 2,17).

"The Jews" (Jewish leaders) question Jesus' authority to cleanse the Temple and they demand an authenticating miracle, "What sign do you show us for doing these things?" (2,18). Jesus declines to work a miracle but makes an enigmatic statement: "Destroy this *sanctuary* (*naos*) and in three days I will raise it" (2,19), which "the Jews" (Jewish authorities) misunderstand as the rebuilding of the material Temple by Jesus (2,20). The *Evangelist* interprets Jesus' saying as a reference to "*the sanctuary (naos) of his body*" (2,21). In other words, the destruction and the rebuilding of the sanctuary (2,19) denote Jesus' future death and resurrection (2,22). It means that the risen Lord will be *the new sanctuary*, the privileged place of encountering God (cf. 1,51) and of "worshipping the Father in Spirit and truth" (4,23-24).

© In short, the Temple-cleansing episode in John's Gospel manifests Jesus as *the Messianic prophet* (at the time of the Temple-purification) and reveals him as *the Son of God* and *the new sanctuary* (in the post-Easter era).[254]

4.1.3. Jesus, the Teacher, the Son of Man, the Son of God and the Mediator of Eternal Life (Jn 3,1-21: Nicodemus-episode)[255]

Nicodemus, a Pharisee and a ruler of the Jews, comes to Jesus by night and acknowledges him as an authentic *teacher* who has come from God (3,1-2) because of the many signs that he has been doing (cf. 2,23). Jesus reveals to him his teaching about *birth from above* (*anôthen*) as a necessary condition for seeing (experiencing) the kingdom/reign of God (3,3). But Nicodemus misunderstands Jesus' statement as a second physical birth ("born again") from his mother's womb (3,4). Jesus explains it as *spiritual birth*, "birth from water and Spirit" (*ex hydatos kai pneumatos* 3,5). The *Spirit's birthing action* is as mysterious as the movement of the *wind* (*pneuma* 3,6-8). This refers to the *new birth* of human beings as "*children of God*" by being "*born from God*" (cf. 1,12-13), now specified as being "*born from the Spirit*" (3,6.8).

Besides being a true teacher from God (3,2), Jesus is also the *unique revealer* of heavenly realities because he is *the Son of Man* who has descended from heaven (3,12-13). "Like the Danielic Son of Man coming on the clouds of heaven (Dan 7,13-14), Jesus is the human being with a mysterious origin who can reveal the heavenly reality of God's reign/kingdom because he has come from God (Jn 3,2.12-13; cf. also 1,18.51)."[256]

When the Israelites were bitten by poisonous snakes in the desert, Moses "*lifted up*" (mounted on a pole) a bronze serpent (Num 21,8-9) so that the affected people could be saved from physical death. Similarly, *the Son of Man* (Jesus) must be "*lifted up*" (on the cross and to heaven) so that those who believe in him (commit themselves to him in faith) may have "*eternal life*" (Jn 3,14-15). "Eternal life" (in the Gospel of John) is not merely "everlasting life" (life without end) but a *qualitatively new life*, the *divine life* of the Father in which the Son of God shares (cf. 5,26) which he mediates to those who believe in him (3,15).

If it is surprising that anyone about to die of poisonous snake-bite escaped death by looking up to the bronze serpent (mounted on a pole) with faith in God's word, it is all the more paradoxical that everyone who believes in the Son of Man (raised on a cross) is assured of *eternal life*. Just as God changed the serpent, a sign of death, into a sign of salvation for the Israelites, now the crucified human Jesus becomes the symbol and sacrament of salvation for all humans. This is part of God's paradoxical plan of salvation for humankind.[257]

Jesus' explanation of this divine paradox is found in the boundless love of God for sinful humankind. God loved humans so much that he gave his "*unique Son*" (*monogenês:* 3,16).[258] God's gift of his unique Son to the humans and his death on the cross for them reveal *God's boundless love* for them and his desire to share his divine life of love with them. This revelation of God's limitless love for human beings is meant to lead them to believe in God's unique Son so that they may have eternal life (3,16-17). In other words, God the Father's love for sinful humans is so great that he sent his "unique Son" so that by laying down his life for them he could *mediate eternal life* to those who believe in him (3,16).

"God sent the Son into the world" (of sinful humanity) "not to condemn the world" but to save it through him (3,17), but humans have loved darkness (of sin) and refused to come to *the light* (of revelation) because their deeds are evil (3,18-20). By refusing to believe in God's "unique Son" who *reveals God's infinite love* for sinful humans, they condemn themselves to the dungeon of darkness and death (3,16-21).

©The Nicodemus-episode highlights *Jesus* as *the true teacher (Sadguru) of birth from above/Spirit, the Son of Man* to be lifted up, the *unique Son of God, the mediator of life and light.*

4.1.4. Jesus, the Messianic Bridegroom, the Son of God and the Life-Giver (Jn 3,22-36: Baptist-episode)[259]

This episode narrates the simultaneous *baptizing ministries* of Jesus in the Judean countryside and John the Baptist at Aenon near Salim in Samaria before his imprisonment (3,22-24). This leads to a *dialogue* between the Baptist and his disciples (3,25-30) and his ensuing *discourse* (3,31-36). Here Jesus is revealed primarily through *John's testimony* (3,26-36; cf. 1,19-36).

When John realizes that his disciples are jealous of Jesus' successful baptizing ministry, John reminds them that he is *not the Messiah* but only his messenger or precursor (3,28; cf. 1,20.23). He states clearly that *Jesus* is *the Messianic bridegroom* and he is only *his friend* (3,29). All those who go to Jesus and become his disciples are God's gift to him (3,27); they may be likened to the bride of the (Messianic) bridegroom (3,29). As a selfless friend of the Messiah, John is ready to decrease so that Jesus may increase (3,30). In brief, in and through his *self-emptying testimony* John the Baptist manifests *Jesus* as *the Messianic bridegroom* (3,25-30).

John's self-emptying leads him to grasp the *mystery of the mission and person of Jesus*, the beloved Son of God and the mediator of eternal life (3,31-36). Here he discloses that Jesus is *more than a human Messiah* since he has "*come from above/heaven*" (3,31), and that he is the *ideal witness* to the heavenly mysteries which "he has seen and heard" (3,32). Jesus is *God's apostle* par excellence because he speaks the words of God who fills him with *the Spirit of God* (3,34). He is the *beloved Son of God* to whom the Father has entrusted everything (3,35). Those who believe in him *have eternal life* (3,36). "Eternal life" here is not a future reality (life after death) but a *present reality* (divine life here and now) which Jesus, the Son of God, *mediates* to the believers (3,15-16.36).

©John the Baptist (as a faithful friend) bears testimony to Jesus as *the Messianic Bridegroom, God's Apostle and Beloved Son, the Mediator of the Spirit and Eternal Life to the believers.*

4.1.5. Jesus, the Samaritan Prophetic Messiah,[260] Giver of Living Water (Holy Spirit) and the Saviour of the World (Jn 4,1-42: Samaritan-episode)[261]

When Jesus learns that reports about his great success in making disciples and baptizing have reached the ears of the Pharisees, he leaves the Judean countryside for Galilee (4,1-3).

Following an inner impulse (divine necessity, *edei*, "*he had to*" 4,4) to go through Samaria, Jesus walks through the scorching Judean desert and reaches the Samaritan city of Sychar at noon. After the tiring journey, he feels thirsty and so he sits beside Jacob's well (4,4-6). A woman comes there to draw water and he asks her to give him a drink (4,7). It shocks her because Jesus is a Jewish rabbi, while she is a Samaritan woman (4,9).[262] Since the Jews regarded the Samaritans to be impure (because of mixed blood through intermarriage with the Gentiles) and the Samaritan women to be perpetually 'unclean' ("the daughters of the Samaritans are menstruants from their cradle"), the Jews would avoid drinking from the vessels used by Samaritan women. Here Jesus goes against the taboos and prejudices between the Jews and the Samaritans and breaks the discriminatory social barrier by asking to drink from the Samaritan woman's vessel (4,7.9). Furthermore, he *promises* to give her "*living water*" (4,10). Since he does not have a bucket to draw water from the deep well of Jacob, she questions him: "From where (*pothen*) do you have this living water?" (4,11). Ironically she asks him if he claims to be greater than Jacob! (4,12). He tells her that the water that he would give her, unlike ordinary water from Jacob's well, would quench her thirst once and for all because it would become a fountain within her (4,13-14).

"*Living water*" refers to moving water, flowing water, fountain water, the water of streams and rivers, as opposed to 'dead water,' that is, stagnant water in ponds, wells or cisterns, since movement is associated with life. "Living water" is the symbol of something spiritual that leads to eternal life: "the water that I shall give her/him will become in her/him a spring of water gushing/leaping up to eternal life" (4,14). Jesus does not say that he is the "*living water*," nor does he identify it with eternal life. Later the Evangelist will clarify that "living water" refers to the *Holy Spirit* that the glorified risen Jesus will give to those who believe in him (cf. 7,37-39).

Although the Samaritan woman may not have understood the symbolical/spiritual meaning of the "living water", she requests Jesus to give it to her (4,15). Now he tells her: "Go, call your man (*andra*) and come here" (4,16) but she answers: "I have no husband" (*andra*) (4,17). Jesus gently challenges her to look into her dissolute life of having had "five men" (*pente gar andras esches*) in the past and of having now one who is not her "husband" (*anêr*) (4,18).[263] Jesus' intuitive knowledge of her immoral life inspires her to confess him as a *prophet* ("I perceive that you are a prophet" 4,19).

Now Jesus engages in an *inter-religious dialogue* with the Samaritan woman about the place and nature of *true worship* (4,20-24). When she asks him about the right *place of worship* (mount Gerizim or Jerusalem), he tells her that what is important in worshipping God (the Father) is not the 'place' (4,21) but the *way* of worship: "True worshippers must worship the Father *in Spirit and truth*" (4,23). Here Jesus is not opposed to external worship (e.g., in the Temple at Jerusalem or on Mount Gerizim), since he himself frequently visits the Temple in Jerusalem to celebrate the Jewish feasts (cf. 2,13; 5,1.14; 7,10.14; 10,22-23; 12,12). He insists that "true worshippers" (whether they are Jews, Samaritans, or Gentiles) must *worship God as "the Father"* (4,23). Since God is "Spirit" (4,24), that is, spiritual, he must be worshipped "*in Spirit and truth*," that is, under the influence and guidance of the Spirit of truth (cf. 14,17; 15,26; 16,13). Since Jesus is "the truth" (14,6), the revelation of God "the Father full of grace and truth" (1,14), and since the greatest gift of truth ("the grace and the truth") is mediated through Jesus (1,17), the latter can enlighten and empower humans to worship God "*in truth*" (4,23-24).

> In short, true worship consists in worshipping God as the Father in a filial manner according to the revelation in and through Jesus, the incarnate Son of God, and under the constant influence of the [indwelling] Spirit of Jesus, the Spirit of truth. It is such *filial worship in the Spirit* of God's incarnate Son that is pleasing to God the Father (4,23-24).[264]

When the woman tells Jesus about the *Samaritan expectation* in the coming of *a prophetic Messiah* who is to reveal and settle all disputes about religious worship (4,25), Jesus manifests his Messianic identity to her: "I am (*egô eimi*), the one speaking to you" (4,26). Significantly, Jesus reveals himself to be the expected Messiah, *the Samaritan Messiah*, to a woman, a Samaritan woman, a sinful Samaritan woman, at the end of an inter-religious dialogue (4,19-26). This is the only instance in the Gospel of John (4,26) in which Jesus openly tells anyone that he is *the Messiah*. A *woman* is the *privileged recipient* of this *unique Messianic self-revelation of Jesus.*

The Samaritan woman goes to her people in the city and invites them to "*come and see… the Christ*" (4,28-29). Because of her witness to *Jesus* as *the Messiah* (4,29), many Samaritans begin to believe in Jesus (4,39) and are persuaded to come and meet him at Jacob's well. Seeing them coming towards him (4,35), he invites his disciples to reap the harvest of the seed/word of God sown by Jesus in the heart of the Samaritan woman and who, in turn, has sown it in the hearts of her people (4,36-38). They gladly invited Jesus to stay in their homes which he gladly accepted and was their guest for two days (4,40). Now by listening to his word "many more believed" (4,41). Because of their close interaction with him during the short stay, the *Samaritans confess* their unshakable faith in *Jesus* as the *universal Saviour*: "we know for certain (*oidamen*) that this is indeed *the Saviour of the world*" (4,42).

Jesus' *prophetic teaching-pedagogy* in 4,4-42 is also noteworthy. Jesus breaks the Jewish-Samaritan social barrier by asking the Samaritan woman for a drink (4,7). Her racial prejudice (4,9), her biting irony (4,11-12), her slowness in understanding (4,13-15) and her immoral life (4,16-18) do not prevent Jesus from engaging in a meaningful *dialogue* with her on true worship of God and the expected Messiah (4,19-26). It is noteworthy that in John's Gospel Jesus *reveals his Messianic identity* only *to the Samaritan woman*: "I am, the one speaking to you" (4,26). The dialogue Jesus had with the Samaritan woman is the longest recorded conversation in Jn (4,7-26), as a result of which she becomes *a disciple of Jesus*. Significantly, the sinful Samaritan woman's encounter with Jesus has transformed her into *an effective missionary* who succeeds in bringing her people to the Messiah through her testimony (4,28-30). Jesus also does a *prophetic act of solidarity with the Samaritans* by *staying with them* for two days (4,40).

©The Samaritan episode reveals Jesus, as *the giver of living water (Holy Spirit), the prophet and teacher of true worship, the Samaritan Messiah and the Saviour of the world.*

4.1.6. Jesus, the Prophet/Messiah and the Lord of Life (Jn 4,43-54: Second Cana Sign)[265]

The opposition of the Jewish leaders to Jesus' Temple-cleansing in Jerusalem (2,18-20) and the negative reaction of the Pharisees to his baptizing ministry in Judean countryside (4,1-2) clearly show that the Jews do not honour him as a *prophet* in his own country (Judea and its capital Jerusalem) (4,44). The Samaritans, however, believe in him (4,39-42) and the Galileans welcome him because of the prophetic act of cleansing the Temple (2,13-17) and the signs done in Jerusalem during the Passover feast (4,45; cf. 2,23).

When Jesus comes back to Cana in Galilee, where he had miraculously changed water into wine, a *royal official* from Capernaum goes to Jesus and begs him to come down and cure his seriously sick son (4,46-47). Jesus replies: "Unless you see signs and wonders you will not believe" (4,48). Jesus tells him (and others like him) *not* to be fascinated by the *miraculous* aspect of the signs, which may mislead them to take him for *a wonder-worker* (cf. 2,23-25), but to see the *symbolic* significance of the signs which manifest him as *the Messiah* (cf. 20,30-31). Disregarding the royal official's obvious desperation (4,47.49), Jesus declines to go down with him to his home in Capernaum but reassures him with the words: "Go; *your son lives*" (4,50). He believes Jesus' word and goes home. Already on the way, he is told by his servants that his son is alive (4,51) and he finds out that his son was cured at the very same hour that Jesus had said the life-giving word: "your son lives" (4,52-53). Jesus *heals the Gentile official's dying son* with a healing word not only as a powerful *prophet* (4,44) but also as *the Lord of life*. Probably at the time of the healing, the royal official (and his family members) might have believed in Jesus only as a mighty prophet (cf. 4,53; 4,44-45), but later, after the resurrection of Jesus, they believed in him as the "Lord" (4,49; 20,28). Thus, the "sign" of Jesus' saving a dying child from death becomes a symbol of his power to grant eternal life to all those (Jews or Gentiles) who believe in him (cf. 20,30-31).

The second Cana-sign of healing the royal official's son manifests Jesus as *the prophet/Messiah and the Lord of life.*

4.1.© Revelation of the Person and Mission of Jesus in Jn 2-4[266]

In Jn 2-4 Jesus manifests himself to various people differently in their diverse life-situations by responding to them creatively.

> To *sum up*, in each one of the six episodes Jesus *reveals* some aspect or other of his *person and mission* through words and deeds, miraculous signs or symbolic actions. The two Cana-signs at the beginning and end of this Section manifest Jesus as *the Messiah* of the Jews and the Gentiles. That he is also the Samaritan Messiah is explicitly stated at 4,25-26. Furthermore, he is confessed as '*the Saviour of the world*' at 4,42. That he is more than a human Messiah/Saviour is hinted at during the cleansing of the temple and Jesus' dialogue with the woman of Samaria because he calls God 'my Father' or 'the Father.' That is to say, these two episodes point not only to Jesus' Messiahship but also to his *divine Sonship*. The central episodes (Jesus' dialogue-discourse with Nicodemus and the Baptist's dialogue-discourse with his disciples) present Jesus not only as of *the Son of Man* and the *Messianic bridegroom* (3,13-15.28-29) but also as *the unique Son of God* and *the mediator of eternal life* to those who believe in him (3,16-18.35-36).[267]

However, what is stressed most in Jn 2-4 as a whole is that *Jesus is the Universal Messiah* (the Messiah of all peoples: Jews, Samaritans and Gentiles), the Saviour of all humans.

4.2. Jesus, the Co-worker/Son of God (Jn 5-10)[268]

The Evangelist explicitly states in the Conclusion (20,30-31) that one of the primary purposes of writing the Gospel is to help the readers to believe and to deepen their faith in Jesus as "*the Son of God*" (cf. 20,31).

The theme of Jesus' *divine Sonship* is introduced already in the Prologue. It proclaims the pre-existence and the divinity of the Word of God: "In the beginning was the Word..., and the Word was *God*" (1,1). Further, the incarnate Word is described as "a *unique one* (*monogenês*) [Word/Son] from the Father" (1,14) and as "a *unique God (monogenês theos)*, who is in the bosom of the Father" (1,18).

Whereas in Jn 2-4 Jesus, the Messiah, did miraculous signs at the request of somebody pleading for his intervention (his mother and the royal official in the first and second Cana sign respectively), in Jn 5-10 Jesus, *the Son of God,* takes the *initiative* to work miracles for the sake of the sick and the hungry, the helpless and the hopeless. Thus, he cures a cripple at the pool of Bethzatha (5,1-9), provides food for the hungry crowd in Galilee (6,1-15), rescues his disciples from drowning in the stormy sea (6,16-21), and gives sight to a blind beggar on a Sabbath (9,1-7). *The Son of God responds spontaneously and compassionately to persons in need*, even without their asking him for any help.

Jn 5-10 consists of the following ***six Episodes***: *1) The Work of Curing a Cripple by the Son of God (on a Sabbath) (5,1-47);*

2) Feeding 5000, Sea-Rescue, Bread of Life (before Passover) (6,1-71); 3) Source of Living Water and the Light of the World (during Tabernacles) (7,1-8,59); 4) Giving Sight to the Man Born Blind (on a Sabbath) (9,1-41); 5) Sheepfold, Gate & the Life-Giving Good Shepherd (10,1-21); 6) The Works & the Identity of the Son of God (during Dedication) (10,22-42).[269] It may be noted that the above six episodes take place on the Sabbath or during important Jewish feasts such as the Passover, Tabernacles and Dedication.

Whereas the miracles in Jn 2-4 were always described as "signs" (which manifest Jesus as the Messiah), those in Jn 5-10 are sometimes referred as "signs" and at other times as "works" (which reveal him as the Son of God). But the "*works*" of Jesus are underscored in Jn 5-10. A*ll the six episodes* in Jn 5-10 mention *Jesus' works* (which disclose his divine Sonship). In the first episode (the curing of the cripple on a Sabbath) and the last (the Jews' rejection of Jesus at the Feast of Dedication), Jesus highlights in detail the significance of his *works* (cf. 5,17.20.36; 10,25.32.33.37.38) and its relationship to his *divine Sonship* (cf. "*the Son of God*" at 5,25; 10,36; "*the Son*" at 5,19.20.21.22.23.26). By presenting himself as *the Coworker of God,* Jesus reveals himself as *the Son of God.*

4.2.1. Jesus, the Co-worker and the Son of God (Jn 5,1-47: Curing a Cripple and Discourse)

This Section (Jn 5,1-47) consists of *two subsections: a) Work of Curing a Cripple on a Sabbath (5,1-18),* and *b) Discourse on God's Coworker/Son and His Witnesses (5,19-47).*

a) *Work of Curing a Cripple on a Sabbath (Jn 5,1-18)*

Jesus sees a multitude of invalids at the pool of Bethzatha in Jerusalem but takes special notice of a *lame man* who has been *ill for 38 years* and has been lying there alone for a long time without anyone to help him. The compassionate Jesus has the *preferential option* for the most marginalised and abandoned man and takes the initiative to cure him of his crippling sickness (5,1-9).

First, Jesus assesses the cripple's *desire to be healed* by asking him, "Do you want to get well?" (5,6). When Jesus tries to arouse in him the will to get well, he expresses his total helplessness. He is a 'nobody' with "nobody to throw" him "into the pool when the water is stirred" (5,7). Secondly, instead of throwing him into the water, Jesus *cures* him through his encouraging and healing *word*: "Rise, take up your mat and walk" (5,8). Jesus' life-giving word empowers him to stand on his own feet without anybody's help. His powerful word gives him the strength not only to get up and walk but also to carry his mat (5,9). Thirdly, through this healing miracle, Jesus reveals himself to be a *caring human being* (like 'the good Samaritan' in Lk 10,25-37).

Jesus cures the cripple by asking him to carry his mat, even though it is a Sabbath (5,1-9). This healing miracle on the Sabbath reveals Jesus not only as a caring person but also as one having *authority* to interpret the *original purpose* of the Sabbath as the *integral well-being* of human beings ("The Sabbath was made for man, not man for the Sabbath": Mk 2,27). Even though the cured cripple is ignorant of the healer's identity (Jn 5,13), Jesus is concerned not only about the cripple's physical health but also about his spiritual well-being. Therefore, he finds him in the Temple and tells him: "See, you have been made well! Do not sin any more" (5,14). But the cured cripple betrays his benefactor by revealing his identity to "the Jews" (*Jewish leaders*) who are hostile to the healer (5,15-16). As a result, they *persecute Jesus* as one who *breaks the Sabbath law* (5,16), turning the miracle story (5,1-9) into a conflict story (5,10-16).

Now Jesus tells his persecutors that by curing the sick, he is not guilty of violating the Sabbath because he is only giving a helping hand to God the Father in his life-giving work even on a Sabbath: "My Father is working still, and I am working" (5,17). But the religious *leaders accuse him of blasphemy* and even try to kill him (5,18; cf. also 10,33). However, instead of running away from the murderous leaders, he courageously defends himself as *God's Co-worker/Son* who faithfully does the works of the Father. Jesus explains how *his works reveal his divine identity: his praxis manifests his person* (5,17.19-30; cf. also 10,31.34-38) and he cites many *witnesses* in his favour (5,31-47).

b) Discourse on God's Co-worker/Son and His Witnesses (Jn 5,19-47).

(i) *The union of the Co-worker/Son of God with the Father* (Jn 5,19-30)

Since the Jewish leaders misunderstand Jesus' statement: "My Father is working still, and I am working" (5,17), he explains its meaning in the discourse that follows in 5,19-30.

> Starting with the metaphor of a father and a son (5,19-20), Jesus shows that he is very dependent on the Father in everything that he does (5,19.30). In traditional societies, an apprentice/son learns his father's trade (e.g., carpentry) by watching him and working under his guidance (5,19) for the father loves the son and shows him all the tricks of the trade (5,20). Similarly,

> Jesus, the Son of God, learns every work from the Father who loves him tenderly and shows him everything that he does (5,19-20.30). God the Father empowers the Son to do the divine works of calling the dead from the tombs and raising them to eternal life or judgement (5,28-29). Because the Son shares in the very life of the Father (5,26), the Son, like the Father, can even raise the dead and give them life (5,21). Likewise, God the Father has given the divine-human Son the divine authority to judge all humans (5,22.27). Hence, to avoid condemnation and enter eternal life, all must listen to the Son (5,24-25).[270]

Here the Johannine Jesus makes it clear that "*the Son*" is *dependent* on "the Father" who loves him (5,19-20), shares his life with him (5,26) and gives him his life-giving and judging functions (5,21-24.28-29; cf. also 6,40).

(ii) *Witnesses to Jesus, the Son of God* (Jn 5,31-47)

Jesus defends himself against the religious authorities' accusation of Sabbath-violation and blasphemy (5,16.18) by presenting a variety of *witnesses* in his favour, such as John the Baptist, his works, the Father, the Scriptures and Moses (5,31-47).

> First of all, *John the Baptist*, "a burning and shining lamp" (5,35), testified to the truth (5,33) that Jesus is "the Lamb of God" (1,29.36) and "the Son of God" (1,34), who baptizes with the Holy Spirit (1,33). Secondly, the *works* that Jesus does bear witness to his mission from God the Father (5,36; cf. also 10,25.36). ... Thirdly, the *Father* himself, who sent him, has testified on Jesus' behalf (5,37), which seems to be a reference to the divine revelation at his baptism (cf. 1,33) [cf. also Mk 1,8.11; Mt 3,17]. Finally, the *Scriptures* bear testimony to Jesus, in which "the Jews" hoped to find eternal life (5,39.47). ["Great is *Torah*, for it gives to them that practice it life in this age and in the age to come" (*Pirqe Aboth* vi,7).] In fact, he claims that *Moses*, whom "the Jews" regarded as the author of the Pentateuch, wrote about him (5,46; cf. Deut 18,18).[271]

©To sum up, *Jesus' work* of *curing the cripple on the Sabbath* and the ensuing *discourse* disclose Jesus as *the Co-worker/Son of God* and *the Revealer of the Father.*

4.2.2. Jesus, the Final Prophet, "I Am", the Bread of Life and the Holy One of God (Jn 6,1-71: Bread of Life-episode)

This *dramatic episode* consists of *five scenes*: *a) The Sign of Feeding the Five Thousand (6,1-15); b) Jesus' Walking on the Stormy Sea (6,16-21); c) Jesus' Dialogue-Discourse on the Bread of Life (6,22-59); d) The Disciples' Desertion of Jesus (6,60-66); e) The Twelve's Faith in Jesus (6,67-71).*[272]

a) Jesus' Sign of Feeding the Five Thousand (Jn 6,1-15)

Seeing the healing signs that Jesus was doing, crowds began following him. Before the feast of the Passover he went up on a mountain and sat down with his disciples (6,1-4). Contemplating the large multitude coming to him, he feels compassion for the hungry. Unlike the Synoptic Jesus who first teaches the crowd and then gives them food to eat (cf. Mk 6,34-44), the Johannine Jesus is keen on feeding them first because food is the urgent need of all hungry persons. Gandhiji used to say that God can appear to a hungry man only in the form of bread. So Jesus takes the initiative to feed the hungry multitude. He asks Philip: "From where [*pothen*] are we to buy bread for these people to eat?" (Jn 6,5). Philip thinks that it would cost an enormous amount of money ("two hundred denarii") (6,7) but Andrew informs Jesus about a boy who has "five barley loaves and two small fish", which, however, are next to nothing in the current situation (6,8-9). To teach the disciples to trust in him, Jesus tells them to make the multitude of about five thousand to recline for a meal (6,10).

Now Jesus took the lad's five loaves and two fish and, after giving thanks to God, distributed them to those who were reclining till they are fully satisfied (6,11-12). It is noteworthy that here it is Jesus himself (not the disciples, as in the Synoptic Gospels) who distributes the food to the crowd (6,11: "*he distributed* them to those who were seated"). Here the miracle of the multiplication of the loaves and the fish seems to take place in the hands of Jesus himself.

Seeing the great "sign" done by Jesus, the people perceive that he is the long-expected (Messianic) *prophet* whom God has sent into the world (6,14; cf. 11,27). The over-enthusiastic crowd is keen to crown him their king but he "withdraws to the mountain by himself" (6,15), making it clear to them that he is *not a political king* who seeks worldly kingdom, royal power and glory.[273] Thus, through the *sign of feeding the five thousand*, Jesus reveals himself as the long-awaited *final prophet* (who is concerned about the poor and the hungry people) but *not* a worldly king.

b) Jesus' Walking on the Stormy Sea (Jn 6,16-21)[274]

When the disciples are struggling hard to row the boat in the turbulent sea at night, Jesus comes to them *walking on the stormy sea* (6,16-19). As they see him approaching the boat, they get frightened, but he tells them: "I am" (*egô eimi*); "do not be afraid" (6,20). "I am" has a double meaning or two levels of meaning: "*It is I*" (I am Jesus) and the *divine* "*I am*".

> At the historical level, the Greek expression *egô eimi* ["I am"] would have meant "It is I" (Jesus). But at the post-Easter level, after Jesus is already confessed as "God" (cf. 20,28), *egô eimi* would be understood as the divine "*I am*". Just as Yahweh in the burning bush revealed to Moses his divine name as "I am" (cf.

> Ex 3,14), Jesus who comes walking on the stormy sea manifests himself as the divine being "I am" (cf. 8,58).[275]

Jesus reassures his disciples not to be frightened (6,20) because he ("*I am*") is present with them. The Lord's coming to their rescue in the tumultuous sea points also to his being a true shepherd (like Yahweh) who protects them from every harm and does not let them perish (cf. 10,28). When the disciples desire to take him into the boat, he makes them cross the sea miraculously and reach their destination immediately (6,21). In short, Jesus reveals himself as *the divine "I am"* by saving his disciples from drowning in the stormy sea and by taking them safely to the shore.

c) *Jesus' Dialogue-Discourse on the Bread of Life (Jn 6,22-59)*

(i) *Dialogue on the Son of Man and the bread of heaven/God* (Jn 6,22-34)

The crowd whom Jesus had fed with plenty of food the previous day comes to Capernaum in search of him (6,22-24). He rebukes them for seeing him as a mere wonder-worker who satisfies their immediate physical needs but failing to see the symbolic significance of the signs (6,26). He advises them not to work for perishable food (like ordinary bread) but for the *imperishable food* which he is going to offer, spiritual food that will endure to eternal life (6,27). This refers to the unique *divine revelation* that will enable believers to have eternal life, which "*the Son of Man*" (the human Jesus) will give them when he will be lifted on the cross (cf. 3,14-15; 8,28; 12,32-34). Jesus is already appointed by God to reveal him as the Father but this supreme revelation will take place especially on the cross (8,28; 12,32). God the Father has already set his seal on this unique revelatory Son of Man (6,27). The cross is the Father's seal by which he attests the truth and the authority of Jesus, the Son of Man. The cross is Christ's credential or signet ring from the Father. Jesus tells the people to believe in him whom God has sent as his revealer (6,29).

The people ask Jesus to do a sign (marvellous miracle) like Moses' manna ("bread from heaven") in the wilderness so that they may believe in him (6,30-31). Jesus tells them that it was not Moses but God who gave them "bread from heaven," and it is his Father who gives them "the true bread from heaven" (6,32). Manna only fore-shadowed the genuine heavenly bread that gives life to the world (6,33). If manna was a symbol of God's gift of the Law through Moses (1,17), the final gift of God's revelation became a reality through Jesus Christ (1,17). If manna was God's gift of "bread from heaven" to the people of Israel in the desert, now God the Father offers humanity his greatest gift, the *true bread from heaven/God* that gives life to the whole world (6,32-33).

(ii) *Discourse on the bread of life (Jn 6,35-51)*

When the people plead with him for this life-giving bread: "Lord, give us this bread always" (6,34), Jesus discloses to them: "I am the bread of life" (6,35). "He is the revelation of life, the bread that nourishes life. He is *the bread of life* which has come down from heaven (6,35.38.41.42) and which will eternally fulfil the hunger and thirst of those who believe in him (6,35) by enabling them to have eternal life (6,40)."[276] Just as anyone's physical hunger is not satisfied by simply seeing a loaf of bread but by eating it, so one's spiritual hunger will not be sated by merely looking at Jesus, the bread of life, but by believing in him and assimilating the revelation of life in him so that the believer may share in the eternal life of the Father and the Son (6,40).

"The Jews", however, murmur against Jesus ("the son of Joseph") and contest his claim to have "come down from heaven" because they claim to know his human origin (his father and his mother) (6,41-42). Jesus exposes their "murmuring" (6,43) as a sign of their unbelief as in the case of their ancestors in the wilderness (Ex 16,2.7; 17,3). The Father who sent him draws people to Jesus; all those who listen and learn from the Father come to him in faith (6,44-45), thus fulfilling the prophetic promise that "all shall be taught by God" (Is 54,13). This does not, however, mean that anyone has ever seen the Father, except the one who is from God (6,46). Only the one who is in the bosom of the Father has seen God (1,18; 6,46). The unique God/Son who is turned toward the face of the Father has made God the Father known (1,1.18).

Anyone who believes in Jesus' revelation of the Father has eternal life (6,47) because Jesus is the *bread of life* (6,48), the *revelation of life*, the bread that *gives life* and *nourishes life*. This bread is quite different from manna. Whereas the Israelites who ate manna in the wilderness lived a normal human lifetime at the end of which they died, those who eat this bread from heaven, the *living bread*, will not die but will continue to live even after death (6,49-51). Compared to Jesus, the living bread, the manna was dead bread and so those who ate it are dead, whereas those who eat the living bread will continue to live forever. Since Jesus, the Son, participates in the divine life of the Father (5,26), those who "eat" this "bread of life" (6,48), that is, assimilate the revelation of life (6,50.51), *will live forever* (6,51).[277]

(iii) *(Eucharistic) discourse on Jesus' flesh and blood (Jn 6,51-58)*

Jesus makes a surprising promise: "the bread that I will give for the life of the world is my flesh" (6,51). It has a *double meaning.* According to Johannine anthropology, a human being is made of "flesh" (*sarx*) and "soul" (*psychê*). Or, every human being is an animated flesh or an enfleshed soul. Jesus' death involves the "giving (up)" of his "flesh" (body) on the cross "for the sake of" (*hyper*) the life of the "world" (humanity) (6,51) and the "laying down" of his "soul" (life) (10,15.17.18; 15,13). But because Jesus is also Spirit-filled (cf. 1,33; 3,34), when he dies he "hands over the Spirit" (19,30). It is by dying on the cross, by giving (up) his flesh (6,51) and laying down his life (15,13), that Jesus gives the life-giving Spirit to human beings (6,63; 19,30). "This is the mystery of life through death (like the fruit-bearing death of the grain of wheat which falls to the ground: 12,24). It is like the death of a loving mother who chooses to die during delivery to give life to her baby. Paradoxically, *Jesus' death on the cross reveals the mystery of life* for the world."[278] In short, Jesus' *death* is *salvific and life-giving.*

Jesus' words "the bread that I will give for the life of the world is my flesh" (6,51) refer to his self-gift in the *Eucharist.* [This declaration of Jesus is a *bridge* between his discourse on "the bread of life" (6,35-51) and the "Eucharistic" discourse (6,51-58).]

"The Jews", however, take "flesh" (in 6,51) literally and so they dispute among themselves: "How can this man give us his flesh to eat?" (6,52). Jesus' answer is given in 6,53-58,[279] in which he interprets the *meaning of the Eucharist* in terms of *(eternal) life.* By insisting that eating his flesh and drinking his blood is the *sine qua non* for "*having (eternal) life*" (6,53-54), he is not telling the Jews to kill him and eat his flesh like cannibals and drink his blood like leeches. The Hebrew expression "flesh and blood" refers to a *mortal human being* (cf. Mt 16,17), and so the expression *eating Jesus' flesh and drinking his blood* means *appropriating* the whole *person/self* revealed in his humanity ("whoever *eats me...*" in v.57 is parallel to "whoever *eats my flesh and drinks my blood...*" in v.54). Only God the Father and the Son have life in themselves (5,26). Therefore, to have eternal life in us (6,53-54), we have to *assimilate and appropriate the incarnate (enfleshed) Son of God.*

In fact, by participating in the Eucharist an intimate loving communion of *mutual immanence* is established between Christ and the communicants ("those... abide in me and I in them": 6,56). Through holy communion, Christ comes into their stomachs, bodies, hearts and lives, and remains in them ("I in them": 6,56). Just as the food that is eaten and assimilated becomes part of the human person, so Christ becomes *one* with the person who receives him. In other words, *the Eucharistic Christ becomes the Christian* who receives the Eucharist. Because of this Eucharistic mystery, a Christian can say: "I and Christ are one," just as Jesus says: "I and the Father are one" (10,30). The life-relationship between Christ and the Christian who appropriates his life ("eats me") is like the life-relationship between the Father and Jesus: "As the living Father sent me, and as I live because of the Father, so whoever eats me will live because of me" (6,57). The Father is "living" because he "has life in himself" (5,26) and by participating in the *life of the Father*, the ultimate source of life, *the Son* "lives" or "has life in himself" (cf. 5,26). The living Father has sent the living Son into this world so that human beings may share in their divine life. The Eucharist enables us to *live the divine life* of God the Father and the incarnate Son (6,57). Jesus is the true bread that has come down from heaven/God by eating which we will live forever (will have everlasting divine life), unlike the manna that the Israelite ancestors ate in the desert which could not grant them immortality (6,58; cf. also vv. 49-51).

d) *The Disciples' Desertion of Jesus (Jn 6,60-66)*

Many of his disciples are scandalized by Jesus' discourse on the bread of life and the Eucharist. So he asks them to examine it in the light of the *Son of Man's Paschal Mystery* (of passion-death-resurrection-ascension) when the *life-giving Spirit* would be given (6,60-63; cf. 7,39; 19,30; 21,22). He reassures them that his words are "spirit and life" (6,63; cf. 6,68), that is, spiritual and living, but some of them do not believe (6,64). He *knows* the identities of both the *unbelieving* disciples and the future *betrayer* (6,64). Faith is a gift from the Father (6,65) because he "draws" (attracts) people to come to Jesus in faith (cf. 6,44). But many of the disciples resist to be drawn to Jesus and they turn back and no longer go about with him (6,66).

e) *The Twelve's Faith in Jesus (Jn 6,67-71)*

When many of Jesus' disciples desert him (6,66), he *challenges the Twelve* to take a personal and collective decision to leave him or to remain with him: "Do you also want to go away?" (6,67). As the spokesman of the Twelve, Simon Peter professes their faith in Jesus: "*Lord*, to whom shall we go? You have the *words of eternal life*, and we have believed and have known that you are *the Holy One of God*" (6,68-69). They do not want to go away because Jesus speaks the words of eternal life (not words about eternal life but words which have the power to give eternal life) because he is the eternal divine Word that has become incarnate (1,1.14) and who shares in the very life of the Father (5,26). In short, Jesus has the *life-giving words* (6,68) and the Twelve have believed and have known experientially (*egnôkamen*) that he is "*the Holy One of God*" (6,69). Simon Peter and his companions believed that, just as Samson was chosen and consecrated ("set apart" LXX: Jg 13,5.7; 16,17: "God's holy one") to free the Israelites from the Philistines, Jesus would liberate them from the Roman rule. But since the term "holy" (*hagios*) is used in the Gospel of John to refer only to God the Father (17,11), the Spirit (1,33; 7,39; 14,26; 20,22) and to Jesus (6,69), the title "the Holy One of God" has a deeper significance in the post-Easter period, namely, he *belongs to the sphere or divine nature of God*. This is clear from the Prologue ("the Word was God [*theos*]": 1,1) and Thomas' confession of faith in the risen Jesus ("My Lord and my God" 20,28).

©We may sum up the *Christology of Jn 6* as follows: Jesus is *the final prophet, the divine "I Am", the Son of Man, the revelatory and Eucharistic bread of life, the donor of the life-giving Spirit, the Lord of the words of eternal life and the Holy One of God.*[280]

4.2.3. *Jesus, the Prophet, the Messiah, the Source of Living Water, the Light of the World and "I Am" (Jn 7,1-8,59: Discussions on Jesus' Mission and Identity)*

In Jn 7-8 there is a lot of *discussion* between Jesus and his brothers, the crowds, "the Jews" and the Pharisees and among themselves *about his mission and identity*, which they fail to grasp because they do not understand his origin and destination.

a) Jesus, the Teacher, the Prophet and the Messiah (Jn 7,1-36)
Now the Jewish feast of Tents/Tabernacles/Booths (which recalled the Israelites' living in tents during their wandering in the wilderness) was near but Jesus was reluctant to go from Galilee to Jerusalem since "the Jews" (Jewish leaders) there were seeking to kill him (7,1-2; cf. 5,18). But his unbelieving "brothers" in Galilee were tempting him to go up to Judea publicly for the most popular festival of Tents and to "show" himself openly to the multitudes,[281] which he refused to do because his appropriate "time" (*kairos*) had not yet come (7,3-9). But later he went up for the feast not publicly but secretly so that "the Jews" (Jewish authorities) would not come to know his whereabouts (7,10-11).

In his absence, there was a lot of hushed talk among the crowds in Jerusalem and there was a *division of opinion* among them: some saying "He is good" (*agathos estin*), but others saying "No, but he leads the crowd astray" (*plana ton ochlon*) (7,12; cf. also 7,47). Here the issue is not whether Jesus is a "good man" (*pace* RSV translation) but whether he is a *"good" prophet* who leads the people to God or a "false" *prophet* who leads them far away from God.[282]

"About the *middle of the feast* Jesus went up into the temple and taught" (7,14). When "the Jews" marvel at his great learning (7,15), he tells them that his *teaching* is not his own but from God who has sent him to teach them in his name and with his authority, and hence Jesus is an *authentic and authoritative teacher* (7,16-18.28-29).

Similarly, while some believe in Jesus as *the Messiah* because of his many "signs" (7,31.41), others refuse to accept him as the Christ because they claim to know Jesus' place of origin ("we know from where [*pothen*] he is" 7,27), namely, "from Galilee" (7,41), and because, according to Scripture, "Christ is a descendant of David and comes from Bethlehem, the village of David" (7,42; cf. 2 Sam 7,12; Mic 5,2). So there is a *division of opinion* among the people about *Jesus' Messianic identity* (7,43).

b) Jesus, the Source of Living Water (Jn 7,37-39)

During the week-long celebration of Tabernacles, the priests daily went down to the pool of Siloam, and with the people in procession, would bring some of its water to the Temple. After going round the altar of holocaust, they would pour the water on the altar. This symbolic action was a reminder to the people of God's gift of water from the rock at Horeb in the wilderness (cf. Ex 17,1-7; Num 20,1-11) and it was also a symbolic prayer of the people to God for rain.

On the *last day of the feast* during the solemn ceremony of the pouring of the water of the Siloam pool on the altar of holocaust, Jesus stood up and proclaimed: "If anyone thirsts let him come to me, and let him drink who believes in me. As the scripture has said, 'Out of his belly/heart shall flow rivers of living water'" (7,37-38).[283] *Jesus* is the *primary source* of the "*living water*" because *Jesus' body* is the *new temple* (cf. 2,21) from which "rivers of living water" will flow (cf. Ezek 47,1-12; Joel 3,18; Zech 14,8; Jn 19,34). The Evangelist tells us clearly that the "*living water*" is the symbol of the *Holy Spirit*, which will be given by the glorified Jesus to those who believe in him (7,39; cf. 19,30; 20,22). Like lady Wisdom (Prov 9,5), Jesus invites those who are thirsty to come to him and drink (Jn 7,37), the only condition being that they should believe in him (7,38).

The "living water," which the believers drink from Jesus, will become *a fountain welling up to eternal life* (4,14). Since the glorified risen Jesus gives the Holy Spirit to the disciples and sends them to continue his mission (cf. 20,21-22), they are meant to be Spirit-filled persons from whom others can drink the "living water." In other words, *Jesus* is the *prime source* (like a *spring* or *fountain*) of "living water" (7,37-38). The *believers* who drink from him will, in turn, become *channels* (like rivers whose source is a spring) of "living water" (the Holy Spirit) (7,39; cf. Is 58,11).[284]

c) *The Compassionate Jesus and the Woman Caught in Adultery (Jn 7,53-8,11)*[285]

A woman caught in the act of adultery is produced before Jesus in the Temple by the scribes and Pharisees who demand that Jesus follow the Mosaic Law which insists that adultery must be punished with death by stoning (cf. Lev 20,10; Deut 22,22-24). Hence from the context (of Jn 8,3-11) it is clear that the scribes and Pharisees were not just asking for Jesus' personal opinion whether the adulterous woman must be stoned to death or not! Of course, they have an ulterior motive of trapping Jesus. If he were to say not to stone her to death, he would be accused of not obeying the Mosaic Law; if he were to say to stone her, he would be branded as non-forgiving!!

It must also be noted that the scribes and the Pharisees do not produce witnesses against her and selectively apply the law of Moses only to the woman but not to the man who committed adultery with her! Jesus, knowing their double standard and hypocrisy, challenges them to stone her if they themselves are not guilty of the sin of adultery: "Let him who is without *sin* among you be the first *to throw a stone at her*" (8,7)! The fact that none of them dares *to throw a stone at her* shows that they too are adulterous men (because Jesus was not talking about any 'sin' but about the '*sin of adultery*' in the context.

When the accusers of the adulterous woman depart (8,9) and she is left alone with Jesus, he gently asks her: "Woman, where are they? Has no one condemned you?" (8,10). When she answers: "No one, Lord," he reassures her with his compassionate words: "Neither do I condemn you; go, and do not sin again" (8,11). He does not condone the sin of adultery but shows *compassion to the sinner*. Thus, he reveals himself not only as the *true prophet* and the *merciful Messiah* (7,40) but also as *the Son of God* who was sent into the sinful world *not to condemn sinners* but *to save them* (cf. 3,17). The sinful woman's experience of the *Lord's compassion and forgiveness* enables her to begin *a new life* (8,11).[286]

d) Jesus, the Light of the World, the Unique Witness and Judge (Jn 8,12-20)

During the celebration of the feast of Tabernacles, four large golden lamps were lit on the top of the Temple, which illuminated its surroundings. They symbolized the "pillar of fire" that led the Israelites in the wilderness at night (Ex 13,21), later interpreted as "the imperishable light of the Law" (Wis 18,3-4). Seeing the *Temple-lights* burning bright at night, Jesus proclaims himself as the light, not merely for the Israelites but the whole of humanity: "I am the *light of the world*; whoever follows me will never walk in darkness but will have *the light of life*" (8,12).

> Just as light dispels darkness, Jesus' revelation of God dispels the darkness of ignorance, evil and sin. Just as physical light is needed for human life to exist, Jesus' *revelation of divine life* is

> necessary for humans to have eternal life, provided they believe in the light/revelation and walk in the light (live in accordance with the revelation).[287]

When the Pharisees object to Jesus' testimony on his own behalf as not valid (8,13; cf. Num 35,30; Deut 17,6), he claims that his *testimony* is *unique* because he knows his divine origin and destination, which they do not know (8,14). Like light that is its own witness, Jesus' self-testimony is true and his Father's testimony concurs with his (8,18; cf. 5,37) and therefore the legal requirement of two witnesses is also verified (8,17-18; cf. 5,31-32; Deut 17,6; 19,15). When the Pharisees ask him: "Where is your Father?" he points to himself as the person in whom the Father ("my Father") is present, both of whom they do not know (8,19; cf. 14,9). Hence Jesus, *the light, the revealer*, is a *reliable* and *unique witness* not only to the Father but also to himself.

Light not only reveals itself but also exposes what is hidden in the darkness. Jesus' revelation brings to light both good and evil deeds and reveals the identity of the doers of good and evil. Hence God's revelation in and through his Son results in a *judgement* of the evil-doers (3,19-21). This judgement is *"true" (reliable)* because God the Father whom the Son reveals is with him (8,16) and the Father has granted him the authority to judge (cf. 5,22.27). In other words, the judgement that Jesus' revelatory presence in the world occasions (cf. 9,39) is ratified by the Father (8,15-16). In short, Jesus, *the Son*, the *revealer of the Father*, is an *authoritative judge.*

e) Jesus as "I am" and the Lifted up Son of Man (Jn 8,21-30)

Jesus contrasts "the Jews" who are "*from below*" with himself who is "*from above*" (8,23; cf. 3,31). He tells them to believe in him as "*I am*" (*egô eimi*) lest they should die in their sins (8,24). They are shocked at Jesus' absolute use of "*I am*" and so they ask him about his identity: "*Who are you?*" (8,25). His puzzling reply is: "Just what I am telling you" (8,25), which is a reference back to what he has said in the previous verse 24 ("I am"). He further affirms that he reveals what he has heard from the one who sent him (8,26). Since "the Jews" fail to understand that he is referring to the Father, he tells them that when they will *lift the Son of Man* (on the cross), they will come to know that he is "*I am*" and he does nothing on his own but only what pleases the Father and he speaks only what the Father has taught him (8,28-29). Hence his actions and words manifest who he is but his death on the cross will especially reveal that he is "*I am*" (*egô eimi*). Paradoxically, it is the death of the Son of Man (the man with a mysterious origin) that manifests *his divine identity* (*egô eimi*).[288]

f) Jesus, the Liberating Truth (Jn 8,31-32)

Jesus tells those who have believed him (that is, in his words), "If you remain in my word, you are truly my disciples, and you will know the truth, and the *truth will make you free*" (8,31). Like fish in water, believers must be immersed in Jesus' word to have an experiential knowledge of the mystery of God manifested in and through Jesus, the unique revealer of the Father (cf. 1,14.17-18; 14,6). Like a sponge in water, they must be permeated by Jesus' word so that his revelation penetrates their whole being. The *liberative* truth that he reveals through his words and deeds, life and death on the cross, is that *God is a loving Father* who has sent his unique Son into the world to save it (3,16). This *saving* truth of the unconditional love of God for sinful humans, manifested in his incarnate and crucified Son Jesus, *liberates* believers from the slavery of sin. Furthermore, Jesus, the Son of God, transforms the slaves of sin into free sons and daughters of God (8,34-36; cf. 1,12-13). In short, Jesus is the *liberating truth*.

g) Jesus, the Divine "I Am" (Jn 8,33-59)

"The Jews" (Jewish authorities) claim not to need liberation because they are the descendants of Abraham (8,33). Jesus contests their claim to have Abraham as their father (8,39) because their plot to murder Jesus proves that they are not Abraham's children but those of the devil, a murderer (8,39-44). When Jesus tells "the Jews" that, if they keep his word, they will never die (8,51), they ask him sarcastically if he is greater than their ancestor Abraham who died (8,52-53). Then he solemnly declares: "Amen, amen, I say to you, before Abraham was, *I Am*" (*egô eimi* 8,58). Just as Yahweh had manifested himself to Moses as "I Am who I Am" (Ex 3,14; cf. also Is 43,10.13), here Jesus reveals his *divine identity* as "*I Am*." Because of his claim to be the *divine "I Am,"* "the Jews" try to stone him for blasphemy but he hides himself and escapes (8,59).

© In Jn 7-8 Jesus manifests himself as *the teacher, the prophet, the Messiah, the source of living water, the light of the world, the liberating truth and the divine "I Am"*.

4.2.4. Jesus, the Light of the World, the Prophet, the Messiah and the Son of Man (Jn 9,1-41: Curing the Blind Man)

During the festival of Tents, Jesus revealed himself as "*the light of the world*" (8,12). The miraculous work of giving sight to the man born blind in Jn 9 illustrates this truth (cf. 9,4-5). There is also discussion whether Jesus is a prophet (9,17) or the Messiah (9,22), a sinner or a man from God (9,30-34). Finally, when "the Jews" cast the cured blind man out of the synagogue, Jesus manifests himself to him as *the Son of Man* (9,35-38).[289]

a) Jesus, the Co-worker of God, the Light of the World and the Giver of Sight and Insight (Jn 9,1-17)

As Jesus passes by, he sees a man blind from his birth (9,1). According to the prevalent Jewish belief at that time, sickness was God's punishment for one's sins. So the disciples ask Jesus: "Rabbi, who sinned, this man or his parents, that he was born blind?" (9,2). Jesus categorically denies their contention that sin is the cause of the man's blindness: "Neither this man sinned, nor his parents" (9,3). And he tells his disciples what must be done in such a situation: "But so that (*all' hina*) the works of God may be manifested in him [the blind man], *we must work* the works of the one who sent me, while it is day" (9,3-4).[290] Jesus tells them about the urgency of doing *the works of God* at the favourable time ("while it is day" 9,4). He regards himself as *God's worker* (cf. 5,17) and he considers *his disciples* as *his co-workers* ("*we* must *work...*" 9,4).

It is by healing the blind beggar that Jesus reveals himself as "*the light of the world*" (9,5). He manifests himself as the light of revelation for humankind groping in darkness by giving sight to the blind man (9,5; cf. 8,12). Likewise, the disciples will be "the light of the world" (cf. Mt 5,14) if they do God's works in favour of those who are living in the darkness of despair.

Jesus helps the blind beggar unasked, not by giving him alms but by enabling him to see by *rubbing his eyes gently* with mud mixed with his spittle (9,6). He combines *work* (anointing the man's eyes with mud) and *words* ("Go, wash in the pool of Siloam") in *giving sight* to the man born blind (9,6-7).

Now "*Siloam*" means the "*sent one*" and *Jesus* is *God's* "*sent one*" *par excellence* in the Gospel of John (3,17.34; 5,36.38; 6,29.57; 7,29; 8,42; 9,4; etc.). The anointed blind man gets *physical sight* and gains *spiritual insight* by believing Jesus' word and obeying him by going to the pool of "Siloam" and washing his eyes in the water (9,7). Jesus, the Word of God, is the light that enlightens every human being (cf. 1:9). His *revelatory and saving mission* consists in *giving sight and insight* to the blind.

b) Jesus, the Prophet and the Messiah (Jn 9,8-34)

Now when the cured blind man is questioned by his neighbours and the Pharisees, he proclaims Jesus as the man who gave him sight (9,10-11.15). Furthermore, he publicly confesses *Jesus* as a *prophet* (9,17) and boldly defends him as a *God-fearing person* who has *come from God* and who *does the will of God* (9,30-33). The Jewish authorities cast him out of the synagogue (9,34) according to their earlier decision to expel from the synagogue anyone who confesses Jesus as the Messiah (9,22). The fact of the cured blind man's expulsion from the synagogue proves that he believed in Jesus and confessed him as *the Messiah*.

c) Jesus, the Son of Man (Jn 9,35-41)

Jesus searches and finds the expelled cured blind man and asks him if he believes in "*the Son of Man*" (9,35). When he admits his ignorance about who the Son of Man is but expresses his desire to believe in him, *Jesus* manifests himself as "*the Son of Man*" whom the healed man has already seen and who is now speaking with him (9,36-37). Now the cured blind man confesses his faith in Jesus, the Son of Man, by saying "Lord, *I believe*" and "he prostrated himself before him" (9,38).

Even though Jesus, the Son of God, was sent into the world not to condemn it but to save it (cf. 3,17), he tells the unbelieving and arrogant Pharisees: "For judgement I came into this world, that those who do not see may see and those who see may become blind" (9,39). "Whereas Jesus, the light, is a sight-giving and comforting Son of Man to the blind and the persecuted, he is a blinding light and a judging Son of Man to the obstinate sinners like the proud Pharisees, who arrogantly claim to see and persecute the believers in Jesus (9,39-41)."[291]

© In this dramatic episode of giving sight to the man born blind and his trial by the Pharisees (Jn 9) Jesus is revealed as *the light of the world, the prophet, the Messiah* and *the Son of Man.*

It is noteworthy that, when the Pharisees question the cured blind man, he bears courageous *testimony to Jesus* as *the prophet* and *the Christ*, and, after he is thrown out of the synagogue for speaking the truth about Jesus, Jesus searches for him till he finds him and manifests himself to him as *the Son of Man*. It shows that a faithful witness to Jesus in conflict situations is given the grace of growing in his faith. The *healed blind man* is *an inspiring example* to all the persecuted Christians in different parts of the world today.

4.2.5. *Jesus, the Life-Giving Good Shepherd (Jn 10,1-21: Shepherd-discourse)*

a) *Jesus, the Genuine Shepherd (Jn 10,1-6)*

In the "figure of speech" (*paroimia,* parabolic allegory) of the sheepfold (10,1-6) Jesus compares a true shepherd (who enters the sheep pen openly through the gate) with a thief or a robber (who climbs in stealthily). *Jesus* manifests himself as *the genuine shepherd* to whom the gatekeeper opens the door. He calls his sheep by name and leads them out to pasture by walking in front of them. He loves them, protects them, cares for them and looks after all their needs.

b) Jesus, the Gate (Jn 10,7-10)

Now Jesus identifies himself as *the gate* (*thyra*) through which the sheep can go in for shelter from thieves at night and go out for pasture during the day (10,7.9). He is not like the door of a prison that curtails their freedom but the gate to liberty and prosperity, the gate to abundant life (cf. 10,10). Jesus is *the gate of salvation* (10,9). The purpose of his earthly mission is to *give abundant life* (10,10), life in its fullness, a *life of love and freedom*, a *qualitatively new life* that not even death can destroy.

c) Jesus, the Life-Giving Good Shepherd (Jn 10,11-18)

Prophet Ezekiel had painted the picture of an *ideal shepherd* as follows:

> A *good shepherd* takes care of his sheep, protects them from wild animals, seeks the lost, brings back the strayed, binds up the injured, heals the sick, strengthens the weak, leads them to green pastures and fresh waters (cf. Ezek 34,1-16).[292]

Jesus' definition of *the good shepherd* goes *beyond* the prophetic portrayal of the ideal shepherd, for he says, "The good shepherd *lays down his life for the sheep*" (10,11; cf. also 10,14-18). Jesus, the good shepherd, is ready and willing not only *to risk his life* to protect his sheep from wild animals, thieves and robbers but also *to sacrifice his own life for his sheep*.[293] This meaning of "laying down his life for the sheep" is confirmed by Jesus' later statement: "Greater love has no one than this, that one *lays down his life for his friends*" (15,13). The intimate and mutual knowledge and love between Jesus, the good shepherd, and his sheep, prompt him *to die for* the sake of *his sheep* (10,14-15). Furthermore, this mutual, loving knowledge is of a pattern with and participation in the mutual, loving knowledge of the Father and his beloved Son Jesus (10,15). Therefore, Jesus is *the good shepherd par excellence.*

Jesus gladly tells "the Jews": "And I have *other sheep* that are *not from this fold*" (*ha ouk estin ek tês aulês tautês*: 10,16).[294] He is the shepherd not only of Israel (*the Jews*) but also of *all the scattered children of God* (*all the Gentiles*), who will be gathered into unity through his life-giving death (cf. 11,50-52).[295] Jesus lays down his life for them of his own free will, voluntarily out of love, not out of any compulsion (10,17-18).

© In short, Jesus reveals himself as *the good shepherd* who knows and loves, feeds and guides, protects and provides for the sheep, and who *sacrifices his life* so that *all may have abundant life.*

4.2.6. *Jesus, the Messiah and the Co-worker/Son of God (Jn 10,22-42: Discussion on Messianic and Divine Identity)*

This episode (10,22-42) occurred in December during the celebration of the Jewish feast of the *Dedication* (*Hanukkah*), which commemorated the cleansing and the re-consecration (re-dedication) of the Temple and the altar by Judas Maccabeus in 164 BCE (1 Mac 4,41; 2 Mac 10,1-8), three years after their desecration by the Syrian ruler Antiochus Epiphanes (1 Mac 1,54).

a) Jesus, the Messiah, the Shepherd and the divine Son of God (Jn 10,22-30)

"The Jews" (Jewish leaders) surround Jesus in the portico of Solomon and ask him to declare openly: "*If you are the Christ, tell us plainly*" (10,24). It implies, in the context of the festival of Dedication, that they want to know if he is a *militant Messiah* who will liberate them from the Roman rule (10,22-24).[296] He declines to make a public declaration of the nature of his Messiahship because they refuse to believe (10,25-26; cf. 5,31-47). The *works* that he does in his Father's name manifest what kind of a Messiah he is (10,25; cf. 5,36). He is *more than a human Messiah* because he is the *divine shepherd* who gives his sheep eternal life and from his hand no onc can snatch them (10,28). Besides, he calls God "my Father" (10,29) and declares: "*I and the Father are one*" (10,30). The Jewish leaders had asked Jesus to tell them clearly if he was the long-awaited "*Messiah*" (10,24); now he reveals to them openly that he is *the Shepherd/Son of God*, intimately united with the Father in action and being, sharing his very life. Here he *discloses his identity* not merely as the *human Messiah* but as the *divine Son of God* (10,30).

b) Jesus, the Co-worker/Son of God (Jn 10,31-39)

When the Jewish leaders pick up stones to throw at Jesus for *blasphemy* (10,31; cf. 8,59) because of *his claim to be divine* (10,33; cf. 5,18), he defends himself by appealing to the Scriptures and the works of the Father that he does (10,32-38). He reminds them that *judges* like Samuel, to whom the word of God had come (cf. 1 Sam 15,10), are called "*gods*" in the Scripture ("You are *gods*, children of the Most High" Ps 82,6). Therefore, Jesus whom God the Father has consecrated and sent into the world as the *Word made flesh* (cf.1,14) cannot be accused of "blaspheming" because he said: "I am the *Son of God*" (10,34-36). If the consecrated Temple in Jerusalem is the place of God's presence in Israel, then Jesus, the Son of God, whom the Father has "consecrated" (*hêgiasen*, literally "made holy") and sent into the world, is the *living presence of God* among human beings (cf. 1,14: "dwelt among us"). The proof that he is "*the Son of God*" is that he is *doing his Father's works* (10,37; cf. 5,17). Furthermore, the Father is in him and he is in the Father (10,38; cf. 14,10-11).

©To sum up, "the *works* that Jesus does *reveal* him as the Son of God, who is ever ready to do the Father's will and works, and in whom the Father himself is actively present. In short, Jesus is *the Co-worker/Son of God* (cf. 5,17)."[297]

4.3. Jesus, the Loving Life-Giver (Jn 11-12)[298]

The *Johannine Jesus* has clearly stated the *goal of his mission* as *life-giving*: "I came that they may have life, and have it abundantly" (10,10). It is because of God's unconditional *love* for sinful humankind that his unique Son has been sent as the Saviour and mediator of eternal life (cf. 3,16-17).

Jesus' love for us is revealed in the second part of John's Gospel: JESUS' HOUR *(PATH OF LOVE)* (Jn 11-20).[299] Already Jn 11 *introduces* Jesus' *affectionate and self-giving love* for his friends (11,3.5.36). His miracle of bringing his dead friend Lazarus back from the dead (11,11) is the immediate reason for the Sanhedrin's decision to do away with Jesus (11,45-53). Like the grain of wheat that falls to the ground and dies to produce much fruit (12,24), Jesus is ready to risk his life and sacrifice it for the sake of his loved ones (11,7-16; cf. 15,13). In sum, Jn 11-12 presents *Jesus* as *the loving life-giver.*

Jn 11-12 consists of ***two episodes***: 1) the ***Lazarus-Episode*** (*the sickness, death and raising of Lazarus to life*, and *the Sanhedrin's decision to kill Jesus* in ***Jn 11***) and 2) the ***ensuing***

events *(Jesus' anointing at Bethany, his entry into Jerusalem, the coming of the Greeks and of "the hour"* in ***Jn 12****).*[300]

The greatest *sign of raising the dead Lazarus to life* brings out dramatically the *spiritual truth* that Jesus is "*the resurrection and the life*" (11,25) and the *paradoxical truth* that *his gift of life* to a dead man (11,38-44) brings about *his own death* (11,45-53). Furthermore, Lazarus' death-resuscitation points forward to Jesus' own death-resurrection. Jesus explains the meaning of Mary's anointing his feet as symbolizing the anointing of his body for burial (12,7). His entry into Jerusalem as "the King of Israel" (12,12) hints at his enthronement as king on the cross ("the King of the Jews" 19,19). The coming of the Greeks "to see Jesus" indicates the imminence of his "hour" (passion-death-resurrection) (12,23.27). The grain of wheat that falls into the earth and dies to bear much fruit symbolizes the salvific fruitfulness of Jesus' death (12,24). In short, for a contemplative believer, *Jn 11-12* contains the *nucleus of the Paschal Mystery* of Jesus.

4.3.1. Jesus, the Loving Life-Giver (Jn 11,1-54: Lazarus-Episode)

a) Sickness, Death and Raising of Lazarus to Life (Jn 11,1-44)

Even though God's love for humanity and the Father's love for Jesus, the Son, have been stated earlier in John's Gospel (3,16.35; 10,17), *Jesus' love for a friend* is explicitly mentioned for the first time in Jn 11. Lazarus' sisters (Martha and Mary) send Jesus the news of their brother's sickness: "Lord, behold, the one whom *you love* (*phileis*) is ill!" (11,3). Jesus' *affectionate love* (*philein*) for Lazarus is confirmed by his later reference to him as our "*friend*" (*philos* 11,11) and the crowd's remark about the weeping Jesus: "Behold how he loved (*ephilei*) him!" (11,36).

Jesus' mysterious message to Martha and Mary is: "This illness is not unto (*pros*) death but in favour of (*hyper)* the glory of God, so that the Son of God may be glorified through it" (11,4). It means that the outcome of this sickness will not be death but God's glory [God's saving presence] through which God's Son will be glorified (cf. 17,1.4-5). It should be noted that the "glorification (*doxasthê*) of the Son of God" is not through Lazarus' illness and death but through the revelation of "the glory (*doxa*) of God" through what Jesus is going to do to Lazarus, which Jesus explains later to his disciples: "I go to wake him out of sleep" [*to raise him from death*] (11,11).

The Evangelist makes *two enigmatic statements*: "Now Jesus loved (*êgapa*) Martha and her sister and Lazarus. So when he heard that he was ill, he stayed two days longer in the place where he was" (11,5-6). Normally, if we get the news of a friend's serious sickness, we will rush to him/her and will do everything possible to prevent him/her from dying but Jesus stays there until his friend Lazarus dies! (cf. 11,11.14). How can we explain Jesus' paradoxical behaviour towards his friends? It is not due to his indifference to them because we are explicitly told that he "loved" them (11,5). Perhaps the clue to the resolution of this enigma is indicated in the kind of "love" that Jesus has for Lazarus and his sisters. While Jesus' *affectionate love* (*phileis*) for Lazarus was mentioned by Martha and Mary at 11,3, Jesus' *selfless love* (*êgapa*) for Lazarus and his sisters is stressed by the Evangelist at 11,5.

Furthermore, Jesus' love for the Father is the guiding principle of his affectionate love for his friends: "I love (*agapô*) the Father and I do as the Father has commanded me" 14,31). Jesus' human love (*philein*) for his friends is a revelation of the generous, self-giving, self-sacrificing, divine love (*agapê*). Instead of rushing to his sick friend to cure him, Jesus discerns that the Father's will is to raise Lazarus from the dead, which would cost Jesus his own life (11,41-44.45-53). Jesus has declared that the Father loves him because he lays down his life voluntarily for the sheep (10,17). He will tell his disciples during the Farewell discourse: "No one has greater love (*agapê*) than this, to lay down one's life for one's friends" (15,13). This is precisely what Jesus does: he is ready to die for his friend Lazarus (cf. 11,7-8.11-16). Such self-giving, self-sacrificing love for his friends (Lazarus, Martha and Mary) is a manifestation of God's love (*agapê*).

Even though the Jewish authorities in Jerusalem have been attempting to stone Jesus or to arrest him and therefore his disciples are scared and they try to dissuade him from going to Bethany in Judea (11,8: cf. 10,31.39), he is *ready to risk his life* (11,7.16) to "awaken" (raise) his friend Lazarus who "has fallen asleep" (11,11), which means that "Lazarus is dead" (11,14). Jesus is sure of not "stumbling" since he has the light to guide his steps (11,9-10). Jesus is aware that, just as there are twelve hours (of daylight) in a day, "the day" (time-span) of his life and ministry is progressing according to the Father's preordained plan. Therefore, Jesus is not afraid of the hours of darkness overtaking him by surprise and of stumbling over unseen obstacles on his way. Like the sunlight that helps a person to walk without falling, the light of God's never-failing revelation lights up Jesus' steps (11,9-10).

When Jesus tells the disciples: "Let us go to him [Lazarus]" (11,15), Thomas tells his fellow disciples (*synmathêtai*, "co-disciples"): "Let us also go so that *we may die with him*" (11,16). When the other disciples of Jesus are afraid to go with Jesus to

Judea because of the Jews' plot to put him to death (cf. 11,8), *Thomas* is a *daring disciple* and a *faithful friend* who is ready to lay down his life for Jesus (cf. 15,13: "Greater love no one has than to lay down his life for his friends"). Thomas' limitless love and daring desire to die with/for Jesus (his Lord and his God, cf. 20,28) will find fulfilment when he will be *martyred* in Mylapore near Chennai, India, in 72 CE (according to early Christian tradition in Kerala).

The bereaved sisters, Martha and Mary, who had expected Jesus to come quickly and cure their seriously sick brother, did not know the reason for his delay (11,5-6) or his plan to raise their dead brother to life (11,11). So when Jesus arrives at Bethany four days after their brother's death and burial (11,17), both the sisters complain to him bitterly: "Lord, if you had been here, my brother would not have died" (11,21.32).

Jesus consoles Martha with the assurance that her brother will rise again (11,23) and he reveals himself to her as "*the resurrection and the life*" (11,25). He asks her to believe this (11,26) and she makes a profound confession of faith in Jesus: "Yes, Lord, I believe that you are the Christ, the Son of God, he who is coming into the world" (11,27).

Jesus' way of consoling the desolate sisters reveals *his tender love* for them. When they pour out their hearts to him without any inhibition (11,21-22.32), gently he enters into dialogue with them (11,23-27.33-34). Touched by their intense grief, he is "deeply moved in spirit and troubled" (11,33.38). Empathizing with Mary and others in tears, he shares their sorrow and *sheds tears* (11,35). These are unmistakable manifestations of his true *humanity* and his *warm and affectionate love* for Lazarus, Martha and Mary (11,36).

Jesus' spontaneous *prayer* to the Father before raising Lazarus from death to life reveals his perfect trust in the Father and his constant, intimate communion with him ("Father, I thank you that you have heard me. I knew [for certain] that you hear me always ..." 11,41-42; cf. also 3,35; 4,34; 5,21.25; 6,38; 10,30). He also prays for the bystanders that they may come to believe that the Father has sent him (11,42; cf. also 17,20-21). And with a confident cry, Jesus commands the dead Lazarus to "come out" of the tomb and he promptly obcys him! (11,43-44). Thus, the miraculous *sign of raising Lazarus* from the dead reveals the *life-giving power of Jesus' word* and his being *the resurrection and the life* (11,25).

b) Sanhedrin's decision to kill Jesus (Jn 11,45-54)

Because Jesus raised the dead Lazarus to life, the chief priests and the Pharisees, agents of the life-denying forces, plot to destroy Jesus' life (11,47-53). Caiaphas, the high priest, advises the members of the Sanhedrin to do away with Jesus: "It is expedient for you that one man should die for the people and that the whole nation should not perish" (11,50). Although Caiaphas wants to sacrifice Jesus on the altar of expediency under the pretext of saving the Jewish nation from perishing [destruction by the Romans], the Evangelist interprets the high priest's statement as an unconscious prophecy regarding *the universal salvific significance of Jesus' death* (11,51-52). In short, because of Jesus' gift of life to a dead man, Jesus will have to face death, which, in turn, will gather together the scattered children of God (11,52). The death of the good shepherd brings about the unity of the dispersed sheep! This is the *paradox of the Paschal mystery* of Jesus.

© Reviewing Jesus' revelation in Jn 11, we may *conclude*: The Lazarus-episode depicts the *loving Jesus, the Christ, the Son of God, the resurrection and the life* and *the Lord of life* (for he raises a dead friend to life by risking his own life, which symbolizes his gift of eternal life to all through his life-giving death). In short, *Jesus* is the *loving life-giver.*

4.3.2. Jesus Anointed for Burial, the Messianic King of Israel and the Son of Man to be Lifted up (Jn 11,55-12,50: Anointing at Bethany, Entry into Jerusalem and the Greeks' Arrival)

a) Jesus' Anointing at Bethany (Jn 12,1-8)

Even though the chief priests and the Pharisees have already given orders to the people to inform them about Jesus' whereabouts so that they could arrest him (11,57), six days before the Passover, he goes to Bethany, the home of his friends Lazarus, Martha and Mary (12,1). While he is reclining for a meal, *Mary anoints his feet* with a precious perfume of pure nard and wipes his feet with her hair (11,2-3). When the hypocritical Judas, hiding his greed under the guise of concern for the poor, criticizes her action as a sheer waste of a large sum of money (12,4-6), Jesus defends her generous and affectionate anointing of his feet as a *prophetic and anticipatory act of anointing his body for burial* (12,7).

b) Jesus' Entry into Jerusalem (Jn 12,12-19)

Unlike Matthew and Mark who narrate *Jesus' entry into Jerusalem* (Mt 21,1-11; Mk 11,1-11) much before his anointing (cf. Mt 26,6-13; Mk 14,3-9), John describes it (Jn 12,12-19) after the anointing at Bethany (12,1-8). This helps us to grasp correctly the *Johannine understanding of Jesus' Messiahship and kingship.*

John has been very reluctant to present Jesus as the kingly Messiah (for he is never called "the Son of David" and he distances himself from the Galilean crowd keen on crowning him their king cf. 6,15). But now that he is anointed for burial (12,7), Jesus does not object to the large crowd of Passover pilgrims' proclamation: "Hosanna! Blessed is he who comes in the name of the Lord, even *the King of Israel*" (12,13; cf. Ps 118,26). The true nature of Jesus' kingship, however, will be revealed only during his passion, particularly during his trial before Pilate (18,28-19,16b) and his crucifixion (cf. the title on the cross "the king of the Jews" 19,19-22).

When the Passover crowds come to meet Jesus waving palm branches and singing "Hosanna!" to "the King of Israel" (12,13), he reveals his understanding of his kingship through his symbolic action of *sitting and riding on a donkey* (12,14-15). This indicates that he is *not a worldly or warrior king* (who enters the city triumphantly, after a military victory, seated on a warhorse) but one who fulfils God's salvific plan for the people of God ("Fear not, daughter of Zion; behold your king is coming, sitting on an ass's colt!" (12,15; cf. Zech 9,9; Is 35,4; 40,9; Zeph 3,14-15).[301] As the *Prince of peace* Jesus enters "Jerusalem" ('the city of peace') and therefore he is "*the King of Israel*" according to the heart of God (*not* according to the religio-political expectations of the Passover crowds who hail him their king).

c) *The Coming of the Greeks (Jn 12,20-36)*

Some Greeks go to Philip (a disciple with a Greek name *Philippos*) and say to him: "Sir, we wish to see Jesus" (12,20-21). Philip and Andrew (another disciple with a Greek name *Andreas*) take the Greeks to Jesus (12,22).[302]

The coming of the Greeks seeking to "see [meet] Jesus" is a signal to him of the arrival of "*the hour*" of his glorification, for he declares: "The hour has come for the Son of Man to be glorified" (12,23). "The arrival of the Greeks and the coming of the hour are closely linked because it is through the glorification of Jesus in his passion, death and resurrection that God's promise of life for all peoples is fulfilled."[303] Jesus is ready to die, like a grain of wheat that falls to the ground and dies, so that he may bear much fruit (12,24; cf. also 12,32). However, as a young man, he recoils at the thought of premature death and prays to the Father to save him from the painful "hour" but accepts it willingly since it is going to glorify the Father's name (12,27-28).

Like a *mother in labour-pain*, who accepts the suffering associated with *giving birth to a new life* (16,21), Jesus prays to the Father: "Father, glorify your name" (12,28). The Father who is present to the suffering Son, reassures him with the words: "I have glorified it, and I will glorify it again" (12,28). God is going to be revealed as *a loving Father* through his Son's suffering and death on the cross for the life of the world. Just as Jesus' life, words and deeds have manifested God's love for humankind and thus have glorified his name 'Father,' so Jesus's voluntary death will reveal the limitless love of the Father for the humans and thus glorify his name (12,28; cf. 17,26). In short, *the hour* of Jesus' passion and death is the *kairos* for the *revelation of divine love and glory*.

The *crucifixion of the Son of Man* may be compared to the '*divine magnetisation*'. Like a magnet that attracts soft iron filings to itself, Jesus, the *"lifted up" Son of Man*, the crucified Christ, will draw all humans to himself (12,32-34) because his death on the cross will disclose his boundless love for them (15,13) and the unfathomable love of the Father for sinful humanity (3,16). "Just as when a photographic negative is developed in the darkroom the picture gradually becomes visible, so the loving Father's face will appear on the face of the crucified Son in the dark hour of his death on Calvary."[304]

> Paradoxically *Jesus' death on the cross* will be *his decisive victory* over death and Satan: Jesus' crucifixion is the crucial battle against the death-dealing forces represented by Satan, the ruler of this world, who will be cast out (12,31) ... The cross will become the standard under which Jesus' followers will have to continue to fight the battles, even though the war is already won because the Satanic ruler of the world is already vanquished.[305]

Jesus tells the crowd about the effect of his death-resurrection on humankind: "When I am *lifted up* from the earth, I will *draw all* to myself" (12,32). Jesus' being "lifted up" refers not only to his *crucifixion* (raised on the cross) (12,33.34) but also to his *glorification* (exaltation) through his resurrection-ascension (12,32; cf. 14,3), which of course is beyond the capacity of the crowd to understand then. Since the Jews believe that the expected Messiah would "remain for ever" (12,34) according to the prophetic predictions (cf. Is 9,3; Ezek 37,25; Dan 7,14), they ask Jesus: "How can you say that the Son of Man must be lifted up? Who is this Son of Man?" (12,34). Since Jesus had already dealt with the "lifting up" of "the Son of Man" earlier (cf. 3,14; 8,28), instead of answering their questions, he insists on the urgency of walking and believing in the light: "Walk while you have the light… *believe in the light*, so that you may *become sons of light*" (12,35-36; cf. 8,12). He tells all to believe in the light of the revelation of God so that they may become "sons (and daughters) of light", that is, guided by the true light, they participate in it and manifest it in their lives and dispel the darkness in society (12,35-36).

After making this final appeal to believe in Jesus, he disappears from the scene ("he departed and hid himself from them") (12,36).

d) Jesus' Summing up Discourse (12,44-50)

After the curtain has fallen at the close of the central dramatic act (Jn 11-12) Jesus cries out, as it were, from behind the curtain and *sums up his revelatory salvific mission and summons all to believe in him* (12,44-50). This summary discourse not only points back to Jesus' discourses in Part I (Jn 2-12: "*Path of Faith*") but also points forward to his final Farewell Discourse (Jn 13-17) in Part II (Jn 11-20: "*Path of Love*"), thus *bridging* the two Parts together.

> This short and straightforward discourse which both discloses the revelatory and saving mission of Jesus (12,45-47.49-50) and invites the audience (readers) to believe in him (12,44) in order to have eternal life and to avoid judgement by his word (12,48), has many *thematic echoes* of the earlier passages (especially *Jesus' discourses*) and a number of *theological resonances* with the *Farewell Discourse* in Jn 13-17 (e.g., faith in Jesus and the Father: 5,24; 12,44; 14,1; seeing Jesus and the Father: 6,40; 12,45; 14,9; Jesus' coming into the world: 1,9; 3,19; 6,14; 12,46; 16,28; 18,37; Jesus as the light of the world: 1,4.9; 3,19; 8,12; 9,5; 12,46; Jesus' saving, not condemnatory, mission: 3,17; 12,47; judgement: 3,18; 12,48; 16,11; the last day: 6,39.44.54; 11,24; 12,48; the commandment or will of the Father connected with eternal life: 6,40; 12,50; 17,2). [306]

4.4. Jesus the Lover's Last Testament (Jn 13-17)

Jn 13-17 is Jesus' *Farewell Address*, which is a discourse delivered in anticipation of his imminent death. Knowing that "the hour" of his departure has come, Jesus reveals his limitless love for his own (13,1). He washes his disciples' feet (13,2-17), pours out his heart to them through a long dialogue-discourse that discloses the revelatory and salvific meaning of his passion-death-resurrection (Jn 13-16). He ends the farewell discourse with a moving final prayer (Jn 17). In other words, Jn 13-17 is *Jesus the lover's last testament.*[307]

> The whole of *Jn 13-17* is meant to be the *revelation of Jesus' love for his own* ("having loved his own who were in the world, he loved them to the end" 13,1), which ultimately reflects the Father's love for Jesus ("As the Father has loved me, so have I loved you" 15,9; "so that the love with which you [Father] loved me may be in them, and I in them" 17,26).[308]

Jn 13-17 consists of ***five subsections***: *1) Jesus' Feet-Washing, Prediction of Betrayal and Denial, New Commandment of Love* (13,1-38); *2) First Part of Jesus' Farewell Discourse* (13,31-14,31); *3) Jesus' Commissioning Discourse* (15,1-16,4d); *4) Second Part of Jesus' Farewell Discourse* (16,4e-33); *5) Jesus' Prayer of the Hour [of His Passion-Death-Resurrection]* (17,1-26).[309]

4.4.1. Jesus' Feet-Washing, Prediction of Betrayal and Denial, New Commandment of Love (Jn 13,1-38)

a) Jesus' Hour and His Love for His Own (Jn 13,1) (Introduction)

Before the feast of Passover, Jesus is aware of the arrival of "*his hour*" of his departure from this world to the Father (through his passion-death-resurrection) (13,1).[310] He is with "his own" (disciples) at the table and he shows his boundless love for them ("he loved them to the end" 13,1) by washing their feet and by revealing to them his innermost thoughts and deepest feelings as he is about to enter his passion.

b) *Jesus' Washing the Disciples' Feet and Its Significance (Jn 13,2-17)*

Aware of Judas' diabolic decision to betray him and conscious of his divine authority and origin and the proximity of his passion and death (13,2-3), Jesus strips himself of his garments and girds himself with a towel around his waist like a slave and washes the feet of his disciples who are about to betray, deny or desert him (13,4-5).[311]

The incarnate Son of God kneels at the feet of sinful human beings to hold, wash and wipe their dusty, dirty feet! His washing their feet demonstrates his unconditional and self-sacrificing love for his own (13,1). Later he will stretch out those same hands to be nailed to a cross. When Simon Peter protests against the Lord's washing his feet, Jesus tells him that it is a *symbolic act of his life-giving death* that would enable Peter to have a "part" (inheritance of eternal life) with him (13,8; cf. 17,1-2). He explains to the disciples that, by washing their feet, as their teacher and Lord, he has set an *example* of *servant leadership*, a new paradigm of *loving service* to be followed (13,12-15). This does not mean mere ritual repetition of washing the feet (once a year on Maundy Thursday) but it does demand that the disciples be loving servants of one another (13,14) to the extent of laying down their lives for others as Jesus did. Such "doers" are declared "*blessed*" by Jesus (13,17). In short, Jesus' washing his disciples' feet has both a *salvific* and an *exemplary* significance.

c) *Jesus' Prediction of Betrayal and Love for the Betrayer (Jn 13,18-30)*

Jesus is deeply disturbed by the thought of betrayal by a chosen disciple and trusted friend who enjoys table-fellowship with him (13,18; cf. Ps 41,9). Thoroughly distressed in spirit, he declares to the disciples: "Amen, amen, I say to you, *one of you will betray me*" (13,21). However, he refuses to reveal the identity of the betrayer (except to the Beloved Disciple) to protect him from possible attack by other disciples like the impetuous Peter (cf. 18,10). Jesus does *not hate the betrayer* but does care for him. As a sign of his special love for him, Jesus gives him a morsel of bread dipped in the dish, but he fails to see its symbolic significance and submits himself to the spell of Satan (13,26-27). So Jesus tells the betrayer: "Do quickly what you are going to do" (13,27). Judas goes out into the darkness of the night (13,30), symbolizing the darkness of evil (cf. 3,19-20).

d) The New Commandment of Love (Jn 13,31-35)

With the departure of the betrayer, Jesus realizes that his passion is soon to begin, in and through which the Son of Man and God will be glorified (13,31-32), that is, his saving presence will be made manifest. Like a dying father or mother who is about to start his/her final journey, Jesus addresses his disciples lovingly as "little children" and tells them that he will be with them only "a little while" (13,33). He tells them what they must do after his death: "A *new commandment* I give you that you *love* one another *as I have loved you*" (13,34). Jesus' new commandment consists of loving like him to the extent of dying for others (cf. 15,13). Such selfless, self-giving, self-sacrificing, *Christlike love* will be the sure identifiable sign of his authentic disciples (13,35).[312] Anyone who does not love like Christ is not a true disciple and hence not a genuine Christian!

e) Jesus' Prediction of Peter's Denials (Jn 13,36-38)

After Jesus announces his imminent departure, he tells the disciples: "Where I am going you cannot come" (13,33). Simon

Peter asks him: "Lord, where are you going?" (13,36), which shows his ignorance of Jesus' impending death. Jesus assures him that, although he cannot follow him now, afterwards he will (13,36). But *Peter* is *presumptuous* about his ability to follow him immediately and he boasts about his readiness even to die for him: "Lord, why can't I follow you now? I will lay down my life for you" (13,37). Now Jesus' *prediction of Peter's triple denial* silences him (13,38). It is only the experience of his frailty and fallibility that will teach Peter not to be proud and presumptuous but to be humble and dependent upon the Lord (cf. 18,17.25-27; 21,15-19).

4.4.2. *Jesus, the Path, the Truth and the Life, the Sender of the Spirit/Paraclete and the Giver of Peace (Jn 13,31-14,31: First Part of the Farewell Discourse)*

a) Jesus, the Path (to the Father), the Truth and the Life (Jn 14,1-14)

Realizing that the announcement of his imminent departure has upset his disciples, he reassures them that he is going to prepare a place for them in his Father's house and promises them that he would return to them and take them home (14,1-4). Jesus reveals himself to them: "I am the path, the truth and the life" (14,6). He is the *path/way* that leads to the Father because he is the *truth* (revelation) of the Father, and his *life* is the manifestation of the Father's life (14,6; cf. 5,26). Anyone who sees him with the eyes of faith sees the Father (14,9). Besides, his words and works manifest the mutual immanence of Jesus and the Father (14,10-11). In short, Jesus, the incarnate Son, is the *transparency* or the *reflection* of the Father for the believers.

b) *Jesus' Promise of the Indwelling of the Spirit/Paraclete, Jesus and the Father, in the 'Lovers' (Jn 14,15-26)*

Jesus assures his disciples (who love him and one another) that he would pray to the Father to give them another Spirit/ Paraclete (14,15-16).

> After having revealed himself as the path/way to the Father, Jesus now promises his loving disciples "*another Paraclete*," "*the Spirit of truth*," to be with them [by their side] and within them [to guide them] forever (14,15-17). Since Jesus is the truth (the revelation of the Father) (14,6), "the Spirit of truth" is the Spirit of *revelation*, whom the Father will give them at Jesus' request. The *indwelling Spirit* will *teach* the believing and loving disciples everything especially by reminding them of all that Jesus has told them during his ministry and the Last Supper (14,26).[313]

Jesus also promises his disciples that he will not leave them orphans but will return to them in just "a little while" (14,18-19). Then they will experience a *loving mutual indwelling* ("you in me and I in you": 14,20).

> Even though in a little while the world will not see him, after his resurrection they will see him alive and they will share in his new life (14,19). On that day, they will experientially know that Jesus is in the Father and they in him and he in them (14,20). After his resurrection, they will recognize Jesus' indwelling and intimate communion with the Father and experience the mutual immanence of Jesus and themselves.[314]

Jesus now gives the disciples a *criterion* to identify his true '*lovers*': "The one who has my commandments and keeps them is the one who loves me" (14,21; cf. also 14,15). Such *a faithful 'lover'* (one who is in love with Jesus) will be loved by the Father and by Jesus himself, and he will manifest himself to him (14,21-23). The constant and unfailing love of the beloved impels the lover to *manifest more* and more of himself to his beloved. This is the *law of love* (both human and divine).

> Such a *loving person* will become the *home/abode* of Jesus and the Father (14,23). A loving person is the living temple of the Triune God of love. If heaven is where God abides, a loving heart is heaven on earth. The God of love can be encountered in every loving person. A *loving person* is the *living revelation of God who is love* (1 Jn 4,8).[315]
>
> Just as Jesus, the incarnate Word of God, reveals through his words and works the love and life of the Father, the loving person who welcomes Jesus' revelation will, in turn, become a *revealer of the Triune God of love.* Every word and deed of such a person attuned to the teaching of Jesus and his Spirit will bear testimony to the loving mission of Jesus (cf. 15,26-27). In short, a loving community of disciples will become '*the Way*' to the Triune God.[316]

c) Jesus' Loving Obedience and Departing Gift of Peace (Jn 14,27-31)

Jesus gives the disciples his *peace* (*eirênê, shâlôm*), that is, *total well-being*, which is different from the peace (absence of war) that the world offers. Jesus establishes peace by overcoming the ruler (Satan) of this sinful world by sacrificing his own life out of loving obedience to the Father (14,27.30-31). Later Jesus will reassure the disciples that, because he has overcome the world (the evil forces), in him they will experience peace even amid tribulation in the world (16,33).

4.4.3. *Jesus, the True Vine, His Commandment of Love and the World's Hatred (Jn 15,1-16,4d: Commissioning Discourse)*

a) *Jesus, the True Vine, and His Commandment of Love (Jn 15,1-17)*

The allegory of the vine begins with the identification of Jesus as "the true vine" (*hê ampelos hê alêthinê*) and his Father as the farmer (*geôrgos,* vine grower) (15,1), who "takes away" (*airei*) every barren branch but "prunes" (*kathairei*) every fruit-bearing branch so that it may bear more fruit (15,2). Jesus tells his disciples that they are already "clean" (*katharoi*) through the word that he has spoken to them (15,3).

The metaphor of *the vine and the branches* indicates *the intimate and mutual communion* between Jesus and his genuine disciples and highlights its intrinsic link with bearing fruit (15,4-5.7-8). Therefore, he tells them: "*Remain in me, and I in you.* As the branch cannot bear fruit by itself, unless it remains in the vine, neither can you unless you remain in me" (15,4). Just as the vine continuously supplies its life-giving sap to the branches to make them fruitful, so Jesus is the source of the apostles' fruitfulness but they have to remain constantly in union with him to participate in his life and become fruitful in their mission.

It is to be noted that Jesus does *not* say, 'I am *like* the vine; you are *like* the branches,' but affirms: "*I am* the vine; *you are* the branches" (15,5; cf. also 15,2: "every branch *in/on me*" [*en emoi*]). Jesus *identifies* himself with the vine and the disciples with the branches which are *part of the vine*, which highlight the *intimate union* between Jesus and the disciples.

> Since the disciples are branches of the vine (Jesus), they become, as it were, *part of Jesus*, the vine. There is no fruit-bearing vine without the branches and no fruitful branch without the vine. Just as Jesus had told the Jews, 'I and the Father are one' (10,30), the true disciple can say, 'I and Jesus are one' (cf. 17,11.22; cf. Gal 2,20). The union between Jesus and the genuine disciple is so complete that they become truly *one in being and mission.* This is one of the greatest mysteries revealed by the Johannine Jesus.[317]

Now *love* is the *basis* of the mutual immanence ("remain in me and I in you" 15,4.5.7) of Jesus and the disciples: "As the Father has loved me, so have I loved you; remain in my love" (15,9). Since the Father has loved the Son and continues to love him (15,9; cf. also 3,35; 17,26), the incarnate Son communicates this divine love in and through his human love for his disciples. In brief, *God the Father* is the *source of love* and *Jesus* is the *channel of love* to the disciples and the latter are invited to *remain in that love* (15,9).

This abiding/remaining in Jesus' love will be possible for the disciples only if they *keep his commandments* just as he has kept his Father's commandments and abides/remains in his love (15,10). Here "commandments" are not understood as some external laws imposed from outside but as the expression of the wish/will of the one who loves and is loved. A lover who fulfils the least wish of the beloved is a true lover and is genuinely 'in love.' Just as Jesus, the beloved Son of God, is always attuned to the Father's will and finds joy in accomplishing it (cf. 4,34; 15,11), so the disciples by lovingly tuning their will to Jesus' will and obeying his commandments will be able to remain in his love. In brief, *loving obedience* is the *condition for abiding in Jesus' love.*

Summing up all his commandments into one, Jesus says: "This is my commandment, that you love one another *as I have loved you*" (15,12). "As (*kathôs*) I have loved you" (15,12; see also 13,34; 15,9) means not only to love 'like' Jesus (regarding him as an example to be imitated) but also 'because' he has loved us as a friend by giving himself totally and sacrificing himself without counting the cost (cf. 15,13). So *Christlike love* means being ready and willing to lay down our lives for one another as friends (15,14). Jesus tells thc disciplcs: "No longer do I call you servants... but I have called you *friends*, for all that I have heard from my Father I have made known to you" (15,15). They are his confidants with whom he shares whatever the Father has confided in him. There is no secret between true friends. Because the disciples are friends of the Lord, they are friends in the Lord. Jesus has chosen them and appointed them to go and bear lasting fruit (15,16). He sends his friends on a *mission of love*. "This I command you that you love one another" (15,17.12). A *Christlike mutual love* for one another is the *only commandment* of *Jesus, the friend*. Christ commands his disciples to form a *community* of "*friends in the Lord*", a loving community of equality and fraternity, fellowship and friendship (15,12.17; cf. also 13,34-35).

b) The World's Hatred and Persecution of Jesus and the Disciples (Jn 15,18-16,4d)

Having revealed the close communion of life and love between Jesus and his disciples through the allegory of the vine and the branches and the new commandment of Christlike love (15,1-17), he predicts that, like Jesus, they too would be *hated and persecuted by the world* (15,18-25).

Jesus tells the disciples clearly: "If the world hates you, know that it has hated me before you" (15,18) and "If they persecuted me, they will persecute you also" (15,20). They are hated by the wicked world because they do not belong to it but belong to Jesus who "chose" them "out of the world" (15,19; cf. 15,16: "I chose you"). They will be persecuted because of their faith in Jesus ("because of my name" 15,21).

The ultimate reason for the world's hatred and persecution of the disciples is its *culpable ignorance* of God the Father who loved the world and sent his Son (3,17; 15,21: "because they do not know him who sent me"; 16,3: "because they have not known the Father nor me"). Despite the Son having revealed the Father's limitless love for the world (3,17), it decided to be deliberately deaf to his revelatory words and wilfully blind to his saving works (15,22-24), which led it to hate not only Jesus but also God (15,15: "They hated me without a cause" cf. Ps 35,19; 69,5).

> The counter-part of the Christians' communion with Christ and Christlike fraternal love (15,1-17) is the world's hatred and persecution (15,18-16,4d). The fate of friends or the destiny of the disciples and the master is identical (15,18-20). If Jesus was the object of the world's hatred, opposition and persecution, their lot will not be any different from his (15,18.20; 17,14). The forces of darkness and hatred cannot stand the light of love revealed in Jesus (15,21) and reflected in his chosen disciples (15,19; cf. 15,16; 17,26).[318]

Now Jesus promises the disciples that when the Paraclete, *the Spirit of truth*, comes from the Father, he will *bear witness* to Jesus, the truth, and those who allow themselves to be guided by God's revelation in Christ and by the Spirit of truth will be Jesus' authentic witnesses in the hostile world (15,26-27). That is to say, Jesus' revelation will continue through the faithful *disciples*, his *Spirit-filled witnesses* (15,27).

Jesus warns the disciples not to be scandalized when they will be thrown out of the synagogues and will even be killed. They are not to be shocked even if their murderer thinks that slaying them will be an offering of worship pleasing to God (16,1-2)! The cold-blooded murders of the Kandhamal Christians and Dr. Graham Staines and his two sons in Orissa are recent examples of Hindutva fanatics' hatred of the disciples of Jesus in India.

4.4.4. Jesus, the Comforter, the Sender of the Spirit, the Revealer of the Father, the Giver of Peace (Jn 16,4e-33: Second Part of the Farewell Discourse)

a) Jesus' Departure and the Disciples' Sorrow (Jn 16,4e-6)

Already in Jn 14 Jesus had tried to console his disciples (disturbed by his declaration of his imminent departure from this world) by telling them: "Let not your hearts be troubled" (14,1.27) and by assuring them that, after preparing a place for them in his Father's house (14,2), he would come back and take them there (14,3) and would not leave them orphans (14,16-17). He had also given them his parting gift of peace (14,27).

Unlike Peter and Thomas who had earlier asked Jesus about the destination of his departure (13,36; 14,5), now none of the disciples asks him: "Where are you going?" (16,5). Jesus is aware that, since *sorrow* has filled their hearts (16,6), their silence is the sign of deep distress.

b) The Works of the Paraclete/Spirit of Truth (Jn 16,7-15)

Jesus tries to *console* his grieving disciples once again by reassuring them that his going away is for their good. Only if he goes away, he will be able to send the *Spirit/Paraclete* (the Helper/Advocate/Counsellor) to them (16,7-11). The Paraclete will convict the world of the sin of unbelief (16,9), judge the world and its ruler (16,11), and convince the disciples of Jesus' righteousness to be vindicated by the Father through his resurrection (16,10). The Spirit of truth will do all this to guide the disciples (*odogêsei hymas*, "will show you the way") in every (salvific) truth by speaking not on his own authority but by listening to the risen Jesus (16,13). By being attuned to Jesus, the truth (14,6), the Spirit of truth (14,17) will announce and interpret to the disciples the things that are to come (16,13). The Spirit will declare to them all that is from Jesus, the Son of God, who has everything in common with the Father (16,15; cf. 3,34; 17,10). The Spirit will glorify Jesus by making the disciples understand the signs of the times by the revelation of truth in and through Jesus (16,14-15).

c) Jesus' Departure for "a Little While" (Jn 16,16-24)

> As a mother who is about to go on a distant trip tries to comfort her crying children by telling them that she would be back within a short time, Jesus consoles the desolate disciples by telling them that he will be *away only for "a little while"* and then they will see him again (16,16). They are, however, at a loss to figure out the meaning of this enigmatic expression "a little while" (16,17-18).[319]

Jesus knows that his departure/death will cause them pain but he assures them that their sorrow will soon be turned into joy (16,20). Using the *metaphor of a woman in labour-pain* who goes through agony for a while but soon forgets her suffering because of the great joy of giving birth to a child (16,21), he promises them that their sorrowful hearts will rejoice when he will see them again (16,22). They will be glad when they will see the risen Lord (cf. 20,20).

d) *Jesus' Plain Speaking and Its Effects on the Disciples (Jn 16,25-33)*

Jesus tells the disciples that he will *speak* to them *plainly* about the Father (16,25). He *reveals* that *the Father loves them tenderly* because they love Jesus affectionately and have believed in him as the Father's emissary. Therefore, the Father will be pleased to answer all their petitions asked in Jesus' name, even without Jesus' active intercession (16,26-27). Jesus tells the disciples *plainly* about *his origin/mission and destination*, "I came from the Father and have come into the world; again, I am leaving the world and going to the Father" (16,28). The disciples exclaim: "Behold! Now you are speaking plainly, not in any figure of speech!" (16,29).

> The primary purpose of this discourse, Jesus tells the disciples, is that they may have *peace* in him (16,33; cf. 14,27), that is, well-being in communion of life with him. And he tells them to take heart when they will face tribulation in the world because he has *conquered the world of evil* (16,33). But this conquest of the world is not with the sword but *with the cross*. That is why Christians all over the world remember the day of Jesus' death on the cross as "*Good* Friday" (not "*Bad* Friday"). Whenever they make the way of the cross, they thank the crucified Lord: "We praise you and we bless you because by your holy cross you have redeemed the world." Christ has conquered the evil [sinful] world not by destroying it with force but *by redeeming it with love*. The disciples are to remember this *victory of love* when they face persecution in the world (16,33).[320]

4.4.5 *Jesus' Prayer of the Hour [of Passion-Death-Resurrection] (Jn 17,1-26)*

Jesus ends his farewell discourse with a *final prayer for himself, his disciples and the future believers.* This *prayer of "the hour"* (of his passion-death-resurrection) in the presence of his disciples reveals his *intimate loving relationship with the Father.*

> The familiar way with which he addresses God is itself revelatory, for he calls him 'Father' (*pater*, *Abba*, which is equivalent to 'dear Father' or 'Daddy' or 'Papa' 17,1), indicating his intimate filial familiarity with God and total trust in him (cf. 11,41). Like a pregnant woman, beginning to experience the labour-pain, intimates her loving husband or empathetic mother, Jesus spontaneously turns to the Father in prayer when he realizes that his long-awaited 'hour' has arrived (17,1; cf. also 12,23.27; 13,1). But unlike at 12,27 when he agonized over the imminence of 'the hour' and was tempted to pray to the Father to save him from 'the hour' of suffering and death (cf. also Mt 26,39), he is now self-possessed and he sees '*the hour*' as the historic time of his *glorification* in and through which the Father will be glorified (17,1; cf. 12,23; 13,31-32).[321]

Already during his ministry, Jesus manifested the Father's glory by accomplishing the God-given work/mission (17,4; cf. 4,34) and particularly through his miraculous signs (2,11; 11,40). But now his Paschal mystery (passion-death-resurrection) is going to be a *new revelation of the glory* (the saving presence of God) (17,1).

Jesus *prays* to the Father *to glorify him* ("your Son") so that he may glorify the Father (17,1) since the Father has given him power over "all flesh" (weak and mortal human beings) to give eternal life to all whom the Father has given him (17,2; cf. 6,37-40). Jesus (the Word of God) enables all believing human beings "to become children of God" (cf. 1,12). If, according to

St. Irenaeus, "*Gloria Dei vivens homo*" (*Against Heresies*, 4:20), "the greatest glory of the Father would be revealed when humans are eternally alive with the divine life. This is made possible through *Jesus' life-giving death*."[322]

Description of *eternal life* as *knowing (ginôskein) the Father and Jesus Christ* (17,3) does not refer to abstract theoretical knowledge about them but personal loving knowledge of them. Eternal life is *an experiential knowing, a loving union* with Jesus Christ and the Father (17,3).

Jesus, the incarnate Son of God, has revealed God as a loving and caring Father ("I have manifested your name": 17,6.26) in a human way. Jesus is the *transparent face of the Father* turned towards humankind ("he who has seen me has seen the Father": 14,7) because he is not only the divine but also the 'enfleshed' Word (1,14; cf. 1 Jn 1,1-3), in whose mortal human life the divine life and glory are made visible (1,14.18).[323]

As Jesus is about to depart from this world, he *prays to the Father for the disciples* in the world that he may *protect* them from the evil one and that they may be *united* (17,9-16), "that they may be one, even as we are one" (17,11). He requests the Father to "s*anctify* them in the truth" (17,17), that is, to set them apart for their revelatory mission in the world (17,17-19).

Jesus *prays* also *for the future believers' unity* so that their life may be patterned on the loving unity of Jesus and the Father, as a result of which the world may come to believe and know Jesus as the apostle of God (17,20-23). The lack of unity in the Church today is a scandal/obstacle that prevents people from believing in Jesus!

Jesus' *final prayer/desire* is that all the disciples/believers may be with him to experience and share his glory with the Father (17,24) whose name and love he is going to make known in a unique manner through his passion-death-resurrection (17,26). "Jesus' *last wish* is that the love with which the Father has loved him may be in all his disciples of all times and places and that Jesus himself may be in them through their participation in the mystery of divine love (17,26)."[324]

© Through his final prayer to the Father, Jesus reveals his loving *intimate Father-Son relationship* and his longing for the glorification of the Father through *the hour* of his passion-death-resurrection. He manifests himself as the *mediator of eternal life* (loving knowledge of the Father through the Son). "He prays not only for his glorification but also for the protection, sanctification, mission, love and unity of the present disciples and the future believers (17,1-26)."[325]

4.5. Jesus' Passion-Death-Resurrection (Jn 18-20)

According to the Synoptic authors, the Passion of Jesus begins with his agony in the garden of Gethsemane and ends with his death and burial on Calvary (Mt 26,36-27,66; Mk 14,32-15,47; Lk 22,39-23,56). Then they narrate his resurrection on Easter Sunday, his appearances to the disciples and his ascension (Mt 28; Mk 16; Lk 24). The outpouring of the Spirit occurs later on Pentecost (Acts 2,1-4). According to this Synoptic understanding of the Paschal Mystery, the passion, death, resurrection, ascension and gift of the Holy Spirit take place in different places and times. Paul interprets Jesus' humiliating suffering and obedient death on the cross as the condition for his exaltation through his resurrection and ascension (cf. Phil 2,8-11).

The Fourth Evangelist, however, describes the significant events in "*the hour*" of Jesus as a *continuous dramatic narrative* but he interprets them as *one mystery.*

> John considers *Jesus' passion-death-resurrection and the gift of the Spirit* as *one mystery (the Paschal Mystery)*, although the events are narrated one after the other in Jn 18-20. According to John, not only Jesus' resurrection and ascension but also his sufferings and death are part of his *glorification* [cf. Jn 13-17 especially 13,31-32; 17,1-5]. Hence the Johannine Jesus is the *sovereign Lord* even during his arrest, trials and death on the cross.[326]

Furthermore, *Jesus' death on the cross* is described as "*handing over the Spirit*" on Good Friday (19,30.34) and the *risen Lord* "*breathes into*" the disciples *the Holy Spirit* already on Easter Sunday (20,22).

> The *theological profile of Jesus* that is painted in the Johannine passion-resurrection narrative highlights not so much his sufferings during the passion [as in the Synoptics] and then his glory after his resurrection but rather *a human-divine Christ glorified already* during his appearance before his arrest-party, during his Jewish and Roman trials, and on the cross, and bearing the marks of the passion even as the risen Lord. His divinity and sovereignty, kingship and Lordship, are revealed already during the passion, and his human care and love for his own are made manifest not only in the passion narrative but also in the episodes connected with the resurrection. The passion and the resurrection illuminate and interpret one another so much that Jesus is glorified already in and through the passion and crucifixion (e.g., the "lifting up" on the cross is already an exaltation) and the risen glorified Lord is still fully human and humane. In other words, the Jesus of the Johannine passion-resurrection is not a hyphenated man-God or God-man but a "*Godman*" who reveals the mystery of his person that is both divine and human and manifests best and brings to perfect completion his revelatory and salvific mission. All that happens

in Jn 18-20 belongs to the *tetelestai* ["It is accomplished"] (19,30) of Jesus, the Man and God, the Revealer and Saviour, the King and Brother, the Teacher and Spirit-giver, the Lord and Lover.[327]

The narrative of "**Jesus' Passion-Death-Resurrection**" (**Jn 18-20**) consists of ***four episodes***: *1) Sovereign Jesus before the Arrest-Party, Peter and Annas* (18,1-27); *2) Jesus the King's Trial before Pilate* (18,28-19,16b); *3) Jesus the King's Crucifixion, Death and Burial* (19,16c-42); *4) Lord Jesus with Mary Magdalene, Disciples and Thomas* (20,1-29).[328]

4.5.1. Sovereign Jesus before the Arrest Party, Peter and Annas (Jn 18,1-27)

This episode (18,1-27) consists of a *diptych (two scenes): a) Jesus before the arrest party* in the garden of Gethsemane (18,1-14), and *b) Peter's Denials and Jesus' Trial before Annas* in the high priests' palace *(*18,12-27*)*, both of which are *connected* through the *bridge-verses* (12-14).

a) Jesus before the arrest party (Jn 18,1-14)

When Jesus sees Judas, the betrayer, the Temple police and a band of armed soldiers, coming to the garden (of Gethsemane), instead of running away from them, he courageously confronts the arrest-party with the question: "Whom do you seek?" (18,1-4). When they reply "Jesus the Nazarene" (18,5), boldly he reveals his identity as "*I am*" (*egô eimi* 18,5), that is, he is "*Jesus of Nazareth*" (whom they are seeking) and the *divine "I am*" (cf. Ex 3,14; Jn 8,58), at which they fall to the ground as at a theophany (18,6). Here Jesus manifests himself as the *sovereign Lord* who is in total control of the situation (18,7-8).

The Johannine Jesus in the garden of Gethsemane is not a man in agony, as in the Synoptic Gospels (Mt 26,36-46; Mk 14,32-42;

> Lk 22,40-46), but the *sovereign, human-divine "Jesus of Nazareth"* at whose self-revelation "*I am*" (*egô eimi* 18,5) his armed adversaries, led by Judas the betrayer, fall upon their faces as during a divine epiphany (18,6; cf. Ezek 1,28). The combination of the human name "Jesus of Nazareth" (18:5.7) and the divine name "I am" (18,5.6.8; cf. Ex 3,14) points paradoxically to the *mystery of Jesus' human-divine person.*[329]

The garden-scene presents Jesus also as the *good shepherd*. His frequent gathering of his disciples in the garden (18,2) reminds us of a shepherd's gathering his flock in the evening to shield them from thieves and wolves (cf. 10,8.10.12). Unlike a hireling who runs away when he sees the wolf coming to attack the sheep, Jesus protects them like a good shepherd who is ready even to lay down his life for them (10,11). He does it voluntarily (10,17-18) because he knows them lovingly (10,14-15). Jesus is aware that the Father has entrusted the disciples to his care and so he must not lose any of them (6,39; 17,12; 18,9). Therefore, when the Temple-police and the Roman soldiers arrive to arrest him, his primary concern is not his own safety but the security of his disciples. Hence he tells the arrest party: "So if you seek me, let these men go" (18,8).

> [T]he garden-scene reveals Jesus as *the good shepherd* (10,11.15.17.18) who *protects* his sheep (18,8-9; cf. 17,12) and *risks* his own life to save their lives. For he not only prevents the disciples from being arrested by the soldiers (18,8) but allows himself to be arrested. He lets his disciples go free by the power of his word (18,8) but lets himself be bound for their sake. He does not allow anyone of those whom the Father has given him to be lost (18,9; cf. 6,39; 10,28; 17,12) or to be snatched by the wolves (cf. 10,12) sent by the Roman and Jewish authorities, but is *ready and willing to suffer and lay down his life* for the protection and salvation of those entrusted to him by the Father (cf. 18,9.11).[330]

In brief, the garden-scene (18,1-11) highlights *Jesus' sovereignty and Lordship, humanity and divinity, the good shepherd's care and concern* for the protection of his sheep/disciples, and his willing *filial submission* to the salvific plan of the Father.[331]

Jesus *lets himself be arrested*, bound and led to Annas, the father-in-law of Caiaphas, the high priest (18,12-14) who had counselled the Sanhedrin to sacrifice Jesus on the altar of expediency (cf. 11,49-50). (*Jesus' arrest concludes* the scene in the garden of Gethsemane and *introduces* the scene in Anna's palace.)

b) Peter's Denials and Jesus' Trial before Annas (Jn 18,15-27)

Jesus' trial before Annas (18,19-24) is *sandwiched* between Peter's denials (18,15-18.25-27). These actions take place *simultaneously.* While Simon Peter denies his being a disciple of Jesus at the entrance to and inside the court of the high priest, Jesus is tried by Annas in the high priest's palace. The *cowardice* of Peter's denials is *contrasted* with the *courage* of Jesus' self-defence.

When the Beloved Disciple brings Simon Peter in, the gate-keeper questions him: "Are not you also one of this man's disciples?" (18,17). Peter flatly denies it by saying: "I am not" (18,17). As he is warming himself with the slaves and the police standing around the charcoal fire in the courtyard, they question him again about his discipleship and he denies it twice more and, with the third denial, the cock crows as Jesus had predicted (18,25-27; cf. 13,38). It is *by disowning his discipleship* that *Peter denies Jesus.* Peter's cowardly act of denial of his being a disciple of Jesus, whom he had earlier confessed as "the Holy One of God" (6,69), is contrasted with Jesus' courageous act of defending himself and his wise silence about his disciples.

When Annas questions Jesus about his disciples and doctrine, Jesus deftly throws the ball back into his court by asking him to call witnesses. During the trial before Annas (18,19-24), Jesus is portrayed as an inspiring *courageous teacher* and as an exemplary *prophetic protestor* who fearlessly exposes Annas' hypocrisy and boldly questions the servant's insulting slap.

> Jesus *refuses to answer* Annas' questions and *challenges* him to look into the real reason for the questioning. Jesus exposes Annas' hypocrisy of conducting a mock trial because he has not called in witnesses to testify for and against Jesus. If he is interested in finding out the truth, he should question those who heard him because Jesus used to speak openly in the synagogues and the Temple (18,20-21). When he is *slapped* by a servant for speaking thus to Annas, Jesus does not suffer the insult in silence but challenges him to prove if,he has spoken wrongly and questions his right to strike him if he has spoken rightly (18,22-23). Although he is under arrest and is bound, bravely he *protests* against the injustice done to him by the hypocritical high priest and against the insult by his stooge, thus setting his cowardly disciples like Peter an excellent *example of prophetic courage.*[332]

©This episode (18,1-27) highlights Jesus as *'I am', the sovereign Lord, the good shepherd, a courageous teacher and a protesting prophet.*

4.5.2. Jesus the King's Trial before Pilate (Jn 18,28-19,16b)

The dramatic episode of ***Jesus' Trial before Pilate*** consists of *seven alternating scenes (outside* and *inside the Roman praetorium): a) Pilate and the Jews' accusation against Jesus as an evildoer* (18,28-32); *b)Pilate and Jesus' kingship* (18,33-38b); *c) Pilate and the Jews' choice of Barabbas, a robber* (18,38c-40); *d) Scourging and mocking of Jesus, the king of the Jews* (19,1-3); *e) Pilate* *and the Jews' cry for the crucifixion of the Son of God* (19,4-7); *f) Pilate and Jesus' origin* (19,8-12); *g) Pilate's proclamation of Jesus' kingship and his condemnation* (19,12-16b).[333]

a) *Pilate and the Jews' Accusation against Jesus as an Evildoer (Jn 18,28-32)*

Early in the morning, the Jewish authorities bring Jesus to the Roman praetorium (18,28). Pilate questions them about Jesus: "What *accusation* do you bring against this *man*?" (18,29). They charge him of being an *evildoer* (18,30), a criminal, who must be put to death (18,31).

b) *Pilate and Jesus' Kingship (Jn 18,33-38b)*

Jesus' kingship is the most dominant Christological motif in the Roman trial. Pilate's first question to Jesus is: "Are you *the king of the Jews?*" (18,33). Although Jesus had given the slip to the Galilean crowd that had wanted to crown him king (6,15), later the Passover crowd in Jerusalem hailed him "*the king of Israel*" (18,13), which the Roman governor might have come to know. Jesus' reply to Pilate implies that he is a *king* (18,37), but *not a worldly king* (18,36).

> The dialogue between Pilate and Jesus discloses the *nature of his kingship* (18,33-38b)... Jesus explicitly tells Pilate that his kingship is *not from this world*; if it were so, his servants would be fighting to prevent him from being handed over to the Jewish authorities (18,36). Jesus does *not* crave for *worldly power nor* is he interested in establishing a *temporal empire* by waging wars with the help of soldiers or armed followers.[334]

Unlike the Roman kingdom built on military might and domination, *Jesus' kingship* is *founded on "truth."* His *mission* is "*to testify to the truth*" (18,39) of God's unlimited love for humans (3,16). This truth/revelation will set them free from the slavery of sin (cf. 8,31-36) and empower them to become children of God (1,12).

c) *Pilate and the Jews' Choice of Barabbas, a Robber (Jn 18,38c-40)*

Pilate is convinced that Jesus is neither a criminal nor a threat to Roman power and so he announces to "the Jews" that he finds *Jesus innocent* (18,38). But instead of letting him go, the Roman governor tries to bargain with the Jewish leaders to release "the king of the Jews" on the occasion of the feast of Passover (18,39). But they cry out for the release of *Barabbas (a robber)* instead of Jesus (whom they contemptuously call "this fellow") (18,40).

d) *Scourging and Mocking of Jesus, the King of the Jews (Jn 19,1-3)*

Although Pilate has publicly declared Jesus innocent (18,38; cf. also 19,4.6), the governor gets him *scourged* by the soldiers who *crown* him with thorns, *slap* him and *mock* him as the *king of the Jews* (19,1-3). Jesus is not a violent king but *suffers violence silently* like the *suffering servant* (cf. Is 53,7). But does not his silent suffering now contradict his courageous protest when he was slapped before Annas (18,22-23)? His present silence shows that he is truly the *suffering* "king of the Jews" (19,3) as the Son of God who is "the King of Israel" (cf. 1,49; 12,13).

e) *Pilate and the Jews' Cry for the Crucifixion of the Son of God (Jn 19,4-7)*

The badly battered Jesus, wearing the crown of thorns and the purple royal robe, is paraded before the people by Pilate who proclaims: "*Behold the man!*" (19,5). This makes the chief priests and the police cry out for his *crucifixion* (19,6), even though the real reason for their demand is his claim to be *the Son of God* (19,7; cf. also 5,18; 10,33.36).

f) Pilate and Jesus' Origin (Jn 19,8-12)

Jesus refuses to answer Pilate's question about his origin: "Where are you from?" (19,9). His silence about his *divine origin* (*pothen*) is a sign of protest against Pilate's indifference to truth (18,38), his bartering him for a bandit (18,39-40) and his unjust scourging (19,1). When Pilate claims to have the power to release him or to crucify him, Jesus courageously *challenges* that assertion and reminds him that he would have no power over him unless it were given to him "from above" (that is, from the emperor and/or from God) (19,10-11). Jesus cannot be intimidated even by the Roman governor. Christ *bears witness to the truth with courage.*

g) Pilate's Proclamation of Jesus' Kingship and His Condemnation (Jn 19,12-16b)

Finally, when "the Jews" accuse Pilate of not being "Caesar's friend" (19,12), he makes Jesus sit on a bench and proclaims him *king of the Jews* about the "sixth hour" (that is, at noon) when the Passover lambs are killed in the Temple (19,13-14). Although the Roman governor's proclamation ("*Behold your King!*" 19,14) is intended to be an insult to "the Jews," it has a deeper theological significance for the Evangelist: Jesus is both the *shepherd/king* who lays down his life for the sheep (cf. 10,11.15.17.18) and the *Passover lamb* (cf. 1,29) that is going to be sacrificed for the salvation of the people. "*Triply betrayed* by his own disciple Judas (18,2.5), by his own people 'the Jews' and the chief priests (18,35; 19,11), and by the Roman governor

Pilate (19:16), the *innocent Jesus is unjustly condemned to death* on the cross!"[335]

©Jesus' trial before Pilate highlights *Jesus' kingship* (18,33.36.37.39; 19,2-3.5.12.14.15). His *innocence* is repeatedly affirmed by the Roman governor (18,18; 19,4.6). Jesus' *humanity* ("*the Man*" 18,29; 19,5), *divinity* ("*the Son of God*" 19,7) and *mysterious origin* (*pothen, "whence"* 19,9) are also stressed.

4.5.3. Jesus the King's Crucifixion, Death and Burial (Jn 19,16c-42)

Like Jesus' trial before Pilate, this ***episode on Calvary*** (***19,16c-42***) is composed of *seven scenes: a) Jesus' crucifixion on Golgotha* (19,16c-18); *b) The title on the cross: "Jesus of Nazareth, the king of the Jews"* (19,19-22); *c) The soldiers and Jesus' garments* (19,23-24); *d) Jesus, his Mother and the Beloved Disciple* (19,25-27); *e) Jesus' thirst and Spirit-giving death* (19,28-30); *f) Water and blood from Jesus' pierced side* (19,31-37); *g) Jesus' royal burial in a garden* (19,38-42).[336]

a) Jesus' Crucifixion on Golgotha (Jn 19,16c-18)

Jesus' *carrying the cross* by himself to "Golgotha" ("the place of the skull": 19,17) symbolises his readiness to embrace death to save mortal humans and to give them life (cf. 10,11.15.17-18; 11,50-52; 15,13). Jesus' crucifixion between two others, one on his right side and the other on his left, shows his *solidarity with the crucified* of human history (19,18). Whereas the Synoptics explicitly mention that those who were crucified with Jesus were robbers (Mt 27,38; Mk 15,27) or criminals (Lk 23,32-33) or that they reviled him (cf. Mt 27,44; Mk 15,32; Lk 23,39), John is silent about their identity and actions. In the Fourth Gospel, the two men hanging on either side of Jesus look like *guards of honour* to the *enthroned king on the cross* in the middle.

b) The Title on the Cross: "Jesus of Nazareth, the King of the Jews" (Jn 19,19-22)

Jesus is a *crucified king* and it is from the cross that he reigns. The primary purpose of Pilate's inscription on the cross: "Jesus of Nazareth, the king of the Jews" 19,19), was to identify the person (cf. 18,5.7) and to indicate the reason for his crucifixion. It was also intended to warn the Jews with kingly ambitions/ pretensions and to humiliate the Jewish leaders (cf. the chief priests' reaction to the title at 19,21). But the Evangelist sees in it a symbolic and theological significance, namely, that the *crucified Jesus* is truly "*the king of the Jews*" because it was *written in three prevailing languages* (Hebrew, Latin and Greek) and because Pilate refused to change it even when the chief priests objected to it (19,20-22). The *truth of Jesus' kingship* is declared by the Roman governor as *irrevocable:* "What I have written I have written" (19,22). This is part of the *Johannine irony* that the veracity of the kingship of the crucified Christ is proclaimed by the very Roman governor who condemned him to be crucified!

c) The Soldiers and Jesus' Garments (Jn 19,23-24)

The soldiers' *dividing* the crucified *Jesus' garments* and *casting lots for his seamless tunic* are affirmed as the *fulfilment of the Scripture* (19,23-24; cf. Ps 22,18). It shows that everything done to the crucified Jesus is per the preordained plan of God.

> If the division of Jesus' [outer] garments into four parts points to his *life-giving physical death* (cf. 13,4), 'the seamless [inner] tunic wholly woven 'from above/top' may symbolize the *divine*

life which Jesus, the Son of God, has from the Father (5,26; cf. 'from above/top' [*anôthen*] 19,23; cf. also 3,3.7.31; 19,11) and which even the soldiers who crucified him cannot destroy ('tear') (19,24).[337]

d) Jesus, His Mother and the Beloved Disciple (Jn 19,25-27)

Now that "the hour" of Jesus has arrived and he is lifted up on the cross, he sees *his mother* and *the Beloved Disciple* standing under the cross and reveals their *new spiritual relationship* as *mother* and *son*. Some Johannine commentators understand Jesus' words from the cross to his mother ("Woman, behold your son!" 19,26) and to the Beloved Disciple ("Behold your mother!" 19,27) as his entrusting her to the disciple's care. But the *revelatory formula* ("seeing" - "saying" - "Behold!") used here (19,26; cf. 1,29.36.47) points to a deeper *symbolic/spiritual significance* in the scene. Many scholars take "the mother of Jesus" to be a symbol of the Church, the mother of the faithful, and the Beloved Disciple to be representing individual Christians, who are entrusted to the Church.

If this were the case, "the mother of Jesus" should have taken the Beloved Disciple to her home, rather than his taking her to his own home (19,27)! If, however, "*the mother of Jesus*" is a *symbol of the Paraclete*, who will remain with the disciples and within them (cf. 14,16-17.26; 15,26; 16,7-15), the Beloved Disciple's taking her "*into his own*" (heart and home) (*eis ta idia* 19,27) makes sense.[338]

In short, *the mother of Jesus* symbolizes *the Holy Spirit* and *the Beloved Disciple* represents *all the disciples* whom Jesus loves.

e) Jesus' Thirst and Spirit-Giving Death (Jn 19,28-30)

Now the crucified Jesus says: "*I thirst*" (19,28). It is quite natural for a crucified person (who has lost a lot of blood) to feel terribly thirsty. This shows Jesus' utter *solidarity with humanity* (cf. the tired, thirsty Jesus' request for a drink from a Samaritan woman at 4,7). But the Evangelist tells us that Jesus said "I thirst" in order *to fulfil the Scripture* (19,28; cf. Ps 69,21).[339] It shows us that Jesus' primary concern even on the cross is to fulfil the Father's will and to complete his work/mission (4,34; 5,36;17,4; 19,28.30). So after drinking the vinegar (sour wine) offered to him, he says: "*it is finished*" (*tetelestai*) (19,30). It has a *double meaning*, namely, "it [the vinegar] is finished" and "it [the mission] is accomplished."[340]

Realizing that his God-given mission has now been accomplished, Jesus bowed his head and "handed over the Spirit" (*paredôken to pneuma*) (19,30). This is generally translated as: "he gave up his spirit" (cf. *RSV*, *NRSV*, etc.). But the Greek text does not say "his spirit" (*to pneuma autou*) but "the Spirit" (*to pneuma*).

> Unlike Lk 23,46 which records Jesus' prayer: "Father, into your hands, I commit my Spirit" (*to pneuma mou*), Jn 19,30 does not specify the Spirit as "my Spirit," nor does it indicate to whom "the Spirit" is given or handed over (*paredôken*). But what is underscored is that, according to the Johannine understanding, *Jesus' death on the cross* is a *Spirit-giving death* (19,30). Just as the risen Jesus breathes the Spirit on the disciples (20,22), the dying Jesus gives the Spirit (19,30). Thus the Johannine Pentecost coincides with Jesus' death-resurrection, just as the crucifixion of Jesus is already his exaltation or glorification.[341]

"*Handing over the Spirit*" (19,30) seems to have a *double meaning*, namely, he *breathed his last* and *gave the Spirit*. In other words, *his death* on the cross is *life-giving* because he gives the Spirit that is life-giving (cf. 6,63). The Spirit that descended like a dove from heaven and remained on Jesus at the time of his baptism (1,32) is handed over when he breathes his last. The question may be asked: "*To whom* did the dying Jesus hand over the Spirit?"

> The immediate context of 19,30 points to the persons who "put a sponge full of vinegar on hyssop and held it to his mouth" (19,29). But to whom do "they" refer in 19,29? In the immediately preceding scene (19,25-27) Jesus' mother, her sister, Mary the wife of Clopas, Mary Magdalene and the Beloved Disciple were "standing by the cross of Jesus" (19,25). Therefore, it is reasonable to believe that they, who were standing close to the crucified Christ, were the ones who offered him a drink when he cried out "I thirst" (19,28). But if the Beloved Disciple had taken Jesus' mother to his home (19,27), the *three women* still *standing under the cross* of Christ are most probably the ones who *gave the thirsty Jesus a drink* and *to whom he gave the Holy Spirit.*[342]

In Jn 4,7-14 the thirsty Jesus, who had asked the Samaritan woman for a drink, promised her "living water," the symbol of the Holy Spirit (cf. 7,38-39). Now the women who offered a drink to the crucified Christ, who said "I thirst", are given the Holy Spirit.

f) Jesus, the Passover Lamb, and Water and Blood from His Pierced Side (Jn 19,31-37)

The Evangelist interprets the fact that the *crucified Jesus' legs* were *not broken* by the soldiers on the day of preparation for the Passover (19,31-33) as the fulfilment of the Scripture which says: "Not a bone of him shall be broken" (19,36), which refers to the Passover lamb (cf. Ex 12,10.46; Ps 34,21; Num 9,12). In other words, the crucified Jesus is *the Passover lamb* since none of his bones was broken. Just as the Israelites were freed from the slavery of Egypt through the Paschal lamb's death and blood, now through the death of Jesus, the new Passover lamb, the whole of humanity is saved from "the sin of the world" (cf. 1,29).

Likewise, the flow of "*blood and water*" from the pierced side of Jesus (19,34-35) indicates that he is *truly dead* in solidarity with all mortals and it symbolizes the *gift of life and Spirit* through his death on the cross because "blood" is the seat and symbol of life (cf. 6,53-54) and living "water" is the sign/symbol of the Spirit (cf. 4,10; 7,37-39).

> In short, *Jesus' death* is both *life-giving* and *Spirit-giving*, especially to those who look on him with faith (19,35.37). Jesus lays down his life (10,11.15) by shedding his blood, the symbol of life (19,34), and pours out the (living) water, the symbol of the life-giving Holy Spirit (19,34; cf. 6,63), so that all may have life in abundance (10,10).[343]

g) Jesus' Royal Burial in a Garden (Jn 19,38-42)

Even though Jesus was condemned to death on a cross like a criminal or an impostor king, Joseph of Arimathea, "a secret disciple" of Jesus ("for fear of the Jews"), goes to Pilate and asks permission to take away Jesus' dead body (19,38). Now Nicodemus, a Pharisee who had first come to Jesus "at night" (probably because of fear), brings "a mixture of myrrh and aloes about one hundred pounds' weight" (19,39). They wrap his body in linen cloths with a large quantity of spices and bury him, according to the Jewish rites, in a new tomb in a nearby garden (19,40-42). Thus they give the *crucified Jesus* ("the king of the Jews") a *royal burial.*

The fact that Joseph of Arimathea and Nicodemus come openly and bury the body of the crucified Jesus shows that the "*lifted up*" Jesus has already started "*drawing all*" to himself (12,32). It means that his *self-sacrificing death*, like the grain of wheat which falls to the ground and dies, has begun to *bear much fruit* (12,24).

©To sum up, *all the scenes on Calvary* are *revelatory* in nature for they manifest important aspects of *Jesus' person and mission: Jesus is the crucified and glorified King of the Jews, the giver of the Spirit, the Passover Lamb, and the fulfilment of the Scriptures.*

4.5.4. Lord Jesus with Mary Magdalene, Disciples and Thomas (Jn 20,1-29)

Jn 20,1-29 consists of *two diptychs (20,1-18.19-29)*: *a)* The *first diptych* depicts the discovery of the empty tomb by Mary Magdalene, the Beloved Disciple and Simon Peter (20,1-10), and Jesus' appearance to Mary there (20,11-18); *b)* The *second diptych* consists of Jesus' appearances to the disciples and to the doubting Thomas in a locked room (20,19-25.24-29), which are connected through the "bridge verses" (24-25) that conclude the first appearance and prepare for the second.

a) Discovery of the Empty Tomb and Jesus' Appearance to Mary Magdalene (Jn 20,1-18)

Mary Magdalene, who had stood under the cross of Jesus (cf. 19,25), comes to his tomb very early in the morning because of her faithful love for him; and she is shocked to see the tombstone rolled away and so she rushes back to report it to Simon Peter and the Beloved Disciple (20,1-2). They come running to the tomb and they too are surprised to find it *empty* (20,3-10)!

In 20,1-18, the *risen Jesus* seems to be *playing hide-and-seek* with his disciples Peter, the Beloved Disciple and Mary Magdalene. First of all, the stone at the entrance to the tomb is rolled away, which makes Mary Magdalene come to the (wrong) conclusion that Jesus' body has been stolen (20,1-2)! Besides, the linen cloths with which his body was wrapped are left behind in the tomb and the napkin with which his face was covered is rolled up in a place by itself (20,5-6)! Even though these details *baffled Simon Peter*, they enabled the *Beloved Disciple to "see and believe"* (20,8). "Seeing" the empty tomb with his wrapping cloths and the rolled up napkin, the Beloved Disciple *"believes" in the resurrection*. The *insight of love* leads him to have a *new faith in the risen Lord.*

Furthermore, the risen Jesus *appears* to Mary Magdalene *like the gardener* and so she fails to recognize him (20,14-15)! He asks her: "Woman, why are you weeping? Whom do you seek?" (20,15), as though he did not know! Her weeping is the manifestation of the intensity of her love for him. Now he calls her affectionately by name "*Mary*" (*Mariam* 20,16), and she responds by calling him lovingly "*my teacher*" (*Rabbouni*) and by *grasping* him like a *beloved* who has found her *lover* (20,17). This dramatic scene reveals the risen Jesus' *humanity* and the warm *friendship* between him and Mary Magdalene.

> That even after the resurrection Jesus remains *human* is seen from the facts that he can be taken for a gardener (20,15) and held in a loving embrace by Mary Magdalene (20,17). Besides, he refers to God as "my God and your God" (20,17). On the other hand, Jesus is twice referred to as "*the Lord*" (*ho kyrios*: 20,2.18) and once as "*my Lord*" (*ho kyrios mou*: 20,13) by Mary Magdalene. This points to the Christological mystery of the *human Jesus* being the *divine Lord.*[344]

Now the risen Jesus asks Mary Magdalene to stop clinging to him and *sends her* to his "*brothers*" with the *Easter mission* of bearing witness to his resurrection and of announcing his imminent ascension to his God and Father, who has become their God and Father (20,17). And she goes to the disciples and tells them: "*I have seen the Lord*" (20,18). Thus the risen Jesus makes his *beloved Mary, a woman disciple*, his *first witness* to the resurrection and his *apostle to the apostles.*

By referring to *his disciples* as "*my brothers*" (*adelphoi mou*) for the first time in this Gospel, Jesus reveals that, through his death-resurrection, a new brotherly relationship is established between him and the disciples, because *his God and Father* has now *become* also *their God and Father* (20,17). It means that they have a new filial relationship and communion with God the Father. Since the same God is the "Father" not only of Jesus but also of the disciples, they have become his "brothers". In short, they have *a new filial bond with God the Father* and *a new brotherly relationship with Jesus*. This is the *good news* of the risen Jesus which Mary Magdalene is commissioned to communicate to his disciples.[345]

b) Jesus' Appearances to the Disciples and to the Doubting Thomas (Jn 20,19-29)

On the evening of Easter Sunday and a week later, the risen Jesus "came" into the locked room and "stood among" the disciples (20,19.26). His "coming" and "standing among them" suggest that he who was dead and buried is now *alive* and *active* among them. Then he shows them his pierced hands and side, which means that the one whom they see now is the same Jesus who was crucified. He greets them: "Peace to you" (*eirênê hymin*) (20,19.21.26). "*Peace*" (*shâlôm*) is the crucified-risen Jesus' gift to the frightened and doubting disciples. The peace that he bestows on them is the fruit of his death on the cross which has reconciled them with God the Father and has made them the Father's children (20,17). Therefore, he is the *mediator or giver of God's peace* to them (20,19.21.26).

Already during the Farewell Discourse Jesus had told them: "Peace I leave with you; *my peace* I give to you; not as the world gives do I give to you" (14,27); "I have said these things to you so that *in me* you may *have peace*" (16,33). Jesus enables his disciples to *share* in *his peace* even amid sufferings; he encourages them to "take heart" because he has "overcome the world" (16,33) through his passion-death-resurrection.

Now the crucified-risen Lord *commissions* his disciples to continue his revelatory-salvific mission on earth ("As the Father has sent me, even so, I send you" 20,21) and he "breathes on them" and says to them: "Receive the Holy Spirit" (20,22). Through the gift of the Holy Spirit, the risen Lord empowers them to "forgive sins" (20,23; cf. 7,39; 19,30).[346]

Since *Thomas*, one of the Twelve, was not present when the risen Jesus appeared to the other disciples (20,24), they told him: "We have seen the Lord" (20,25). But he insists that unless he *sees and touches the marks of the crucifixion* on his hands and side, he *will not believe* (20,25). Because of this, he is often branded as the "doubting Thomas"! But if it is remembered that he was a *loving and committed disciple* who was *ready even to die with Jesus* (cf. "Let us also go that we may die with him" 11,16), his insistence on "*seeing*" and "*touching*" him (20,25) highlights *his longing* to have a *personal experience* of the crucified-risen Jesus (which the other disciples had: "he showed them his hands and his side" 20,20).

Eight days later, the risen Jesus appears to Thomas and asks him to verify the marks of the crucifixion: "Put your finger here, and see my hands; and put your hand, and place it in my side, and do not be unbelieving but believing" (*kai mê ginou apistos alla pistos* 20,27). It is noteworthy that, as soon as Thomas sees the crucified-risen Jesus and hears his challenging words, instead touching the marks of the crucifixion in his hands and the wound in his side, he *publicly professes his faith in him*: "*My Lord and my God*" (20,28). This is the *climactic confession* in the *Lordship and divinity* of the *crucified-risen Jesus* in the Gospel of John.[347] It is to be noted here that the Fourth Evangelist docs *not say* that Thomas *touched* the wound of Jesus. This is confirmed by what the risen Lord tells Thomas: "Because you have *seen me*, you *have believed*;[348] *blessed* are those who have *not seen* and *yet have believed*" (20,29). *All* (post-Apostolic) *believers* down the centuries are included in this *last* "*beatitude*" in John's Gospel.

It may be recalled here that *after washing the disciples' feet* during the Last Supper, Jesus declared the *first "beatitude"*: "If you know these things, *blessed* are you if you *do* them" (13,17), that is, those who manifest their *love in deeds (of service)* are blessed.

Unlike the Matthean and Lukan Gospels which have *nine* (Mt 5,3-11) and *four* (Lk 6,20-23) "*beatitudes*" respectively, the Johannine Gospel has *only two "beatitudes"*: the first on "*loving*" (Jn 13,17) and the second on "*believing*" (Jn 20,29). If we *believe* in Jesus and *love/serve* one another like him, we would be *doubly blessed*! In short, *a blessed/happy Christian life* consists in *committing oneself to Christ in faith* and *serving others with love like Christ.*

©Looking back at the whole of *Jn 20,1-29*, we may conclude that the *risen Jesus* is revealed as *the Lover and Brother, the Giver of Peace and the Holy Spirit, the Lord and God.*

4.* CONCLUSION: Jesus, the Messiah, Son of God and Life-Giver (Jn 20,30-31)

It is almost universally accepted by Johannine scholars that *Jn 20,30-31* forms the "*Conclusion*" of the whole Gospel. Jn 20,30 states that "Jesus *did many other signs*," to which the disciples were eyewitnesses, "which are *not written*" in this Gospel, since it is *not* meant to be *biographical.*

John's Gospel was written with a *twofold purpose*. The *first* is "so that *you may believe* that *Jesus* is *the Christ, the Son of God*" (20,31abc). "The *immediate purpose* of the whole Gospel of John is to persuade the readers *to believe* (if they are not yet Christians) and *to deepen their faith* (if they are already Christians) in Jesus as the Christ and the Son of God."[349] The first title "*the Christ*" ("Messiah") manifests the *human* aspect and the second title "*the Son of God*" reveals the *divine* dimension of Jesus. The *final purpose* is "that believing *you may have life in his name*" (20,31d). This life-giving purpose of his mission is stated by Jesus himself: "I have come that they may *have life* and have it *abundantly*" (10,10; cf. also 3,16.36). *Salvation* in Jn is interpreted in terms of "*(eternal) life*". "Hence, ultimately every word and deed of the Johannine Jesus must be read and interpreted, prayed and contemplated, under the guidance of the life-giving Spirit (6,63; 16,13), in relation to eternal life, which is manifested in the life-death-resurrection of Jesus."[350] In short, the "*Conclusion*" of John's Gospel underscores *Jesus' Messianic and divine identity* and his *life-giving mission.*

4.6. The Caring Risen Lord (Jn 21)

Jn 21, which is added after the Conclusion (20,30-31), has ***two Sections:*** *1) Epilogue* (21,1-23), and *2) Editorial Conclusion* (21,24-25).

4.6.1. Epilogue (Jn 21,1-23) consists of *two scenes: a) The Miraculous Catch of Fish at the Sea of Galilee (21,1-14)*, and *b) The Risen Lord's Commissioning of Simon Peter and the Beloved Disciple (21,15-23).*

a) The Miraculous Catch of Fish at the Sea of Galilee (Jn 21,1-14)

According to the Gospel of John, the risen Lord had already appeared twice to the disciples who were behind closed doors in Jerusalem for fear of the Jews (20,19-23.26-29). This time he manifests himself to a group of *seven disciples* through a *miraculous catch of fish* in the Sea of Galilee and through serving them *breakfast* at the seashore (21,1-14).

The seven disciples' *fishing expedition*, led by Simon Peter, proves to be *an utter failure* because "that night they caught nothing" (21,2-3)! As they return to the shore tired and hungry, empty-handed and disappointed, the risen Jesus stands on the shore (unrecognized by them 21,4). He asks them affectionately, "Children, you haven't *anything to eat* (*mê ti prosphagion echête;*) have you?" (21,5). (Please note that in the original Greek text mê (interrogative) *expects the answer "No"; mê echête;* you haven't..., have you?") His question implies that he is aware of their predicament and shows a genuine *concern* for them. When they reply with a monosyllabic "*no*" (*ou* 21,5), Jesus tells them what to do, "Cast the net to the right side of the boat, and you will find some" (21,6). As they do that, they have such a big catch that they are unable to haul it in (21,6). Thus, "the *miraculous catch of fish* reveals the *power of Jesus' word to change penury into plenty*. When the disciples act on his word, their plight of having "no" fish (21,5) is transformed into having "so many fish" (21,6)."[351]

Realizing that his disciples must be very tired and hungry after nightlong labour, the risen Lord *prepares breakfast* (of bread and fish) for them and *serves* them lovingly (21,9-13).[352]

> Jesus not only cooks the fish on the charcoal fire and invites them to have breakfast but also *serves* them himself (21,12-13) *like a loving mother*, who serves food to her children when they return home after hard work. It is in and through such a *caring* attitude for and concrete *service* of his disciples that the risen Lord *reveals* himself (21,14).[353]

©To sum up, through the miraculous catch of fish and by serving breakfast to the disciples, the risen *Jesus* manifests himself to them as the *caring, loving and serving Lord.*

b) The Risen Lord's Commissioning of Simon Peter and the Beloved Disciple (Jn 21,15-23)

Already in the miraculous catch of fish (21,1-14), Simon Peter and the Beloved Disciple play different roles. While it is Peter who takes the *initiative* to go fishing (21,3), it is the Beloved Disciple who *recognizes the risen Jesus* during the big catch of fish and tells Peter: "*It is the Lord*" (21,7), at which Simon "comes swimming" to Jesus, while the other disciples come in the boat, dragging the net full of fish (21,7-8). Again, it is Simon who "*hauls the net ashore*" and brings to Jesus some of the fish for the disciples' breakfast (21,10-11).

In the next scene (21,15-23) the *risen Jesus* asks *Simon* three times if he *loves* him and, on getting an affirmative answer, the

Lord *commissions* him to be *the universal pastor* (21,15-17: "Feed *my lambs*" (*boske ta arnia mou*) [leaders]; "Shepherd *my sheep*" (*poimaine ta probata mou*) [believers]; "Feed *my little sheep (boske ta probatia mou)* [new converts]. (Please note that *probatia* in the original Greek text at 21,17 is *different* from *probata* at 21,16.) Then Jesus (the good shepherd) hints at the necessity for Simon Peter (the shepherd) to sacrifice his life for the sheep (21,18-19; cf. 10,11.17-28). In the end, Jesus tells him: "*Follow me*" (21,19), that is, all thc way to death on the cross out of love for the sheep.

Whereas the risen Lord has commissioned the loving Simon to be the universal shepherd (21,15-19), he assigns the *Beloved Disciple* the unique mission to "*remain*" *(menein)* until his second "coming" (21,20-23). This "*abiding*" mission of the Beloved Disciple is fulfilled by his "*witnessing*" and "*writing*" the Gospel (21,24; cf. 20,30-31).[354]

4.6.2. Editorial Conclusion (Jn 21,24-25)

This *second (Editorial) conclusion* (21,24-25) consists of *two kinds of conclusions: a)* a *testimonial conclusion* about the *author* of the Fourth Gospel (21,24), and b) a *hyperbolic conclusion* about the innumerable things done by Jesus (21,25).

a) Testimonial Conclusion (Jn 21,24)[355]

It is to be noted that 21,24 does *not* say: "This *was* the disciple who *bore witness* to these things... and we know that his testimony *was* true" but affirms in the *present tense*: "This *is* (*estin*) the disciple who *is bearing witness* (*ho martyrôn*) to these things and who wrote (*ho grapsas*) these things, and *we know* (*oidamen*) that his testimony (*martyria*) *is* (*estin*) true". The Johannine community and/or its leaders attest ("*we know*" [for certain] *oidamen*) to the truth of the *Beloved Disciple's lasting testimony* ("the one bearing witness" *ho martyrôn*) and to *his authorship of the Gospel* ("the one who wrote these things" *ho grapsas tauta:* 21,23; cf. 20,30-31). The *author's name* is not mentioned in this Gospel but he is explicitly stated to be "*the disciple whom Jesus loved*" (21,20.24; cf. 13,23-25; 19,26-27; 20,2).

b) Hyperbolic Conclusion (Jn 21,25)

While an *authoritative group* attested ("*we* know") the *authenticity* of *the Beloved Disciple's testimony* and *authorship* of this Gospel (21,24), now an *individual* ("*I* suppose") concludes the Gospel with a *hyperbole*: "But there are also many other things that Jesus did; if they were to be written one by one, I suppose that the world itself could not contain the books that would be written" (21,25).

> The first part of v.25 seems to be a poor imitation of the original conclusion of the Gospel by the Evangelist in 20,30. Probably the *redactor* wrote 21,25 to tell the reader that Jn 21 belonged to the "many other signs/things" (20,30; 21,25) done by Jesus. The impossibility of writing down everything that Jesus did is highlighted by this *hyperbolic conclusion*.[356]

This *hyperbole* is similar to the *exaggerated statement* reported to have been made by Rabbi Johanan ben Zakkai about his teacher (around 80 A.D.):

> If all the heavens were sheets of paper, and all the trees were pens for writing, and all the seas were ink, that would not suffice to write down the wisdom I have received from my teacher; and yet I have taken no more from the wisdom of the sages than a fly does when it dips into the sea and bears away a tiny drop.[357]

4.©. John's Good News of the Universal Messiah, the Son of Man, the Incarnate Word/Son of God and the Loving Life-Giver[358]

The Johannine Jesus' *person* and *mission* are revealed in a *variety of ways*: through *titles* and *self-designations, signs* and *works, dialogues* and *discourses* (as we have seen above). *Many Christological titles* are found in the Gospel of John: *the Word, the Lamb of God, Teacher, the Prophet, the Messiah, the King of Israel, the Son of God, the unique Son of God, the Son, the Son of Man, the Saviour of the world, the Holy One of God, the Lord and God.*

There are *seven self-designations of Jesus*: "I am *the bread of life*" (6,35.48), "I am *the light of the world*" (8,12; 9,5), "I am *the gate of the sheep*" (10,7.9), "I am *the good shepherd*" (10,11.14), "I am *the resurrection and the life*" (11,25), "I am *the path, the truth and the life*" (14,6), "I am *the true vine*" (15,1.5).[359] The meaning of these claims is made clear by Jesus' miraculous *signs* and revelatory *discourses.* For instance, his *sign of feeding the hungry* crowd in the wilderness points to Jesus as the *bread of life*; his *giving sight to the man born blind* manifests him as the *light of the world*; Jesus' *raising the dead Lazarus to life* reveals him as *the resurrection and the life.* The *other self-designations* of Jesus are explained in the discourses in which they occur (e.g., the gate and the good shepherd in 10,7-18; the path, the truth and the life in 14,1-31; the true vine in 15,1-8).

The *personal identity and life-giving mission of Jesus* are *summed up* by the Evangelist in the *Conclusion*: "These things are written that you *may believe* that *Jesus* is *the Christ, the Son of God*, and believing you *may have life* in his name" (20,31). In short, the purpose of the Gospel of John is to manifest that

Jesus is *the Messiah* and *the Son of God*, and to help those who believe in him to *have eternal life*. This is confirmed by *Jesus' revelation* to Martha: "I am the resurrection and the life" (11,25) and by *Martha's confession*: "I believe that you are the Christ, the Son of God..." (11,27). But these *titles* have distinctive meanings in the Johannine Gospel.

4.©.1. Jesus, the Universal Messiah/Christ[360]

John's Gospel has many references to Jesus as the *Messiah/ Christ* (*ho Christos* e.g., 1,41; 4,25-26; 7,31.41-42; 11,27; 20,31; cf. also 1,20.25; 3,28; 4,29; 7,26-27; 9,22; 10,24; 12,34). Jesus is *the Universal Messiah* (of *the Jews, Samaritans and the Gentiles*, especially in Jn 2-4, as we have seen) but its significance is also related to the other titles like "the Son of Man" and "the Son of God."

4.©.2. Jesus, the Son of Man[361]

Jesus is the Messiah with a *mysterious origin* because he is "the one who has *descended from heaven, the Son of Man*" (3,13) and he "*comes from above*" (3,31), which, however, no one knows ("when the Christ comes, no one will know *whence* [*pothen*] he comes" 7,27). This *Messiah/Son of Man* will be *lifted up*, which means that Jesus is a *crucified/exalted Messianic Son of Man* (3,14; 8,28; 12,32-34).[362] Thus, the frequent *self-designation* of Jesus as "the Son of Man" (1,51; 3,13,14; 5,27; 6,27.53; 8,28; 9,35; 12,23.24) modifies the meaning of his Messiahship, especially his *origin* and *destiny*.

4.©.3. Jesus, the Son of God[363]

The title "*the Son of God*" occurs many times and in significant places in the Gospel of John (1,34.49; 5,25; 10,36; 11,4.27; 19,7;

20,31). This Christological title has to be interpreted in its context and in the light of the titles like "the *unique* (*monogenês*) *Son of God*" (3,16.18) and "*the Son*" (3,17.35.36; 5,19.20.21.22.23.26; 6,40; 8,36;14,13; 17,1).

Sometimes "*the Son of God*" has a *double meaning*. For example, when Nathanael exclaims: "Rabbi, you are the Son of God! You are the King of Israel!" (1,49), he understands the last two titles as synonymous, which mean that Jesus, the *King* of Israel, is the *adopted* Son of God. Similarly, when Martha confesses Jesus as "the Messiah, the Son of God, he who is coming into the world" (11,27), she means that Jesus is the *expected* Messiah. However, in the *post-resurrectional* period, "*the Son of God*" in Nathanael's and Martha's confessions would mean that Jesus is *divine* (cf. 20,31). Likewise, John the Baptist's testimony that Jesus is "the Son (chosen one) of God" (1,34) has a similar *double meaning*.[364]

Sometimes the Fourth Evangelist highlights the *unique filial relationship* between the *incarnate Son* and *God the Father*. For instance, he states in the Prologue: "The Word became flesh and dwelt among us, and we have seen his glory, glory as of a *unique one (son)* from the Father" (*monogenous para patros*: 1,14), and he concludes the Prologue by confessing: "a *unique God/Son* (*monogenês theos/hyios*), the one who is *in the bosom of the Father*, he has made him known" (1,18). Hence Jesus, the *unique Son of God*, is the *revealer par excellence* of God the Father.

Furthermore, Jesus himself declares: "God so loved the world that he gave his *unique Son* (*ho hyios ho monogenês*) that whoever believes in him may not perish but may have eternal life" (3,16; cf. 3,18: "*the unique Son of God*" *ho monogenês hyios tou theou*). The purpose of the loving God sending his *unique Son* into the world is to *save* the world by giving *eternal life* to all those who believe in him (3,17).[365]

Often the Johannine Jesus claims *divine identity*. For instance, he tells "the Jews": "Truly, truly, I say to you, before Abraham was, *I am*" (8,58), for which they try to stone him as a blasphemer (8,59). Again, when "the Jews" accuse Jesus of blasphemy when he says: "*I and the Father are one*" (10,30), he declares: "*I am the Son of God*" (10,36) and "*the Father is in me and I am in the Father*" (10,38). This shows that Jesus is conscious of his being the *divine Son* of the Father and that they have an intimate *mutual indwelling* relationship. Frequently, God "*the Father*" and "*the Son*" are mentioned together to indicate their *divine paternal-filial relationship* (e.g., 3,35; 5,19-23.26). Jesus, the *incarnate Son*, is the *revealer* of the Father (1,14.18; 14,8-11).

4.©.4. *Jesus, the Loving Life-Giver*[366]

We have seen above that the *final purpose* of writing the Fourth Gospel is to enable the readers to have *(eternal) life* (*zôê*) in and through Jesus, the Christ, the Son of God (20,31). God *the Father* is the *source* of (divine/eternal) *life* and Jesus, the Son of God, shares in the Father's life ("For as the Father has life in himself, so he has *granted* the Son also to have life in himself": 5,26) and the Son *mediates* this divine life to believing humans. Jesus himself has explicitly stated that the reason why he has come into this world is to *impart life in abundance* ("I came that they may have life and have it abundantly": 10,10; cf. 3,16: "that whoever believes in him may have eternal life"). This *life in abundance* is symbolized by the amazing signs of the *abundance of wine and bread* provided by Jesus during the Cana-wedding (2,1-11) and the feeding of the five thousand

(6,4-14) respectively. The *life-giving power of Jesus' word* is manifested in the miraculous signs of the healing of the royal official's dying son (4,46-54) and the raising of the dead Lazarus to life (11,38-44). The raising of Lazarus from the dead reveals Jesus as "*the resurrection and the life*" (11,25), a qualitatively new life that will outlive physical death (11,26) because it is a participation in the *eternal life*, the *divine life* of the Father and the Son (5,21.24-29). Jesus is not only the *revealer* (8,12; 14,6) but also the *mediator or giver of eternal life* (17,2-3). To *mediate God's own life* (*zôê*) to human beings, the incarnate Son of God, *the good shepherd*, has to voluntarily *sacrifice* ("*lay down*") *his physical life* (*psychê*) (10,11.15.17; cf. 11,50-52). *Jesus' self-sacrificial death* reveals that he is *a loving life-giver* (13,1; cf.15,13: "Greater love than this no one has that he lays down his life for his friends").

In short, the *Johannine Jesus* is the *human Christ* and the *divine Son* and therefore he *reveals God the Father* and *mediates eternal life* to believers. *John's Christology* may be summed up in the confession of faith: *Jesus* is *the Christ*, *the Son of God* and *the Life-Giver* (cf. 20,31).[367]

©.

CONCLUSION[368]

All the four Gospels present *Jesus Christ* as both *human* and *divine.* All the Evangelists believe that Jesus has a *God-given salvific mission* which he has accomplished in and through his life and ministry, death and resurrection.

The four Evangelists are *unanimous* in affirming that Jesus is the "*Christ/Messiah*" but his *Messiahship* is understood/ interpreted *differently* in each Gospel. Jesus is a *mysterious* Messiah in Mark, a *Davidic* Messiah in Matthew, a *prophetic* Messiah in Luke and a *universal* Messiah in John. They are *complementary* aspects of *Jesus' Messiahship.*

Similarly, Jesus is presented as "*the Son of God*" in all the Gospels. Even though he is confessed as "the Son of God" in every Gospel, the title may have *different connotations* depending on the *context* in the Gospel. Often it has also *two* (*historical* and *post-resurrectional*) *levels* of meaning (e.g., in the testimony John the Baptist, in the confessions of disciples like Nathanael, Simon Peter, Martha of Bethany, the centurion, etc.). During Jesus' baptism and transfiguration, God the Father reveals Jesus to be his *beloved Son* but its deeper meaning of his being the *unique Son of God* would be understood only in the light of Easter and under the guidance of the Holy Spirit. By the time the Gospels were written, the Evangelists and the Christian communities believed in and proclaimed Jesus Christ's *truly divine Sonship* and *unique filial relationship* with God the Father.

Jesus is not only "the Son of God" but also "*the Son of Man*" in all the four Gospels, which has *many meanings* depending on the context. It is Jesus' preferred *self-designation*. It points to Jesus being *truly human* (a member of the human race) and a *suffering human being* in solidarity with others (cf. his *passion-predictions*). Sometimes it refers to his (*divine*) *authority* even during his ministry (e.g., to teach in the Temple, to work miracles even on the Sabbath, to forgive sins). At times it indicates his *mysterious origin* and his *sitting at the right hand of God* after his resurrection. At his final coming (*parousia*) he will be a *glorious (humandivine) being* who will *gather the elect* and *judge the nations*. Thus, "the Son of Man" in the Gospels means that Jesus is *truly human* but *more than human*. Therefore, "*the Son of Man*" is a "*bridge*" between the *human Messiah* and the *divine Son of God*.

Jesus' salvific mission is repeatedly mentioned in all the Gospels. But the *nature of his mission* is presented *differently* in the *Synoptic* and *Johannine Gospels*. The *Synoptic* authors underscore the *liberative* aspect and the *Johannine* Evangelist underlines the *life-giving* dimension of *salvation*. In short, the *divinehuman Jesus Christ* is *the living liberator* in the Gospels of Mark, Matthew and Luke and *the loving life-giver* in the Gospel of John.[369]

In the *Synoptic* Gospels Jesus' *mission* consists primarily in *establishing* the *reign/kingdom of God* here on earth, whereas in the *Johannine* Gospel it means *giving eternal life* (life in its fullness/abundance) here and now and hereafter.

In the *Synoptic* Gospels Jesus not only *announced/proclaimed* the good news of *God's kingdom/rule* of justice, love, freedom and fraternity but also revealed its real presence in his *loving attitude* towards all men, women and children, and in his *compassionate actions* in favour of the poor, the hungry, the sick, the marginalized, the oppressed, the exploited, the despised and the sinners. All of them experienced the *presence of the loving and compassionate God in him*. The *reign of the loving God*, which was manifested already in Jesus' ministry, was finally established in *his passion-death-resurrection*. The *paschal mystery* is the *climax* of the *saving/liberative mission* of Jesus in the Synoptic Gospels.

In the Johannine Gospel the God-given *mission* of the divinehuman Jesus, the universal Saviour, consists in *revealing God as a loving Father* and in *mediating eternal life* to all who believe in him (3,16; 10,10; 20,31).[370]

In the Gospel of John, the *source* of (divine/eternal) *life* is God *the Father* and its mediator to believing human beings is Jesus, the Son of God, who shares in the Father's life (5,26). Jesus himself has clearly affirmed that the *purpose of his coming into this world* is to enable humans to "have *life*, and have it *abundantly*" (10,10). This *abundant life* is symbolized by the *abundance of wine and bread* provided miraculously by Jesus during the wedding at Cana (2,1-11) and the feeding of the five thousand (6,4-14) respectively. The miraculous sign of the curing of the royal official's dying son (4,46-54) manifests the *life-giving power of Jesus' word*. The raising of the dead Lazarus to life reveals Jesus as "*the resurrection and the life*" (11,25).

Jesus is both the *revealer* (8,12; 14,6) and the *giver of eternal life* (17,2-3). In order to *mediate God's life* (*zôê*) to humans, *the good shepherd sacrifices* ("*lays down*") *his physical life* (*psychê*) (10,11.15.17). Since there is no greater love than to lay down one's life for one's friends (15,13), *Jesus' voluntary self-sacrificial death* reveals that he is *the loving life-giver par excellence* (cf. 13,1).

ENDNOTES

***ACRONYMS* of *Books* by George Mlakuzhyil S.J.:**

AL	:	*Abundant Life in the Gospel of John* (Delhi 2007).
BLG	:	*Be a Life-Giver: A Retreat on John's Gospel* (Mumbai 2012).
CLS	:	*The Christocentric Literary Structure of the Fourth Gospel* (First Edition) (Rome 1987).
CLDS	:	*Christocentric Literary-Dramatic Structure of John's Gospel* (Second Enlarged Edition) (Rome 2011).
GJCS	:	*The Gospel of John: Commentary for Students* (Delhi 2013).
IGL	:	*Initiation to the Gospel of Life: A Guide to John's Gospel* (Mumbai 2008).
PAL	:	*Path to Abundant Life in the Gospel of John: A Guide to Study, Prayer, Preaching and Retreat* (Delhi 2005).
GNJCPI	:	T. K. John S.J. & George Mlakuzhyil S.J., *The Good News of Jesus Christ for the People of India* (Delhi 2021).

[1] "*Primarily*, the *gospels* tell us *how an evangelist conceived of and presented Jesus to a Christian community* in the last third of the first century, a presentation that indirectly gives us an insight into that community's life at the time when the gospel was written" (R. E. Brown, "Johannine Ecclesiology - The Community's Origins", 380 [*italics* added] [retrieved on 18-07-2019].

[2] Cf. T. K. John S.J. & George Mlakuzhyil S.J., *The Good News of Jesus Christ for the People of India [GNJCPI]* (Delhi 2021).

[3] We will be dealing with *Jesus only* in the *four Gospels* (cf. Richard A. Burridge, *Four Gospels, One Jesus? A Symbolic Reading, 2nd edition* [London 2005]; Mark L. Strauss, *Four Portraits, One Jesus: A Survey of Jesus and the Gospels* [Michigan 2015]: Zondervan: Kindle Edition).

Some authors have examined the Christologies in all the books of the NT (e.g., Frank J. Matera, *New Testament Christology* [Kentucky 1999]). Others have studied the Christology of the NT from the perspective of the Christological titles like Prophet, Messiah, Son of Man, Son of God, Lord, etc. (e.g., V. Taylor, *The Names of Jesus* [London 1954]; Oscar Cullmann, *The Christology of the New Testament*, 2nd edition [London 1963]; Raymond E. Brown, *An Introduction to New Testament Christology* [New York 1994]).

[4] *The New Jerome Biblical Commentary [NJBC]*, edited by Raymond E. Brown, Joseph A. Fitzmyer & Roland E. Murphy, (London/New York 1995),1357-58 [*italics* added].

[5] *Ibid.*, 1358 [*italics* added].

[6] Cf. Richard A. Burridge compares the four Gospel portraits of Jesus to *four pictures* of Sir Winston Churchill (in his country house in Kent, England):

"Four pictures, all different – each with its own story evoking its own atmosphere and provoking its own response in the viewer – yet all are of one and the same man… So we are introduced to the *statesman*, the *family man*, the *man of war*, or the *solitary painter*, yet all recognizably *Churchill*, and some things (the cigar perhaps) are common to all four pictures… So in these simple portraits we have diversity and continuity, inspiration and selectivity, artistic licence within limits." (*op. cit.*, 2 [*italics* added]).

[7] Mark L. Strauss, *op. cit.*, 24 [*italics* added].

[8] *Ibid.*, 21.

[9] Cf. T. K. John S.J. & George Mlakuzhyil S.J., *GNJCPI.*

[10] Even though *traditionally* the New Testament gives the *Gospel of Matthew* as the *first*, followed by the other Gospels of Mark, Luke and John, there is literary evidence to show that Matthew and Luke used Mark's Gospel as *one* of their sources. That is to say, Mt and Lk are *dependent* on Mk. Therefore, we prefer to present '**Mark's Jesus Christ**' ***first.***

[11] "Although there is no outline of Mark's Gospel with which all commentators agree, most recognize that Peter's confession at Caesarea Philippi (8,27-30) is a turning point in the narrative. Previous to this episode, Jesus' initial proclamation that the kingdom of God is at hand (1,15) provides the narrative's leitmotif, which identifies Jesus as the powerful herald of God's kingdom who, unlike the scribes, has been endowed with authority to teach, preach, and heal" (Frank J. Matera, *op. cit.,* 6).

[12] After Peter's Messianic confession, the Section on Jesus' passion predictions of "the Son of Man" and the disciples' failure to understand (on the way to Jerusalem) forms the 2nd part of the Gospel (8,31-10,52).

[13] The passion-death-resurrection (foretold in the 2nd part) is narrated in the 3rd part of the Gospel (11,1-16,8) (in Jerusalem).

[14] It may be noted that *hyios theou* ("Son of God") at 1,1 and 15,39 is without the definitive article "the" (*ho*). It means that he is "God's Son" ("divine"). But during Jesus' baptism and transfiguration, the Father reveals him as "my Son, the beloved" (*ho hyios mou ho agapêtos:* 1,11; 9,7). During his trial before the Sanhedrin, the high priest asks him, "Are you the Christ, the Son of the Blessed One?" (*sy ei ho Christos ho hyios tou eulogêtou:* 14,61).

[15] The Greek expression *hê basileia tou theou* highlights the reality of "the reign/rule of God" rather than the territory (empire) of "the kingdom of God."

[16] John Fuellenbach, *The Kingdom of God: The Message of Jesus Today* (New York 1997), 80.

[17] Frank J. Matera, *op. cit.,* 10 [*italics* added].

[18] Daniel J. Harrington, "The Gospel according to Mark," in: *NJBC*, 600.

[19] Frank J. Matera, *op. cit.*, 11.

[20] In the 1950s my father used to insist that the *Dalit labourers* working in our field must *sit and eat meals with the family members*, even though some of our relatives and neighbours used to raise objections against it!

[21] Frank J. Matera, *op. cit.*, 12-13 [*italics* added].

[22] Ibid., 14 [*italics* added].

[23] Cf. Daniel J. Harrington, *op. cit.*, in: *NJBC*, 609.

[24] "*The Little Sisters of Jesus*" living in a small house in Varanasi (on the bank of the river Ganges) *share their food with any beggar* (poor man or woman or child) who comes to their convent during their meals. What an edifying example it is for all priests and Religious to follow!

[25] Frank J. Matera, *op. cit.*, 16 [*italics* added].

[26] Are the priests/pastors in parishes and principals in the Christian schools and colleges in India today concerned about feeding the hungry and educating the poor children? Or are many of them busy catering to the rich and enriching themselves? They seem to be like the disciples who failed to understand the meaning of Jesus' miraculous feeding of the crowd with five "loaves" (cf. 6,52)!

[27] Frank J. Matera, *op. cit.*, 16-17 [*italics* added].

[28] *Ibid.*, 17.

[29] *Ibid.*, 18.

[30] '*Satan*' (in Hebrew) means "adversary". Hence, by addressing Peter "Satan," Jesus reprimands him for being his "adversary"!

[31] These three "passion predictions" deal primarily with Jesus' suffering, death and resurrection but they are also applicable to the sufferings of his faithful disciples in history.

[32] Every Pope is supposed to be "the servant of servants" (*servus servorum*). Pope Francis is a shining example of Christian "servant-leadership" in the Church today.

[33] Mark L. Strauss, *op. cit.*, 187.

[34] "*Den of robbers [spêlaion lêstôn]* is better translated as 'bandits' stronghold,' conveying more the original sense of Jeremiah that the rulers plunder the people like bandits and then seek refuge in the Temple" (*The New Oxford Annotated Bible, NRSV,* footnote on Mk 11,17).

[35] Frank J. Matera, *op. cit.,* 20.

[36] Cf. Daniel J. Harrington, *op. cit.*, in: *NJBC*, 623-25.

[37] Mark L. Strauss, *op. cit.,* 189-190 [*italics* added].

[38] *Ibid.*, 190 [*italics* added].

[39] Frank J. Matera, *op. cit.,* 20 [*italics* added].

[40] According to Jn 12,3 it was *Mary of Bethany* who *anointed Jesus' feet* with a costly ointment.

[41] Cf. V. Sevasahayam, *Doing Dalit Theology in Biblical Key* (ISPCK, Delhi, 1997), 36-44: "New Thrusts of Dalit Theology" based on Mk 14,3-9.

[42] Cf. Daniel J. Harrington, *op. cit.*, in: *NJBC*, 626.

[43] *Awakened leaders of Dalits and Tribals* must have the courage, like the assertive Christ, to *challenge the unjust oppressive powers* if the leaders are serious about the liberation of their suffering brothers and sisters.

[44] A Dalit is sometimes stripped and paraded in the village by the so called high castes to insult the whole Dalit community.

[45] Here, as in Mk 1,1, *hyios theou* ("son of God") does not have the definite article *ho* ("the) before *hyios* ("son"). Hence the Gentile centurion might have understood it as referring to Jesus' divinity as "a son of God". But for Mark, Jesus is "the Son of God" since God the Father declared Jesus to be "my Son the beloved" (*ho hyios mou ho agapêtos:* Mk 1,11; 9,7) during his Baptism and Transfiguration. There is a correspondence between Mark's proclamation of "Jesus, Son of God" (1,1) in the very first verse of the Gospel, and God the Father's declaration "my beloved Son" at the beginning (1,11) and middle (9,7) of the Gospel, and the Centurion's confession: "Truly this one was son of God" (15,39) towards the end of the Gospel.

[46] Earlier evil spirits had cried out, "You are the Son of God" (Mk 3,11) and "the Son of the Most High" (5,7). During Jesus' trial before

the Sanhedrin, the high priest had questioned Jesus: "Are you the Christ, the Son of the Blessed One?" (14,61). But when Jesus answered him, "I am", he was accused of blasphemy (14,64)!

[47] Mark L. Strauss, *op. cit.*, 191-92.

[48] This is the "good news of Jesus, Son of God" (1,1; cf. also 1,11).

[49] Mark L. Strauss, *op. cit.*, 192.

[50] *Ibid.*, 193.

[51] Cf. Bruce M. Metzger, *A Textual Commentary on the Greek New Testament*, 2nd ed. (Stuttgart 1994), Mk 16,9-20.

[52] Cf. Frank J. Matera, *op. cit.*, 24-26 and Mark L. Strauss, *op. cit.*, 194-96. Cf. Jack Dean Kingsbury, *The Christology of Mark's Gospel* (Philadelphia 1983), for a detailed study of the Christological titles.

[53] Mk 2,10.28; 8,31.38; 9,9.12.31; 10,33.45; 13,26; 14,21.21.41.62.

[54] The Greek *ho hyios tou anthrôpou* ("the Son of Man") is a literal translation of the Aramaic *bar nasa* or the Hebrew *ben adam*, which means, a member of the genus man [humanity]. In the OT "the son of man" is often used as an equivalent to "man". For example, "What is *man* that you are mindful of him, and the *son of man* that you consider him?" (Ps 8,4[5]).

[55] Raymond E. Brown, *Introduction to New Testament Christology*, 91.

[56] Mark L. Strauss, *op. cit.*, 195 [*italics* added].

[57] Frank J. Matera, *op. cit.*, 26 [*italics* added].

[58] Cf. Mark L. Strauss, *op. cit.*, 194.

[59] Frank J. Matera, *op. cit.*, 6.

[60] "Matthew groups his narrative sections around these five discourses, providing a pattern of alternating narrative and discourse throughout the Gospel" (Mark L. Strauss, *op. cit.*, 219). This is not always true, since the *last section* consists only of *one narrative* of Jesus' Passion, Death and Resurrection (Mt 26,1-28,28), whose *new beginning* is clearly indicated at 26,1 ("When Jesus had *finished* all these sayings...").

[61] Cf. *ibid*, 220-22 and Frank J. Matera, *op. cit.*, 26-28 for the threefold division of Mt 4,12-28,20 and subdivisions (based on the criteria of alternating narrative and discourse, names of places and movement of Jesus). But we have a modified *fourfold division* (as shown below).

[62] Frank J. Matera, *op. cit.,* 29.

[63] Cf. *ibid.,* 30 and n. 60 on p. 263.

[64] Even though John the Baptist might have used "fire" in Mt 3,11 to symbolize judgement (cf. 3,10.12; cf. also Gen 19,24), at Pentecost the Holy Spirit appears to the disciples in the form of "tongues of fire" and rests on them which enables them to speak in tongues (Acts 2,3-4), implying that they are purified and empowered.

[65]Frank J. Matera, *op. cit.,* 32 [*italics* added].

[66] The "kingdom of heaven" is a reverent circumlocution (to avoid mentioning the name of God) for the "kingdom of God" (cf. Mt 12,28; 19,24; 21,31.43). It refers to God's reign/rule of justice and peace on earth (not in heaven).

[67] *DBCNT*, 101.

[68] Frank J. Matera, *op. cit.,* 34 [*italics* added].

[69] Cf. *DBCNT*, 107-8.

[70] Frank J. Matera, *op. cit.,* 34 [*italics* added]. Cf. also Tobias Hägerland, "John's Gospel: A Two-Level Drama," *JSNT* [Journal of the Study of the New Testament], (2003), 309-322.

[71] Cf. Frank J. Matera, *op. cit.,* 35.

[72] Mark L. Strauss, *op. cit.,* 230 [*italics* added].

[73] *Ibid.,* 230.

[74] *DBCNT*, 120.

[75] *NJBC*, 654.

[76] C. H. Dodd, *The Parables of the Kingdom* (New York 1961), 5.

[77] Frank J. Matera, *op. cit.,* 37.

[78] *Ibid.,* 37.

[79] "*Compassion* in the Gospel of Matthew means a deep inward movement, as if something *touched the inner recesses of one's being.* What moved Jesus within compelled him to express himself in outward action as well. Hence his *acts of compassion* were *much more than* mere *feeling pity*" (*DBCNT*, 127; *italics* added).

[80] The expression "the Son of Man" occurs 81 times in the four Gospels (30x in Mt, 14x in Mk, 25x in Lk & 12x in Jn).

[81] *Later* Matthew will portray Jesus as the *suffering Son of Man* and the *glorious judge* in the Parousia (see below).

[82] At the historical context, the second title did not necessarily mean that Jesus was divine but that, Jesus, the Messiah, was like a son very dear to God. But in the post-Easter period, the title has a deeper meaning of Jesus being the divine Son of God (which reflects the faith of the Matthean community).

Since the title "The Son of the living God" is found only in Mt (but not in Mk or Lk), probably it was not part of the original confession of Simon but was added by Matthew. This is confirmed by the fact that Jesus asks the disciples not to reveal his identity as "the Christ" (16,20) but not as "the Son of God."

[83] At the end of Jesus' temptations, he ordered the devil: "Begone, Satan!" (Mt 4,10: *hypage, satana*); now he orders Peter: "Begone behind me, Satan!" (16,23: *hypage hopisô mou, satana*). "The Greek verb *dei* ["must" at 16,21] suggests that Jesus' passion, death, and resurrection are God's will for the Messiah... In trying to dissuade Jesus from his messianic destiny, Peter unwittingly plays the role of Satan (16,22-23)" (Frank J. Matera, *op. cit.*, 38-39). By opposing God's plan of salvation through Jesus' Paschal mystery (suffering-death-resurrection), Peter acts as an "*Adversary*" (*Satan*)! So Jesus orders Peter to get out of his way!

[84] Since the discourse is more ecclesial than Christological, we shall examine it only briefly, highlighting what it says about the person and mission of Jesus.

[85] Adrian Leske, "Matthew," in: *The International Bible Commentary [IBC]*, ed. by William R. Farmer (Collegeville 1998), 1308.

[86] The future passive tense (*paradothêsetai*) (Mt 20,18) is normally translated as "will be delivered" (e.g., RSV) but here it hints at the betrayal by Judas (one of the Twelve), who is often referred to as "the betrayer" (*ho paradidous*) (26,26.46.48; 27,3; cf. also 25,24-26).

[87] Some years ago when an Indian Archbishop was made a Cardinal, he is reported to have said: "Finally, I have become *a Prince of the Church*"!

[88] *DBCNT*, 140-41.

[89] Normally this episode is *wrongly entitled* (by translators and commentators) as "Jesus' *triumphal* entry into Jerusalem"! Many

parishes have *triumphalist processions* on *Palm Sunday* and on the feast of "Christ the King"! Regrettably they forget that Jesus is *not* a *worldly king* but a *crucified king* (cf. Mt 27,37)!

[90] It is to be noted that when Matthew quotes Zech 9,9, he leaves out the words "triumphant and victorious is he" but retains the words "*humble*, and mounted on an ass..." (Mt 21,5). It proves that Mt interprets Jesus' entry *not* as a "*triumphal*" but as a "*humble*" one! Generally, victorious kings and generals do not ride on an ass but on a war horse. It was reported that an Indian Catholic Bishop rode a decorated horse when he went to take charge of his diocese! What a counter-witness it is to Jesus Christ who rode on a donkey!

[91] "Son of David" is one of the favourite titles for the Messiah in Mt (1,1; 9,27; 12,23; 15,22; 20,30.31; 21,9.15; 22,42).

[92] This recognition of Jesus "the prophet" prepares the readers of the Gospel for the next episode of the cleansing of the Temple as a prophetic act (see below).

[93] At the time of Jesus, there was a popular belief that the Temple would be cleansed by the Messiah (cf. *Ps Sol* 17:30) (cf. Adrian Leske, "Matthew," in: *IBC*, 1312).

[94] *DBCNT*, 141.

[95] *Ibid.*, 142.

[96] Mark L. Strauss, *op. cit.*, 233 [*italics* added]. Jesus' interpretation of the sudden withering of the fig tree as an example of the power of faith may be a later Matthean reinterpretation of the meaning of the miracle to instruct the Christians to pray with unshakable faith (cf. 21,20-22).

[97] *DBCNT*, 143.

[98] *Ibid.*, 146.

[99] It is surprising that, in spite of Jesus' prohibition to call any one "father," even today most Christian *priests* insist on being addressed "*father*" (which fosters *paternalism* in their dealings with the faithful)! If all Christians are brothers and sisters, how can the priests claim to be "fathers" of the faithful? Likewise, if *Jesus* is the only "*Lord*," why should *bishops* be addressed "*Your Lordship*"? Like Jesus who washed his disciples' feet and like Pope Francis who washed the feet

of the prisoners and women, all bishops and priests are called to be *servant-leaders*: "He who is *greatest* among you shall be *your servant*" (Mt 23,11).

[100] The prediction of the destruction of Jerusalem and that of the temple are linked together (cf. Mt 23,38 & 24,2).

[101] Adrian Leske, "Matthew," in: *IBC*, 1318.

[102] *NJBC*, 669 [*italics* added].

[103] The present passive verb (*paradidotai, "is delivered up"*) points to his experience of it as if it were happening to him right now. That is why it is called "prophetic awareness". This fourth passion prediction in Mt 26,2 is not found in Mk.

[104] Their meeting in the palace of Caiaphas is mentioned only in Mt (not in Mk). It highlights the religious leaders' secret scheming and deliberate decision to do away with Jesus at the earliest opportune moment.

[105] In Jn 12,1-3 the man's name is "*Lazarus*" (not "Simon the leper" as in Mk and Mt) and the woman is Lazarus' sister "*Mary*" and she anointed Jesus' *feet* (not "his head," as in Mk and Mt).

[106] It is only Matthew that mentions "the disciples" (Mt 26,8) as the ones who were indignant at the woman who "wasted" the precious ointment, whereas Mark refers to those who were at table (Mk 14,4) and John names "Judas" as the accuser (Jn 12,4-5).

[107] This is Matthew's shortened version of Mk 14,12-17.

[108] It is only in Mt (not in Mk) that Judas also asks Jesus, "Is it I, Rabbi" and Jesus answers him, "You have said so", which underscores his hypocrisy.

[109] Cf. "Passover *Seder*," *Wikipedia* (retrieved on 19-08-2018).

[110] Notice that in Mt 26,31 Peter says: "I will *never* (*oudepote*)..., whereas in Mk 14,29 he says: "*not* I" (*ouk egô*).

[111] We know from Jn 18,10 that it was "Simon Peter" who had the sword and cut off the slave Malchus' ear.

[112] This is reported only in Matthew (not in the other Gospels). Another version of Judas' suicide is given in Acts 1,18-19.

[113] It is based on Mk 15,1-15 but with *some additions* like the request of Pilate's wife not to condemn Jesus, "the righteous man" (Mt 27,19), Pilate's washing his hands and the people's reaction (Mt 27,24-25).

[114] "Jesus, like Dalits, was stripped of his right to protect his decency and dignity by being dispossessed of his clothes" (*DBCNT*, 158).

[115] Frank J. Matera, *op. cit.*, 43.

[116] We may wonder why the angel at Jesus' tomb and the risen Lord insist on the disciples' going to *Galilee* in order to meet him. First of all, it was in "Galilee of the Gentiles" (Mt 4,15-16) that Jesus started his mission of proclaiming the presence of the Kingdom of God (4,17). Secondly, it was from this Galilee that Jesus called his first disciples to follow him (cf. 4,18-22). Hence it is fitting that he chose Galilee from which to send the Eleven disciples to "*disciple* [*mathêteusate:* make disciples of] all the nations" (*panta ta ethnê:* Gentiles) (cf. 28,19).

[117] This is my own *literal* translation of the Greek text in Mt 28,19-20. It is to be noted that there is only one imperative verb *mathêteusate* ("disciple" used as a verb, which is normally translated as "make disciples"), all the others are participles (*poreuthentes* "going," *baptizontes* "baptizing" or "immersing," *didaskontes* "teaching"). Hence the emphasis is on *mathêteusate ('discipling').*

[118] *DBCNT,* 162 [*italics* added].

[119] Unfortunately, the Catholic ritual of "baptizing" children and adults by pouring a few drops of water on their head has lost its baptismal symbolism! I wish the Catholic Church would go back to the Early Church's meaningful practice of baptising catechumens by immersion. Dipping the catechumen in the water and lifting him/her up from it would symbolize *dying with Christ* and *rising with him* to new life, that is, *participating* in the *Paschal mystery* of Jesus.

[120] Cf. Frank J. Matera, *op. cit.,* 26-47, especially 44-47; Mark L. Strauss, *op. cit.,* 239-42. Besides *titles*, Jesus' *words* (e.g., preaching, teaching) and *deeds* (miracles, passion-death-resurrection) *reveal* a lot about *Jesus' person and mission* (as we have seen above).

[121] Besides these *primary* titles, there are also other *secondary* titles such as "Teacher," "Prophet," "Lord," etc. in Mt.

[122] Cf. Frank J. Matera, *op. cit.,* 44; Mark L. Strauss, *op. cit.,* 239-40.

[123] Frank J. Matera, *op. cit.,* 44 [*italics* added].

[124] *Ibid.* [*italics* added].

[125] Cf. Mt 8,20; 9,6; 11,19; 12,8.32; 13,37; 20,28.

[126] Gerald O'Collins, *Christology: A Biblical, Historical, and Systematic Study of Jesus* (New York 1995), 126 [*italics* added].

Even though only Mk 14,36 reports Jesus' addressing God in prayer using the Aramaic *Abba* (*ho patêr,* Father), in Mt 11,26 he prays to God by calling Him "Father" (*ho patêr*), which is the Greek equivalent of *Abba*.

[127] It may be noted that *theou hyios* ("God's son") both in Mt 14,33 and 27,54 does *not* have the definite article *ho* (the). Historically speaking, it is probable that the disciples, who were amazed at Jesus' calming the stormy sea, concluded him to be a wonder-worker with divine authority. Similarly, seeing the earthquake at the death of Jesus, the Gentile centurion might have thought of Jesus as "a son of God". But in the post-resurrection period the Evangelist sees a deeper Christological significance in their confessions as "the Son of God" who has a "truly" unique filial relationship with God.

[128] St. Paul makes an *experiential confession of faith* in the *personal presence of Christ in him* when he says: "It is no longer I who live, but *Christ* who *lives in me*" (Gal 2,20).

[129] This is a modified version of the Outlines by Mark L. Strauss, *op. cit.*, 260-61; Frank J. Matera, *op. cit.*, 51; Robert J. Karris, "The Gospel according to Luke," in: *NJBC*, 677-78.

[130] "The prologue sets out the *purpose* of the work, which is to confirm for Theophilus the *truth* of the gospel. Luke stresses the historical reliability of his story, claiming to have received his information from eyewitnesses and to have carefully investigated these accounts to ensure their veracity" (Mark L. Strauss, *op. cit.*, 263, *italics* added).

[131] *Ibid.*, 263.

[132] Robert J. Karris, *op. cit.*, in: *NJBC*, 679. Since the "*Birth of Jesus, the Saviour*" (cf. Lk 2,10-11) is in "*Fulfilment of God's Promises,*" it is better to *combine* the *two titles* into *one* (as given above).

[133] Mark L. Strauss, *op. cit.*, 264 [*italics* added]. "The first part of the infancy narrative clearly indicates that the birth of the Messiah and of his predecessor is the continuation of God's faithfulness to

Israel and not a disruption of salvation history. Jesus is the Davidic Messiah who will fulfil the promises God made to Abraham" (Frank J. Matera, *op. cit.*, 52).

[134] Mark L. Strauss, *op. cit.*, 264 [*italics* added]

[135] *Ibid.*

[136] *Ibid.*, 265 [*italics* added].

[137] A "diptych" is a double painting on two connected panels.

[138] "Hannah also testified to this truth by offering a joyful prayer to God in which she said, "He (Lord) raises up the poor (*dal*) from the dust..." (1 Sam 2,8). Hannah addressed herself as the lowly (Dalit) in Hebrew (*dal*), who had been living in a hopeless situation like that of Elizabeth. Elizabeth lived through the curse of barrenness all through her life, and endured the disgrace from her people. But now God has taken away her disgrace by looking at her "favourably" (v 25)" (*DBCNT*, 207).

[139] A literal translation of the Greek text (Lk 1,35bcd) is given above. Just as the expressions *pneuma hagion* (1,35b) and *dynamis hypsistou* (1,35c), which are parallel to each other, do not have the definite article *ho* (the), so *hyios theou* has no article (*ho*). Also *dio kai* (1,35d) is translated literally as "and therefore" since it shows the connection with 1,35bc and the reason why "the holy one to be born (*to gennômenon hagion*) will be called Son of God" (*klêthêsetai hyios theou*) (1,35d). The "*holy*" child (that is going to be born) is "Son of God" because he was conceived by the power of the *Holy* Spirit. [It is to be noted that, since *hagion* is a neuter adjective, it qualifies *to gennômenon*, and not *hyios*, which is a masculine noun.]

[140] "So it was that Mary, a virgin, poor and from an unimportant village, was chosen by God for his greatest intervention in history. When the call came, after stating the truth about herself, Mary responded firmly to the call... Her submission to the divine will is remarkably complete" (*DBCNT*, 207).

[141] Elizabeth calls Mary "the mother of my Lord" (1,43), anticipating the title "Lord" used by Christian believers to address the risen Christ (cf. Frank J. Matera, *op. cit.*, 53).

[142] *Ibid.*, 53.

[143] The Greek word *katalyma* (Lk 2,7) means a "*guest-room*" in a house (cf. Lk 22,11; cf. also Mk 14,14), and *not* an "*inn*" (as it is normally translated, e.g., RSV), for which Luke employs another Greek word *pandocheion* (cf. Lk 10,34).

[144] It is to be noted that *euangelizomai* ("I goodnews") is a *verb* whose *direct object* is *charan megalên* ("*great joy*") and the indirect object is *hymin* ("to you").

[145] Frank J. Matera, *op. cit.*, 53-54 [*italics* added].

[146] *DBCNT*, 210.

[147] *Ibid.*, 213 [*italics* added].

[148] It also brings to fulfilment Zechariah's prophecy about John's mission (cf. Lk 1,76-78).

[149] *DBCNT*, 213 [*italics* added].

[150] While John's baptising "with water" (*hydati)* is only a symbolic purification, Jesus' baptising (immersing) "in Holy Spirit and fire" (*en pneumati hagio kai pyri)* brings about a real purification of the person and his inner transformation (cf. Acts 2,3-4). N.B. The Greek expression *en pneumati hagiô kai pyri* is a *hendiadys* (in which one idea or reality is expressed by *two words* connected by 'and', e.g., Today is "nice and cool," which means, "nicely cool").

[151] Robert J. Karris, op. cit., in: *NJBC*, 686. At Pentecost Luke reports how the 'fire' of the Holy Spirit transforms human beings (cf. Acts 2,1-4.14-18).

[152] It is noteworthy that the Greek noun used for the "dove" is *not* the masculine *peristeros* (cock dove) but the feminine *peristera* (female dove) (Lk 3,22; cf. also Mk 1,10; Mt 3,16). In Jn 1,32 John the Baptist bears witness saying: "I saw the Spirit descend as a [female] *dove* (*hôs peristeran*) from heaven and remained on him" (cf. also Jn 1,33). And based on this revelatory experience John testifies that "this is the Son of God" (Jn 1,34).

[153] "You are my son" was said of king David in the royal Ps 2,7 but Jesus is more than the adopted son of God because he was conceived by the virgin through the Holy Spirit and therefore "holy" and "will be called Son of God" (cf. explanation of Lk 1,35 above).

[154] Cf. Mark L. Strauss, *op. cit.*, 268; Robert J. Karris, *op. cit.*, in: *NJBC*, 688.

[155] Mark L. Strauss, *op. cit.*, 269.

[156] This is *my literal translation* of the Greek text (cited by Luke from the Septuagint [LXX]) to highlight the repetition of significant terms so that we can understand the nuances of the Lukan text.

[157] It is noteworthy that purposefully *Jesus leaves out* the second part of Is 61,2 ("and the day of vengeance of our God": 61,2b); it points to God *not* being a *vengeful* God but being a *compassionate* God.

[158] "The *Jubilee year* was held every 50 years. During it fields lay fallow, persons returned to their homes, debts were cancelled, and slaves were set *free*. The image derived from it underscored *restoration*, beginning, faith in the sovereignty of God, and conviction that the structures of social and economic life must reflect *God's reign*" (Robert J. Karris, op. cit., in: *NJBC*, 690 [*italics* added]).

[159] Mark L. Strauss, *op. cit.*, 270.

[160] "Jesus' action of 'touching' the person [leper Lk 5,12-13], who was considered an untouchable, amounts to the restoration of that person from absolute social death" (*DBCNT*, 221).

[161] In Jn 3,29 John the Baptist compares *Jesus* to the *bridegroom* and the *disciples* to his *bride*.

[162] Jesus' saying that "new wine must be put into fresh wineskins" (Lk 5,38) means that "the gospel is radically new and must be allowed to express itself in its own way" (I. Howard Marshall, *The Gospel of Luke: A Commentary on the Greek Text* (Exeter 1978), 227-8).

[163] Cf. Mk 2,27-28: "The Sabbath was made for man, not man for the Sabbath; so the Son of man is lord even of the Sabbath."

[164] Robert J. Karris, op. cit., in: *NJBC*, 694.

[165] Cf. *ibid.*, 694.

[166] "The kingdom of God here and in a number of places in the Gospel means the end of exploitation of the poor which hindered their becoming full human beings. This reality of the reign of God makes the poor 'blessed', because it will put an end to their poverty..." (*DBCNT*, 224).

[167] Mark L. Strauss, *op. cit.*, 271 [*italics* added].

[168] In the original Greek (cf. Lk 8,5-8) the "*seed*" is always used in the *singular* (*sporos*) and the corresponding *verb* is also *singular*. Hence the author seems to be stressing the fact that the "*seed*" (the kingdom of God) is the *same* but the *fruit* it produces depends on the *soil* (*footpath, rock, thorns, good soil*) in which it is sown (cf. 8,11-15).

[169] This *allegorical interpretation* of the parable is the Lukan attempt at making it relevant primarily for the members of the Christian community in the post-resurrectional period.

[170] The verb "*rebuked*" (*epetimêsen*) is normally used for exorcising evil spirits (cf. Lk 4,35.49). This shows that Jesus has divine power and authority not only over evil spirits but also over violent natural forces like the raging storm and the mighty waves.

[171] Robert J. Karris, op. cit., in: *NJBC*, 698 [*italics* added].

[172] *DBCNT*, 229.

[173] Ashish Mehta, "In His End, a Message," *The Indian Express* (10 Feb. 2020), p. 8. Regarding the lasting impact of the crucified Christ on Mahatma Gandhi, Ashish Mehta says: "The image of Christ crucified endured with him. After seeing a painting of the crucified Christ in the Sistine Chapel of Rome, he commented, 'I saw there at once that nations like individuals could only be made through the agony of the cross and in no other way.'" (*ibid.*)

[174] Mark L. Strauss, *op. cit.*, 272.

[175] Frank J. Matera, *op. cit.,* 58 [*italics* added].

[176] Cf. Jack Dean Kingsbury, "Jesus as the 'Prophetic Messiah' in Luke's Gospel," in: *The Future of Christology: Essays in Honour of Leander E. Kech,* ed. Abraham J. Malherbe and Wayne Meeks (Minneapolis 1993), 29-42.

[177] Elsewhere "Lord" is a title used for the risen Jesus (e.g., 24,34; Acts 1,6).

[178] I have coined a new word '*humandivine*' [*without hyphen* in the middle] to show that Jesus Christ is not a hyphenated ['*human-divine*'] person but one integral person.

[179] Mark L. Strauss, *op. cit.*, 273.

[180] Since Jesus is "*the Christ*" (cf. Lk 9,20), the one "*anointed*" by the Holy Spirit (cf. 4,18), his disciples are called not simply to follow

(walk behind) the historical Jesus to Jerusalem but to follow the "way" of the Messiah (Christ). *All the disciples* of all places and times have to follow "*Christ's Way*" in order to be true *Christians.*

[181] Robert J. Karris, op. cit., in: *NJBC*, 701 [*italics* added].

[182] Cf. *ibid.*, 700-711; I. H. Marshall, *op. cit.*, 402-709.

[183] Since ancient and reliable manuscripts support both the readings, it is difficult to decide whether 70 or 72 was the original number in the Lukan text. Gen 10,2-31 ("the table of the nations of the world") seems to be the OT text behind the number; the uncertainty is created by the fact that MT (Masoretic Text in Hebrew) has 70 but LXX (Septuagint, Greek translation of the OT) has 72 (cf. Robert J. Karris, op. cit., in: *NJBC*, 701).

[184] Just as Jesus gave the Twelve power and authority to cast out demons and cure sicknesses and to preach the kingdom of God (Lk 9,1-2), he empowers also the seventy(-two) to do the same (10,9.17-20), indicating thereby that not only the Twelve (and their successors, the Bishops) but also the seventy(-two) (and the future missionaries, lay or religious) share in Jesus' power and authority. Hence it is high time that the Church hierarchy (especially the Bishops) re-examine their exclusive claim of authority and power over the Christians, the people of Christ.

The mission-requirements of both the Twelve and the seventy(-two) are also similar; both must depend not on their own provisions but on God's providence and on the people's hospitality to whom they are sent (cf. Lk 9,3-5 and 10,4-11).

[185] Samuel Oyin Abogunrin, "Luke," in: *IBC,* 1406.

[186] Robert J. Karris, op. cit., in: *NJBC*, 702.

[187] George Mlakuzhyil S.J., "*Abba* (Papa), Our Father in Heaven (and on Earth)," in: *The Lord's Prayer and Its Emerging Concerns,* ed. Assisi Saldanha (Bangalore 2008), 12 [*italics* added].

[188] George Mlakuzhyil S.J., "Abba, the Christian Mantra," *VJTR* 38 (1974), 396-97.

[189] The above "*woes*" against the Pharisees and scribes of Jesus' time are applicable to some *Pharisaic leaders* in the Church today! But unfortunately there are not enough courageous *prophetical lay-leaders*

to challenge such *Church leaders* who behave like the *hypocritical national leaders* in our country!

[190] *The Diplomat.com,* retrieved on 12-09-2020.

[191] *DBCNT*, 241.

[192] As we saw above (cf. Lk 3,16), the Greek expression *en pneumati hagiô kai pyri* is a *hendiadys* (in which one idea is expressed by *two words* connected by '*and*').

[193] During the farewell discourse in the Last Supper room Jesus bequeaths his peace to his disciples: "Peace I leave with you; my peace I give to you" (Jn 14,27), and the risen Lord greets them by saying: "Peace be with you" (Jn 20,19.21) and empowers them to forgive sinners and thus restore peace to them (cf. Jn 20,23).

[194] Robert J. Karris, op. cit., in: *NJBC*, 705. Following the principle of "what is right", *reconciliation* is recommended also in Lk 12,57-59.

[195] "Lo, *these three years* I have come seeking fruit on this fig tree, and I find none" (13,7) may refer to *Jesus' three-year long ministry* to which many have not responded with repentance. They are like the *fruitless tree* that will be "*cut down*," if it continues to be barren (13,7-8).

[196] I. H. Marshall, *op. cit.*, 568.

[197] In the Greek text *legô gar hymin* (Lk 14,24: "For I tell *you*"), "*you*" is plural (*hymin*, *not* singular *soi*) and hence it is not a reference to the servant but to the people (audience), and "I" points simultaneously to the householder and to Jesus, and therefore "*my banquet*" (14,24) refers to the "*great banquet*" (cf. 14,16), which is the symbol of the *eschatological banquet* "in the kingdom of God" (cf. 14,15).

[198] "Uncompromising loyalty was the first condition to be a member of the family/community of Jesus' disciples. This is what is meant by the prophetic use of the expression "hate" in verse 26. Discipleship had to take primacy over all other close relations. It was equal to a perpetual death on 'cross,' which was the price of being a disciple of Jesus (v 27)" (*DBCNT*, 245).

[199] *Renunciation of all possessions* is a *necessary condition for true discipleship*. For instance, the "*rich ruler*" could not become Christ's disciple because he was *unwilling to renounce all* his wealth (cf. Lk 18,18-23).

[200] It is similar to the context of the Dalit Christians (who were converted to Christ) for which they were criticized by the so-called upper caste Christians.

[201] The pitiable condition of the Prodigal son (feeding the rich man's pigs) is similar to that of the Dalits. "This is like the state of Indian Dalits who have become aware of their non-human state because of which they have named themselves 'Dalit'" (*DBCNT*, 246).

[202] Samuel Oyin Abogunrin, "Luke," in: *IBC,*1416.

[203] Normally this parable (Lk 16,1-8) is called the "the parable of the *dishonest* steward" but his master praises him not for his dishonesty but for his "*shrewdness/prudence*" (16,8).

[204] If the manager of the master's estate had included *his own exorbitant commission* in the contracts with the tenants in terms of annual produce like olive oil and wheat, he was *unjust* in doing so. Now by *reducing* the amount of oil and wheat due to be paid by the debtors, the manager is *forgoing part of his unjust commission* and therefore he is acting *prudently* or *shrewdly* to assure for himself a better future: "so that people may receive me into their houses when I am out of stewardship" (Lk 16,4). Hence we can understand why the master commends the steward's shrewdness (16,8).

[205] *Disproportionate distribution of wealth* among the Indian population exposes the *unbridled greed of the rich.*

[206] "The reference to the Samaritan and his identification as a "foreigner" [*allogenês*, "of another race"] (Lk 17,18) is a striking reminder of the all-encompassing love implicit in Jesus' compassionate ministry. It brings to mind once again the outsider who was casting out demons in the name of Jesus (9,49-50), the parable of the Good Samaritan in which the "foreigner" is identified as the real "neighbour" (10,25-37), and the criticisms levelled at Jesus' reception of the tax collectors and sinners (15,1-2)" (Samuel Oyin Abogunrin, "Luke," in: *IBC*, 1418).

[207] Robert J. Karris, *op. cit.*, in: *NJBC*, 709 [*italics* added].

[208] *The NIV Bible Commentary*, Vol 2: *New Testament*, ed. by Richard Polcyn & Verlyn D. Verbrugge (London 1994), 268 [*italics* added].

[209] Robert J. Karris, *op. cit.*, in: *NJBC*, 710.

[210] A *mina* (*mna*) [translated as a "pound"] was about 100 denarii, that is, about 100 days' wages of a labourer.

[211] Robert J. Karris, *op. cit.*, in: *NJBC*, 711.

[212] *DBCNT*, 252 [*italics* added].

[213] This is a literal translation of the Greek text (*en ouranô eirênê kai doxa en hypsistois*) in Lk 19,38, which has a *chiastic* (inverted parallel) *structure* (AB B'A'), where the first element A ("in heaven") is parallel to A' ("in the highest") and the central elements B ("peace") and B' ("glory") are parallel to each other.

[214] I. H. Marshall, *op. cit.*, 715-16 [*italics* added].

[215] Robert J. Karris, *op. cit.*, in: *NJBC*, 712.

[216] Frank J. Matera, *op. cit.*, 59 [*italics* in the original].

[217] Lk 19,47 and 21,37-38 form an *inclusion* (which signals the beginning and end of this Section 19,47-21,38).

[218] This is confirmed by the following parable (cf. Lk 20,9-18; cf. especially v. 13: "I will send *my beloved son*").

[219] These *themes* are developed almost like a "*winding staircase*": *a), b), a'), b'), c), b"), a")*.

[220] Robert J. Karris, *op. cit.*, in: *NJBC*, 714.

[221] Cf. I. H. Marshall, *op. cit.*, 780, for the different interpretations of "this generation" (*hê genea hautê*) by various Biblical scholars.

[222] This is the reason for Luke to *alternate* the prediction of the *destruction of the Temple/Jerusalem* and final *glorious coming of the Son of Man* (as we have seen above).

[223] Frank J. Matera, *op. cit.*, 61 [*italics* added].

[224] This explains why the celebration of the Eucharist in the early Church was known as "the breaking of the bread" (Acts 3,42).

[225] Robert J. Karris, *op. cit.*, in: *NJBC*, 715-16.

[226] Cf. I. H. Marshall, *op. cit.*, 806.

[227] The Greek word for "you" in Lk 22,31 is plural (*hymas*) but "you" in Lk 22,32 is singular (*sou*).

[228] Jesus' predictions of betrayal by Judas and denials by Peter indicate his super-human knowledge of his disciples and their future failures.

[229] Verses 43-44 are missing from most manuscripts. It must be noted that the Lukan text (vv. 40-42.45-46) has a ***concentric*** *plan: (a), (b),* ***(c)****, (b') (a')*, whose ***centre*** is (***c***): ***Jesus' prayer to the Father***.

[230] Mark L. Strauss, *op. cit.*, 280.

[231] "The core and substance of their mission [Lk 24,47-48] was: "repentance and forgiveness of sins to be proclaimed in his name to all nations beginning from Jerusalem" (v 47). All that Jesus had done, the apostles had seen with their eyes, therefore their role was going to be his witnesses (v 48, see Acts 1,6-8,22)" (*DBCNT*, 264).

[232] The noun "*joy*" (*chara*) occurs 8 times in Lk (1,14; 2,10; 8,13; 10,17; 15,7.10;24,41.52) and the verb "*rejoice*" (*chairô*) 12 times (1,14.28; 6,23; 10,20.20; 13,7; 15,5.32; 19,6.37; 22,5.8).

[233] Mark L. Strauss, *op. cit.*, 281 [*italics* added].

[234] *Ibid.*, 282 [*italics* added for "*suffering Messiah*"].

[235] "Son of Man" occurs in Lk's Gospel 25 times.

[236] Frank J. Matera, *op. cit.*, 63 [*italics* added].

[237] *Ibid.*, 63 [*italics* added]. The angel announces to the shepherds in Bethlehem the good news of the birth of Jesus: "to you is born today in the city of David a *Saviour*, who is *Christ the Lord*" (Lk 2,11).

[238] Mark L. Strauss, *op. cit.*, 282 [*italics* added]. The title "*the Son of Man*" is also important especially because it "*bridges*" the two titles "the Messiah" and "the Son of God" (as we have seen above).

[239] Cf. George Mlakuzhyil S.J., *GJCS*, xi-xxvi, for a brief "Introduction" to the authorship, purpose, destination, nature, literary-dramatic features and plan of John's Gospel.

[240] Cf. George Mlakuzhyil S.J., *CLDS*, 349-499 for elaborate discussion of the *literary-dramatic plan* of John's Gospel.

[241] Cf. *IGL*, 17-18; cf. *CLDS*, 580-681 for detailed discussion of the Christ-centred theology in the Plan of John's Gospel.

[242] Cf. *AL*, 15-21.

[243] This is very significant for developing a *new theology of religions* and a *Logos Christology* (cf. George Mlakuzhyil S.J., *GNJCG*, ***4.0.1. Prologue*** in Chapter 4).

[244] *IGL*, 25.

[245] The Greek text of Jn 1,45 states explicitly: *hon egrapsen Môysês en tô nomô* ("*about whom Moses wrote in the Law*"), which refers back to Deut 18,18 ("*I will raise up for them a prophet like you* from among their brethren"), which does not refer to any one of the prophets but to the *final Moses-like eschatological prophet.*

[246] Normally, Jn 1,46 (*ek Nazaret dynatai ti agathon einai*) is translated as: "Can anything good come out of Nazareth?" (e.g., RSV, NRSV), even though the original Greek text does not have the verb "come" but "be" (*einai*). The last two words of Philip (in the Greek text of 1,45) were "from Nazareth", which surprises Nathanael and so he questions/ exclaims: "From Nazareth!" (1,46).

[247] *CLDS,* 584-88.

[248] Cf. *AL,* 47-93; *PAL,* 57-103.

[249] *Jesus' self-revelation* to the *followers of different faiths* (Jews, Samaritans, Gentiles) through signs, dialogues and discourses will give us new light on *inter-faith dialogue* with *Hindus, Muslims,* Sikhs (cf. *GNJCPI*, Chapter 4).

[250] *AL,* 47; cf. *CLDS*, 430-441 for detailed explanation of the division of Jn 2-4 into six episodes.

[251] Cf. *IGL*, 33-34.

[252] Jesus as the *bridegroom* (cf. Jn 2,11; 3,29) will be very *meaningful for the women (lay and Religious)* in India to enter into *mystical intimacy with him.*

[253] Cf. *IGL*, 34-35.

[254] Cf. *AL*, 56-57.

[255] Cf. *IGL*, 35-36.

[256] *AL*, 61.

[257] Cf. *ibid.*, 61-62.

[258] "*Unique Son*" is my translation of the original Greek *monogenês hyios*, which is normally translated as "only begotten Son" (cf. KJ: Jn 1,18; 3,16.18) or "only Son" (cf. RSV: Jn 1,18; 3,16.18)." *Monogenês* literally means "one of its kind," which must be distinguished from *monos*, meaning "only" (cf. Jn 17,3).

[259] Cf. *AL,* 64-65.

[260] "The Samaritans did not expect a Messiah in the sense of the anointed king of the Davidic house. They expected a Taheb (*Ta'eb,* the one who returns), seemingly the Prophet-like-Moses. This belief was the fifth article in the Samaritan creed." (R. E. Brown, *The Gospel according to John,* I, 172.)

[261] Cf. *IGL*, 38-40; *AL*, 68-78.

[262] It is like a Brahmin asking for a drink from a Dalit woman at a village well in India!

[263] It is to be noted that in Jn 4,16-18 the Greek word *anêr/andra* has a *double meaning* (male "*man*" or "*husband*"). Jesus tells the woman to bring her "man" (4,16) but she gives an evasive answer that she has no "husband" (4,17). Now Jesus tells her that her reply of not having a "husband" is true, since she has had five "men" and the one she now has is not her "husband"! Hence Jn 4,16-18 has nothing to do with "Israelite custom of levirate marriage" (as affirmed in *DBCNT*, 281).

[264] *AL*, 73.

[265] Cf. *IGL*, 40-41; *AL*, 81-82.

[266] Cf. *AL*, 83-92.

[267] *AL*, 92 [*italics* added]. N.B. Jesus as 'the Son of God' and 'the life-giver' will be dealt with in greater detail in Jn 5-10 and Jn 11-12 respectively.

[268] Cf. *IGL*, 49-69; *AL*, 94-175; *PAL*, 105-84.

[269] Cf. *AL*, 96; cf. also *CLDS*, 441-461.

[270] *IGL*, 52-53.

[271] *Ibid.*, 53.

[272] *AL*, 106; *CLDS*, 461.

[273] Jesus considers the crowd's attempt to make him king a temptation (like his second temptation by the devil in Lk 4,5-7) and so he leaves the crowd and goes to the mountain to be alone with God in prayer.

[274] Normally this episode (Jn 6,16-21) is entitled "Walking on the Water" in most of the Bible translations (e.g., RSV). But "water" (*hydôr*) is never mentioned in the Greek text, whereas "sea" (*thalassa*) occurs four times (vv. 16.17.18.19) and the Evangelist explicitly states: "they saw *Jesus walking on the sea*" (Jn 6,19: *theôrousin ton Iêsoun peripatounta epi tês thalassês*). *Stormy "sea"* is a symbol of a life-threatening force,

signalling the danger of death for those struggling to save themselves from getting drowned.

[275] *AL*, 109.

[276] *Ibid.*, 111.

[277] *Ibid.*, 112.

[278] *Ibid.*, 113.

[279] Jn 6,53-58 may be regarded as the Johannine equivalent of the Synoptic and Pauline institution narratives of the Eucharist (Mt 26,26-29; Mk 14,22-25; Lk 22,15-20; 1 Cor 11,23-25), since there are many Eucharistic terms found in all the narratives (e.g., "bread," "to eat," "flesh/body," "drink," "blood," "give," "for".

[280] Cf. *AL*, 116-17 for more Christological details in Jn 6,1-71.

[281] This is like the devil's third temptation of Jesus to jump down from the pinnacle of the temple for show (cf. Lk 4,9) but in Jn 7,4-5 it is not the devil but Jesus' own unbelieving "brothers" (kith and kin) who tempt him to show off to the world, which he wisely resists (cf. Jn 7,6-9).

[282] This interpretation of Jesus as *a good prophet* is confirmed by the people's confession later: "He is *truly the prophet*" (*alêthôs ho prophêtês:* Jn 7,40). The Pharisees, however, accuse Jesus as the one who "led astray" (through his teaching) even the Temple police who were sent to arrest him, which they failed to do because no one ever spoke like Jesus (cf. Jn 7,46-47). When Nicodemus tries to defend Jesus (7,51), the other Pharisees insult him by calling him a 'Galilean' and silence him by telling a blatant lie that "no prophet is to rise from Galilee" (7,52), even though prophet Jonah was from Gath-hepher in Galilee (cf. 2 Kgs 14,25)!

[283] The Greek text does *not* say "out of the *believer's* heart" but "out of *his* belly/heart" (*ek tês koilias autou: Jn* 7,38).

[284] Cf. *AL*, 129.

[285] This story is not found in the earliest manuscripts of John's Gospel.

[286] Cf. George Mlakuzhyil S.J., *GJCS*, 64. As in Israel in Jesus' time, so in India today it is mostly the woman, not the man, who is accused and condemned of committing adultery because of the belief that the woman seduces the man (and not *vice versa*)! But the *compassionate*

Jesus saves the sinful woman from being stoned to death and sends her away in peace to begin a new life without sin (Jn 8,7-11).

[287] *AL*, 130.

[288]In the Gospel of Mark too it is when Jesus dies on the cross that the Centurion confesses: "Truly this man was Son of God" (15,39).

[289] *IGL*, 58-59.

[290] Normally the original Greek text (which has no punctuation marks) of Jn 9,3 is translated *wrongly* by putting a *comma* after "his parents", and a *full stop* after "in him" (cf. *RSV*), which means that the man was born blind in order that "God's works" many be revealed in the blind man! This is an atrocious allegation against God that he has caused the man to be born blind! But by putting a *full stop* after "his parents" and a *comma* after "in him" (v. 3b) (as we have done), vv. 3b-4 would mean that the reason why "we must do the works" of God is that they "may be made manifest in him" (in the healing of the blind man). No sickness glorifies God but its healing does, and therefore "we must" collaborate with God in curing the sick. This is what doctors and nurses do today in the clinics and hospitals.

[291] *IGL*, 60.

[292] *AL*, 159-160.

[293] "The *laying down of the shepherd's life* in John 10 is primarily about the *imminent reality of Jesus' death* rather than the mere risking of his life" (Christopher W. Skinner, "'The Good Shepherd Lays Down His Life for the Sheep' (Jn 10,11.15.17): Questioning the Limits of a Johannine Metaphor," 17 [*italics* added], (pp. 1-17, retrieved on 26-11-2019).

[294] Cf. R. E. Brown, "Other Sheep Not of This Fold: The Johannine Perspective on Christian Diversity in the Late First Century", *JBL* 97/1 (1978) 5-22.

[295] Cf. *AL*, 161.

[296] "The Jews expected the Messiah who would be royal and militant to liberate them from the colonial rule of the Romans and restore the land to them. The Jewish interrogation implied that if Jesus were the Messiah of that type, they insisted that he should openly declare it (v. 24). But Jesus explains his different Messiahship not in terms of

kingship and militancy but in terms of his commitment to his sheep without allowing them to be snatched away from him and his gift of eternal life to them (vv. 27-28)" (*DBCNT*, 293).

[297] *AL*, 166 [*italics* in the original text].

[298] *IGL*, 70-84; *AL*, 176-211; *CLDS*, 461-68.

[299] *CLDS*, 497.

[300] Cf. *Ibid.*, 461-68.

[301] It is to be noted that, while quoting Zech 9,9, John purposely leaves out the clause "triumphant and victorious is he" after the announcement "behold, your king is coming," and before the description "sitting on an ass's colt!" (Jn 12,15). This clearly shows that, according to the Johannine understanding of this episode (Jn 12,12-19), it is *not* Jesus' "*triumphal entry* into Jerusalem", as the title given in many of the NT translations (e.g., *RSV, GNB*)!

[302] It is remarkable that the same two Jewish disciples, Andrew and Philip, who had brought Simon Peter and Nathanael respectively to Jesus (Jn 1,40-42.43-46), now play a prominent role in leading the Greek disciples to him (12,20-22).

[303] *DBCNT*, 296.

[304] *AL*, 199.

[305] *Ibid.*, 198.

[306] *CLDS*, 623 [*italics* added].

[307] Here '*lover*' is used not in the romantic/sentimental sense but to mean '*the one who loves*' (cf. 13,1).

[308] *AL*, 208.

[309] Cf. *CLDS*, 468-80 for the reasons for the division of Jn 13-17 into 5 subsections.

[310] Although the "hour" of Jesus was mentioned a few times in Jn 2-12, it was said that his "hour" had "not yet come" (2,4; 7,30; 8,20) or that it was near (12,23.27).

[311] *IGL*, 87.

[312] "In the traditional commandment ("love others as you love yourself"), the norm for loving others is the qualitative intensity of loving oneself. But in the new commandment it is Jesus' unique way

of loving others that is shown as the distinctive model [13,34-35] … Focussing on the love of the other as Jesus did will make his disciples distinct and different" (*DBCNT*, 298).

[313] *AL*, 221-22.

[314] *Ibid.*, 222.

[315] *Ibid.*

[316] *Ibid.*, 223. It may be recalled that Luke refers to the early Christians as "the Way" (*hê hodos*) (Acts 19,9.23; 22,4; 24,14.22).

[317] *Ibid.*, 229-30 [*italics* in the original text].

[318] *CLDS*, 644.

[319] *AL*, 239.

[320] *Ibid.*, 237. "Jesus' conquering the world of evil forces in the face of persecutions and sufferings will be the inspiring and guiding example for his disciples to take courage and face their afflictions (Jn 16,33)" (*DBCNT*, 302).

[321] *AL*, 243-44.

[322] *Ibid.*, 244.

[323] George Mlakuzhyil S.J., "Mission in the Gospel of John," *Vidyajyoti Journal of Theological Reflection [VJTR]*, 57 (1993), 263.

[324] *IGL*, 97.

[325] *Ibid.*,103.

[326] *AL*, 253 [*italics* in the original].

[327] *CLDS*, 661-62 [*italics* added].

[328] *Ibid.*, 480-91.

[329] *Ibid.*, 650 [the last *italics* added].

[330] *AL*, 255-56.

[331] "Jesus does not resort to easy short-cut and immediate solutions and that is why he chides Peter for having cut off the right ear of the slave of the high priest (v 10). But he is determined to fulfil the will of his Father by drinking with full consent the cup his Father has given him (v 11)" (*DBCNT*, 304).

[332] *AL*, 258-59 [*italics* in the original text].

[333] Cf. *Ibid.*, 262.

[334] *Ibid.*, 263-64.

[335] *Ibid.*, 265.

[336] Cf. *Ibid.*, 272.

[337] *Ibid.*, 274.

[338] *Ibid.*, 366, n. 17.

[339] *Jesus' fulfilment of the Scripture* is explicitly stated by the Evangelist in many of the events on Calvary (Jn 19,24.28.36).

[340] "Jesus willingly accepted the mission given him by the Father, selflessly worked for that mission, bravely faced all the oppositions and persecutions, accomplished fruitfully the mission. That is why he could fittingly utter from the cross, "It is finished" [Jn 19,30: *tetelestai*, "accomplished"]" (*DBCNT*, 307).

[341] *CLDS*, 659-60.

[342] *AL*, 275.

[343] *Ibid.*, 276.

[344] *Ibid.*, 282.

[345] Cf. *Ibid.*, 282-83.

[346] Cf. *IGL*, 112.

[347] "Thomas' confession in the Lordship and divinity of Jesus reflects the post-Easter faith of the Johannine community in the crucified-risen Jesus." (George Mlakuzhyil S.J., *GJCS*, 132.)

[348] Jesus' statement to Thomas (Jn 20,29a) implies that he believed *not because* he *touched* him but *because* he *saw* him. What is underlined in this episode is that Thomas too had a *personal experience of the risen Lord*, like the one the other disciples had ("We *have seen* the Lord" 20,25; cf. also 20,18). Hence it is an *artistic aberration* when many *paintings and films* portray the *"doubting" Thomas putting his finger into the wound* of Jesus' pierced side!!

[349] *AL*, 295.

[350] *Ibid.*, 296-97.

[351] *Ibid.*, 300; cf. also *IGL*, 120-21.

[352] The Evangelist states the simple fact: "When they [the disciples] got out on land, they saw a charcoal fire there, with fish lying on it, and bread" (21,9). It means that Jesus was cooking the fish on the fire

(preparing breakfast) for the disciples. (The author is not interested in satisfying our curiosity how Jesus got the fish and bread, how he did 'the cutting and cleaning and marinating'!)

[353] *AL*, 300 (*italics* in the original text).

[354] Cf. *AL*, 303-10 and *IGL*, 123-29 for detailed explanation of the *different roles/missions* of *Simon Peter* and the *Beloved Disciple* in Jn 21.

[355] Cf. *AL*, 311-12.

[356] *Ibid*., 313.

[357] Cited by R. E. Brown, *The Gospel according to John*, II, 1130.

[358] Cf. *CLDS*, 578-670, for detailed description of the development of these Johannine Christological themes in Jn 1-21.

[359] The eighth one is the absolute "*I am*" (*egô eimi*), which points to Jesus' *divine origin*: "Before Abraham was, *I am*" (*egô eimi*: Jn 8,58), which is *different* from the *seven self-designations* mentioned above.

[360] Cf. *CLDS*, 504-19 for the development of "*Christ/Messiah*" in Jn.

[361] Cf. *ibid*., 534-39 for the development of "*the Son of Man*" in Jn.

[362] *Jesus' crucifixion and death* in the Fourth Gospel are presented as *his glorification and return to the Father*. Similarly, the three "*passion predictions*" in the Synoptic Gospels (Mk 8,31; 9,31; 10,33-34 and parallels) are replaced in John's Gospel with three instances of Jesus' predictions about his (the Son of Man's) being "*lifted up*"(Jn 3,14; 8,28; 12,32). The verb "to be lifted up" (*hypsothênai*) has *double entendre* because it refers to Jesus' being physically *elevated* from the earth *to the cross* (by the soldiers) and also simultaneously his being *exalted or glorified* (by God the Father).

[363] Cf. *CLDS*, 519-31 for the development of "*the Son of God*" and "*the Son*" in Jn.

[364] "From aha-encounters with Jesus as the Messiah/Christ among those who would become his followers to later affirmations of his divine agency and being, the Johannine view of Jesus' oneness with the Father is clear" (Paul N. Anderson, "On Jewish Preexistence, the Jesus of History, and the Christ of Faith – A Response to Boccaccini", p. 18).

[365] Cf. Don Trest, "The Distinctive Sonship Soteriology of Jesus in the Fourth Gospel," a paper (pp. 1-71), academia.edu, (retrieved on 10-12-2019).

[366] Cf. AL, 176-82; cf. also CLDS, 501-681.

[367] "According to John's Gospel, it is by *believing in Jesus Christ* that we can *have eternal life* or *live life to the full* (3,17.36; 20,31) and it is by *loving like Christ* that we can *give life to others* (15,12)" (George Mlakuzhyil S.J., *Be a Life-Giver [BLG]*, 9 [*italics* in the original]).

[368] Since an *appropriate* "**Conclusion**" © has been given at the **end** of **each of the Chapters 1-4** (cf. **1.©**, **2.©**, **3.©**, **4.©**) and of most *Sections* in every Chapter, only a **concise "Conclusion"** here is sufficient to highlight a few *outstanding aspects* of *Jesus Christ's person and mission in the Gospels.*

[369] This is a matter of *emphasis, not* of *exclusion*, since the *liberative* and *life-giving* aspects of *Jesus' mission* do not exclude one another.

[370] See ***4.©.4. Jesus, the Loving Life-Giver*** in **Chapter 4** above. Cf. also *IGL*, 209-19: "Jesus' mission in Jn".

www.ingramcontent.com/pod-product-compliance
Ingram Content Group UK Ltd.
Pitfield, Milton Keynes, MK11 3LW, UK
UKHW041859190726
13854UKWH00002B/989